Understanding and Preventing Online Sexual Exploitation of Children

Over the last decade there has been dramatically increased interest in the ways that technology has been used in the abuse and exploitation of children, due in part to increasing numbers of convictions for child pornography-related offences.

Opinion swings between those who feel that there is a danger of distorting the threat posed to children by technology, and those for whom it appears that the threat has been grossly underestimated. Current literature surrounding the debate at times seems to create more questions than answers and what quickly becomes apparent is that the data we have to inform our understanding is partial, potentially context specific, and at times seemingly contradictory.

This book broadens our understanding of the complex nature of online sexual exploitation of children and considers the risk that those engaged in Internet-related offences pose to children in both the online and offline environments. It focuses on cutting-edge research and conceptual thinking that views perpetrators within context, examines those impacted by such offending, describes emerging legal and policy issues, and proposes innovative strategies for prevention within a dynamic global environment.

Understanding and Preventing Online Sexual Exploitation of Children responds to the growing call for help across all practice areas, from judicial to therapeutic, and will provide an invaluable resource for practitioners and policy makers working in the field, as well as students and academics studying sexual exploitation and cyber crime.

Ethel Quayle is Senior Lecturer in Clinical Psychology at the University of Edinburgh and a trained clinical psychologist.

Kurt M. Ribisl is Associate Professor in Health Behaviour and Health Education at the Gillings School of Global Public Health, University of North Carolina.

Understanding and Preventing Online Sexual Exploitation of Children

Edited by Ethel Quayle
and Kurt M. Ribisl

Routledge
Taylor & Francis Group

LONDON AND NEW YORK

First published 2012
by Routledge
2 Park Square, Milton Park, Abingdon, Oxon, OX14 4RN

Simultaneously published in the USA and Canada
by Routledge
711 Third Avenue, New York, NY 10017

Routledge is an imprint of the Taylor & Francis Group, an informa business

British Library Cataloguing in Publication Data
A catalogue record for this book is available from the British Library

Library of Congress Cataloging in Publication Data
A catalog record for this book has been requested

ISBN: 978–0–415–68940–3 hbk
ISBN: 978–0–415–68941–0 pbk
ISBN: 978–0–203–12776–6 ebk

Typeset in Times New Roman
by Keystroke, Station Road, Codsall, Wolverhampton

MIX
Paper from
responsible sources
FSC
www.fsc.org   FSC® C004839

Printed and bound in Great Britain by
CPI Antony Rowe, Chippenham, Wiltshire

Contents

Foreword

I have been a prosecutor for nearly twenty-five years, and in my career I have handled a full range of criminal offenses, everything from simple larceny to international drug trafficking. I have incarcerated rapists, airline hijackers, armed career criminals, and corrupt federal agents. From my experience with these cases, an offender's motive, intent, and purpose are generally clear from the facts and easily grasped. The grade of seriousness attributed to these offenses is not a matter of real dispute. And, when it comes to sentencing factors, lawyers, probation officers, and sentencing judges typically disagree only at the margins. Child pornography collectors, however, seem to stand in distinct contrast to this norm because the seriousness of their crimes is not commonly understood.

Within the realm of judges, lawyers, and probation officers in the United States, child pornography offenders are currently the subject of significant debate, largely flowing from differing opinions concerning how dangerous these offenders are. For those of us who are witness to these crimes through investigation and prosecution, however, evidence suggests that many of these offenders are quite dangerous, especially if they participate in an online group, forum, or social networking site centered on pedophilic interests. In these online forums the discussion of child sexual abuse flows as freely as might the discussion of hydrangeas in a gardening forum. The talk in child abuse forums, however, is distinctively worrisome. In one online group investigated recently, for instance, a member posted a survey asking, "have you thought about whether or not you would abduct a preteen girl/boy," with over 50 percent of the responders answering, "I would absolutely do it" or "if the circumstances were right, I'd do it." In another investigation, a member of an online assemblage of producers and traders of child pornography talked about how he was eagerly anticipating the opportunity to molest his daughter, who had not been born yet. He posted a message exclaiming "o man do i have some news i have a new baby about to be added to the game i will share her pics when i get some." Shortly thereafter, a sonogram image of his unborn daughter in the womb was posted. And a member of yet another online forum posted a solicitation to his fellow members offering to pay $1,000 per hour, up to a maximum of $50,000, for access to a child, with the restriction that the child be a blond-haired, blue-eyed girl between 7 and 9 years of age.

The US Department of Justice's Child Exploitation and Obscenity Section, which I have led for the last ten years, is a group of prosecutors, computer forensic specialists, and other experts dedicated to addressing federal crimes against children. Our investigative efforts are conducted in close partnership with the Federal Bureau of Investigation's Innocent Images National Initiative, the U.S. Immigration and Customs Enforcement Child Exploitation Section, and the U.S. Postal Inspection Service's child exploitation unit, as well as our foreign law enforcement colleagues, since online child exploitation offenses are increasingly international in scope. In recent years, much of our investigative effort has been directed towards child pornography offenders operating online in groups.

Forums with large memberships dedicated to the sexual abuse of children and the exchange of its graphic imagery are ubiquitous on the Internet. Indeed, groups of people with pedophilic interests have taken extensively to social networking platforms. In all of these groups, we consistently find certain common characteristics: they are a thriving marketplace for the exchange of child pornography; they are hierarchical and members' upward progression is achieved most readily by producing child pornography and distributing it to other members; and communication between members typically normalizes, encourages, and facilitates the sexual abuse of children. Given these characteristics, law enforcement officers addressing child pornography are confident that online collectives like these and the individuals who belong to them are worthy of careful attention because they pose a real risk to children.

This attention may be well placed against online forums, but what about individual collectors? Law enforcement in the United States has been bringing prosecutions against child pornography possessors for decades now, and our record indicates that many collectors are abusing children as well. But there are more primary reasons to address child pornography collectors. Even if collectors never abused children (which, of course, is not the case), they would still directly contribute to the exploitation and even the sexual abuse of children, and would merit criminal justice action. Our Supreme Court long ago noted that the heart of a child pornography case is the endless sexual exploitation of a child through the ongoing mass circulation of images of their abuse. *New York* v. *Ferber*, 458 U.S. 747, 758 (1982) ("the use of children as subjects of pornographic materials is harmful to the physiological, emotional, and mental health of the child"). In the words of one victim, a child who was raped and bound repeatedly by her father for two years starting when she was 10:

> thinking about all those sick perverts viewing my body being ravished and hurt like that makes me feel like I was raped by each and every one of them. I was so young . . . It terrifies me that people enjoy viewing things like this . . . Each person who has found enjoyment in these sick images needs to be brought to justice . . . even though I don't know them, they are hurting me still. They have exploited me in the most horrible way.

The Supreme Court also observed that perhaps the only practical way to stop the production of child pornography is to give severe sentences to child pornography offenders, the individuals who stimulate the demand for a constant stream of new images that can only be produced by sexually abusing a child. *Ferber*, 458 U.S. at 760 ("The most expeditious if not the only practical method of law enforcement may be to dry up the market for this material by imposing severe criminal penalties on persons selling, advertising, or otherwise promoting the product"). The traffic of child pornography on the Internet indeed exhibits the characteristics of a marketplace, and each person who draws from this virtual market is compelling the production of new images. Many offenders compulsively collect images. The collections are often meticulously organized by name of the child, sex of the child, age of the child, or type of sexual activity depicted in the image of the child. Collectors use these images much like currency, trading images for new ones that are highly coveted. The drive in this underground market is to collect new images. It is easy to see how this would drive the abuse of children to satisfy the never-ending demand for new images, and would turn collectors into producers, creating images of their own sexual abuse of children in order to have new, and therefore valuable currency on the Internet. In full view of this condition, law enforcement is convinced that collectors of child pornography should be addressed seriously.

Others with professional interest in the matter of child pornography offenders, however, are far less convinced. In February of this year the Associated Press published an article on the debate that is simmering in the United States. Among other things, the article claimed, "[d]efense attorneys, legal scholars and even some federal judges bemoan the prosecution and sentencing developments as draconian for failing to distinguish between hardcore producers of child pornography and hapless Web surfers with mental problems" (Paul Elias, "Child Porn Prosecutions Soaring," Associated Press, February 5, 2011, available in Westlaw at 2/5/11 ALPERTCA 19:05:25). An article appearing in the ABA Journal entitled "A reluctant rebellion," raised questions about the child pornography sentencing guidelines (Mark Hansen, "A reluctant rebellion," ABA Journal, June 2009 at http://www.abajournal.com/magazine/article/areluctantrebellion/). The author acknowledges that producers of child pornography – those known to be molesting a child – are committing serious offenses, but cites a number of critics who depict the individuals collecting, trading, viewing, and possessing these images as "otherwise law abiding" citizens who merely enjoy an odd and even deviant form of sex, but do so in the "privacy of [their] own home." The article suggests that serious sentences for these offenses are motivated by a puritan ideal and "polite society's disgust and revulsion" with pornography. This sentiment is summed up by one jurist, who commented, "our federal legal system has lost its bearings on the subject of computer-based child pornography. Our 'social revulsion' against these 'misfits' downloading these images is perhaps somewhat more rational than the thousands of witchcraft trials and burnings conducted in Europe and here from the Thirteenth to the Eighteenth Centuries, but it borders on the same thing" (*United States* v. *Paull*, 551 F.3d 516, 533 (6th Cir. 2009) (Merritt, J., dissenting)).

It may not be a "rebellion," but the intellectual debate in the United States about the nature of child pornography offenses, what penalties are appropriate for those crimes, and the risks posed by those who commit those crimes is rising. The debate is understandable, because research concerning issues such as the link between child pornography offenses and contact sexual abuse offenses and the extent to which child pornography offenses stimulate a demand for the production of new child pornography images, has not yet definitively resolved these questions. Moreover, it is clear to even the hard enforcement end of this debate that we cannot prosecute this crime problem to eradication. We must instead try to prevent it.

Recognizing that a better understanding of child pornography offenders will help us not only better to investigate and prosecute these offenders but also better to prevent their crimes in the first place, in 2007 I began to pursue the goal of organizing a symposium of experts from around the world who have examined child pornography offenses and offenders through psychology, social science, and analytical research. In November 2007, as part of the US delegation to the Roma/Lyon Group of the G8, I put forth such a proposal to the Law Enforcement Projects Subgroup. As proposed, the purpose of the symposium was to provide an opportunity for experts from G8 countries and beyond to share their individual research findings and experiences and to develop international consensus on the risks to children associated with child pornography, among other things. The project was formally approved by the Heads of Delegation in February 2008.

The Global Symposium for Examining the Relationship Between Online and Offline Offenses and Preventing the Sexual Exploitation of Children was hosted in the United States by the University of North Carolina Chapel Hill, Injury Prevention Research Center, in Chapel Hill, North Carolina, from April 5 to April 7, 2009. It was made possible through the financial and administrative support of the US Department of Justice's Office of Justice Programs. Participating in the symposium were forty-five substantive experts from the fields of psychology, social science, and analytical research, with expertise in child pornography crimes, offenders, and/or victims. Eleven countries were represented. The main objectives of this symposium were to: examine the risk factors associated with child pornography offenders; develop findings on the role of the Internet and child pornography in child sexual abuse offenses; develop findings on the broader context in which child pornography offenses occur; and develop areas for further research.

The substantive portions of the symposium were divided into three theme sessions, spanned over two days. The three themes were: (1) the broader context; (2) conceptualizing risk; and (3) the relationship between online and offline sexual offenses against children. Within each thematic session, three experts chosen on the basis of their research and analytical work in the thematic area gave plenary presentations on that work. Each symposium participant was provided an abstract of the presentations before the symposium and also received position papers to assist in preparing for the symposium. After the presentations, all symposium participants were divided into small discussion groups that conducted a critical examination of the presentations and developed a synthesis of current knowledge, identified gaps in knowledge in the subject area, and analyzed future research needs. The participants then developed a final synthesis on all three themes, and during the final plenary session, short presentations were made by three of the facilitators on the various points of consensus and divergence, and the recommendations for future research that arose from the various breakout groups. After each of these presentations, participants engaged in a general discussion, among the entire group of experts, on the points of consensus and divergence and recommendations. In this way, the group ensured that there was indeed consensus on the points and recommendations. These points and recommendations were later shared with the G8 Justice Ministers, who on May 30, 2009, issued a Minster's Declaration announcing the results of the symposium.

From this gathering of experts also sprung the idea for this book. *Understanding and Preventing Online Sexual Exploitation of Children* responds to the growing call for help across all practice areas, from judicial to therapeutic. The book broadens our understanding of the complex nature of online sexual exploitation in meaningful and directly useful ways. And, particularly with its view on a public health approach to addressing online sexual exploitation of children, this book may change professional discourse on the problem entirely. Debate will continue, but each chapter of this book and the research supporting it will bring answers to those who seek them.

The debaters and anyone looking for a better understanding of online child sexual exploitation owe a profound debt of gratitude to the book's many contributors and especially its editors, Professors Ethel Quayle and Kurt Ribisl. Professors Quayle and Ribisl provided the vision and will that made the symposium a success and this extremely valuable book a reality

Drew Oosterbaan
Chief, Child Exploitation and Obscenity Section,
US Department of Justice

Part 1

Abusive images and their emergence as a significant problem

1 An introduction to the problem

Ethel Quayle, University of Edinburgh
School of Health in Social Science

Roberta Sinclair, National Child
Exploitation Coordination Centre

Overview

This chapter is about photographs: still and moving sexualized images of children, variously called child pornography, abuse images or child exploitation materials. In the chapter we will look critically at some of the assumptions which underlie the criminalization of these materials; the ways in which they are used by offenders; the content of these images; desistance from their use; social contexts for their use; and, the thorny problem of self-generated content. Inevitably, in trying to address these issues, we will touch upon areas covered by other chapters in this book as well as making reference to some of the same literature, much of it written since 2000.

The last ten years have seen a substantial increase in the number of international research publications, policy documents and legislative changes in relation to these photographs. This increased interest in part reflects the growing number of people in the criminal justice system convicted of crimes related to the production, distribution and possession of child pornography (Wolak et al., 2008), a perceived threat that children are at risk of victimization related to technological change (Altobelli, 2010) and possible concern about children and young people's engagement with Internet media, and their capacity to generate content (Ostrager, 2010). However, as early as 2001, Adler was raising concerns as to whether the proliferation of laws in the United States related to child pornography was potentially problematic, making us look at children through paedophilic eyes and, more recently, McKee (2010) has asserted that there is no element of culture today that is not claimed by someone to cause harm to children. There are many reasons underlying such concerns. In May 2008 the Australian Federal police removed a series of artworks by internationally renowned photomedia artist Bill Henson from the walls of a Sydney gallery just hours before his exhibition was due to open. They did so in response to an allegation that the invitation to the opening carried an image of child pornography (Hinkson, 2009). In addition there are very different concerns that a preoccupation with media and harm to children diverts attention and resources away from the more substantial problems related to contact sexual offences against children (Wolak et al., 2008). At times it appears that there is a polarization of opinion expressed as concerns about either the presence of

(Internet Safety Technical Taskforce, 2008), or lack of (Jenkins, 2009), moral panic about these crimes.

One of the challenges in talking about these photographs, and the people who produce and use them, relates to language. Whilst most national and supranational laws use the term child pornography (Akdeniz, 2008), we still see reference to obscenity (Adler, 2008) and indecent content. Outside the United States, and the legal system, there is a growing preference for calling these photographs child abuse images (Jones and Skogrand, 2005), child exploitation materials (Carr, 2009) and indecent images of children (IIOC: Long et al., under review). This is thought to more adequately capture the content of these images and the ways that they are used, and moves us away from uncritical comparisons with adult pornography (Taylor and Quayle, 2003). There are equally a variety of terms used to describe the producers and users of such materials: paedophiles (Seto, 2010; Holt et al., 2010); online sex offenders (Babchishin et al., 2010; Bourke and Hernandez, 2008); Internet sexual offenders (Elliott, Beech, Mandeville-Norden et al., 2009); and Internet-based sexual offenders (Henry et al., 2010). This becomes even more confusing with reference to people whose offences involve downloading abusive images of children as well as the commission of a contact offence or the sexual abuse of a child who is photographed and the image uploaded onto the Internet. Sheldon and Howitt (2008) described these people as 'mixed offenders' as they had committed both contact and Internet child pornography offences, while Wolak et al. (2005) used the term 'dual offenders'. Does this matter? At its most simplistic, it makes comparison between samples a challenge as it is not immediately apparent whether reference is being made to populations with the same characteristics. However, on another level it reflects some concerns as to whether we are adopting a criminal justice stance or a clinical stance (Kramer, 2010), which is also reflected in the use of language such as minor-attracted people or adults (Goode, 2009) and whether we should always define such children as 'victims' (e.g. Riegel, 2010; Malón, 2009).

Harm or rights?

One assumption underpinning the interest in abuse images is that of harm. This may be expressed as harm towards the child who was depicted in the image, but equally harm has been argued to take place when someone views the image of the child, even without any contact having taken place. The reasoning is that there is the potential for additional harm, as looking at images may increase the likelihood of the commission of a contact offence against a child at some point in the near, or distant, future. Such arguments have become enshrined in the laws of many countries with, for example, the US Department of Justice prosecuting possession under the rationale that (1) possession leads to contact offences; (2) demand drives supply; and (3) the availability constitutes continued and indirect abuse of the child depicted (Bausbaum, 2010). Mirkin (2009) has challenged assumptions of harm, arguing that the majority of images depict children not engaged in acts that are harmful in themselves (such as individual or group masturbation), with Malón's

(2009) and Riegel's (2010) discussion of the 'participating victim' adding to the broader debate.

However, the harm argument presents problems for us when we consider images of children that we might argue are exploitative (such as photographs taken without the child's knowledge on the beach or in a changing room), but where no actual contact has taken place. In such a context the child, or the person looking after it, may never know that the images have been taken or their potential for distribution. A further challenge lies in the criminalization of 'non-photographic pornographic images of children' (NPPIC) which became a new offence in the United Kingdom under the Coroner and Justice Act 2009. Ost (2010) argues that it is difficult to find a legitimate basis for the prevention of completely fabricated NPPIC through the application of the harm principle, and that moral-based arguments are not convincing since legal moralism, or moral paternalism, should not be acceptable grounds for criminalization. However, the argument that NPPIC, or virtual child pornography, perpetuates a market for pornography involving actual children and thereby causes substantial indirect harm to society is firmly held by many concerned with its use and criminalization (Mains, 2010).

Concern with harm is not a spurious argument. One might argue that conduct should be criminalized only if it is directly harmful, although it is the case that some criminal wrongdoing does take place without causing any direct harm (e.g. trespass). In such cases, as with some abusive images, a case is made for indirect harm as a justification for criminalization. Stewart (2010) alleges that this strategy justifies the criminalization of a wide range of conduct on the basis of the fear, worry and anxiety it generates among those who are not the direct victims. His alternative is to recognize that people have the right to be treated in a certain way because they are persons, as well as rights that are based on their interests and are subordinate to the harm principle. This is enshrined in Article 3 of the United Nations Optional Protocol to the Convention on the Rights of the Child on the Sale of Children, Child Prostitution and Child Pornography, which entered into force in 2002 and states that each 'State Party shall ensure that, as a minimum, producing, distributing, disseminating, importing, exporting, offering, selling or possessing for the above purposes child pornography as defined in Article 2 are fully covered under its criminal or penal law, whether these offences are committed domestically or transnationally or on an individual or organized basis'.

It might have been thought that such arguments about 'harm', 'rights' and the morality of abusive images (King, 2008; Oswell, 2006) might have led to further research on the children within the images, but it is of interest that such research is limited and largely pre-dates the Internet (see Renold and Creighton, 2003). An exception to this is the work of Svedin and Back (2003) with a sample of Swedish children (see chapter 2 for a more substantial discussion). While it would be unfair to say that there has not been a considerable investment made in many countries to understand the risks posed to children by technology-mediated communication (e.g. Livingstone et al., 2010; Wolak et al., 2008) outside activities by law enforcement the focus for intervention has largely been on educating children about grooming or online sexual solicitation (Davidson et al., 2009 as an example). In the larger context of child protection, education interventions seem to provide the most adequate evidence base (Finkelhor, 2009), but outside of educating children about the dangers of self-generated content or 'sexting', very little seems to have been written about child protection strategies in the context of abusive images. Here, industry does seem to have played an increasing role by entering into voluntary or mandated agreements in many countries to block websites or remove content (Eneman, 2010).

The use of abusive images

It is very difficult to ascertain the numbers of abusive and exploitative images of children available through the Internet, or indeed the number of children that may be involved in their production, but it does seem self-evident that the nature of the Internet means that such content is cumulative, with more and more images being added to what is already available (Taylor and Quayle, 2003). Few studies have examined these images, which in part may be due to the difficulties in researchers gaining access without committing an offence (Adler, 2008; Blevins and Anton, 2008; Jenkins, 2009) along with the ethical challenges posed by repeat viewing. It might seem that the seriousness of the problem has largely been measured in terms of the number of offenders in the criminal justice system and the proportion of these who have already committed a contact offence or who are deemed at risk of committing one. Where the images in their possession have been explored this is most often in relation to what it might tell us about the offender: the nature of their sexual interests and fantasies, their sexual orientation, and the intensity of their interest or preoccupation. All of this reflects a legitimate concern with the offender and the nature of the offence, but unlike the research on solicitation or grooming, does little to help us understand what has happened from the perspective of the child (see Leonard, 2010).

Paradoxically, more recent interest in the images of these children has arisen as a means of better understanding the offender's motivation and sexual orientation without having to rely on self-report measures such as questionnaires or interviews (Glasgow, 2010 and chapter 10). Research using indirect measures such as the polygraph (Buschman, Bogaerts et al., 2010; Buschman, Wilcox et al., 2010) would seem to indicate that when questioned, Internet sex offenders overestimate the ages of the children in the images that they have downloaded as well as the severity of the exploitation or abuse, or the number of children with whom they have committed a contact offence. Such inconsistencies in the reporting of offence-related behaviour may be construed positively as a protective measure, indicating awareness of the 'wrongness' of the behaviour and decreasing the risk of subsequent offending (Harkins et al., 2010). It may also be framed as impression management, or even lying (e.g. Lippert et al., 2010). In part, this fuels our concern that an interest in abuse images is a good indicator of paedophilic interest (Seto, 2010) and that the content of images may prove to relate to who might also commit contact offences and how such offences might find expression (Long et al., under review).

The ongoing concern with how similar, or different, Internet sex offenders are from contact offenders dominates much of the current research (e.g. Neutze et al., 2010). It is apparent that a proportion of people who commit an online offence involving abuse images share similar characteristics to those who offend in the offline environment. Henry et al. (2010) performed a cluster analysis of the scores of a standard psychometric screening battery (part of the Sex Offender Treatment Evaluation Project (STEP) test battery, Beech et al., 1999) provided by the UK National Probation Service on 422 men convicted of Internet sex offences. The majority were convicted of downloading indecent images of children, with thirty-eight convicted of taking images and one man of enticement. Three clusters were identified which were labelled: normal, inadequate, and deviant. Those in the normal cluster were more emotionally stable and less pro-offending in attitude but scored higher for social desirability than men in the inadequate or deviant clusters. The inadequate cluster was characterized by socio-affective difficulties, deficits in levels of self-esteem and emotional loneliness. The deviant group were characterized by very poor victim empathy. The authors felt that their results were similar to the clusters found in contact offender groups. In addition Seto et al. (2011) found that approximately half of a sample of Canadian online offenders admitted to committing a contact sexual offence and 12.2 per cent had an official history of contact sexual offences.

However, it is evident that there are differences between Internet and contact offenders related to demographic characteristics such as age, level of education and measures of intelligence (Eke et al., 2010) as well as psychological variables such as cognitive distortions, emotional dysregulation, empathy and impression management (Howitt and Sheldon, 2007; Bates and Metcalf, 2007; Middleton et al., 2006). Babchishin et al. (2010) in their meta-analysis of twenty-seven samples found that online offenders tended to be Caucasian males younger than the general population, who, although they did not differ in terms of education, were more likely to be unemployed. Both online and offline offenders were more likely to have experienced physical and sexual abuse than the general population. In comparison with offline offenders, online offenders had greater victim empathy, greater sexual deviancy and lower impression management. These authors concluded that youth and unemployment are risk factors for online sexual offending and that this was consistent with typical crime patterns.

Research on the offence histories of Internet offenders and the likelihood of future offending would suggest that with a longer period post-offence more offenders are detected for new offences, with recidivism for contact sexual offences predicted by criminal history, and in particular violent offence history and the age of the offender at the time of their first conviction (Eke et al., 2010). Importantly, this study also examined failures on conditional release, in particular where offenders put themselves in 'risky' situations, such as being alone with children. The finding that one-quarter of the extended sample was charged with failures was consistent with the findings from other sex offender groups. Such failures included breaches of conditions about being alone with children, accessing the Internet and contacting children and downloading child abuse materials, as well as other violations which were non-sexual or indicated non-compliance. This is of interest because while 34 per cent of offenders had a charge for any type of further offence, only 4 per cent were charged with any new contact sexual offence and 7 per cent were charged with new child pornography-related offences. While a modified version of a widely used actuarial risk assessment measure (Risk Matrix 2000; Thornton, 2007) is able significantly to predict contact sexual offending in child pornography offenders (Barnett et al., 2010) the base rate in this sample of 514 offenders was low (1.4 per cent). In a UK sample of seventy-three Internet sex offenders, none of the offenders were convicted of a further offence in a 1.5–4-year follow-up (Osborn et al., 2010). Similarly, Endrass et al. (2009) in a study of 231 men charged with child pornography offences examined recidivism six years after the index offence. In this study 4.8 per cent of the sample had prior convictions for sexual or violent offences, and 1 per cent for a contact offence against a child. Using a broad definition of recidivism, 3 per cent recidivated with a violent or sexual offence, 3.9 per cent with a non-contact sexual offence, and 0.8 per cent with a contact offence, leading these authors to conclude that downloading child pornography alone is not a risk factor for the commission of a contact offence.

Elliott, Beech, Mandeville-Norden et al. (2009) compared 505 Internet sex offenders and 526 contact offenders on a range of psychological measures relating to offence supportive beliefs, empathic concern, interpersonal functioning and emotional management. Contact offending was predicted by an increase in scores of scales of locus of control, perspective taking, empathic concern, over assertiveness, victim empathy distortions, cognitive distortions and cognitive impulsivity. An increase in scores on scales of fantasy, under assertiveness and motor impulsivity were predictive of an Internet offence type. Eke et al. (2010) also report on an unpublished study by Faust et al. (2009) who examined potential risk factors in a sample of 870 child pornography offenders. They identified five variables as being significant predictors of re-arrest for a sexual crime: they included lower education, being single, having non-Internet child pornography, prior sexual offender treatment, and not having pictures of 'adolescent minors'. It is unclear whether this might suggest an older group of offenders, but it does link with concerns about whether we should distinguish men who access images of prepubescent children from those who access images of pubescent or sexually mature young people (Seto, 2010). This also touches upon some of the challenges as to how 'child' is operationalized in national and supranational law (Gillespie, 2010). While analyses of images by law enforcement agencies would suggest that the typical child depicted is a pre-pubescent girl (e.g. Wolak et al., 2005; 2009; Baartz, 2008), an analysis of a sample of seized images within one UK law enforcement database would suggest that the odds of the abuse images being of females versus males were about 4 to 1, and the odds of the images being of white children versus non-white children were about 10 to 1. Of those white female children, approximately 48 per cent were pubescent (Quayle and Jones, 2011). It may be that in many instances we can at best approximate the content of image collections, given the potential volume of images collected and the limited forensic resources of most specialist police units and Glasgow (2010) has suggested that the volume, complexity and inaccessibility of digital evidence has deterred a systematic analysis of the relationship between downloaded material and potential risk.

Image content

Challenges to a systematic analysis stem from difficulties in describing the content of images in any systematic way beyond the age or gender of the child or children. The adoption by the UK Sentencing Advisory Panel (SAP) of the COPINE scale (Taylor et al., 2001) as an objective measure of content was probably not a reflection of the integrity of the scale but rather the absence of anything else (Quayle, 2008). The original COPINE scale had ten levels ranging from indicative images to ones depicting sadism or bestiality. In 2002, in England and Wales, the SAP published their advice to the Court of Appeal on offences involving child pornography. The SAP believed that the nature of the material should be the key factor in deciding the level of sentence, and adapted the COPINE scale to five levels. They dropped levels 1 to 3 completely, arguing that nakedness alone was not indicative of indecency. The proposed structure was therefore that COPINE levels 5 to 6 constitute sentencing level 1 and COPINE levels 7 onwards each constitute an individual sentencing stage (Gillespie, 2003). In spite of concern over its use and the confusion as to whether it is the original scale or the SAP guidelines that are being referred to (Kennington, 2010), having some objective measure does allow us to make comparisons between samples and have some sense of both preferred materials and also (although rarely referred to) the types of sexual activity that the depicted child has been exposed to. Niveau (2010) included data on the files downloaded by thirty-six men from pay-for-view web pages and peer-to-peer networks. Using the original COPINE scale, all files depicted explicit sexual acts between adults and children, although in all cases non-paedophilic pornographic material was also found. Eight participants possessed material corresponding to level 9 (gross assault) or below, whereas the twenty-eight others (78 per cent) collected material classified as level 10, which implies the depiction of at least one scene of humiliation, sadism or other deviant acts committed on a child.

Two further studies have examined image content in samples of men who had committed child pornography offences. Osborn et al. (2010) measured risk using Risk Assessment 2000 and Static 99 with seventy-three offenders. Offenders who were categorized low or medium risk were more frequently reported to have Level 4 and 5 images (Sentencing Guidelines Council, 2007), with one-third of low-risk offenders viewing images at Level 5, depicting sadism or bestiality. The authors signal that this result may be an artefact of the sampling process, but that it may indicate that the images are a by-product of the offence and may not be indicative of more entrenched offending behaviour or an impaired ability to desist. These results appear different from a second UK sample of twenty-two contact offenders and twenty non-contact offenders all found in possession of child abuse images and all of whom were arrested after 2000 (Long et al., under review). The range of the number of images collected was 4–130,745 with contact offenders possessing significantly fewer images at each level of the SAP scale (apart from Level 5). As non-contact offenders were found to have significantly more still images in total than contact offenders, the amount that offenders possessed was calculated as a percentage to explore offenders' possession across the five levels. Contact offenders were found to have a significantly higher percentage of Level 3 and Level 4 still images than non-contact offenders. Non-contact offenders could be distinguished by the larger number of Level 1 images downloaded. Possession of Level 1 and Level 3 images were the best predictors of non-contact and contact offending respectively. There was also a high correlation between the content of still and moving image possession in that offenders who possessed penetrative still images were also likely to possess moving images of penetrative sex. With contact offenders, the more severe the contact offence, the higher the SAP level of the images possessed. Offenders who had penetrated their victims were more likely to possess Level 3 (non-penetrative sexual activity between adults and children), and gender and age of the children within the images were directly associated with those of the contact offence victims. Contact offenders tended to view content with a smaller victim range and were polymorphic with regard to gender. Non-contact offenders had been downloading content for longer than contact offenders and the duration of the collecting behaviour was associated with more images at Level 5.

At face value these two studies appear to contradict each other. In Osborn et al.'s (2010) study one-third of the people who were looking at images of children depicting sadistic abuse or bestiality were found to be at 'low risk' of recidivating, whereas in Long et al.'s study, those who looked at images depicting non-penetrative and penetrative sexual activity between adults and children were more likely to commit a contact offence against a child. In the latter study there was a high correlation between the content of the image, in terms of the sexual offence committed as well as the gender and age of the child, and the sexual assault committed against a further child in the offline environment. This is the first evidence of congruence between images sought and collected and the type of offence committed against a child. The numbers in this study were small and the authors are currently gathering a larger data set, but it will be of interest to see whether these results are further supported.

These studies raise additional concerns about how images are used to determine the sentence given to the offender and whether the sentence should be based on principles of harm or on the likelihood of recidivism. It is apparent that in reality these might yield very different decisions. A more extensive critique of the UK sentencing guidelines can be found in Hebenton et al. (2009) and a further typology of abuse images, extending the COPINE Scale, has been provided by Stapleton (2010).

Desistance

While the above research reflects an ongoing concern with risk and the relationship between viewing images and the commission of a contact offence, it may also be relevant to ask why some men do not seem to progress to offline offences and if there is a possibility that some individuals will, in fact, desist from future offending. Any process model (e.g. Quayle and Taylor, 2003) has to acknowledge that a fraction of people who download abuse images are likely to stop doing so at some point. This may be because the images as stimuli are no longer arousing, although, as Elliott and Beech (2009) have noted, research has been very mixed in its support for any such habituation effect. Alternative explanations include the idea of 'periodically prurient' offenders, whose interest in abuse images is part of a wider interest in all forms of sexual materials, including 'extreme' pornography (Elliott and Beech, 2009). However 'desistance' may also relate to how some people clearly struggle with their sexual feelings and behaviours and will try to avoid situations that facilitate accessing related content (Goode, 2009). This may also be why some men will opt for using various monitoring software as a way of managing their online sexual behaviour (Elliott et al., 2010). However, why do many people who have accessed abuse images not go on to commit contact offences against children if their image choice is indicative of preferential sexual interest in children (Seto et al., 2006)? Eke et al. (2010) suggest that:

> Individuals who seek out child pornography are exhibiting their sexual interest in children in illegal behavior, but some of these individuals may not have the characteristics generally associated with a willingness or ability to engage in more serious illegal behavior involving direct contact with a victim who may show distress, resist, or disclose the sexual contact, resulting in severe personal and legal consequences.
>
> (476)

At present it is difficult to know whether this may also relate to: lack of access to an easily accessible victim; high levels of engagement in online behaviour to the exclusion of other activities; and/or a disconnect between moral values that protect against the commission of a contact offence but not against accessing images that are sexually exploitative or abusive, or the possibility that for some people, the images are simply sufficient to meet their needs.

There is inadequate evidence to provide a strong case for the latter, although this may warrant further investigation. Elliott et al.'s (2009) study with a large sample of convicted Internet and contact sexual offenders indicated that an increase in scores on scales of fantasy, under assertiveness, and motor impulsivity were predictive of an Internet offence type. In a comparative study by Sheldon and Howitt (2007), Internet sex offenders were more likely to be professionally employed; have more years in education; few criminal convictions; report some childhood difficulties and heterosexual sexualized play; and have high levels of paedophile fantasies and cognitive distortions but few criminal convictions of any kind. In this group paedophilic fantasies were related to sex play experiences and closely related themes between early childhood sexual experience and later adult abusive behaviour were evident. The fantasy questionnaire used was different from that in Elliott et al.'s (2009) study and may have been measuring a different construct, but it is of interest that one intervention study did find that:

The average post-stage score on the fantasy subscale of the Interpersonal Reactivity Inventory (Davis, 1983) rose slightly from the pre-stage score (13.26–13.89 within a normative range of 5–16). This scale assesses the degree to which offenders over-identify with fictional characters and it may be that these results indicate that this is a particularly difficult trait to change in those who seek pseudo-intimacy through online interactions.

(Middleton et al., 2009: 14)

Is it possible that for these people the photographs provide an escape into fantasy, which may be underpinned by earlier childhood experiences, and that this is what matters rather than actual coercive contact with a child? Whether, as suggested by Elliott and Beech (2009), this might change over time through normative contact with a 'deviant community' is unclear.

This clearly relates to the function that the images have for the individual and whether downloading is simply a substitute for an actual child as a source of sexual arousal and gratification. Within the offender literature there is evidence from both self-reports (Seto et al., 2010) as well as through bio-signal measures (both polygraph and phallometric) (Buschman et al., 2010; Seto et al., 2006) that sexual photographs of children are arousing, and that this arousal can differentiate between men who use sexual images and those whose preference is contact offending (Seto et al., 2006). There is also evidence that gynophilic men (men preferentially attracted to adult women) on phallometric tests demonstrate the greatest arousal to stimuli of adult women, with systematically decreasing arousal as the female stimuli become younger, and essentially no arousal to any age categories of males or to neutral (non-erotic) stimuli (Lykins et al., 2010). This study also demonstrated that arousal to both pubescent and prepubescent girls were significantly greater than to neutral stimuli ($p < .001$ for both). This would seem to support the fact that in a laboratory setting gynophilic men reliably produce a detectable response to prepubescent girls. With Internet offenders, images appear to be selected to meet some preferred criteria (unlike in a laboratory setting where the images are pre-selected by the researcher). The criteria may relate to a characteristic of the child or children (such as age, gender, ethnic group, physical attributes as in body mass or hair colour) or of the depicted activity (which, for example, defined the levels in the COPINE scale). Glasgow (2010) has argued that these image preferences offer a golden opportunity to analyse unequivocal evidence of sexual deviance known to be associated with risk.

So for a large proportion of these people images are highly arousing, more easily accessible than a child, easier to match in terms of preferred sexual characteristics and scripts, and enable both fantasy and 'safe' sexual activity. Fantasy also seems to be important in relation to online solicitation or grooming. An exploratory study of 'chat room' sex offenders suggested two subgroups (Briggs et al., 2010). The first was described as a contact-driven group, motivated to engage in offline sexual behaviour, and a fantasy-driven group motivated to engage in cybersex without an express wish to meet children offline. Photographs cannot refuse, resist or fail to comply with the wishes of the viewer or bring with them the risk of disclosure.

These photographs also appear to meet other needs. Surjadi et al. (2010), using the Internet Offender-Function Questionnaire (IO-FQ), found that in their sample of forty-three Internet offenders, avoidance of real life was the most salient function, which the authors acknowledge may correspond to a more general underlying construct. Other studies have also suggested that avoidant behaviour may be important in Internet sex offending (Quayle et al., 2006) although McCoy and Fremouw (2010) have contested the evidence for sex functioning as a coping strategy for sexual offenders.

Social contexts for image use

Much of the existing research has tended to focus on the Internet offender as an individual, as opposed to someone within a specific social context. Yet some of the earliest studies of this population (e.g. Durkin, 1997; Durkin and Bryant, 1999; Jenkins, 2001) related to the importance of communication with other members of online communities. A replication of Durkin and Bryant's (1999) original study of an online 'boy-lover' forum would suggest that contrary to expectations, the use of a Usenet newsgroup as a communicative medium has not declined over a decade and that within the forum the use of previously identified justifications for sexual interest in children is still common (O'Halloran and Quayle, 2010). Holt et al. (2010), in an analysis of postings to five 'paedophile' web forums, examined their subculture and enculturation process. The results suggested that the online world of these forum members was shaped by four interrelated normative orders including marginalization, sexuality, law, and security, which were used to generate justifications for behaviour, affect attitudes towards sexual relationships with children, and structure identity. The authors suggest that this affects attitudes and beliefs, and justifies involvement in 'deviance' through a rejection of larger social norms. Clearly not all Internet sex offenders use the Internet in such a way. In Surjadi et al.'s (2010) study there was little evidence of supportive relationships having an important function for these offenders. However, Seto et al. (2010) found that, 'a substantial number of child pornography offenders, particularly in the police sample, participated in online communities and traded child pornography with others' (p. 177). Similarly, in a qualitative study of a small sample of men who produced abuse images, it was found that the social function of image taking to share with the community was the one most frequently referred to by participants (Sheehan and Sullivan, 2010).

Such research would suggest that individuals who have an interest in abuse images may receive significant reinforcement from their online relationships with others who share this interest (Taylor and Quayle, 2003). It also suggests that offender relationships (and associated social rewards) may be strengthened by the mutual provision of rare or personally produced images (Quayle and Taylor, 2002; Sheehan and Sullivan, 2010). Furthermore, individuals who engage with others using socially facilitative online applications demonstrate greater involvement in a wide range of offence-related activities than those who do not. It is hypothesized that, through their desire to develop and maintain online social connections, some offenders may feel compelled to produce child sexual exploitation material that they can then share with their online associates (Carr, 2009 and Chapter 6). As such, contact offending may result as much from a desire to please other members of an online social network as from a desire for sexual engagement with a child (Elliott and Beech, 2009). Clearly, such a finding would have significant implications for policing, offender treatment and child protection activities.

One critical aspect of these social relationships may lie in Internet-initiated incitement and conspiracy to commit child sexual abuse. Gallagher (2007) presented the first research on cases where offenders initiate contact with other individuals over the Internet and incite or conspire with them to commit a contact offence. This study was an attempt to describe a typology of such offences through an examination of police data. However, the research was limited because it examined a disparate number of cases and was unable to explore the relationships between individual members, how these were formed both in the online and offline environment, how these changed over time and how they influenced others. In a further comparative study by McCarthy (2010) of 'contact and non-contact child pornography offenders', contact offenders were more likely than non-contact offenders to communicate both online and in person with others who shared their sexual interests in minors and abuse images. Contact offenders were also more likely to use the Internet to locate potential children and engage in grooming behaviour by sending electronic files containing both child and adult pornography.

It would also seem to be the case that Internet-facilitated commercial sexual exploitation (IF-CSEC) also has an important social element to it. Mitchell et al. (2011) report on telephone interviews with law enforcement related to 1,051 individual arrest cases. Of these, 569 were identified as IF-CSEC. These fell into two main categories: those who used the Internet to purchase or sell access to identified children for sexual purposes, including child pornography production (36 per cent), and those who used the Internet to purchase or sell child pornography images they possessed but did not produce (64 per cent). The study reported that offenders attempting to profit were more likely than those purchasing to: have prior arrests for sexual and non-sexual offences; a history of violence; produce child pornography; *joined forces with other offenders*; and include female offenders. These findings require further investigation.

Self-generated content

One final consideration is self-generated, or user-generated, content. Baines (2008), in her law enforcement response for the Third World Congress, noted that self-generated content by children and young people was becoming of considerable concern. It is of interest that in current analyses of identified children, the National Center for Missing and Exploited Children in the United States is now excluding young people who have uploaded their images, as this was distorting their data (Collins, personal communication, November 2010). In a US nationally representative survey by the Pew Research Center (Lenhart, 2009) 4 per cent of teenagers aged 12–17 who own a mobile phone reported that they have sent sexually suggestive nude or nearly nude images of themselves to someone else via text messaging and 15 per cent have received such images. This increases to 8 per cent and 30 per cent respectively in those who are 17 years old, with teenagers who pay their own bills more likely to send sexual images. This activity is frequently referred to as 'sexting': the practice of sending or posting sexually suggestive text messages and images, including nude or semi-nude photographs, via cellular telephones or over the Internet (Levick and Moon, 2010). Typically, the young person takes a picture of himself or herself with a mobile phone camera (or other digital camera), or has someone else take the picture. This is then stored as a digital image and transmitted via mobile phone as a text message, photo-send function or electronic mail. Additionally, the subject may use a mobile phone to post the image to a social networking website like Facebook or MySpace (McBeth, 2010). Leary (2007; 2010) has referred to this material as 'self-produced child pornography'. Self-produced child pornography is images that possess the following criteria: they meet the legal definition of child pornography and were originally produced by a minor with no coercion, grooming or adult participation whatsoever. The definition does not focus exclusively on the young person who makes the image but also those, 'juveniles in the distribution chain who may coerce production, or later possess, distribute, or utilize such images' (p. 492). Leary (2010) highlights that the term sexting has been used variously to describe: one minor sending one picture to a perceived significant other; a minor taking and/or distributing pictures of him/herself and others engaged in sexually explicit conduct; a minor extensively forwarding or disseminating a nude picture of another youth without his/her knowledge; a minor posting such pictures on a web site; an older teen asking (or coercing) another youth for such pictures; a person impersonating a classmate to 'dupe' and or blackmail other minors into sending pictures; adults sending pictures or videos to minors or possessing sexually explicit pictures of juveniles; and adults sending sexually suggestive text or images to other adults. These are all different activities, only some of which would be deemed illegal in many jurisdictions.

Of relevance to this chapter, Leary (2010) asks questions about the specific harms caused by 'self-produced child pornography' and whether it may be understood as normal self-exploration or an inconsistent criminalization of legal sexual activity. She argues that young people risk significant harm when they engage in self-produced child pornography either in the initial sending or subsequent transmissions. This relates to the fact that an image exists out of the subject's control for the remainder of his or her life. The harm remains because of the pictures' existence and distribution. Leary (2010) states that, 'The visual images created in self-produced child pornography manifest analogous harms. While children are no doubt more severely harmed in the production stage of conventional child pornography, children in self-produced child pornography are harmed. Those images document the youth's participation in the production and that is exacerbated by the circulation throughout the Internet' (p. 526). However Wastler (2010) has argued that even though self-produced images create a lasting permanent record that may cause future emotional and psychological harm to the minor, the circulation of such images does not 'revictimize' the juvenile with every viewing. Humbach (2009) discusses many recent cases in the US where young people have been prosecuted for taking photographs of themselves while engaging in lawful sexual activity and the harms that might follow from a possible child pornography conviction. He concludes:

> In the end, it cannot be ignored that there are also generational factors at work in the prosecutions of teens for sexting and autopornography. The prosecutorial and judicial personnel who are acting in these prosecutions are typically two or more generations removed from the teenagers whose sexual expression is condemned and whose prospects are drastically affected. Ultimately, however, efforts such as these are generally futile. The future and its values belong to those whose lives lie mostly ahead of them.
>
> (Humbach, 2009: 485)

However, Heverly (2008) has pointed out that there is little, if any, explicit recognition among young people that digital media may not only be used by them, but in fact may use them. This is expressed very powerfully in the following: 'when young people become the subject (or object, if you will) of digital media, they are used by it; when a digital media artefact – a digital media file of any type, for example video, audio, still image, text – that features them is created, part of them becomes entangled with the digital media and forms the substance of it' (p. 199). Heverly (2008) distinguishes between those young people who actively create media files in which they are embedded and those for whom the activity is passive. This brings us back to Leary's (2010) point that such media files may not only be used by the person or people within the images but also by other young people or adults within the distribution chain. Ostrager (2010) suggests that within this group of producers and distributors of self-generated content there is a need to distinguish between a person who is a 'mass sexter' and someone who is a 'repeat sexter'. He suggests a three-tier approach. Tier one includes young people who sext a picture to one person or possess one picture but who do not disseminate it. Tier two are described as mass sexters who send a graphic picture to up to ten people, or a repeat sexter who sends to up to five people in one month. Tier three are juveniles that send mass texts to eleven or more people or a repeat sexter who disseminates to six or more people at different times within one month. While it would seem that the numbers chosen to justify whether someone falls into either of the tiers is somewhat arbitrary, there does appear to be a legitimate concern to distinguish between sexting as a serious offence which poses a danger to others and when it is simply the product of a legitimate sexual relationship.

Conclusion

While from 2000 onwards we have seen a growing body of evidence that relates to the Internet sex offender, much less investment has been made into research on the photographs and the children in them. This is peculiar, given the importance of the assumption of harm in both legislation and sentencing, as well as it being the driver behind much service development (for example, in the UK, the Child Exploitation and Online Protection (CEOP) Centre delivers a multi-agency service dedicated to tackling the exploitation of children, and one of their main operational units is their 'Harm Reduction Faculty'). Nor has there been much research about the content of images collected and what this might tell us about the sexual interests of the offender, the relationship of images to risk, and the commission of further offences against children. It is difficult to know why this has happened and why we have largely ignored, outside of securing a conviction, the photographs and moving images that in any other context might be thought of as evidential material.

References

Adler, A. (2001). The perverse law of child pornography. *Columbia Law Review, 209*, 1–101.
—— (2008). All porn all the time. *31 NYU Rev. L. and Soc. Change* 695.
Akdeniz, Y. (2008) *Internet Child Pornography and the Law. National and International Responses.* Aldershot: Ashgate.
Altobelli, T. (2010) Cyber-abuse – a new worldwide threat to children's rights. *Family Court, 48*(3), 459–81.
Baartz, D. (2008). *Australians, the Internet and Technology-enabled Child Sex Abuse: A Statistical Profile.* Canberra: Australian Federal Police.
Babchishin, K.M., Hanson, R.K. and Hermann, C.A. (2010) The characteristics of online sex offenders: A meta-analysis of online sex offenders. *Sexual Abuse: A Journal of Research and Treatment.* 1–32.
Baines, V. (2008). *Online Child Sexual Abuse: The Law Enforcement Response.* Bangkok: ECPAT International.
Barnett, G.D., Wakeling, H.C. and Howard, P.D. (2010). An examination of the predictive validity of the Risk Matrix 2000 in England and Wales. *Sexual Abuse: A Journal of Research and Treatment.*
Bates, A. and Metcalf, C. (2007). A psychometric comparison of internet and non-internet sex offenders from a community treatment sample. *Journal of Sexual Aggression, 13*, 11–20.
Bausbaum, J.P. (2010). Inequitable sentencing for possession of child pornography: A failure to distinguish voyeurs from pederasts. *Hastings Law Journal, 61*(5), 1281–305.
Beech, A.R., Fisher, D. and Beckett, R.C. (1999). *Step 3: An Evaluation of the Prison Sex Offender Treatment Programme.* London: Home Office.
Blevins, J.L. and Anton, F. (2008). Muted voices in the legislative process: The role of scholarship in in US Congressional efforts to protect children from internet pornography. *New Media Society, 10*, 115–37.
Bourke, M.L. and Hernandez, A.E. (2009). The 'Butner Study' redux: A report of the incidence of hands-on child victimization by child pornography offenders. *Journal of Family Violence, 24*, 183–91.
Briggs, P., Simon, W.T. and Simonsen, S. (2010). An exploratory study of Internet-initiated sexual offenses and the chat room sex offender: Has the Internet enabled a new typology of sex offender? *Sexual Abuse: A Journal of Research and Treatment, 22 (4)*, 72–91.
Buschman, J., Wilcox, D., Krapohl, D., Oelrich, M. and Hackett, S. (2010). Cybersex offender risk assessment. An explorative study. *Journal of Sexual Aggression, 16 (2)*, 197–210.

Buschman, J., Bogaerts, S., Foulger, S., Wilcox, D., Sosnowski, D. and Cushman, B. (2010). Sexual history disclosure polygraph examinations with cybercrime offences: A first Dutch explorative study. *International Journal of Offender Therapy Comp Criminol, 54*, 395–411

Carr, A. (2009). The social dimension of the online trade of child sexual exploitation material. Paper presented at the global symposium for examining the relationship between online and offline offences and preventing the sexual exploitation of children. Chapel Hill, North Carolina, 6–7 April.

Davidson, J., Martellozzo, E. and Lorenz, M. (2009). *Evaluation of CEOP ThinkUKnow Internet Safety Programme and Exploration of Young People's Internet Safety Knowledge.* Available online from http://www.cats-rp.org.uk/pdf%20files/Internet%20safety%20report%204-2010.pdf.

Davis, M.H. (1983). Measuring individual differences in empathy: Evidence for a multiple dimensional approach. *Journal of Personality and Social Psychology, 44*, 113–26.

Durkin, K.F. (1997). Misuse of the Internet by pedophiles: Implications for law probation practice. *Federal Probation, 61*, 14–18.

Durkin, K.F. and Bryant, C. (1999). Propagandizing pederasty: A thematic analysis of online exculpatory accounts of unrepentant paedophiles. *Deviant Behaviour: An Inter-Disciplinary Journal, 20*(2), 103–27.

Eke, A.W., Seto, M.C. and Williams, J. (2010). Examining the criminal history and future offending of child pornography offenders: An extended prospective follow-up study. *Law and Human Behavior*, 1–13.

Eliott, I., Findlater, D. and Hughes, T. (2010). Practice report: A review of e-Safety remote computer monitoring for UK sex offenders. *Journal of Sexual Aggression,16*(2), 237–48.

Elliott, I.A. and Beech, A.R. (2009). Understanding online child pornography use: Applying sexual offender theory to Internet offenders. *Aggression and Violent Behavior, 14*, 180–93.

Elliott, I.A., Beech, A.R., Mandeville-Norden, T. and Hayes, E. (2009). Psychological profiles of internet sexual offenders. *Sexual Abuse: A Journal of Research and Treatment, 21,* 76–92.

Endrass, J., Urbaniok, F., Hamermeister, L.C., Benz, C., Elbert, T., Laubacher, A. and Rosseger, A. (2009). The consumption of Internet child pornography and violent and sex offending. *BMC Psychiatry, 9*, 43

Eneman, M. (2010) Internet service provider (ISP) filtering of child abuse material: A critical reflection of its effectiveness. *Journal of Sexual Aggression, 16*(2), 223–37.

Faust, E., Renaud, C. and Bickart, W. (2009). Predictors of Re-offence among a Sample of Federally Convicted Child Pornography Offenders. Paper presented at the 28th Annual Conference of the Association for the Treatment of Sexual Abusers, Dallas, TX.

Finkelhor, D. (2009). The prevention of childhood sexual abuse. *The Future of Children, 19*(2), 169–94.

Gallagher, B. (2007). Internet-initiated incitement and conspiracy to commit child sexual abuse (CSA): the typology, extent and nature of known cases. *Journal of Sexual Aggression, 13*(2), 101–19.

Gillespie A.A. (2003). Sentences for offences involving child pornography. *Criminal Law Review*, 81–93.

—— (2010). Legal definitions of child pornography. *Journal of Sexual Aggression, 16*(1), 19–32.

Glasgow, D. (2010). The potential of digital evidence to contribute to risk assessment of internet offenders. *Journal of Sexual Aggression, 16*(1), 223–37.

Goode, S.D. (2009). *Understanding and Addressing Sexual Attraction to Children: A Study of Paedophiles in Contemporary Society*. Abingdon: Routledge.

Harkins, L., Beech, A.R. and Goodwill, A.M. (2010). Examining the influence of denial, motivation, and risk on sexual recidivism. *Sexual Abuse: A Journal of Research and Treatment, 22*, 78–94.

Hebenton, B., Shaw, D. and Pease, K. (2009). Offences involving indecent photographs and pseudo-photographs of children: An analysis of sentencing guidelines. *Psychology, Crime and Law, 15*(5), 425–40.

Henry, O., Mandeville-Norden, R., Hayes, E. and Egan, V. (2010). Do internet based sexual offenders reduce to normal, inadequate and deviant groups? *Journal of Sexual Aggression, 6*(1), 33–46.

Heverly, R.A. (2008). Growing up digital: Control and the pieces of a digital life. In T. McPherson (ed.), *Digital Youth, Innovation, and the Unexpected. The John D. and Catherine T. MacArthur Foundation Series on Digital Media and Learning*. Cambridge, MA: The MIT Press, pp. 199–218.

Hinkson, M. (2009). Australia's Bill Henson scandal: notes on the new cultural attitude to images. *Visual Studies, 24*(3), 202–13.

Holt, T.J., Blevins, K.R. and Burkert, N. (2010). Considering the pedophile culture online. *Sexual Abuse, 22*(1), 3–24.

Howitt, D. and Sheldon, K. (2007). The role of cognitive distortions in paedophilic offending: Internet and contact offenders compared. *Psychology, Crime and Law, 13*(5), 469–86.

Humbach, J.A. (2009). 'Sexting' and the First Amendment. *37 Hastings Const. L.Q.* 433–86.

Internet Safety Technical Taskforce (2008). *Enhancing Child Safety and Online Technologies: Final Report of the Internet Safety Technical Task Force to the Multi-state Working Group on Social Networking of State Attorneys General of the United States*. The Berkman Center for Internet and Society at Harvard University.

Jenkins, P. (2001). *Beyond Tolerance: Child Pornography on the Internet*. New York: New York University Press.

—— (2009). Failure to launch: Why do some social issues fail to detonate moral panics? *British Journal of Criminology, 49*, 35–47.

Jones, V. and Skogrand, E. (2005). *Position Paper Regarding Online Images of Sexual Abuse and other Internet Related Sexual Exploitation of Children*. Copenhagen: Save the Children Europe Group.

Kennington, R. (2010). Not the Copine scale. *NOTA News, 63*, 4.

King, P.J. (2008). No plaything: Ethical issues concerning child-pornography. *Ethic Theory and Moral Practice, 11*, 327–45.

Kramer, R. (2010). APA guidelines ignored in development of diagnostic criteria for pedohebephilia. *Archives of Sexual Behavior, 40*(2), 433–5.

Leary, M.G. (2007). Self-produced child pornography: The appropriate societal response to juvenile self-exploitation, *Va. J. Soc. Pol'y and L., 15*(1), 12–14.

—— (2010). Sexting or self-produced child pornography? The dialog continues – structured prosecutorial discretion within a multidisciplinary response. *Va. J. Soc. Pol'y and L., 17*, 486–566.

Lenhart (2009). *Teens and Sexting*. Pew Research Centre. Available online at http://www.pewinternet.org/~/media//Files/Reports/2009/PIP_Teens_and_Sexting.pdf.

Leonard, M.M. (2010). 'I did what I was directed to do but he didn't touch me': The impact of being a victim of internet offending. *Journal of Sexual Aggression, 16*(2), 249–56.

Levick, M. and Moon, K. (2010). Prosecuting sexting as child pornography: A critique. *Val. U. L. Rev., 44*, 1035–54.

Lippert, T., Cross, T.P., Jones, L. and Walsh, W. (2010). Suspect confession of child sexual abuse to investigators. *Child Maltreatment, 15*(2), 161–70.

Livingstone, S., Haddon, L., Görzig A. and Ólafsson, K. (2010). Risks and safety on the Internet. *Risks and Safety on the Internet: The Perspective of European Children. Initial Findings*. LSE, London: EU Kids Online.

Long, M.L., Alison, L.A., McManus, M.A. and McCallum, C. (under review). Child pornography offenders: A comparison between contact and non-contact offenders' possession of indecent images of children. *Sexual Abuse: A Journal of Research and Treatment*.

Lykins, A.D., Cantor, J.M., Kuban, M.E., Blak, T., Dickey, R., Klassen, P.E. and Blanchard, R. (2010). Sexual arousal to female children in gynephilic men. *Sexual Abuse: A Journal of Research and Treatment, 22*(3), 279–89.

McBeth, I.A. (2010). Prosecute the cheerleader, save the world? Asserting federal jurisdiction over child pornography crimes committed through 'sexting'. *U. Rich. L. Rev., 44*, 1327–63.

McCarthy, J. (2010). Internet sexual activity: A comparison between contact and non-contact child pornography offenders. *Journal of Sexual Aggression, 16*(2), 181–96.

McCoy, K. and Fremouw, W. (2010). The relation between negative affect and sexual offending: A critical review. *Clinical Psychology Review, 30*(3), 317–25.

McKee, A. (2010). Everything is child abuse. *Media International Australia, 135*, 131–40.

Mains, B.A. (2010). Virtual child pornography, and the first amendment: How developments in technology and shifting First Amendment jurisprudence have affected the criminalisation of child pornography. *Hastings Constitutional L.Q.*, 809–36.

Malón, A. (2009). The 'participating victim' in the study of erotic experiences between children and adults: An historical analysis. *Archives of Sexual Behavior, 40*(1), 169–88.

Middleton, D., Elliott, I., Mandeville-Norden, R. and Beech, A.R. (2006). An investigation into the applicability of the Ward and Siegert Pathways Model of child sexual abuse with Internet offenders. *Psychology, Crime and Law, 12*(6), 589–603.

Middleton, D., Elliott, I., Mandeville-Norden, R. and Hayes, E. (2009). Does treatment work with Internet sex offenders? Emerging findings from the Internet Sex Offender Treatment Programme (i-SOTP). *Journal of Sexual Aggression, 15*(1), 5–19.

Mirkin, H. (2009). The social, political, and legal construction of the concept of child pornography. *Journal of Homosexuality, 56*(2), 233–67.

Mitchell, K.J., Jones, L.M., Finkelhor, D. and Wolak, J. (2011). Internet-facilitated commercial sexual exploitation of children: Findings from a nationally representative sample of law enforcement agencies in the United States (2010). *Sexual Abuse: A Journal of Research and Treatment, 23*(1), 43–71.

Neutze, J., Seto, M.L., Schaefer, G.A., Mundt, I.A. and Beier, K. (2010). Predictors of child pornography offences and child sexual abuse in a community sample of pedophiles and hebephiles. *Sexual Abuse: A Journal of Research and Treatment, 22*(4), 3–24.

Niveau, G. (2010). Cyber-pedocriminality: Characteristics of a sample of Internet child pornography offenders. *Child Abuse and Neglect, 34*, 570–75.

O'Halloran, E., and Quayle, E. (2010). A content analysis of a 'boy-love' support forum: Revisiting Durkin and Bryant. *Journal of Sexual Aggression, 16*, 71–85.

Osborn, J., Elliott, I.A. and Beech, A.R. (2010). The use of actuarial risk assessment measures with UK Internet child pornography offenders. *Journal of Aggression, Conflict and Peace Research, 2*(3), 16–24.

Ost, S. (2010). Criminalising fabricated images of child pornography: A matter of harm or morality? *Legal Studies, 30*(2), 230–56.

Ostrager, B. (2010). SMS.OMG! TTYL: Translating the law to accommodate today's teens and the evolution from texting to sexting. *Family Court Review, 48*(4), 712–26.

Oswell, D. (2006). When images matter: Internet child pornography, forms of observation and an ethics of the virtual. *Information, Communication and Society, 9*(2), 244–65.

Quayle, E. (2008). Internet offending. In D.R. Laws and W. O'Donohue (eds), *Sexual Deviance*. New York: Guilford Press, pp. 439–58.

Quayle, E. and Jones, T. (2011). Sexualized images of children on the Internet. *Sexual Abuse: A Journal of Research and Treatment, 23*(1), 7–21.

Quayle, E and Taylor, M. (2002). Child pornography and the Internet: Perpetuating a cycle of abuse. *Deviant Behavior, 23*(4), 331–62.

—— (2003). Model of problematic Internet use in people with a sexual interest in children. *CyberPsychology & Behavior, 6*(1), 93–106.

Quayle, E., Vaughan, M. and Taylor, M. (2006). Sex offenders, Internet child abuse images and emotional avoidance: The importance of values. *Aggression and Violent Behaviour, 11*(1), 1–11.

Renold, E. and Creighton, S.J. (2003). *Images of Abuse: A Review of the Evidence on Child Pornography*. London: NSPCC.

Riegel, D.L. (2010). The participating victim: Complement to Malón. *Archives of Sexual Behavior, 39,* 1027–8.

Sentencing Guidelines Council. (2007). *Sexual Offences Act 2003: Definitive Guideline*. London: Sentencing Guidelines Secretariat.

Seto, M. (2010). Child pornography use and Internet solicitation in the diagnosis of pedophilia. *Archives of Sexual Behavior, 39,* 591–3.

Seto, M.C., Cantor, J.M., and Blanchard, R. (2006). Child pornography offences are a valid diagnostic indicator of pedophilia. *Journal of Abnormal Psychology, 115,* 610–15.

Seto, M.C., Hanson, R.K., Babchishin, K.M. (2011). Contact sexual offending by men with online sexual offenses. *Sex Abuse, 23*(1), 124–45.

Seto, M. C., Reeves, L. and Jung, S. (2010). Motives for child pornography offending: The explanations given by the offenders. *Journal of Sexual Aggression, 16,* 169–80.

Sheehan, V. and Sullivan, J. (2010). A qualitative analysis of child sex offenders involved in the manufacture of indecent images of children. *Journal of Sexual Aggression, 16*(2), 143–68.

Sheldon, K. and Howitt, D. (2007). *Sex Offenders and the Internet*. Chichester: Wiley.

—— (2008). Sexual fantasy in paedophile offenders: Can any model explain satisfactorily new findings from a study of Internet and contact sexual offenders? *Legal and Criminological Psychology, 13,* 137–58.

Stapleton, A. (2010). Knowing it when you (don't) see it: Mapping the pornographic child in order to diffuse the paedophilic gaze. *Global Media Journal: Australian Edition, 4*(2), 1–21.

Stewart, H. (2010). The limits of the harm principle. *Criminal Law and Philosophy, 4,* 17–35.

Surjadi, B., Bullens, R., Van Horn, J. and Bogaerts, S. (2010). Internet offending: Sexual and non-sexual functions within a Dutch sample. *Journal of Sexual Aggression, 16*(1), 47–58.

Svedin, C.G. and Back, K. (2003). *Why Didn't They Tell Us? Sexual Abuse in Child Pornography*. Stockholm : Save the Children Sweden.

Taylor, M. and Quayle, E. (2003). *Child Pornography: An Internet Crime*. Brighton: Routledge.

Taylor, M., Holland, G. and Quayle, E. (2001). Typology of paedophile picture collections. *The Police Journal, 74*(2), 97–107.

Thornton, D. (2007). Scoring guide for the Risk Matrix 2000.9/SVC. Available online at http://www.cfcp.bham.ac.uk/Extras/SCORING%20GUIDE%20FOR%20RISK%20MATRIX%202000.9-%20SVC%20-%20(ver.%20Feb%202007).pdf.

Wastler, S. (2010). The harm in 'sexting'? Analyzing the constitutionality of child pornography statutes that prohibit the voluntary production, possession, and dissemination of sexually explicit images by teenagers. *Harv. J.L. and Gender, 33*, 687–702.

Wolak, J., Finkelhor, D. and Mitchell, K.J. (2005). *Child-pornography Possessors Arrested in Internet-Related Crimes: Findings from the National Juvenile Online Victimization Study*. Washington: National Center for Missing and Exploited Children.

—— (2009). Trends in arrests of 'online predators'. Crime Against Children Research Center. Available from http://www.unh.edu/ccrc/pdf/cv194.pdf.

Wolak, J., Finkelhor, D., Mitchell, K. and Ybarra, M. (2008). Online 'predators' and their victims: Myths, realities, and implications for prevention and treatment. *American Psychologist, 63*(2): 111–28.

2   Children within the images

Linda Jonsson, Linköping University

Carl Göran Svedin, Linköping University

Overview

Children in sexual images

The near infinite numbers of sexual images on the Internet showing under-aged children raises many questions, not least who the children in the images are. The concept of sexual images is often equated with sexual abusive images or child pornography and vice versa, which is why it can be confusing as to how we should describe the children within the images. As well as the need for clear definitions there is also a pressing need for further research in the field of identified children in the images.

Around the world 2,025 children have been identified in what Interpol has defined as child pornographic images (Interpol, International Child Sexual Exploitation Image Database, 2011). This is just a fraction of the children in all of the child sexual images that exist. The children depicted in the images are both girls and boys, with different ethnicity and different skin colour, and of all ages (Fig. 2.1). This gives us an indication that the problem is global in nature and not confined just to particular groups of children. Though it seems that there are some differences, there are some characteristics that are more common when it comes to children in sexual images. The Child Exploitation and Online Protection Centre (CEOP) has developed a database, ChildBase, which includes child abusive images gathered from police seizures across the United Kingdom. The database is continually updated. Recently a study was conducted (Quayle and Jones, 2011) which included 10 per cent of the, at that time, 247,950 images to find out more about the characteristics of the children in the images. Quayle and Jones found that the odds for the images to show a female child compared to a male was 4 to 1. It was ten times more likely that the depicted child was white vs non-white. The children in the images were divided into three age groups – pubescent, prepubescent and very young – and the most common group was prepubescent, which generally means having the appearance of children less than 10 years of age. The smallest group was the very young (0.7 per cent girls and 1.6 per cent boys) which means babies or children of less than 2 years of age.

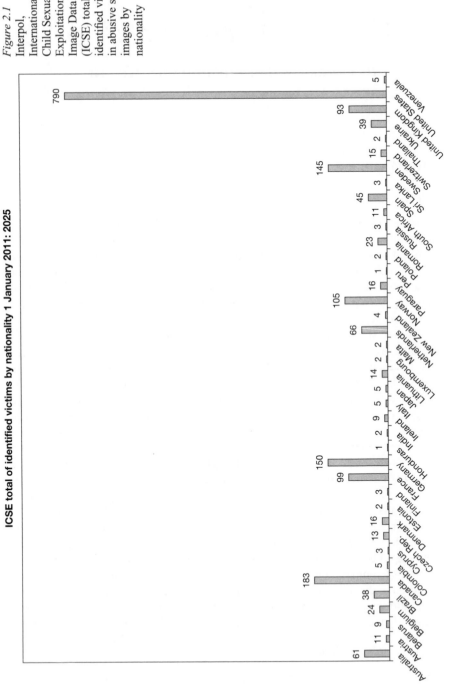

Figure 2.1
Interpol,
International
Child Sexual
Exploitation
Image Data Base
(ICSE) total
identified victims
in abusive sexual
images by
nationality

ICSE total of identified victims by nationality 1 January 2011: 2025

Anna, Alice and Björn: examples of children in sexual images

The histories that lie behind online sexual images might be quite different. Anna, Alice, and Björn are all children who have had sexual images of themselves placed online, but the images were produced and distributed in very different ways.

Anna

Anna, 14 years old, came to a child psychiatric clinic after her parents discovered her having webcam sex with an older man. Her parents were concerned about Anna frequently being absent from school and avoiding her old friends. She spent more and more time in front of the computer and had hundreds of friends online. Around twenty online contacts had led to sexual encounters offline with boys of her own age but also with older men. Anna described herself as very sexually curious and found it exciting with all the attention she was getting from men. Anna had published images of herself nude but also when masturbating. She considered starting to ask for compensation for sexual favours. When the therapist asked her about the images she said that she was proud of them but wouldn't like any family or friends to know about them.

Alice

Alice and Jens had been together for several months, and had filmed themselves having sex. Alice also sent nude pictures to Jens's mobile phone. When their relationship ended, Alice asked to have the pictures and films back but Jens refused. Instead, he posted them on various websites. As a consequence, Alice was contacted by men who asked her for sexual favours. Some students at her school also knew about the images that flourished online, which Alice found very embarrassing.

Björn

When Björn was 5 years old his father wanted him to 'suck him off'. That was the first time. After that the father kept abusing Björn sexually until he was 11 years old. On two occasions the partner of Björn's father had sexual intercourse with him. Björn also had to watch pornographic films together with his father. Many of the sexual abuses were filmed or photographed. Björn did not tell anyone about the abuse. The abuse was uncovered when the police learned about the images. Björn was 15 years old at that time.

These examples illustrate three different ways in which sexual images of under-aged children can arise. For Anna her self-produced and self-distributed images were part of a game and something she enjoyed doing. Initially she did not consider it a problem. Alice's example illustrates how images can be produced in a consensual way, without the presence of violence, but may later be used in a way which was not originally planned. Finally, in Björn's case the images were taken during sexual abuse and the perpetrator produced and distributed the images.

Fig. 2.2 illustrates these different processes. All situations include children in sexually abusive images and possibly material that could be classified as child pornography, since the images in many countries would be considered illegal material.

In addition to the examples above there are images of nude children, for example taken by a person on a beach, without the knowledge of the child. The purposes of the images are sexual and therefore they could be considered to be child pornography. These images should not be confused with domestic pictures of nude children that most families have at home.

In this chapter we will describe children in sexual images under the age of 18 years old, based on material from a Swedish project aimed at gaining knowledge about children and online sexual abuse: The Online Project (Jonsson et al., 2009) and a study concerning identified children in child pornographic images (Svedin and Back, 2003).

Self-produced sexual material

Posting sexual images online: a risk behaviour

Research studies (e.g. Svedin and Priebe, 2009; Daneback and Månsson, 2009) reveal that most youth do not have experience of exposing themselves sexually online. In a Swedish study consisting of 3,500 young people in secondary school (aged about 17–19), approximately 10 per cent had experience of posting images of themselves in which they were undressed. A larger proportion, 11.9 per cent of

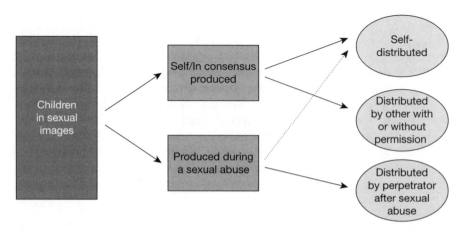

Figure 2.2 Children in sexual images

the male students and 16.4 per cent of the female students, answered that they had posed nude in front of a webcam or mobile phone. A smaller proportion (6.1 per cent of the males and 4.9 per cent of the females) stated that they had masturbated in front of a webcam or mobile phone. The participants who had exposed themselves sexually showed worse psychosocial health, lower self-esteem, lower sense of coherence, and an experience of less care and more control than the rest of the participants (Svedin and Priebe, 2009). Researchers have studied young people with risk behaviour online and found that those who provide personal information, e.g. name, telephone numbers, images, etc., or chat about sex with unknown people online are at greater risk for sexual solicitations and therefore are at greater risk of being sexually abused (Wolak et al., 2008). Also Svedin and Priebe (2009) consider posting sexual images online as risk behaviour and therefore must be taken seriously.

The Online Project at Child and Adolescent Psychiatric Unit, BUP Elefanten

BUP Elefanten is a child and adolescent psychiatric clinic at the university hospital of Linköping, Sweden. The unit specializes in the treatment of children who are victims of sexual abuse and/or physical abuse. With financial support from World Childhood Foundation and Telia Sonera, the Online Project was established to gain knowledge about child victims of online sexual abuse. The project started in 2006 and finished in 2010 and included work with researchers and professionals who have been in touch with victimized children as well as abused children. In total, thirty-one children were offered support and treatment at BUP Elefanten. For research purposes, eleven teenage girls, who had suffered sexual abuse via information technology (IT) or who had shown risky online behaviour, were interviewed. Thirty-two interviews were conducted with staff who worked at child and adolescent psychiatric units or social services. All contacts that were made are described in the two reports from the project: *Abused Online* (Nyman, 2006) and *Children and Sexual Abuse via IT* (Jonsson et al., 2009).

The purpose of the project was to learn more about child victims of sexual abuse via IT and what the consequences of these abuses could entail. Early in the project it was evident that abuse connected to IT could take many forms. Based on the different characteristics, the children were divided into four groups:

- children sexually bullied/harassed online;
- children exploited in images of sexual abuse and other sexualized images;
- children suffering sexual abuse online or offline via online contacts;
- and children receiving compensation for online or offline sex via online contacts.

In certain cases a child had been abused in several ways and therefore belonged to more than one group. Later in our work we found other types of situations which possibly belong in another type of category, e.g. trafficked children.

In many of the above-mentioned groups there existed sexual images of different types. Some of the material had been produced and distributed by the perpetrator but in most examples the children themselves had produced and distributed the images. The material was in many cases not produced with any occurrence of violence or sexual abuse. Some of this material could probably be classified as child pornography. Moreover, in some cases the material was produced with consent, but afterwards used in an abusive way.

The images

The children in the project (interviewed or in treatment at the unit) described the pictures as ranging from nude pictures to pictures and films in which they had sex with themselves or one or more partners. A few of the children had received compensation, e.g. money or top-ups for their mobile phone cards, for the images.

Most children were not very willing to talk about the actual images. They felt ashamed and knew that there could be risks connected with the publication of the pictures. In an interview Sara explained that she likes the images but that she never talks about what she is doing since it would not be accepted among her family or friends.

> The pictures are pretty in one way, but of course, if I showed them to you now it would feel embarrassing and you would probably be disgusted.
>
> (Sara, 16)

Our experience is that some of the children in sexual images are very concerned about the images being widely distributed, and some are not. Children who showed little concern about the images often suggested that they had not had any negative experiences in connection with them and that they felt that they were in control.

Cathrine, 15, was interviewed about her use of her mobile phone and the Internet. She said that she daily sent 'funny pictures' to friends on her mobile phone, sometimes showing her naked in different sexual poses.

> the risk that some of my friends would spread my pictures is out of the question. Everyone is sending pictures to one another . . . But I wouldn't publish a nude picture or a picture when I am having sex on the Internet. That is risky since you don't know who will find it.

Cathrine was also asked in the interview if she had had webcam sex. She laughed and said: 'Who hasn't? Why do you think the webcam was invented?'

In contrast to Sara and Cathrine, we also had contact with children who were very preoccupied and worried about their images online. Who will see me? What will my parents say? What will happen later in life when I am searching for a job? In many of the cases in which the children were concerned about their images they had often had experiences suggesting that the images had been used in an undesired way. In many cases they also feared that someone else with access to the images would distribute them. We also had contact with children who dropped out of school, fearing that the images would be discovered, or children who suffered harassment and had to change school when the images surfaced. A father called the clinic asking for help because his son had told him that he had had webcam sex with someone he thought was a girl who later turned out to be an older man. The abused boy was very ashamed and feared that the man had distributed the film. The boy stopped going to school and quit sports training and seeing friends. He spent all his days searching for the film on various homosexual sites online. He also became very aggressive, especially to his mother, who had to contact both social services and the acute psychiatric service.

Aware of the risks – but not

Most of the children in the Online Project were well informed about the dangers of the Internet and knew that if they, for example, published a sexual image, this was associated with risk. The child's own risk-taking and personal activities were some of the most characteristic features of all the children in the project. Even where there was a high degree of risk-taking the children often tried to protect themselves: for example, by having an online nickname not related to their real name. One girl interviewed said that she would never post sexual images online but did not hesitate when it came to selling sex. She argued that the pictures were permanent but the communication and physical meetings with her customers were of a temporary nature.

We found that many children felt safe online because they believed that they were anonymous. This might also contribute to the children saying/writing things, or posting pictures and films, which they probably would not have done outside the Internet. The children were aware of the fact that they were taking risks but not aware of the consequences.

Someone seeing me

The children in the Online Project all displayed a great need for attention and recognition: that someone would 'see' them. Many of the children had been brought up in family situations with insufficient attachment and/or neglect. From the outside many families looked as though they functioned well but often the contact between the parents and the child was lacking, e.g. they seldom talked with each other, or the child did not feel that they could trust their parents. The child often felt alone, worried and abandoned due to life experiences in the family, such as divorce, illness or death of a family member. Their need for affirmation could immediately be provided for online. Through all of the compliments they received, the child felt chosen and unique, something they had lacked at home or among friends

> He said that I had such a beautiful language. No one has ever said that to me before.
>
> (Emma, 13)

Curiosity about sex

To be curious about sex is natural when it comes to adolescents. Through the Internet most teenagers have access to pornographic sites or social networking sites where sex is a common subject of discussion. Some of the children in the project have experienced insecurity about their sexual identity and have then used the Internet to find answers to their questions about for example, normality. For some children their curiosity and interest in sex has made them publish sexual images or have webcam sex. Some children have lived in sexualized home environments where other family members have posted sexual images online, which might have contributed to difficulties for the children in knowing what is acceptable or what not to do.

Lured and manipulated

> It was like I was brainwashed. But I wasn't aware of it then.
>
> (Lotta, 14)

Many of the children in the Online Project have been in contact with people online who have manipulated them. They have not realized the consequences of their interaction until it has been too late. The fact that adolescents are still in their bio-psycho-social development and lack extensive life experience may contribute to them having difficulties with assessing the intentions of their online contacts. Moreover, the Internet provides fewer clues as how to interpret someone's intentions compared to real life. Most likely these children would not have given nude pictures away in an offline situation.

In a well-publicized Swedish criminal case, the Alexandra case (see Leander et al., 2008), a man lured in hundreds of Swedish teenage girls saying he was a model agent called Alexandra. The girls sent him nude pictures and hoped for modelling contracts that never materialized. Alexandra often paid for the pictures, which was a sign of how serious 'her' interest was for some of the girls. Some of the contacts with Alexandra also resulted in sexual meetings offline. The girls knew they were going to meet a man who would pay them for sex. Some had realized that Alexandra and the man was the same person, but some had not and thought that the man was a male friend of Alexandra.

Threat

The endless possibilities to interact with people online are important to mention when it comes to self-produced images. The children in sexual images might have experienced an online contact that was initially a friendship where the child's needs were central, but which gradually developed into something they could not escape. The child might have felt pressured or threatened. Often the threat is implicit and the child thinks they cannot terminate the contact, but in some cases the threat is explicitly made by the perpetrator.

Don't tell if not asked

Research and clinical experience (see, for example, Svedin and Back, 2003, Priebe and Svedin, 2008) show that children seldom disclose sexual abuse. In cases of online sexual abuse the experience is the same. Most of the children in the project had not told anyone about the online sexual abuse or about sexual images unless they had been asked about it. No child had contacted the clinic by themselves. They have always been referred by, for example, social services.

In the interviews with staff at child and adolescent psychiatric units and social services some of the staff emphasized the difficulties asking children about what had happened. They felt limited in their knowledge about sexual abuse but also about IT. Some said that they therefore did not know what to ask for.

> Well, I don't know what the pictures were or where they were, but they were of that sexual kind.
> (Counsellor at a child and adolescent psychiatric unit)

Von Weiler et al (2010) studied the care and treatment of child victims of sexual pornographic exploitation in Germany. Of the interviewed professionals 50 per cent agreed that cases involving child abusive images were more complex and challenging than 'mere' cases of child sexual abuse. Some professionals said they would not introduce the topic of abusive images in therapy. They reported that they felt uncomfortable and insecure as to how and when to address the issue of images and were afraid to re-traumatize the child.

Shame and guilt

What was common to many of the children in the Online Project was their feelings of shame and guilt. Since many of the children had been active participants in the interaction with the abuser, the situation was experienced as very confusing. The child thought that what had happened was their fault since they, in some cases, felt that they had initiated the contact or produced and distributed the images. Since they thought it was their fault they felt they had no right to complain. When a case was revealed many children worried about the parents' reactions and also felt as if they had let their parents down, since they were taking risks online despite knowing of the dangers.

Consequences of online sexual abuse

In the Online Project the children who were victims of online sexual abuse show the same symptoms as children who are subject to sexual abuse offline. These were symptom, such as anxiety, fear, depression, low self-esteem, aggression, sexual-ized behaviour and self harming, that are often reported among child victims of offline sexual abuse (Horner, 2010). Many of the children in the Online Project have been diagnosed with post-traumatic stress disorder (PTSD), which entails the traumatic event being re-experienced through painful recollections and nightmares or as physiological reactions. The children avoided stimuli that could be associated with the trauma or have had continuous sleeping difficulties. Many children also had difficulties with trusting other people and suffered severe anxiety. Many had poor self-esteem and felt shame, guilt, uneasiness and confusion. For some children the risky online behaviour was in itself a sign that they were not feeling very well. Some of the children initially stated that they were unaffected by the abuse and free from symptoms. Several of them significantly overstated their well-being in questionnaires. But we also experienced the opposite, when the child told the therapist when they were in treatment that they were fine, but answered differently in questionnaires assessing their well-being.

Children in sexually abusive images

The Svedin and Back study

In the 1990s two major child pornographic rings were revealed in Sweden: first, the Huddinge child pornography ring and, second, the Norrköping pornographic ring. After the cases were prosecuted cooperation was established between the National Police (National Bureau of Investigation) and the child and adolescent psychiatric unit at the university hospital of Linköping. An agreement was reached whereby the police would inform the clinic when they were able to identify any child in the seized material. When a child has been sexually abused and images are produced there is a great deal of evidence that the actual abuse has taken place, and this gives unique possibilities for investigating how children are recruited and what children remember of their participation in relation to the actual course of events depicted in the images, as well as shedding light upon the psychosocial health of the children. This was one of the backgrounds to the Svedin and Back (2003) study: to compare what the child disclosed with the content of the images that had been taken of them. In the study all the court documents, pre-investigative protocols, police interviews and seized material were carefully scrutinized. Parents and children were interviewed and completed questionnaires concerning psychosocial health. For the parents the Child Behaviour Checklist (CBCL) was used; for the children the Youth Self-Report was used (Achenbach, 1991a; 1991b). For more details about the study see: *Children Who Don't Tell?* (Svedin and Back, 1996) and *Why Didn't They Tell Us?* (Svedin and Back, 2003).

The children

In the Svedin and Back study (2003) thirty children who were victims of documented sexual abuse were included (11 girls and 19 boys). When the children were abused they were aged between 6 months to 14 years old. Fourteen were living with both their parents during the time of the sexual abuse and sixteen lived together with one biological parent, alone or in combination with a step-parent. The parents of twenty-two of the children were gainfully employed and often this was true of both parents. They worked, among others things, as computer technicians, engineers, assistant nurses, teachers, office clerks, cashiers or carpenters/joiners, or were self-employed. Seven children had parents who did not work and the reason for this was either the shortage of work or physical and/or psychological ill-health experienced by the parents. Five of the children lived in very deprived socio-economic conditions; of those two lived in extreme poverty.

Most of the children in the study originated from, at least from the outside, fairly ordinary home conditions. There had, however, been periods of stress within the families and parental neglect – as a consequence of divorce, a death in the family, and overwork or burden of work. There had sometimes been a need for respite assistance and help with children, occasionally coupled with parental gullibility. In three cases there was a noticeable lack of supervision and care. In these cases an unknown perpetrator initiated contact with children in the wider society.

The perpetrators

The perpetrators comprised eleven men and two women. When they were found guilty, they were on average 39 years old, with an age range of 21 to 58 years. Six of the male perpetrators had worked with children, either during working hours or in their leisure time as children and youth leaders, or at day nurseries. It was evaluated that seven of the perpetrators suffered from mental difficulties, of which two had such serious symptoms that they consequently received forensic psychiatric care. Five perpetrators regarded or defined themselves as paedophiles, and all of them had earlier worked with children and youth activities. Two of these, two men, had previously been found guilty of sexual crimes against children. These two also stated that they travelled to Southeast Asia in order to 'socialize with children/boys'.

Most of the children had an existing relationship with the perpetrator, e.g. family member, relative, friend of the family and so on. Out of the thirty children, in only three cases (10 per cent) the perpetrator was someone who from the beginning was largely unknown to the child or the child's family. He made contact with children in public places or at jumble sales. For a majority of the children, the perpetrator had made himself invaluable to the family, offering support, babysitting or adult friendship, and becoming more or less part of the family. Any suspicions on the part of the parents were allayed through the perpetrator becoming a trusted person, for example as a workmate, nursery staff or relative, and appreciated and liked by adults as well as children. Of their own accord the children made contact with the perpetrator, who engaged with them, gave them attention and things to do, all of which they appreciated. In the majority of cases one can see that the perpetrator acted like a cuckoo in marginalizing the parents. For a time, the perpetrator became an important person or even the most important adult person for the child.

The sexual abuse

It is only the substantiated sexual abuse that can be proved. Only one child talked about an incident of sexual abuse that was not documented in the seized material, and none of the perpetrators said more about the abuse than this material actually showed. There is good reason to think that significantly more sexual abuse took place. For example, a girl placed in a foster home later talked about a serious case of repeated sexual abuse that was not substantiated. On average, the sexual abuse continued for twenty-two months (range 1–100 months).

The acts that the children were subject to varied greatly, but they generally covered all forms of sexual activity, from sexual molestation in the form of perpetrators touching children's genitals to full oral, genital and anal intercourse. Other children had been persuaded to engage in sexual activities with one another before the camera. The children had been photographed with a variety of objects, such as burning cigarettes in the rectum, pens or pennants in the vagina and anus. Some children had had to masturbate the perpetrator and others had had ejaculate sprayed onto their faces or their dummy/pacifier dipped in seminal fluid. One child was forced to urinate, and another to empty its bowels (compulsive purging).

Disclosure

No child had disclosed that they had been sexually abused before they were identified through the seized images. In the police interviews with the children, only two of them began to talk spontaneously, and there were five others who eventually gave a fairly complete account without being shown the pictures or the investigator saying that he/she knew what had happened (from the seized material). Five children denied that anything had occurred. All the children's accounts were fragmentary, and the children showed great difficulty in talking about their contact with the suspected perpetrator. They often said that they did not remember what had happened; we do not know whether this meant that they did not have any memory of the incidents or if it was too difficult to put it into words. Nevertheless, it became apparent that what the children least 'wanted to remember', was the most unpleasant or abusive activities, and these were probably the most shameful and guilt-ridden. It was shown that the more interviews the children took part in, the more they talked. It was as if they first needed to 'sort out the memories which emerged' and only later could put into words what had happened. The interview can be likened to an onion that is peeled – layer after layer peeled gently away.

Children's psychosocial health

Before disclosure

In the study there was no detailed knowledge about how the children felt and functioned *before the sexual abuse* started. Few children had symptoms or diffi-culties that their parents noticed. One child had various behavioural problems, another had truancy problems, while a further child was described as having fits of crying, conflict with other children, hyper-sexualized behaviour, but nothing that occasioned, for example, the school to raise the alarm.

During the period of sexual abuse

Parents described the majority of children as largely free of problems during the period of abuse, and no child displayed symptoms that could be interpreted as indicating sexual abuse. Ten children exhibited signs that they did not feel well. One girl had various symptoms both before and during the period of sexual abuse, symptoms that later became more pronounced at the time of disclosure. Other parents remembered that, for example, their son was more quiet and introverted than usual and another described that her daughter had problems taking care of her hygiene. In addition to sexual abuse, three children who experienced parental neglect displayed obvious symptoms and behaviour problems. In two cases this was detailed in child psychiatric investigations and the third in a statement of opinion, and this was all confirmed by teachers and school psychologists. It is, however, less clear to what extent parents understood that their children experienced problems. When the sexual abuse was being carried out, two of the boys had a noticeably increased rate of truancy from school. One of the boys started to misuse butane gas; and according to their schools, all of them had evident problems. Restlessness, low-spiritedness, a lack of appetite, tiredness, concentration diffi-culties, aggressiveness, bullying, running about, advanced sexual behaviour in the form of interest, gestures and language, were all symptoms that were noted. On one occasion, a boy arrived at school with a whole bag full of condoms.

During the period between the last instance of sexual abuse and the disclosure of this abuse

Some children had problems during this period. One paternal grandmother said that her granddaughter, then aged between 10 and 12 years, did not feel at all well (the sexual abuse ceased when she was 11 years old). Later, all through secondary school, the girl felt unwell. She was depressed, had difficulties in sleeping and sometimes thought about suicide. Only a few days before the disclosure of sexual abuse the girl had asked her mother to make an appointment with the child psychiatric clinic. One boy, on his own initiative and because of his misuse of butane gas, was placed into a foster home during the period between the time of the sexual abuse and its disclosure. He himself felt that his mother could not take care of him.

In connection with the disclosure

When the disclosure of sexual abuse happened as a result of the police making contact, it was a shock for both the children and their parents. All described a period of worsened mental health, irrespective of how they had felt earlier. The children had hoped that their parents would never know anything. All the children interviewed described how shame and a sense of guilt predominated, while simultaneously an intense anger against the perpetrator began to stream forth. The period after the disclosure of sexual abuse was chaotic as a consequence of the upset in connection with the interviews, court cases, contacts with social services, child and youth psychiatric clinics, the criminal victims' support agency or the Save the Children organization. All felt poorly and unwell. This demonstrates how essential it is to have well-thought-out, first-rate support for children during this period. None of the children criticized the interviewers, but they found it hard having to remember and speak about such very shameful sexual abuse and exploitation. One girl was critical that after being called for interview and having to talk about very difficult experiences, an experience in which her whole world was turned upside down, she was obliged to travel alone by means of public transport to get home again. This girl was also upset that she could not herself determine the time of the interview. She had thought that her account of sexual abuse could wait until she was old enough to leave her family and could manage her own life independently. Another girl recounted that she nearly fainted during the interview because it was such a horrible experience.

For the three boys who had also had unsatisfactory family care and nurturing, the disclosure of sexual abuse was associated with great mental stress. One boy went to his school nurse and when asked if there was anything wrong with him said, 'Everything is utter confusion inside me'. Another of these boys had nightmares, screamed in his sleep and was frightened that the perpetrator would try to seek revenge. All three boys were afraid of what might happen when the perpetrator had served his prison sentence and could return to the area in which they lived. One of the boys declared during an interview that in spite of fear of the perpetrator, 'it was a great relief to speak (about the sexual abuse) at the police questioning'. The children's reactions varied accordingly, from relief that everything about the sexual abuse was now fully disclosed to very strong denial and despair about the need to confront what had taken place. One boy spontaneously explained his relief after the disclosure, and comforted his mother by saying 'it is all over now'.

One girl explained how she had decided to speak about her sexual abuse when she became an adult and had moved away from home. Now, when she was completely unprepared, she was shown pictures of the serious sexual abuse to which she had been subjected, and found this viewing very difficult. Another girl emphasized that she was relieved that everything was now in the open but, at the same time, during the interview her attitude seemed to imply that she was also 'proud' of what had happened and took the responsibility upon herself, thus protecting the perpetrator – at least initially.

It was difficult for children to drop the defences or justifications that they had employed over many years. When disclosure was made by the unprepared child, defences such as repression, denial or the isolation of feelings were no longer viable and instead the child was confronted with a storm of bewildering emotions. Many of the children were very disgusted when they saw their pictures and felt ashamed, along with feelings of having been utterly deceived by the perpetrator. One boy reacted during most of the initial interview with intense anxiety and denial. He would not accept that it was he who was in the pictures that were shown to him. Three children also displayed great fear of the perpetrator at the time of disclosure.

It was only when the legal proceedings were over that life slowly began to return to normal. Many of the children, however, took a break from their studies, as everything that had happened in connection with the disclosure of sexual abuse had tangible consequences for their schoolwork. According to parents, it took up to one year before matters began to sort themselves out and things settled down. 'It was as if a year was lost', as one parent put it. With parental support, the companionship of friends, through recreation activities and therapeutic contacts, many children nevertheless recovered surprisingly well. Other children had great difficulties working through their experiences. This was especially the case for the three boys who simultaneously experienced neglectful care, and for those children who were subjected to the gravest sexual abuse.

Sixteen of the twenty-one children who were interviewed also had contact with the criminal victims' support organization, the Save the Children Fund's boy centre in Stockholm, and with child and youth psychiatric outpatient clinics. This ranged from passing contact in crisis situations and brief investigative contact to longer therapeutic counselling of up to two years in duration.

After disclosure

After seventeen months, on average, from the disclosure of sexual abuse, the children's mental health or ill-health was registered through interviews with parents and the children. This was assessed using the parental form CBCL (Child Behaviour Check List) and the children's self-completion form YSR (Youth Self Report) (Achenbach, 1991a; 1991b).

The time that elapsed between the disclosure and the interviews ranged from one to forty-two months, so the children were found at different stages of their recovery process and consequently their reported mental health differed. Twelve children's scores on the CBCL and YSR indicated mental ill-health difficulties (over the mean value of 14 points) and seven showed ill-health that was judged as serious and clinical. According to the parents, the most usual symptoms exhibited by the children were the following (ranked by importance): obstinacy, sulkiness or irritability, 88 per cent; opinionated, contrariness, 82 per cent; preferring to be alone, 76 per cent; demanding lots of attention, 65 per cent; swearing or using dirty words, 65 per cent; making oneself out to be or playing the buffoon, 59 per cent; daydreams, retreating into their own worlds, 53 per cent: being slightly envious or jealous, 53 per cent: and teasing, 53 per cent. Parents reported few of the symptoms that are usually associated with sexual abuse, that is to say the signs/symptoms that are manifestations of post-traumatic stress syndrome (e.g. nightmares, 29 per cent) or sexualized behaviour (e.g. playing with their genitals when others are looking, 6 per cent).

Five of the ten children that filled in the YSR reported symptoms of mental ill-health that were higher than the average for boys and girls respectively (38 and 44 points). The commonest symptoms that the children mentioned were: I am stubborn and contradict others, 90 per cent; I swear or used dirty words, 90 per cent; I have difficulty in concentrating or being attentive, 80 per cent; I talk too much, 80 per cent; I care too much about appearing clean and tidy, 80 per cent; I show off or boast and want to impress, 70 per cent; I daydream quite a lot, 70 per cent; I am shy, 70 per cent; I'd rather be alone than with others, 60 per cent; I am secretive and keep very much to myself, 60 per cent; I have a furious temper, 60 per cent; and finally, I think too much about sex, 60 per cent.

Sixteen of the twenty-two children whom we had satisfactory information about showed signs of mental ill-health that exceeded what is average for Swedish children. In those cases where there is information from both parents and children, there was a good concurrence of the accounts of what happened. It is noticeable, however, that no parents noted that their children had an increased interest in sex, while six out of ten children reported being troubled by thinking too much about sex. Based on the classification of Burgess et al. (1981), of the twenty-two children that we had information about from parents, children or other substantiated information, we can see that four of the children integrated the experiences of sexual abuse (had put it behind them, could talk about what happened without symptoms of distress); three children essentially demonstrated avoidance behaviour (did not want to talk about what had happened or became distressed when somebody tried to talk about what happened or avoided situations that reminded them of the events); while nine children showed a repetition of symptoms, that is to say, they still had symptoms and behavioural difficulties as a consequence of what had happened. Six children were difficult to classify because of insufficient information.

Children do not tell

One of the major findings in the Svedin and Back study (2003) is the fact that these children seldom told about the sexual abuse, and that sometimes the children continued to deny what had happened even when, for example, a police investigator showed a boy a photograph in which he appeared naked. The boy repeated twenty-four times, 'That cannot be me.'

Based on their maturity and age in combination with the seriousness of the sexual abuse, it was evaluated that twenty-three children could have been able to relate what had taken place. All these children were, on average, subjected to twenty-two months of sexual abuse. Later, it took on average a further nineteen months before the sexual abuse was discovered. These children kept their experiences to themselves during a period, in all, of around eighty-one years of life (eighty-one years and four months). The average time before disclosure was forty-one months, with a range of between one month and 176 months. Not one of the children spontaneously disclosed any instance of sexual abuse. The children had kept this to themselves and had not talked about this to parents, friends, siblings, relatives or another adult. This is a very compelling argument that children do not at all, or very reluctantly, talk about sexual abuse. This is also a very formidable contrast to the idea that children invent or make false accusations of sexual abuse. False allegations have been said to vary between 6 to 35 per cent (Weiner, 2003); in contrast, research shows that only 7 to 10 per cent of experienced abuse is reported to the authorities (Priebe and Svedin, 2008; Svedin and Priebe, 2009) and our study underlines that many children stay silent and tolerate sexual abuse. Based on the information from this study, the three categories (secrecy, helplessness. and entrapment and accommodation) of so-called 'child sexual abuse accommodation syndrome', as described by Summit (1983), are the most appropriate way of describing children's adjustment to sexual abuse.

What, then, is it that makes children reluctant to disclose such sexual abuse, or later in interviews not to talk about it? The literature usually mentions the child's insufficient comprehension of having participated in something that is wrong, emotional reasons, memory loss, or a deliberate attempt to forget or not remember. These same explanations can also be used to account for why children do not talk during interviews, but this is also contingent upon the quality and the setting/situation of the interview.

Our experience, based on the study and from everyday clinical practice, is that usually there are various reasons why children do not tell, but that these are also in themselves coherent in different ways. What can be viewed superficially as memory loss, when investigated, is instead an inability to recollect 'visual pictures' from memory, or a deliberate avoidance of remembering. This in turn depends on various types of emotion and consequence that are associated with the incidents that the child will not remember.

Conclusion and discussion

The children in the images

Children who figure in sexual images are a worldwide phenomenon on a very large scale. It is important not to generalize when it comes to describing who the children in the images are. To start with, the children depicted are of all ages and different ethnic groups, as well as coming from different psychosocial backgrounds. In addition, the context in which the images are taken may be very different. Some images, for example some of the self-produced and self-distributed material, might not have caused the child any apparent harm. On the other hand, the images produced in connection with sexual abuse can be connected to both physical and psychological pain.

It is important to differentiate between material that was produced and distributed willingly and not related to sexual abuse, and material that involved sexual abuse. In a recent study by Wolak and Finkelhor (2011), of 550 cases of self-produced material obtained from a national survey of law enforcement agencies, the authors could see two major groupings in the material: aggravated and experimental. In the aggravated group the images involved additional criminal or abusive elements that were not included in the experimental group. The children in the Online Project who produced their own sexual material could belong in both the experimental and the aggravated groups. Most often they knew they were taking risks and that the publishing of the images could entail dangers. However, it did not appear that they fully understood the consequences. All of the children had longed for affirmation and acknowledgement and had a need to be 'seen'. This finding is supported by a Swedish interview study (Nigård, 2009) carried out among youth 18–25 years old who had experiences of posting images on porno-graphic sites. Nigård describes the need to be seen as a kind of 'self-medication', that is linked to individualization and narcissism. She also mentions two other themes that were common in the interviews with the youth: sexual exposure as a 'cultural lay-off' and the 'pornographic script and ambivalence'. Sexual exposure as a cultural lay-off means that the exposure can be seen as a phenomenon with everyday overtones. The informants, for example, described the important social function that the pornographic website had. But Nigård also mentions that it is 'normal' to watch pornography among youth and that sex need not necessarily be associated with love. The last theme Nigård mentions is 'the pornographic script and ambivalence', especially among the female informants. The girls gave conflicting explanations for the exposure. One girl, for example, said that the images she posted were not sexual, but in fact they were posted in a sexual context which, according to Nigård, might be associated with the risk of being perceived and treated as a 'whore'. Ambivalence to posting images online was also found in the Online Project but here posting was not necessarily on pornographic websites.

The children in the Svedin and Back study were portrayed in sexually abusive images produced during sexual abuse, and this differs from most of the children in the Online Project. The first and most obvious difference relates to age. The children in the Svedin and Back study were younger than the children in the Online Project. A second difference was that all the images depicted very serious child sexual abuse, such as the anal penetration of a 5-year-old boy. Being very young in the abusive images and thereby almost impossible to be recognized was, for some of the children, a relief. One girl stated, 'I was so young that only my mother can recognize me from those images.' To be beyond recognition supported this girl's ability to move forward in life. Yet for the older children the possibility of having the images disseminated for others to see created anxiety and panic. In the Svedin and Back study the perpetrators were, in almost all cases, a family member or someone in the child's physical environment, whereas most of the children in the Online Project had made contact with the perpetrator online or the abuser was a girlfriend or boyfriend.

The silence and feelings of shame and guilt

There are some common denominators that colour many of the children's stories; the silence and the shame and guilt the children felt. The results from both the Svedin and Back study as well as the material from the Online Project speak clearly when it comes to the fact that children do not talk about such abusive experiences. Even the children who were depicted in images of abusive situations sometimes denied that anything had taken place. There might be many explanations for this reaction. Probably most children do remember what happened but avoid talking about the abuse. The Svedin and Back study showed that the seriousness of the experienced abuse is also of importance to what the child discloses. It is easier to talk about less serious abuse than more serious contact offences. This finding is also supported by other studies (Priebe and Svedin, 2008). Both Svedin and Back's study and the results from the Online Project demonstrate that it is embarrassing to talk about sexual abuse and that many of the children feel as if it is their fault or that they did not do anything to stop the abuse. The children described their feeling of being active participants in what had happened. In the Svedin and Back study, some of the children described how they did what they were asked to, and in the Online Projects material the children often also stated that they acted as was asked of them or on their own initiative. Leonard (2010) describes a girl whose father had directed her to take obscene photographs. At the court hearing, professionals described her father as a perpetrator of child abuse, which was something that the girl could not relate to. Instead, she felt guilty for touching herself and said that she was the one who took off her clothes. In addition to confused feelings of guilt and shame it must be acknowledged how difficult it is for a child to refuse the wishes of an adult, even if they feel what is being asked of them is wrong. It is also important to remember the possibility that the child has been threatened, something that may be of importance both in the therapeutic situation and in the police investigation (Lyon, 1996).

The images might entail consequences

For all children, no matter what the history of the images or the child is, the images may cause concerns and worries. If the images are a documentation of a sexual abuse they can be seen as an additional complication of the experience of the abuse and something that the child needs to be given an opportunity to talk about. On the other hand, it should not be taken for granted that all children depicted in sexual images online are traumatized or will show symptoms of psychological or physical illness. In the Svedin and Back study few children, according to their parents, showed any symptoms or difficulties during the time of the abuse. Instead a period of worsening health for the children was described during the time of disclosure and afterwards.

Some children appear not to be concerned at all about their sexual images, while others can feel considerable discomfort and worry. For those who experience distress, the fact that there are numerous 'unknown perpetrators' looking at photographs of their abuse might be something they are concerned about. Leonard (2010) describes children who were being psychically sick, as well as having frequent panic attacks when thinking of what people might be doing while watching the pictures.

Future challenges

There are few signs that the interest for children in sexually abusive images is decreasing. To be able to stop the abusive production of images of child sexual abuse will require preventive work to locate both potential perpetrators and victims. We need to learn more about the children who produce their own images, as well as gain an increased understanding of risk-taking behaviours that could lead to unwanted experiences and how we, as adults, might intervene to minimize those risks. There is still a lack of research in relation to the children in sexual images, especially for the children in images depicting their sexual abuse.

There needs to be capacity in every country to offer different levels of professional support to children who have been involved in the production of sexual images. This is a considerable challenge since the children from both the projects described were more reluctant to engage in treatment. This requires additional education for all professionals who might have contact with the abused children, so they can feel secure in what to look for and ask about. In the von Weiler study (2010) one major conclusion was that the professionals who get in contact with child victims of child pornographic exploitation are still at a loss as to how to treat the children to the fullest extent. The author demands an increase in knowledge among professionals, but also specialized counselling and therapy for the victims.

Children in sexual abuse images might not be a homogeneous group and this is especially the case where the images are produced under different circumstances. What all the children have got in common is their right to be seen, not by a perpetrator, but by adults and authorities that can ensure their safety and support them to better health and a good life.

References

Achenbach, T.M. (1991a). *Manual for the Youth Self-Report and 1991 Profile.* Burlington, Vermont: University of Vermont, Department of Psychiatry.
—— (1991b). *Manual for the Child Behavior Checklist/4-18 and 1991 Profile.* Burlington, Vermont: University of Vermont, Department of Psychiatry.
Burgess, A.W., Groth, A.N., and McCausland, M.P. (1981). Child sex initiation rings. *American Journal of Orthopsychiatry, 51*, 110–19.
Daneback, K. and Månsson, S.-A. (2009). *Kärlek och sexualitet på Internet 2009.* Chap. 5. Se mig. Unga om sex och Internet.Ungdomsstyrelsen.
Horner, G. (2010). Child sexual abuse: consequences and implications. *Journal of Pediatric Health Care, 24*(5), 358–64.
Interpol-International Child Sexual Exploitation Image Data Base (2011). Personal communication. Anders Persson, ICSE Co-cordinator, 6 January.
Jonsson, L., Warfvinge, C. and Banck, L. (2009). *Children and Sexual Abuse via IT.* County Council of Östergötland. BUP Elefanten 2009.
Leander, L., Christiansson, S.Å., and Granhag, P.A. (2008). Internet-initiated sexual abuse: adolescent victims' reports about on- and off-line sexual activities. *Applied Cognitive Psychology, 22*, 1260–74.
Leonard, M. (2010). 'I did what I was directed to do but he didn't touch me': The impact of being a victim of Internet offending. *Journal of Sexual Aggression, 2*, 249–56.

Lyon, T. (1996). The effect of threats on children's disclosure of sexual abuse. *The APSAC Advisor*, 9, 9–15.

Nigård, P. (2009). *Frivillig sexuell exponering på internet*. Chap. 7. Se mig. Om unga sex och internet. Ungdomsstyrelsen 2009:9

Nyman, A. (2006). *Abused Online*. Linköping: BUP-Elefanten och Landstinget i Östergötland

Priebe, G., and Svedin, C.G. (2008). Child sexual abuse is largely hidden from the adult society. An epidemiological study of adolescents' disclosures. *Child Abuse and Neglect*, 32:1095–1108.

Quayle, E. and Jones, T. (2011). Sexualised images of children on the Internet. *Sexual Abuse: A Journal of Research and Treatment.*23 (1), 7–21.

Summit, R.C. (1983). The child sexual abuse accommodation syndrome. *Child Abuse and Neglect* 7(3):177–93.

Svedin, C.G. and Back, K. (1996). *Children Who Don't Speak Out About Children Being Used in Child Pornography*. Stockholm: Save the Children.

—— (2003). *Varför berättar de inte? Om att utnyttjas i barnpornografi*. (*Why Didn't They Tell Us?: On Sexual Abuse in Child Pornography*). Stockholm: Save the Children/ Linköping: BUP Elefanten.

Svedin, C.G. and Priebe, G. (2009). *Unga, sex och Internet*. Chap. 3. Se mig. Unga om sex och Internet. Ungdomsstyrelsen.

von Weiler, J., Haardt-Becker, A. and Schulte, S. (2010). Care and treatment of child victims of child pornographic exploitation (CPE) in Germany. *Journal of Sexual Aggression*, 16, 211–22.

Weiner, I.B. (2003). *Handbook of Psychology*. New Jersey: John Wiley and Sons.

Wolak, J. and Finkelhor, D. (2011). *Sexting: A Typology*. Crime against Children Research Center: University of New Hampshire.

Wolak, J., Finkelhor, D. and Mitchell, K. (2004). Internet-initiated sex crimes against minors: Implications for prevention based on findings from a national study. *Journal of Adolescent Health*, 35, 424.e11–20. Available online at: http://www.unh.edu.ccrc.57.

Wolak, J., Finkelhor, D., Mitchell, K.J. and Ybarra, M.L. (2008). Online 'predators' and their victims. Myths, realities, and implications for prevention and treatment. *American Psychologist*, 63, 111–28.

3 Understanding the emergence of the Internet sex offender

How useful are current theories in understanding the problem?

Anthony R. Beech, University of Birmingham

Ian A. Elliott, Lucy Faithfull Foundation

Overview

The most important and urgent problems of the technology of today are no longer
the satisfactions of the primary needs or of archetypal wishes, but the reparation of
the evils and damages by the technology of yesterday.

(Dennis Gabor, *Innovations: Scientific, Technological and Social*, 1970)

In 1969 the Internet, or more precisely the ARPANet, consisted of just four
computers linked together (Wiggins, 1995), designed to allow general communication between those machines. Half a century later, there are over 1.8 billion
Internet users worldwide (Internet World Stats, 2010). Although the technology
itself is morally neutral, and while it can be assumed that a lot of online behaviour
is generally positive (or at least does not victimize others), online technologies
facilitate a whole host of criminal activities (see Jewkes and Yar, 2010), and hence
are becoming a modern source of a range of societal problems.

One of the most high-profile online types of crime is the increasing incor-
poration of the Internet in child sexual abuse. It is of note that this has increased
considerably in the past five years (Motivans and Kyckelhahn, 2007; Wolak et al.,
2009), and although this group of sexual offenders remains a small proportion of
all identified sex offenders, there is increasing concern about how to assess,
manage, and treat such 'online offenders' (Elliott and Babchishin, in press). The
extent of the problem is indicated by recent analyses of peer-to-peer (P2P)
networks showing that enquiries regarding sexually explicit material involving
children account for between one in 200 and one in 500 queries (Steel, 2009).
Interpol's Child Abuse Image Database (ICAID), a global database for the forensic
analysis of digital images of child abuse, now contains over 500,000 images
submitted from thirty-six member countries (Interpol, 2009). While, from fairly
recent figures, the UK Internet Watch Foundation (IWF) has identified 2,755
worldwide Internet domains containing images of child sexual abuse (IWF, 2009).
The perceived anonymity, speed and global character of the Internet and the ability

to set up virtual social groups all contribute to an environment that challenges conventional notions of social organization and control (Taylor and Quayle, 2003) and create a substantial potential for criminal behaviour.

The types of abusive behaviour related to the Internet include the dissemination of sexually explicit material involving children; engagement in inappropriate (sexual) communications with children; and establishing and developing social networks with other individuals with a sexual interest in children (Durkin, 1997; Lanning, 2001). It is clearly the case that not all those who use the Internet for the sexual exploitation of children are motivated by the same ends. Some, as far as we know, appear to restrict their abuse behaviour to the viewing of images online, fuelling a whole industry that abuses children in order to generate images in the process. Some use the Internet for the purpose of contacting and abusing children through chat rooms, and other web-based social networking sites; some set up websites for commercial services or to fuel their collection/masturbatory interests; while others see the distribution of child abuse images as a relatively easy way of making money, as part of a wider repertoire of criminal activity.

Based on such observations, and earlier work by Krone (2004), Lanning (2001) and Sullivan and Beech (2003), we (Elliott and Beech, 2009) have suggested that there are four broad types of individual who by their use of the Internet propagate sexually abusive behaviours against children: (1) *periodically prurient* offenders, consisting of those accessing impulsively, or out of a general curiosity, and who carry out this behaviour sporadically, potentially as part of a broader interest in pornography (including 'extreme' pornography) that may, or may not always, be related to a specific sexual interest in children; (2) *fantasy driven/online-only* offenders, consisting of those who access/trade images to fuel a sexual interest in children, but who have no known history of contact sexual offending (e.g. Osborn et al., 2010; Seto et al., 2011; Webb et al., 2007); (3) *direct victimization* offenders, consisting of those who utilize online technologies as part of a larger pattern of contact, and non-contact, sexual offending, including sexually explicit material involving children, and the gaining and subsequently abusing of the trust of an individual or children online in order to facilitate the later commission of contact sexual offences (Krone, 2004); (4) *commercial exploitation* offenders, consisting of the criminally minded who produce or trade images to make money (Lanning, 2001).

For the purposes of this chapter, we will focus on trying to understand the motivations *periodically prurient* and *fantasy driven/online-only* to provide a better understanding of why these individuals carry out these kinds of behaviour using current theories of sexual offending. We will not consider *direct victimization* offenders in any detail as theories as to why these individuals have committed contact sexual offences have been extensively described elsewhere (see Ward et al., 2006, for a more complete understanding of those who carry out contact sexual offences). *Commercial exploitation* offenders will not be reviewed in detail as this form of offending is typically associated with a wider pattern of criminal behaviour, generally driven by financial profit rather than a sexual interest in children per se (Jewkes and Yar, 2010; Lanning, 2001).

Given that the thrust of our argument is the usefulness of current theory in understanding the motivation of *periodically prurient* and *fantasy driven/online-only* offenders, in the next section of the chapter we will outline perhaps the most contemporary theories of child sexual abuse. Of course, this is not to say that older, more general criminological theories might not also be of use. For example, we would note that Cohen and Felson's (1979) *Routine Activity Theory* suggests that predatory criminal behaviour requires both a motivated offender and an environment that lacks both supervision and guardianship, as well as an environment where a vast array of targets are easily accessible, which certainly appears to be the case as regards those who use the Internet for sexually abusive purposes. For the purposes of the chapter, however, we will focus on current sex offender theory, specifically the *integrated theory of sexual offending* (Ward and Beech, 2006), which gives a broad overview of how Internet offending arises and is maintained, and the *Pathways Model* by Ward and Siegert (2002), which will more specifically help us to understand the motivations of *periodically prurient* and *fantasy driven/online-only* offenders. Current ideas that examine the offence process itself will also be discussed in order to assess whether these can advance our understanding of these types of offenders, and help us combat 'the evils and damages' arising from criminological activity on the Internet.

Applying the integrated theory of sexual offending to understanding the online exploitation of children

The integrated theory of sexual offending (ITSO: Ward and Beech, 2006; see Fig. 3.1 for a brief schematic of the ITSO) may provide a broad framework to understanding why individuals may sexually exploit children. Briefly, this theory suggests that biological (genetic and evolutionary) factors combine with social learning factors (the social, cultural and physical environment and our role within these – our own 'ecological niche') to shape directly individual neuropsychological functioning. If biological inheritance and environmental factors interact in a way that compromises the integrity and function of neuropsychological mechanisms (i.e. typically by sexual, physical and emotional abuse), then surface clinical phenomena become evident. Ward and Beech describe three specific interlocking neuropsychological mechanisms (motivational/emotional, action selection and control, and perception and memory systems) originally proposed by Pennington (2002), underpinning thoughts, feelings and behaviours.

The *action selection and control* system, instantiated in the frontal cortex, the basal ganglia and parts of the thalamus, allows the individual to form and implement action plans designed to achieve goals and to control behaviour, thoughts and emotions in service of those goals. The *perception and memory* system, instantiated in the hippocampal formation and the posterior neocortex, processes incoming sensory information and constructs representations of objects and events. The *motivational/emotional* system, instantiated in the cortical, limbic and brainstem structures, allows goals and values to influence both the perception and memory and the action selection control systems, and to adjust motivational states to changes in the environment of the organism. For sexual offenders, the clinical

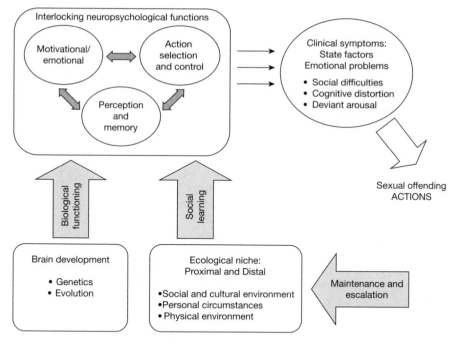

Figure 3.1 A schematic representation of the integrated theory of sexual offending

phenomena that develop when these mechanisms become compromised are typically: failures in self-regulatory control (self-regulation of behaviours and emotions); anti-social thinking patterns (offence-related cognitions); and inter-personal problems (difficulty relating to others); deviant sexual interest/arousal arise through the confluence of problems in these three areas (Ward and Beech, 2006; Whitaker et al., 2008).

In the ITSO, the term *ecological niche* is used to refer to the potentially adverse social and cultural circumstances, personal circumstances and physical environments in which an individual functions; sexually risky behaviours result from the complex relationships between neuropsychological function and the individual's ecological niche. Here, the theory suggests the importance of *distal* factors (where childhood influences affect the psychological and social development of the individual directly) and *proximal* factors (which actually create the circumstances where an offence is likely to occur) necessary for s sexual offence to occur. We will now examine these factors in more detail.

Distal ecological niche (risk) factors in the ITSO

As for distal factors, at the present time relatively little research exists into the developmental histories of Internet offenders. Some research suggests that the reported experiences of abusive sexual experiences in childhood are lower for

Internet offenders compared to contact sexual offenders. Webb et al. (2007) for example, found that around that just over 25 per cent of their sample of Internet offenders had been the victims of sexual abuse during childhood compared to a third of their sample of contact offenders, although this difference was not significant, given the small sample size. Sheldon and Howitt (2007) found that the age at which Internet offenders were sexually victimized tended to be older than contact-only offenders, and that extra-familial abuse was more likely to be reported in the Internet group compared to contact offenders. More recently, Babchishin et al. (2011) reported that Internet-only offenders reported significantly higher frequencies of both physical and sexual abuse compared to males in the general population. They also found that rates of childhood sexual abuse were not significantly different between contact and Internet offenders, while contact sexual offenders tended to report more physical abuse compared to Internet offenders (41 per cent vs 24 per cent). Elliott and Babchishin (in press) suggest that current research may account for only some of the distal factors here, in that in addition to looking at previous abusive experiences they suggest that there should now be a focus on examining the effects of early sexualized behaviour (e.g. Howitt and Sheldon, 2007). Examining other abuse issues, such as sexual activities with other children (Sperry and Gilbert, 2005) and early exposure to pornography (Elliott and Beech, 2009), may increase our understanding of the role of early sexualization for this group.

Proximal ecological niche (risk) factors in the ITSO

Arguably the primary *proximal* factor related to the maintenance of online sexually explicit material of children is the use of the Internet itself. Problematic Internet use (PIU) is defined as a behaviour 'focused on a particular online activity or application, such as online pornography or online gambling' (Davis et al., 2002: 332). The acquisition of skills, such as improving search terms to access abusive materials, and improving methods to reduce the risk of detection (Quayle and Taylor, 2003) would appear to be key. These strategies represent a change to the ecological niche on the part of the individual, in terms of changing both the person's physical environment and their ability to control that environment. Both of these strategies for Internet offenders would appear to increase the likelihood that the individual will be exposed to more sexually explicit material of children.

As Internet pornography represents an immediate stimulus–response condition from which the individual can obtain and receive reinforcement, the behavioural response becomes stronger. This can lead to obsessive thoughts about the Internet, diminished impulse control as well as social isolation and a loss of interest in offline activities (Davis et al., 2002). Other proximal factors typically are seen as perceptions of anonymity and ease of access to pornographic material. Davis et al. (2002) suggest that the main proximal factors related to PIU consist of the following: (1) diminished impulse control; (2) acute loneliness/depression; (3) social comfort; (4) distraction.

Quayle and Taylor (2003) have developed a model of PIU for Internet offenders, which has been modified by Elliott and Beech (2009). In brief, the PIU model suggests that *distal* factors (e.g. sexual, physical abuse, early sexualization) and problems arising from difficulties in neuropsychological function (e.g. loneliness, problematic cognitions, dissatisfaction with persona, disinhibition) when coupled with specific *proximal* Internet factors (e.g. perceptions of anonymity, ease of access to pornographic material) cause the escalation of PIU. In the Quayle and Taylor model, social-cognitive factors, such as increased risk-taking, reduction in offline contact, increased empowerment and validation/normalization, coupled with process factors relating to the Internet (e.g. the acquisition of skills), lead to online sexual behaviours. These can be legal (e.g. cybersex or adult pornography) or illegal (e.g. viewing sexually explicit material of children; online child seduction and procurement). Subsequent engagement with 'like-minded' online communities facilitates such behaviours and equips individuals with the skills to avoid detection, while distorted attitudes related to these behaviours are reinforced and remain unchallenged (Quayle and Taylor, 2003).

Greater use of the Internet, as described in the PIU model, is associated with a decrease in social engagement with the real world (e.g. family members and other social relationships) that represent another material change to the offender's social environment, which may both increase depression and loneliness, and also limits any 'reality checks' on the appropriateness of the behaviour. At the same time, engagement with facilitating online communities possibly leads to escalation in behaviour from downloading sexually explicit material of children to the possibility of contact offending. Although evidence would suggest that this probably only happens in a minority of cases (Seto and Eke, 2005; Taylor and Quayle, 2003).

The feeling of a lack of control over behaviour whilst online is often referred to by Internet offenders as an 'addiction' to sexually explicit material. In fact, some have called for Internet addiction to be recognized in the American Psychiatric *Association's Diagnostic and Statistical Manual of Mental Disorders* (5th edition) (Block, 2008). This is, however, a point of some contention for academics both in the fields of human–computer interaction and in psychiatric mental health, with some arguing that the evidence for Internet addiction is clear (e.g. Young, 2008), others that the Internet is simply a tool that facilitates more traditional offline addictions, such as gambling (e.g. Widyanto and Griffiths, 2006). In terms of sex offender behaviour, conceptualizing the viewing of sexually explicit material of children in a context of an online addiction may serve to remove personal liability for behaviour and reinforce it in the offender's mind, generating cognitive distortions about responsibility (i.e. that they cannot be blamed for actions over which they had no control or that are seen as pathologically inevitable).

Perhaps a more clinically useful way to explore the phenomenon of sex offenders feeling 'out of control', particularly on the Internet, is through the concept of 'Flow' (Csikszentmihalyi, 1996) – an optimal experience of a state of deep concentration where consciousness is unusually well ordered; in lay terms, the feeling of being 'in the zone'. Specifically addressing the issue of sexual arousal, Csikszentmihalyi (1996) notes that there is nothing wrong with indulging our biological responses and the resulting pleasure it provides, so long as we retain sufficient control over attention and maintain our ability to prioritize other goals where necessary. Hence, being in the *flow state* is not a lack of self-control, but a state of complete conscious attention over the completion of a single prioritized task at hand, where attention is narrowed towards goal achievement, action and awareness become merged, distractions are excluded from consciousness, we become less aware of ourselves and less self-conscious, and our perception of time and duration become distorted to the extent that hours can appear to pass like minutes. Problematic issues occur if the task being prioritized is a problematic or malevolent one to begin with (such as searching for sexually explicit material of children online), or one that could lead to an unwanted and unexpected outcome, that is escalating from *legal* adult pornography to extreme *illegal* pornography online.

The antecedents of flow require the task to have clear goals and milestones, immediate feedback to action, as well as a balance between challenges and skills – if the task is too difficult, then we become anxious; too easy, then we become bored (Csikszentmihalyi, 1996). Once online goals are established, online feedback is immediate and information-seeking behaviour is constantly balanced against the user's skill in achieving success (Pace, 2004). For sexual online goals, preference for material will be intangibly linked to the extent of arousal and novel sexual material can be sought and immediately obtained. The challenge presented, of finding that 'perfect' image or the missing image in a set of images, drives action, narrows attention and as a consequence the individual enters the 'flow state'. Offline goals and tasks are ignored as irrelevant distractions, time becomes insignificant, and the whole of the individual's consciousness is tuned to the task of maximizing their online sexual experience.

We will now examine Ward and Siegert's (2002) Pathways model of child sexual abuse, which may help us get a better idea of the motivation of different types of Internet offenders.

Ward and Siegert's pathways model explanation of online sexually abusive behaviours

The pathways model suggests that there are four independent etiological pathways associated with a set of interacting primary psychological mechanisms that can culminate in sexually abusive behaviour. These pathways are: (1) *intimacy deficits*, where individuals exhibiting this pathway offend at times of social isolation, rejection or when adult relationships are compromised; (2) *emotional dysregulation*, where individuals have difficulties in the self-regulation of emotions and behaviour; (3) *antisocial cognitions*, where individuals possess general pro-criminal attitudes and beliefs, and their offending reflects these antisocial tendencies; (4) *deviant sexual scripts*, where individuals have subtle distortions of the cognitive scripts that guide their sexual conduct (often through being sexually and emotionally abused as a child), and where interpersonal closeness is only achieved via sexual contact.

Although sexual offending will involve all of these deficits, to some degree, one of these 'primary' mechanisms will be the main causal influence, the others only exerting a harmful effect due to the driving force of the primary deficit (Ward and Sorbello, 2003; Ward et al., 2006). It is also of note that Ward and Siegert suggest that there is a fifth pathway where all of the dysfunctional mechanisms are in play at the same time; these are the types of motivation typically observed in fixated paedophilic child molesters (i.e. feeling that their emotional needs are better met by children than adults, deviant sexual arousal to children, difficulties in emotional and behavioural regulation, distorted schemas that children are interested in having sex with adults). Lanning (1992) was one of the first to suggest the role viewing sexually explicit material of children plays in sexual fantasy and deviant arousal. Internet offenders are thought to select images that fit pre-existing fantasies, which are typically related to an increase in masturbation, and can be regarded by some as an alternative to contact offences. In some rare cases they may act as a 'blue-print' for contact offences (Quayle and Taylor, 2002). We will now examine the motivations of *fantasy driven/online only* and *periodically prurient* offenders.

Understanding the motivations of 'fantasy driven/online only' offender

The Internet: Absolute communication, absolute isolation.

(Paul Carvel)

With regard to the *fantasy driven/on-line only offender*, the *intimacy deficit* pathway in Ward and Siegert's model may begin to provide an explanation of why individuals carry out such offences. The Internet appears to provide a social outlet for individuals who have difficulties initiating, and maintaining, relationships with other appropriate adults. Putnam (2000), for example, notes that online sexual behaviours can be particularly significant for individuals who have trouble obtaining face-to-face sexual contact, and hence those with intimacy deficits may be prone to developing online sexual habits. Research suggests that these offenders are often overly self-conscious, lack assertiveness, lack empathy in relationships and demonstrate low levels of self-efficacy (Laulik et al., 2007), are emotionally lonely, inadequate and have poor self-esteem (Middleton et al., 2006).

Laulik et al. (2007) report that the levels of these interpersonal problems increase as the amount of time online increases at the expense of offline activities. Prolonged time spent online serves as a mood-enhancing technique (Kennedy-Souza, 1998). These problems coupled with either an established or nascent interest in children may lead some of these individuals to access sexually explicit material of children online. Middleton et al. (2006) suggest that the images to some online consumers of sexually explicit material of children (*online-only*) represent less of a threat than initiating and/or maintaining age-appropriate relationships, and consequently a form of pseudo-intimacy can develop between the offender and particular images of children.

It is of note, however, that Babchishin et al. (2011) in their meta-analysis, found no significant differences between Internet-only and contact offenders in terms of emotional loneliness or self-reported levels of self-esteem. As for the form of a perceived relationship with a real or online image, Howitt and Sheldon (2007) found that a sample of Internet-only offenders could not be differentiated from those who have crossed over (*direct victimization*) on the overall level of their distorted attitudes (cognitive distortions) related to adults having sexual contact with children. Interestingly, Howitt and Sheldon found that *online-only* offenders were significantly more likely than *direct victimization* offenders to endorse items relating to the willingness and ability of children to consent to sexual activity with adults. Babchishin et al. (2011), however, found that contact offenders were more likely to have lower rates of victim empathy and more cognitive distortions compared to Internet offenders.

Understanding the motivations of the 'periodically prurient' offender

> The Internet is so big, so powerful and pointless that for some people it is a complete substitute for life.
>
> (Andrew Brown)

The *emotional dysregulation* pathway may partially describe *periodically prurient offenders* in that this pathway describes individuals who have difficulties in the self-regulation of emotions and behaviour, which seems to be a strong motivation in those who browse the Internet looking for deviant pornography. Hence these individuals will often turn to online activities as a way of dealing with difficult emotional states, such as depression, anxiety and stress (Morahan-Martin and Schumacher, 2000; Quayle et al., 2006). A cognitive style relating to the self, and the world around the individual, which includes problems such as self-doubt, low self-efficacy and negative self-appraisal (e.g. 'I'm only good on the Internet'; 'The Internet is the only place I am respected'; 'Nobody loves me offline'), could perhaps describe this group. Quayle and Taylor (2002) describe how Internet offenders in their sample reported that they could escape from unpleasant realities by viewing sexually explicit material of children, describing how they 'shut themselves off' from their personal circumstances, finding pleasure in online sexual arousal and masturbation (i.e. using sex as a coping strategy, Webb et al., 2007). Regarding the use of child pornography, Middleton et al. have suggested that for individuals in this group, strong negative mood states result in a lack of control and, in conjunction with sexual desire, can lead to the individual seeking contact with children to meet their sexual needs. Self-esteem can be high or low in this group, depending on the psychological make-up of the individual, and this is observed as co-morbidity with low self-esteem.

Although, there is currently a gap in the literature relating to impulsivity in Internet offenders, especially in our knowledge of how the online environment may affect impulse control, this is likely to be a specific concern for our *periodically prurient* group. It is also worth adding that the perceived anonymity, and the nature of the online environment, can have a further powerful disinhibiting effect on some Internet users (Danet, 1998). Consequently, the online environment might be a place where risk-taking behaviour is more likely to take place (Taylor et al., 2001). Different fields of study, however, propose different mechanisms for impulsive behaviour and self-control. In the field of behavioural economics, Loewenstein

(1996) suggests that as transient visceral influences (e.g. sexual arousal, hunger, drug-craving) intensify, there is a related increase in that individual's attention and motivational focus on activities and forms of consumption that are associated with that visceral factor, in that at a sufficient level of intensity it would appear that individuals will give up almost all goods not associated with that factor for even a small amount of goods from the associated factor. As an example, Loewenstein cites evidence from cocaine addicts that privilege their use of the drug over nourishment, sleep, money, responsibility and even survival (Gawin, 1991). A second effect of visceral influences is a collapsing of time-perspective and short-term trade-offs in favour of immediate compared to delayed goals (Loewenstein, 1996). Further, Ariely and Loewenstein (2006) found that during states of sexual arousal, adult males are more likely to report a willingness to engage in risky sexual activities, are more willing to take morally dubious measures to procure sex, and are more willing to engage in activities that were not sexually appealing whilst not in a state of sexual arousal. Deficits in these areas then have a direct consequential impact on the offender's environment and their ability to function within it.

Hence Internet offenders, while in a state of sexual arousal, may be likely to prioritize online sexual gratification over their offline relationships, other biological needs (e.g. sleep, food) and even, for those detected, their civil freedom. Laws (2003) outlined the mechanisms in which this behavioural economic approach to impulsive behaviour can lead to sexual offending during periods of intense sexual arousal and concluded that it is likely to represent a key mechanism in the escalation from sexual arousal to engaging in sexually deviant behaviour. Quayle and Taylor (2002) highlighted an interesting post-offence phenomenon for Internet offenders, noting that a number of their interviewees stopped looking at the pictures directly after masturbation and either switched the computer off or moved on to a non-sexual topic, suggesting that once the individual comes out of the arousal state the immediate need to view sexually explicit material is removed and attention returns to non-sexual functions.

Researchers have found that low self-control and, more generally, impulsivity are related to and even predict general criminality (Andrews and Bonta, 2006; Caspi et al., 1995; Pratt and Cullen, 2000). Hence some Internet sexual offenders (i.e. the periodically prurient type, who also carry out other types of criminal behaviours) will carry out other extremely risky behaviours, for example downloading sexually explicit material of children in a public library. As such, one plausible explanation for the lower observed rates of contact sex offences (as well as recidivism) in Internet offenders compared to hands-on offences may be greater self-control.

Explanations of the offence process in Internet offending

In this section we will describe theory related to sexual offence processes, in particular Ward and Hudson's (1998) self-regulation model. This model suggests that not all sexual offenders are motivated by the same reasons to offend/not offend (i.e. goals), and the strategies individuals use to do this. The interaction between goal and strategy creates four pathways, as follows: (1) the *approach-explicit* goal offender employs *active* strategies and is primarily motivated to offend, constantly seeking opportunities to do this, and purposefully manipulating their environment to set up such offences; (2) the *approach-automatic* offender, although motivated to offend, only does so when the opportunity presents itself, and hence does not employ specific strategies to create opportunities; (3) the *avoidant-active* offender takes purposeful action to avoid offending, but employs poor strategies to do so, such as masturbating to fantasies of children, the employment of which produce 'ironic effects' and actually increase risk; (4) the *avoidant-passive* offender would prefer not to offend but does nothing to prevent himself from doing so.

Elliott and Beech (2009) note the benefits of applying Ward and Hudson's model to Internet sexual offending, specifically the distinction made between under-regulation/misregulation in goal-related behaviours. Passive under-regulation of behaviour, with its related disinhibition and impulsive behaviours, is something that is clearly relevant to the Internet offender population. Internet offenders often explain their abusive behaviours in a passive manner, even placing the responsibility for their behaviour onto the technology itself (Quayle and Taylor, 2002). Similarly, active misregulation of behaviour is also prevalent, as evidenced by those Internet offenders who often view sexually explicit material of children as well as demonstrating other online behaviours, as a coping mechanism to address various shortcomings in their immediate lives, such as boredom, anxiety or depression (e.g. Quayle et al., 2006).

Ward and Hudson's distinction between approach and explicit goals does, however, create difficulties with regards to this population, as it depends on how the crime is defined. That is, whether Internet offenders are *approach-explicit* offenders whose goal is to seek out and download illegal material or *avoidant-active* offenders who carry out such behaviours to avoid contact offending. Ward and Hudson (1998), in their model, suggest that viewing sexually explicit material of children represents a maladaptive strategy to avoid contact offending against children, and that fantasy rehearsal and masturbation make failure to achieve these avoidant goals more likely. However, it is clear that many Internet offenders express their sexual interest through solely viewing/downloading sexually explicit material of children, and are unlikely to commit contact offences. Hence, many of these offenders will display approach goal behaviours towards Internet offending, by either actively and deliberately searching for images to satisfy their sexual desire/interest (the *online-only* group), or by under-regulating their behaviour and offending impulsively or opportunistically (the *periodically prurient* group).

Conclusions

In this chapter we have attempted to illustrate how current theories of sexual offending may advance our understanding of the online exploitation of children. We have suggested that the ITSO may be a useful overall framework for under-standing more about where Internet abuser problems arise, and how interactions between proximal environmental factors and an individual's neuropsychological function can lead to problematic Internet use. We further noted the usefulness of Wards and Siegert's pathways model in understanding those who use the Internet because of their intimacy and/or emotional dysregulation problems. We have also examined theories of the offence process itself, again in order to see whether this approach is useful in understanding the processes by which individuals carry out such offences. We have also briefly described more general theories such as flow theory (Csikszentmihalyi, 1996), which may be useful in understanding why individuals carry out, and continue to carry out, such actions, despite the high levels of risk associated with these behaviours.

Such conceptualizations we would also suggest are useful in providing a framework for understanding the risk both these populations present (see Chapter 9 for a full discussion of these issues). Calder (2004) notes that the move from viewing abusive images of children on the Internet to contact offending is a massive one. While it would appear that not all offenders who masturbate to indecent images of children will inevitably progress to contact sexual offences, the subjective risk of them doing so may increase as the conditional pairing of online fantasy with masturbation and orgasm may lower their inhibitions about doing so (Sullivan and Beech, 2003). Certainly, making the distinction between: (1) the typology of Internet offenders; and (2) approach and avoidant goal setting in Internet offenders will represent a key issue for the understanding of the risk of cross-over from online to offline sexual abuse, and represents another area in need of research development for Internet offender behaviour.

We would also note the importance of situational and environmental factors involved in online abusive behaviours. As Wortley and Smallbone (2006) note, many professionals in criminal justice settings have focused only on personal dimensions of sexual crime, overlooking the contributions of an individual's immediate circumstances. Although it would be unwise to dismiss wholesale decades of work developing the type of etiological theory described above, we do however run the risk that by continually endeavouring to apply sex offender theory (developed from contact offender work) to Internet offenders, we are not capturing the individual qualities of these types of online offence that could allow us to construct better methods of prevention, assessment and treatment. Here it is worth noting that many online offenders do not score highly on measures of clinical symptoms related to sexually offensive behaviour. For example, Middleton et al. (2006) found that 40 per cent of their sample did not display elevated scores in any of their self-report tests of the clinical symptoms described in the ITSO model (i.e. cognitive distortions, emotional dysregulation, intimacy deficits and deviant sexual scripts). As there certainly appears to be a subset of this population which does not share the clinical symptoms outlined in the etiological theory described in this chapter, we would suggest that further investigation of criminological situational factors specific to the online environment is important to this understanding (as discussed in Chapter 11 of this volume).

In conclusion, we are beginning to understand the characteristics of Internet offenders as they relate to our extensive knowledge of contact sexual abusers. The next step is to develop our understanding of those characteristics that are specific to the Internet offender. Given its central role in the *modus operandi* of the offence, we know very little about the effects of surfing the Internet itself as a cognitive task (and the role of 'flow' in this), and consequently what effect it may have on behaviour. Our understanding of this behaviour would be significantly improved by increasing our understanding of pornography use in general – what the function of pornography is in fantasy and masturbation, what 'normal' pornography use is within the general public (although it is starting to be examined by Turner-Moore et al. (2010) in a sample of over 6,000 non-offending males), and how we might be able to account for the phenomenon of escalation from legal adult to extreme pornography and the viewing of sexually explicit material of children. However, these difficulties in self-management appear to have a limit, as the low observed rates of contact sex offences (as well as online recidivism) committed by Internet offenders may indicate well-functioning self-control in the offline world.

References

Andrews, D. A. and Bonta, J. (2006). *The Psychology of Criminal Conduct.* 4th edn. Cincinnati, OH: Anderson.

Ariely, D. and Loewenstein, G. (2006). The heat of the moment. The effect of sexual arousal on sexual decision making. *Journal of Behavioral Decision Making, 19*, 87–98.

Babchishin, K.M., Hanson, R.K. and Hermann, C.A. (2011). The characteristics of online sex offenders: A meta-analysis. *Sexual Abuse: A Journal of Research and Treatment, 23*, 92–123.

Block, J.J. (2008). Issues for DSM-V: Internet addiction [Editorial]. *American Journal of Psychiatry, 165*, 306–7.

Calder, M.C. (2004). The Internet: Potential, problems and pathways to hands-on sexual offending. In M.C. Calder (ed.), *Child Sexual Abuse and the Internet: Tackling the New Frontier.* Lyme Regis, Russell House Publishing, pp. 1–24.

Caspi, A., Henry, B., McGee, R.O. and Moffitt, T.E. (1995). Temperamental origins of child and adolescent behavior problems: From age three to fifteen. *Child Development, 66*, 55–68. Available online at http://www.jstor.org/stable/1131190.

Cohen, L.E., and Felson, M. (1979). Social change and crime rate trends: A routine activity approach. *American Sociological Review, 44*, 588–608. Available online at http://www.jstor.org/stable/2094589.

Csikszentmihalyi, M. (1996). *Creativity: Flow and the Psychology of Discovery and Invention.* New York: HarperCollins.

Danet, B. (1998). Text as mask: Gender, play, and performance on the Internet. In S.G. Jones (ed.), *CyberSociety 2.0: Revisiting Computer-mediated Communication and Community.* London: Sage, pp. 129–58.

Davis, R.A., Flett, G.L. and Besser, A. (2002). Validation of a new scale for measuring problematic Internet use: Implications for pre-employment screening. *CyberPsychology and Behavior, 5*, 331–45.

Durkin, K.F. (1997). Misuse of the Internet by pedophiles: Implications for law enforcement and probation practice. *Federal Probation, 61*, 14–18.

Elliott, I.A. and Babchishin, K.M. (in press). Psychological profiles and processes in viewers of Internet child pornography. In B.K. Schwartz (ed.), *The Sex Offender, Volume 7.* New York: Civic Research Institute.

Elliott, I.A. and Beech, A.R. (2009). Understanding online child pornography use: Applying sexual offender theory to Internet offenders. *Aggression and Violent Behavior, 14*, 180–93.

Gawin, F.H. (1991). Cocaine addiction: Psychology and neurophysiology. *Science, 251*, 1580–6. Available online at http://www.jstor.org/stable/2875724.

Howitt, D. and Sheldon, K. (2007). The role of cognitive distortions in paedophilic offending: Internet and contact offenders compared. *Psychology, Crime and Law, 13*, 469–86.

Internet Watch Foundation (2009). 2009 Annual and Charity Report Retrieved, May 19, 2010. Available online at http://www.iwf.org.uk/documents/20100511_iwf_2009_annual_and_charity_report.pdf.

Internet World Stats (2010). Available online from http://www.internetworldstats.com/stats.htm.

Interpol (2008). Databases. Fact Sheet (COM/FS/2008–07/GI–04). Available online at http://www.interpol.int/Public/ICPO/FactSheets/GI04.pdf

Jewkes, Y. and Yar, M. (2010). *Handbook of Internet Crime*. Cullompton: Willan.

Kennedy-Souza, B.L. (1998). Internet addiction disorder. *Interpersonal Computing and Technology: An Electronic Journal for the 21st Century, 6*, 1–2.

Krone, T. (2004). A typology of online child pornography offending. *Trends and Issues in Crime and Criminal Justice, 279*, 1–6.

Lanning, K. (1992). *Investigator's Guide to Allegations of 'Ritual Child Abuse'*. Quantico, VA: Behavioral Science Unit, National Centre for the Analysis of Violent Crime, FBI Academy.

—— (2001). *Child Molesters: A Behavioral Analysis*. 4th edn. Arlington, VA: National Center for Missing and Exploited Children. Available online at http://www.missing kids.com/en_US/publications/NC70.pdf.

Laulik, S., Allam, J. and Sheridan, L. (2007). An investigation into maladaptive personality functioning in Internet sex offenders. *Psychology, Crime and Law, 13*, 523–35.

Laws, D.R. (2003). Behavioral economic approaches to the assessment and treatment of sexual deviation. In T. Ward, D.R. Laws and S.M. Hudson, *Sexual Deviance: Issues and Controversies*. London: Sage, pp. 65–81.

Loewenstein, G. (1996). Out of control: Visceral influences on behavior. *Organizational and Human Decision Processes, 65*, 272–92.

Middleton, D., Elliott, I.A., Mandeville-Norden, R. and Beech, A.R. (2006). An investigation into the application of the Ward and Siegert pathways model of child sexual abuse with Internet offenders. *Psychology, Crime and Law, 12*, 589–603.

Morahan-Martin, J. and Schumacher, P. (2000). Incidents and correlates of pathological Internet use among college students. *Computers in Human Behavior, 13*, 13–29.

Motivans, M. and Kyckelhahn, T. (2007). *Federal Prosecution of Child Sex Exploitation Offenders, 2006* (Report No. NCJ219412). Available online at http://bjs.ojp.usdoj.gov/index.cfm?ty=pbdetail&iid=886.

Osborn, J. Elliott, I.A., Middleton, D. and Beech, A.R. (2010). The use of actuarial risk assessment measures with UK Internet child pornography offenders. *The Journal of Aggression, Conflict and Peace Studies, 2*, 16–24.

Pace, S. (2004). A grounded theory of the flow experiences of web users. *International Journal of Human-Computer Studies, 60*, 327–63.

Pennington, B.F. (2002). *The Development of Psychopathology: Nature And nurture*. New York: Guilford Press.

Pratt, T.C. and Cullen, F.T. (2000). The empirical status of Gottfredson and Hirschi's general theory of crime: A meta-analysis. *Criminology, 38*, 931–64.

Putnam, D.E. (2000). Initiation and maintenance of online sexual compulsivity: Implications for assessment and treatment. *CyberPsychology and Behavior, 3*, 553–63.

Quayle, E. and Taylor, M. (2002). Child pornography and the Internet: Perpetuating a cycle of abuse. *Deviant Behavior, 23*, 331–61.

—— (2003). Model of problematic Internet use in people with a sexual interest in children. *CyberPsychology and Behavior, 6*, 93–106.

Quayle, E., Vaughan, M. and Taylor, M. (2006). Sex offenders, Internet child abuse images and emotional avoidance: The importance of values. *Aggression and Violent Behavior, 11*, 1–11.

Seto, M.C. and Eke, A.W. (2005). The criminal histories and later offending of child pornography offenders. *Sexual Abuse: A Journal of Research and Treatment, 17*, 201–10.

Seto, M.C., Hanson, R.K. and Babchishin, K.M. (2011). Contact sexual offending by men with online sexual offenses. *Sexual Abuse: A Journal of Research and Treatment, 23*, 124–45.

Sheldon, K. and Howitt, D. (2007). *Sex Offenders and the Internet*. Chichester: Wiley.

Sperry, D.M. and Gilbert, B.O. (2005). Child peer sexual abuse: preliminary data on outcomes and disclosure experiences. *Child Abuse and Neglect, 29*, 889–904.

Steel, C.M.S. (2009). Web-based child pornography: Quantification and qualification of demand. International. *Journal of Digital Crime and Forensics, 1*, 58–69.

Sullivan, J. and Beech, A.R. (2003). Are collectors of child abuse images a risk to children? In A. MacVean and P. Spindler (eds), *Policing Paedophiles on the Internet*. London: The New Police Bookshop, pp. 11–20.

Taylor, M. and Quayle, E. (2003). *Child Pornography: An Internet Crime*. Hove: Brunner-Routledge.

Taylor, M., Holland, G. and Quayle, E. (2001). A typology of paedophile picture collections. *The Police Journal, 74*, 97–107.

Turner-Moore, T., Smith, P. and Waterman, M. (2010). The computerized interview for sexual thoughts: A tool to explore sexual fantasies. Poster Presented at the 29th Annual Conference of the Association for the Treatment of Sexual Abusers, Phoenix, AZ, October 2010.

Ward, T. and Beech, A.R. (2006). An integrated theory of sexual offending. *Aggression and Violent Behavior, 11*, 44–63.

Ward, T. and Hudson, S.M. (1998). The construction and development of theory in the sexual offending area: A meta-theoretical framework. *Sexual Abuse: A Journal of Research and Treatment, 10*, 47–63.

Ward, T. and Siegert, R. J. (2002). Toward a comprehensive theory of child sexual abuse: A theory knitting perspective. *Psychology, Crime, and Law, 9*, 319–51.

Ward, T. and Sorbello, L. (2003). Explaining child sexual abuse: Integration and elaboration. In T. Ward, D.R. Laws and S.M. Hudson (eds), *Sexual Deviance: Issues and Controversies in Sexual Deviance*. London: Sage, pp. 3–20.

Ward, T., Polaschek, D. and Beech, A.R. (2006). *Theories of Sexual Offending*. Chichester: Wiley.

Webb, L., Craisatti, J. and Keen, S. (2007). Characteristics of Internet child pornography offenders: A comparison with child molesters. *Sexual Abuse: A Journal of Research and Treatment, 19*, 449–65.

Whitaker, D.J., Brenda, L., Hanson, R.K., Baker, C.K., McMahon, P.M., Ryan, G. et al. (2008). Risk factors for the perpetration of child sexual abuse: A review and meta-analysis. *Child Abuse and Neglect, 32*, 529–48.

Widyanto, L. and Griffiths, M. (2006). Internet addiction: A critical review. *International*

Journal of Mental Health and Addiction, 4, 31–51.

Wiggins, R.W. (1995). The unfolding Net. *Internet World*, 6, 43–46.

Wolak, J., Finkelhor, D. and Mitchell, K. (2009). *Trends in Arrests of 'Online Predators'.* Crime Against Children Research Center. Available online at http://www.unh.edu/news/NJOV2.pdf.

Wortley, R.K. and Smallbone, S. (2006). Applying situational principles to sexual offenses against children. In R.K. Wortley and S. Smallbone (eds), *Situational Prevention of Child Sexual Abuse*. Morsey, NY: Criminal Justice Press, pp. 7–36.

Young, K.S. (2008). Internet sex addiction: Risk factors, stages of development and treatment. *American Behavioral Scientist*, 52, 21–37.

4 Child pornography in international law

Alisdair A. Gillespie, Leicester
De Montfort Law School

Overview

Increasingly in recent years individual countries have paid considerable attention to introducing laws to combat the production and dissemination of child pornography.[1] At the same time, there has been increased attention paid to this at the international level, including the development of international law. This chapter considers how international law seeks to combat child pornography.

What is international law?

Perhaps the first question to ask is what is international law? In this short chapter it is not possible to discuss this in depth but it is worth outlining briefly because although it has a long history (Aust, 2005) there continue to be some who question whether it can be truly classified as law (Aust, 2005) rather than politics. The question is asked principally because many of the concepts of domestic law are not readily translated into international law, especially the concept of enforceability, with international law sometimes being easily flouted by countries. Certainly it must be conceded that the boundary between international law, politics and custom is obscure at best but to state that international law does not exist is no longer a tenable statement.

International law is a system of laws that are primarily addressed to states (i.e. other countries) and not to individuals. Its primary purpose is to regulate how individual states interact with each other and the wider community, and thus much of its earliest form concerned trade (and indeed this remains perhaps one of the most important aspects of international law) and how representatives of each country were to be treated (and the concept of ambassadorial representation and diplomatic immunity continues to be an important and controversial part of international law: see, for example, Cassese, 2005). International law continues to be primarily focused on the responsibilities of a state rather than an individual and this will be explored in the context of child pornography momentarily. It should be noted, however, that in recent times there has been a slight shift in certain forms of international law, away from its traditional role of focusing on the actions of the state and towards regulating the actions of the individual (Cassese, 2005).

One of the earliest examples of this shift can be seen in the aftermath of the Second World War where perhaps the first recognition that international law could regulate the actions of an individual was the decision of the allied powers to try members of the Nazi party for war crimes at the Nuremberg International Military Tribunal (Aust, 2005). From this has developed a species of international law known as international criminal law. It may be thought that international criminal law would be relevant for the purposes of considering how international law tackles child pornography but it does not, in fact, fall within its remit. International criminal law is a specific type of jurisdiction that refers to crimes against the international community and thus it currently covers issues such as war crimes, crimes against humanity, genocide, torture, aggression and terrorism (Cassese, 2008). So far the sexual exploitation of children does not come within the definition of international criminal law although where sexual violence is inflicted in a systematic way to obtain political goals it is beginning to be classed as falling within crimes against humanity (see the judgments of the *International Criminal Tribunal for the former Yugoslavia* in *Furundžija* (IT-95-17/1-T) and *Kunarac and others* (IT-96-23-T)). As child pornography does not appear to be used as an instrument of the state or a state agent it would not fall within international criminal law.

Child pornography would seem to be a classic example of when a criminal law response is required. The exclusion of child pornography from the definition of international criminal law does not contradict this position and perhaps demonstrates the difficulty one has in mapping domestic theories of law into the international arena. Criminal law, save where it is a crime against the international community, is not considered to be a separate form of law in its own right but rather is recognized as an instrument of existing branches of international law. In the context of sexual exploitation, criminal law can be considered to be an instrument of international human rights law and this is a point that has been expressly recognized by the European Court of Human Rights (ECtHR) who have stated that the criminal law is sometimes the only effective method of protecting an individual's right to personal autonomy (see *X and Y* v *Netherlands* (1986) 8 EHRR 235 and *MC* v *Bulgaria* (2005) 40 EHRR 20).

International human rights law, as with international law in general, is not addressed to an individual citizen but rather continues to be addressed to the state itself. Where the law differs, however, is in its nature: international human rights instruments commit the state to providing its citizens with defined rights. So whilst the instrument itself is not addressed to individuals, the individual citizen will be afforded a degree of protection by the state. International human rights law differs from domestic legislation in that breach of the right is not actionable against another individual but against the state. The international instruments require the state to put forward a framework of protection and thus a breach is where the state has failed to provide this adequate protection. Thus, for example, a breach may be triggered by a private citizen sexually assaulting another person where it can be shown that the framework of laws created by the state was not adequate or where there was a failure to investigate or prosecute the offender. Thus the basis of the rights is an expectation that the state will use its own laws – including criminal law – to help create a system that deters harm being caused and requires their effective investigation, prosecution and punishment. The precise obligations on the state by international instruments relating to child pornography are discussed below.

Jurisdiction

The distinction between international criminal law and criminal law as an instrument of international human rights law was discussed above. One central difference between these forms relates to jurisdiction. Those accused of breaching international criminal law can be tried either at the International Criminal Court or by those countries that recognize the principle of universal jurisdiction (Cassese, 2008). Universal jurisdiction is the doctrine adopted by some countries that allows them to try a citizen of any state who comes within their borders irrespective of whether their own citizens were affected by the actions of the individual (Hirst, 2003). Where the crime is not one under international criminal law, then general principles of jurisdiction apply.

Ordinary principles of jurisdiction dictate that a country exercises jurisdiction in matters that take place within its own territory. Hirst (2003) provides perhaps the most important treatise on the issue of domestic jurisdiction. Precisely what amounts to its jurisdiction is itself the subject of international law (broadly it covers the landmass of a country and its territorial waters (roughly equating to 12 nautical miles) and its airspace) with special provision being made for aircraft and ships (which will, by their very nature, be in international airspace or waters for parts of some journeys) (for a fuller discussion see Hirst, 2003). It is not necessary for us to understand the exact principles of jurisdiction and the exceptions to territorial jurisdiction save that acknowledging the ordinary principles mean that a state can ordinarily only prosecute crimes that take place within their territory.

A difficulty with child pornography, and indeed other forms of child sexual exploitation, is that it is known that the crimes are not necessarily easily detectable and, perhaps of more concern, that there are some countries where adequate child protection mechanisms are still not in place. This can provide a challenge to the ordinary rules of jurisdiction. Let us take an example:

Peter, a national of the UK, goes to Cambodia where he films himself having sexual intercourse with a 10-year-old boy. He also takes indecent photographs of five other children, all engaged in sexual activity. He returns to England, and after five months, his photographs are detected.

England and Wales criminalizes the possession of child pornography (s.160, Criminal Justice Act 1988) and thus Peter will be culpable for this offence since the photographs are being possessed in the territory of England. However, possession does not fully capture Peter's behaviour. England could choose, at Cambodia's request, to extradite Peter to their territory (i.e. send Peter to Cambodia for trial) but this is historically problematic. States must ordinarily have extradition treaties governing the circumstances when people will be extradited (and some countries do not allow the extradition of their citizens), and there must be a realistic prospect of a conviction. If the police, for the example above, in Cambodia do not take the matter seriously or do not identify the children so that they can give evidence in a trial, it is quite possible that Peter will be acquitted. The reluctance of some countries to prosecute incidents of child sexual abuse posed a problem that international law sought to solve.

Whilst a state will ordinarily only prosecute a person for an act committed within its territory, as a sovereign entity it has the right to pass whatever laws it wishes. Accordingly, state X could prosecute a person for doing an act in state Y so long as that person comes within its physical borders. This is known as extraterritoriality, i.e. the ability of a state to prosecute for acts that took place outside its territory. Traditionally, extraterritoriality has been exercised on the basis of the citizenship of the offender, something known as the active personality basis (Fredette, 2009; Hirst, 2003). If this was adopted then, to return to our example above, Peter could be prosecuted in England as one of its citizens for the illegal activities that took place in Cambodia. Exercising extraterritorial jurisdiction can be problematic since it can be difficult to gather evidence but for offences of child pornography this is often easier because the illicit material itself usually provides the evidence (in the example of Peter, his illegal sexual activity with a child and the fact that he took, rather than merely possessed, indecent photographs of children).

Exercising jurisdiction under the active personality principle does not always assist, however, as there may be circumstances where it continues to leave a country unable to act even where it would seem to have a legitimate interest. Let us take a second example:

Michael is a citizen of Italy. When he was visiting Mexico he took indecent photographs of Rebecca, a 12-year-old British citizen. When back in Britain, Rebecca reports Michael's actions. Michael visits Thomas, a friend of his, in London four months later.

If the active personality test for extraterritorial jurisdiction is used then in the example above the UK police cannot arrest Michael when he enters the United Kingdom. Michael is not a UK citizen and thus the courts would not be able to prosecute him for his activities in Mexico. Only the Mexican or Italian authorities could prosecute him; Mexico under ordinary principles of jurisdiction and Italy by exercising its own extraterritorial powers. However, it may be difficult for either jurisdiction to gather the appropriate evidence.

Extraterritoriality can also be exercised under the passive personality principle. This is based not on the nationality of the offender but on the nationality of the victim. Therefore if England were to exercise extraterritoriality on the basis of passive personality then in the example above, Michael could be arrested when he entered England (its territory) because it would apply its laws to those who harm one of its own citizens (Rebecca). Of course, in reality extraterritorial jurisdiction would have to be exercised under both an active and passive personality since if only the passive personality were adopted then in the original example, Peter would not be liable.

Traditionally, many countries, including the United Kingdom, have not adopted the passive personality principle (Hirst, 2003). However, it is notable that in international law there is a growing consensus for its use in the area of child sexual exploitation, including child pornography. The Optional Protocol to the CRC on the Sale of Children, Child Pornography and Child Prostitution and the Council of Europe Convention on the Protection of Children against Sexual Exploitation and Sexual Abuse (considered below) both require states to exercise jurisdiction on both the active and passive personality principles (Articles 4.2(b) and 20.2 respectively).

There are some difficulties with extraterritoriality, including the requirement in some countries for dual criminality (i.e. the requirement that the act is illegal in both the country prosecuting and the country where the activity was alleged to have occurred: Svensson, 2006; Hirst, 2003) or the principle of subordination (put simply, the principle that decides which country has 'greater' claim to prosecuting the offender: Blakesley and Stigall, 2004). It is not possible in this chapter to consider these issues but it should be noted that they do need to be addressed under international law (see the comments of Maalla, 2009), and it is necessary for international law to identify ways in which these rules can be developed without it interfering with the ability of states to prosecute in an extraterritorial manner. It is now recognized that extending jurisdiction is an important feature of combating the sexual exploitation of children, including child pornography (see the comments of Petit, 2004 and Maalla, 2009, both of whom have held the office of UN Special Rapporteur on, *inter alia*, child pornography).

Global instruments

Perhaps the most important international law instrument dedicated to the rights of the child is the UN Convention on the Rights of the Child (CRC). The CRC was not the first instrument specifically to consider the fact that children have distinct rights, with the League of Nations producing a Declaration of the Rights of the Child in 1924. This was followed by a 1959 Declaration by the United Nations General Assembly but a declaration is non-binding and is, in essence, simply a statement of general purpose. For some twenty years there was resistance to the idea of a binding human rights instrument (Buck, 2011) and it took another decade for an instrument to be agreed, with the CRC being declared open for signature in January 1990. The CRC has achieved almost universal approval with 193 states having signed it, with only Somalia and the United States of America failing to sign it (although the USA has signed the Optional Protocol to the CRC discussed below).

Article 34 of the CRC requires states to 'protect the child from all forms of sexual exploitation and sexual abuse' and it makes specific reference to preventing 'the exploitative use of children in pornographic performances and materials' which is a welcome signal that child pornography is a breach of the CRC. However, Article 34 lacks considerable detail. It does not state how a state should protect the child, what forms of protection are considered preferable or indeed what the meaning of the term 'exploitative use of children in pornographic . . . materials' is. Does this, for example, mean that the non-exploitative use of children in pornography is accepted and, if so, what do exploitation and pornography mean? The article was deliberately written widely so as to provide flexibility (Gillespie, 2011) but despite the fact that some argue that it can be used as the basis of protecting a child from sexual exploitation (Jones, 1998) its vagueness means it is difficult to enforce the right. In reality, it is perhaps more of a statement of intent. That said, the inclusion of Article 34 was an important milestone on the protection of children from child pornography in international law and also for ensuring that international law enforcement agencies (most notably Interpol) began actively to work in this area.

After the CRC, perhaps the next significant global instrument to be drafted was the International Labour Organization's Convention 182 drafted in 1999. This was passed at a time when it was estimated that there were upwards of 80 million children who were, in essence, child slaves in harmful situations (NGO Group, 2001). Whilst the ILO Convention does at least attempt to protect children, a criticism of it is that it arguably treats some forms of child sexual exploitation as employment, albeit categorized as the 'worst form of child labour' (Article 3(b) of Convention 182 expressly refers to 'child labour' including 'the use, procuring or offering of a child for prostitution, for the production of pornography or for pornographic performances'). The Convention mandates states to take steps to protect children from these worst forms of labour (Article 7) but it can be questioned whether it is appropriate to label this abuse as 'labour', i.e. work. Surely it would be more appropriate to recognize this as commercial sexual abuse or exploitation instead? While it may seem a question of semantics, sometimes labels can be relevant. Referring to labour would, it is submitted, suggest that the object is perhaps legitimate (labour or employment) but the methods are inappropriate ('worst forms'). However, the sexual exploitation of children, and particularly in the context of the ILO the commercial sexual exploitation of children, is not a legitimate objective and it should be recognized that this is not labour but abuse. The payment of money cannot transform something from abuse to employment and the ILO Convention perhaps blurs this distinction. Others have criticized the instrument for failing to acknowledge the fact that a minor lacks the capacity to consent to commercial sexual acts (Bakirci, 2007) although that would, of course, be based on the legal concept of consent. Bakirci also questions whether there is a risk that this labels victims as 'child sex workers' which may, in some cultures, cause them to be treated differently (ibid.). For all these reasons it is to be regretted that the ILO used such terminology.

The most significant global instrument that specifically relates to child pornography is the Optional Protocol to the CRC on the Sale of Children, Child Prostitution, and Child Pornography (OPSC). The CRC was a broad instrument and despite the inclusion of Article 34, it was never intended that the specific details of protecting children from sexual exploitation would be covered in the CRC itself. Shortly after the implementation of the CRC, work started on a protocol to it, eventually resulting in the OPSC (see Gillespie, 2011 for a brief history of its drafting).

The OPSC covers many forms of sexual abuse and exploitation and specifically refers to child pornography. Article 2(c) of the OPSC defines child pornography as 'any representation, of whatever means, of a child engaged in real or simulated explicit sexual activities or any representation of the sexual parts of a child for primarily sexual purposes'. This is a wide definition, and is indeed wider than many other international instruments (Gillespie, 2010) and it would cover not just image-based child pornography but also text and audio descriptions too. That said, the fact that 'child' is not defined further does raise questions about whether representations of fictitious children (so-called 'virtual child pornography') would be covered by this definition. Age is not defined under the OPSC but since it is a protocol to the CRC the age within the CRC would apply, that being 18 unless domestic law prescribes a lower age for the age of majority (Article 1). It is notable however that Article 1 refers to the age of majority (the age at which a person legally becomes an adult) and not, for example, age of consent, and thus even where the age of consent is lower than 18 in a country, the OPSC will define a child as under 18 for the purposes of child pornography.

The OPSC refers to a number of actions that states are required to carry out in respect of child pornography. It is not possible to critique these in detail but it is worth noting what requirements are imposed on countries. The first of relevance is Article 3(b) which requires the production, distribution, dissemination, import, export, sale or possession of child pornography for one of those purposes to be criminalized. This covers most of the significant actions regarding child pornography, with 'production' encompassing the creation of material (including photographing the child). An interesting question is what 'import' and 'export' means in an online environment: would it cover a situation where D, in country X, downloads a photograph from a server hosted in country Y? Perhaps the most surprising aspect of the OPSC is the vague definition surrounding possession. The wording of Article 3(b) suggests that simple possession (rather than possession with intent to distribute, etc.) is not required to be criminalized. This is different from many other instruments and it is notable that the UN Special Rapporteur has called for simple possession to be criminalized (Petit, 2004) and indeed the latest Special Rapporteur has suggested that states go further and should criminalize the intentional viewing of images (Maalla, 2009). However this is only an opinion of the Special Rapporteurs and the OPSC itself currently does not require states to criminalize these matters.

Article 4 requires states to secure jurisdiction, including extraterritorial jurisdiction. The meaning of this was discussed earlier but it is notable that Article 4.2(b) expressly refers to securing extraterritorial jurisdiction by reference to the nationality of the victim. Articles 5 to 7 take this further by requiring states to consider (and to cooperate) with extradition requests and also to cooperate with each other in the investigation and prosecution of crimes. Article 10.1 also relates to international cooperation and requires states to consider bilateral and multilateral cooperation in the prevention, detection, investigation and prosecution of those who commit an offence, inter alia, involving child pornography.

An important provision of the OPSC is Article 8.2 which states that where the actual age of a child is not known this should not prevent a state from investigating the case. This could be important in cases relating to child pornography where few victims are traced. Article 8 also requires states to treat identifiable victims in sensitive ways and ensure that their criminal justice system take their rights into account. Article 10.2 supports this by requiring states to 'assist child victims in their physical and psychological recovery, social reintegration and repatriation'. This is an important provision as it reminds states that the focus should not just be on the prosecution of offenders but that states have a responsibility to those who are victims of these offences.

Regional instruments

Whilst it has been seen that a number of global instruments exist to combat child pornography, regional groupings have also attempted to address these issues. Areas of the world have developed their own regional bodies, i.e. collectives of geographically proximate states that come together and pass instruments that they collectively agree to obey. These instruments form part of international law but they obviously bind only those countries within the collective and thus have a regional remit (although it should be noted that occasionally some regional instruments will have an extra-regional reach, perhaps most notably the Council of Europe Convention on Cybercrime that was signed by countries outside the Council of Europe including the USA).

In a chapter of this size it is not possible to identify precisely all the instruments that seek to tackle child pornography. As with global instruments there appear to be some instruments that seek to protect children in general and some that specifically address the issue of child pornography.

An example of a general instrument is the thirty-five-country Organization of American States' American Convention on the Human Rights, first drafted in 1969. Along with general rights akin to those set out in the European Convention on Human Rights (such as Article 5, which provides for the right to humane treatment, including requiring an individual's physical, mental and moral integrity to be respected), Article 19 provides specifically for the rights of the child, stating 'Every minor child has the right to the measures of protection required by his condition as a minor'. This is somewhat opaque but could certainly be used as the basis for requiring specific protection to be given to children from sexual exploitation, including child pornography. That said, a general provision is perhaps not as important or as helpful as having the matter expressly dealt with, even in circumstances where the relevant bodies will 'read-across' to other instruments (for example, the CRC or OPSC) to determine the extent of rights (discussed in the enforcement section below).

Others adopt a hybrid approach. For example, Article 16(1) of the African Charter on the Rights and Welfare of the Child provides that state parties 'shall take specific legislative, administrative, social and educational measures to protect the child from all forms of . . . sexual abuse, while in the care of the child'. While this definition is not expanded upon, child pornography must be considered to be a form of sexual abuse and accordingly Article 16(1) would mandate African nations creating laws specifically addressing child pornography. However Article 27 is the more notable provision. This relates to sexual exploitation and Article 27(1) mandates states to 'protect the child from all forms of sexual exploitation and sexual abuse and shall in particular take measures to prevent . . . (c) the use of children in pornographic activities, performances and materials'. Accordingly, the African Charter expressly deals with the issue of child pornography. It differs from, for example, the OPSC in that it does not require specific action to be taken (e.g. it does not expressly require the prohibition of the production, distribution and possession of the material) and perhaps this is something that would be a useful addition should the Charter be updated. However, it is an important recognition of the problem of child pornography and an early one: the African Charter was drafted in 1990 although it did not come into force until 1999. The African Charter is also supplemented by the African Youth Charter, Article 23(l) of which requires signatory states to 'enact and enforce legislation that protect girls and young women from . . . prostitution and pornography'. This Article, of course, does not mention males, and it is in the context of a particular difficulty in some African countries of failing to afford females adequate protection, but the wording is notable in that it requires the state to both enact *and enforce* legislation.

Arguably the region that has paid most attention to the issue of child sexual exploitation, particularly child pornography, is that of Europe. There are two organizations that are relevant to Europe; the Council of Europe (CoE) and the European Union (EU). Technically, these are two separate bodies, with the CoE being the elder and larger of the two (it was created in 1949 and currently consists of forty-seven countries). That said, it is a prerequisite of joining the EU that a member is first a member of the CoE and the two bodies work increasingly closely together. Both the CoE and the EU have enacted international instruments that specifically relate to the issue of the sexual exploitation of a child, including through child pornography.

The CoE's most notable international instrument is the European Convention on Human Rights (ECHR). Whilst this does not expressly govern the issue of child pornography or indeed the sexual exploitation of a child, it does provide for both the freedom from inhumane or degrading treatment (Article 3) and the integrity of the person (Article 8: right to respect for, *inter alia*, private life). It will be seen from the section on enforcement that it is possible that these provisions can be used to frame a protection from sexual exploitation. However the CoE has a number of other instruments and two have direct relevance to us. The first is the Convention on Cybercrime (CETS No. 185) which was drafted in 2001. This instrument was designed specifically to tackle the emerging issue of crimes committed, or facilitated, by information and communication technologies (ICT). Article 9 of the Convention requires states to establish criminal offences relating to the production, making available, distribution, procuring or possession of child pornography. This was one of the first instruments that required states to take specific action in respect of individual offences. It should be noted that the Cybercrime Convention allows member states to define a child as someone aged 16 although ordinarily it should be 18 (see Article 9.3). Similarly it permits states to decline to criminalize the procurement or possession of child pornography (Article 9.4).

The Cybercrime Convention was also limited to child pornography that was produced, hosted, stored or disseminated by ICT. It would not cover material that did not have a link to ICT. A later and more specific instrument is the Convention on the Protection of Children against Sexual Exploitation and Sexual Abuse (CETS No. 201) which was drafted in 2007. This Treaty, as its name suggests, was designed specifically to address the issue of the sexual exploitation of children and Article 20 of the Convention requires member states to create criminal offences relating to the production, offering, making available, distribution, procurement, possession of or deliberate access to child pornography (Article 20.1). This Convention does not permit states the opportunity not to criminalize possession, save where it amounts to so-called virtual child pornography (Article 20.3). The age of a child is 18 (Article 3), although where a child has reached the age of consent in that country, if an image has been taken with its consent, then a country may decide not to criminalize someone who possesses (but does not distribute) the image so long as the child consents to the possession (Article 20.3).

The requirement in both conventions to introduce criminal offences relating to specific conduct is very reminiscent of the OPSC and it is submitted that it does ensure that the matter is addressed specifically by each country, as its obligations are clear. That said, as will be seen, there are still difficulties with enforcement and this means that some member states of the Council of Europe have not fulfilled their obligation. The Convention on the Protection of Children is also notable for mandating not only the criminalization of child pornography but also requiring states to take preventive measures (Article 4), assist victims (Article 14) and ensure investigating officers are adequately trained in these crimes and do not prejudice the welfare of the child during an investigation (Article 30). It also specifically addresses the issues of jurisdiction, extradition and the cooperation of states. In this way it can be said that the Convention truly provides a framework of protection for a child.

The EU was initially a body that was set up to establish a common market for trade and employment but it has gradually assumed competence to act in other areas, including the sexual exploitation of children. One of its earliest instruments in this field was a Council Decision on combating child pornography (2000/375/ JHA), which put forward a broad policy basis for combating child pornography, including the establishment of dedicated police units (Article 1). However, the most notable instrument was probably the Framework Decision on combating the sexual exploitation of children, including through child pornography (2004/68/ JHA). Unlike the Council Decision this required member states to take specific action to combat child pornography. This included, for example, specifically criminalizing the production, distribution, supply, acquisition or possession of child pornography (Article 3.1) although member states were permitted not to criminalize activities relating to so-called virtual child pornography (Article 3.2) or the production or possession of a photograph of a child who had reached the age of consent in that country so long as the child consented to its production and possession (Article 3.2). The Decision also required effective investigation strategies (Article 4), sanctions (Articles 5 and 7), that extraterritorial jurisdiction be exercised (Article 8) and that assistance be given to victims (Article 9).

Decisions of the EU, including Framework Decisions, are supposedly binding on member states, though an internal report showed that this was not the case and that a number of EU states were not complying with the law (EU, 2007). The Treaty of Lisbon increases the enforcement procedures for non-common-market issues and the EU is currently negotiating the text of an instrument to replace the current Framework Decision. Known as a Directive it will be binding on all member states and the Court of Justice of the European Union should have competence to enforce its provisions if matters are referred to it by either domestic courts or the European Commission.

The proposed Directive is very similar to the instrument that it replaces, at least in the context of child pornography (the Directive is wider than the Framework Decision in that it encapsulates, for example, the enticement or luring of a child over the Internet, aka 'grooming'). The Directive will require member states to establish laws that make it a criminal offence to acquire or possess, knowingly obtain access to, distribute, supply or make available or produce child pornography (Article 5). The definition of child pornography is realistically not different although reference to 'lasciviousness' is replaced by the depiction of the sexual organs of a child for primarily sexual purposes (Article 2(b)). In practice this may not make too much difference (Gillespie, 2010) but it is perhaps a clearer definition. The position of so-called virtual child pornography is also clarified in that it expressly forms part of the definition (Article 2(1)). The Directive will also include the wider issues of investigation, jurisdiction and victim support, and indeed these are arguably strengthened with the provision of more detail as to the responsibilities of a member state.

Whilst the Directive is broadly similar, there are a number of differences between the Directive and the Framework Decision. Perhaps the most notable is that the Directive will include minimum maximum penalties. In other words, it will define the minimum term of imprisonment that a member state can impose as its maximum sentence for a crime. This is an attempt to bring consistency to the laws of the EU and to ensure that offences are recognized as serious. Another significant difference is that the proposed Directive does not permit member states to opt out of the criminalization of either so-called virtual child pornography or the production or possession of photographs of children over the age of consent but below 18. The latter is consistent with the OPSC but is significantly more restrictive than the CoE Convention on the Protection of Children. The most controversial difference and the one that is the subject of most debate at the moment is the proposal that member states should block access to child pornography (Article 25). In this chapter it is not possible to discuss this in depth but it has to be recognized that the blocking of material is considered controversial in many states as it is viewed as censorship and, to many, a distraction from the primary aim of removing material (Eneman, 2010 provides a useful summary of the arguments). That said, it is used in some countries (for example, England and Wales) where its use is justified as a means of disrupting access to the material and preventing offenders 'stumbling' across the material (see the work of the Internet Watch Foundation).

Enforceability

Perhaps one of the most controversial aspects of international law is its enforceability and it will be remembered from the beginning of the chapter that this is one of the reasons why questions continue to be asked as to whether international law truly amounts to law. The enforceability of international law differs between the individual instruments depending on the text contained within that treaty. Whilst some instruments do appear to be more enforceable than others the context of this has to be understood. For example, the proposed EU Directive on the sexual exploitation of children will be binding on member states of the EU but this is simply because EU law operates on shared sovereignty: the member states agreeing, at the time of accession, to transfer some sovereignty to the EU in certain matters including enforcement. If a member state left the EU, then their obligations under the Directive would end. Similarly, decisions of the European Court of Human Rights and the Inter-American Court of Human Rights (IACHR) are theoretically binding and thus it would seem that violations of international law adjudicated by those courts are enforceable, but this is simply because signatory courts agree to abide by these judgments. If a country refuses to accept a judgment, and certainly in the context of the ECtHR a number of countries do routinely fail to adhere to the full extent of the judgment, then the matter realistically ceases to be an issue of law and becomes an issue of international politics.

Convention on the Rights of the Child

It has been noted previously that the most important human rights instrument for children is the CRC, but this does not expressly cover issues relating to child pornography. The most important global instrument specifically covering child pornography is its optional protocol on the sexual abuse of children, the OPSC. The CRC, and therefore the OPSC, has limited enforceability. No court has direct jurisdiction over the CRC and it has been remarked that its sole enforceability is through its reporting system (Buck, 2011).

The reporting system operates on the individual states submitting a report to the Committee on the Rights of the Child every five years (Gillespie, 2011). There does not appear, however, to be any sanction where a state fails to submit a report (Buck, 2011), the system simply proceeding on the basis of reminders and public statements that a report has not been submitted. The Committee spends a day examining the reports and this will include seeking representations from the country submitting the report (Buck, 2011).

The effectiveness of the reporting system as a system of enforcing the OPSC and detecting its breaches is perhaps open to question. It has been noted that the system relies on the individual countries preparing their own reports and whilst there is public scrutiny of these reports, there is limited opportunity to gather additional evidence (one mechanism would be through visits by the UN Special Rapporteur (Gillespie, 2011), although this relies on them being invited into the state). The primary source of evidence therefore would seem to be the reports themselves, and this may include information that is dubious at best (see, for example, Buck, 2011, where he notes that in their report North Korea indicated that there had been no cases of sexual exploitation against children, which seems somewhat improbable). Even where a state does prepare a comprehensive report, it must by necessity include broad issues (not least because the report is limited to 120 pages: see Buck, 2011) and thus there must be a real concern that individual breaches of the Convention may not be detected. Some international human rights instruments, including global instruments, provide a right of petition, i.e. the right of an individual to raise an issue to the attention of the relevant organization (Buck, 2011), and this at least means that the enforcing body is aware of individual allegations of a breach.

Would a right of petition be a positive development for the OPSC? Certainly, it would mean that individual breaches could be brought to the attention of the Committee of the Rights of the Child although it should be noted that this is not a court and thus it is questionable whether they could do anything more than take note of the breach. There would be questions about whether the Committee was able to investigate any breach and also whether it would substantially impact on the work of the Committee. The Committee is already under pressure in terms of work with it being noted that there is slow progress on the scrutiny of reports (Buck, 2011), although the UN has promised to provide further funds to the Committee to increase its efficiency (Rehman, 2010). Could a right of petition make the work of the Committee untenable? At least one former member of the Committee believes that the Committee could cope (Sahovic, 2009), but this would almost certainly require significant additional resources. There is currently a proposal to provide a right of individual petition (Štefánek, 2010) although this will require an addition protocol to be included within the CRC (with the right of petition arising only in those countries that sign this protocol). The extent to which the Committee could cope with an increased workload will feature in the discussion surrounding the creation of any new protocol but a note of caution must be sounded. As noted above, even if a right of petition is introduced it does not necessarily follow that there will be direct enforcement: a country could presumably refuse to cooperate with the Committee, disagree with its conclusion and decline to provide a remedy, the latter of which is eminently possible since the Committee is not, of course, a court.

Regional instruments

At the regional level the position as to enforceability is also somewhat vague. No dedicated court has been created by any of the regions to discuss the issue of children's rights. However, it is quite possible that there could be horizontal effect given to the various treaties, including potentially the global instruments. For example, there exist two notable courts of human rights: the Inter-American Court of Human Rights and the European Court of Human Rights. Each theoretically has a specific remit and this does not expressly include the regional instruments for that particular geo-political area. So, for example, whilst the ECtHR is the court for the Council of Europe its remit is in respect of the European Convention on Human Rights and not the Convention on Cybercrime or Convention on the Protection of Children against Sexual Exploitation and Sexual Abuse. Neither of these instruments empower the ECtHR with specific jurisdiction to rule on breaches of the rights contained within these instruments. Similarly, the IACHR is limited to the adjudication of the American Convention on Human Rights.

Courts can, of course, take into account the fact that countries have signed conventions, including global instruments. Accordingly, in *Villagran-Morales* v. *Guatemala* (judgment of 19 November 1999) the IACHR judicially noted that Guatemala was a signatory of the CRC (at para. 184 of the judgment) and based its ruling in part on that. Similar reasoning has been adopted by the ECtHR. Perhaps one of the most notable examples of this is in *KT* v *Norway* (2009) 49 EHRR 4, where the ECtHR expressly considered aspects of the CRC and noted, 'the Court cannot but note the emphasis placed on effectiveness in art. 19 [of the CRC]' (at p. 105). However, whilst the court is able to use the CRC and other conventions as a way of supporting its judgment it should be noted that this is not providing direct enforcement of these rights. A person cannot petition the IACHR or ECtHR arguing that their rights under the CRC, OPSC or a regional convention (e.g. the Convention on the Protection of Children against Sexual Exploitation and Sexual Abuse) have been breached; instead, the case must be brought within the core instrument of that court's competence (identified above). It will be remembered that Article 19 of the American Convention on Human Rights includes an article on the rights of the child, so making the process of bringing a case easier, but it must still be framed in that context. The European Convention on Human Rights does not include an article that expressly governs children's rights and thus a complaint would have to be framed in an alternative way, for example, alleging inhuman or degrading treatment (Article 3) or an infringement of the right to respect for private life (Article 8) which includes physical integrity (see, most notably, *X and Y* v *Netherlands* (1986) 8 EHRR 235 and *KU* v *Finland* (2009) 48 EHRR 52, which expressly related to the inclusion of a child's personal details on a sex site).

Conclusion

The enforceability of international law perhaps demonstrates the biggest weakness of its applicability to child pornography. It is very easy for countries to sign treaties and conventions and make pledges to tackle child pornography but it is also very easy for countries simply to ignore them. Does this mean that international law has no place in tackling child pornography? What we know of child pornography is that the reverse must be true. The global nature of child pornography means that individual countries cannot tackle child pornography by themselves. Countries must cooperate in order to identify those who are producing material and identify solutions that will allow offenders to be dealt with.

There is considerable overlap between the different instruments, and identifying the differences between the various instruments is sometimes difficult. It is not just overlap between global and regional instruments; there can also be overlap at a regional level. A good example of this is the fact that the Council of Europe Convention on Cybercrime and Convention on the Protection of Children against Sexual Exploitation and Sexual Abuse put forward two different definitions of child pornography which require different forms of action. Which law should signatory states adhere to? Where a country also signs the OPSC (as most Council of Europe countries have) then the overlap is even greater.

It has been remarked that some instruments provide a 'gold standard' of rights (Watson, 2009), meaning that they put forward the ideal rights a child should have. While this can be a laudable policy statement, it may also create the position whereby a country can sign a convention committing itself to providing these rights but then fail to implement them because they are unachievable given its current socio-economic and political situation. Whilst international law should seek to offer the most appropriate protection to a child it must be questioned whether there is not some merit in an international instrument that puts forward a minimum requirement for all signatory states. Thus pressure could be placed on countries to ensure that their law achieves this minimum degree of protection (which some states do not currently reach). Once that minimum threshold is reached (which may reduce difficulties with extraterritorial jurisdiction for those states that require dual criminality) then the next objective would be to increase protection by abiding to some of the other instruments.

Abbreviations

CoE	Council of Europe
CRC	[UN] Convention on the Rights of the Child
ECtHR	European Court of Human Rights
IACHR	Inter-American Court of Human Rights
ILO	International Labour Organization
OPSC	Optional Protocol to the CRC on the Sale of Children, Child Prostitution and Child Pornography

Note

1   In this chapter the term 'child pornography' is used notwithstanding that it is a problematic term (Taylor and Quayle, 2003: 3) because, as will be seen, this is the term that is used within international instruments. The use of the term is not to be taken as the author minimizing the harm that is caused by this form of material.

References

Aust, A. (2005). *Handbook of International Law*, Cambridge: Cambridge University Press.

Bakirci, K. (2007). *Child Pornography and Prostitution: Is this Crime or Work that Should Be Regulated? Journal of Financial Crime, 14*, 5–11.

Blakesley, C.L. and Stigall, D. (2004). Wings for talons: The case for the extraterritorial jurisdiction over sexual exploitation of children through cyberspace. *The Wayne Law Review, 50*, 109–59.

Buck, T. (ed.) (2011). *International Child Law*. 2nd edn. London: Routledge.

Cassese, A. (2008). *International Criminal Law*. 2nd edn. Oxford: Oxford University Press.

Eneman, M. (2010). Internet service provider filtering of child-abusive material: A critical reflection on its effectiveness. *Journal of Sexual Aggression, 16*, 223–36.

EU (2007) Report from Commission based on Article 12 of the Council Framework Decision of 22 December 2003 on combating the sexual exploitation of children and child pornography. COM (2007) 716.

Fredette, K. (2009). International legislative efforts to combat child sex tourism. *Boston College International & Comparative Law Review, 32*, 16–43.

Gillespie, A.A. (2010). Defining child pornography: Challenges for the law. *Child and Family Law Quarterly, 22*, 200–22.

—— (2011). Sexual exploitation. In T. Buck (ed.). *International Child Law*. 2nd edn. London: Routledge.

Hirst, M. (2003). *Jurisdiction and the Ambit of the Criminal Law*. Oxford: Oxford University Press.

Jones, L.M. (1998). Regulating child pornography on the Internet – the implications of Article 34 of the United Nations Convention on the Rights of the Child. *The International Journal of Children's Rights, 6*, 55–79.

Maalla, N.M. (2009). *Report Submitted by the Special Rapporteur on the Sale of Children, Child Prostitution and Child Pornography*. UN Human Rights Council. A/HRC/12/23.

NGO Group (2001). *The New ILO Worst Forms of Child Labour Convention 1999*. Geneva: NGO Group for the Convention on the Rights of the Child.

Petit, J.M. (2004). *Rights of the Child: Report Submitted by the Special Rapporteur on the Sale of Children, Child Prostitution and Child Pornography*. UN Economic and Social Council. E/CN.4/2005/78.

Rehman, J. (2010). *International Human Rights Law*. 2nd edn. London: Longman.

Sahovic, N.V. (2009). *Feasibility of a Communication Procedure under the Convention on the Rights of the Child*. UN Human Rights Council. A/HRC/WG.7/1/CRP.1.

Štefánek, D. (2010). *Report of the Open-ended Working Group to Explore the Possibility of Elaborating an Optional Protocol to the Convention on the Rights of the Child to Provide a Communications Procedure*. UN General Assembly. A/HRC/13/43.

Svensson, N.L. (2006). Extraterritorial accountability: An assessment of the effectiveness of child sex tourism laws. *Loyola of Los Angeles International & Comparative Law Review, 28*, 641–4.

Taylor, M. and Quayle, E. (2003). *Child Pornography: An Internet Crime*. Hove: Brunner-Routledge.

Watson, A.M.S. (2009). Too many children left behind: The inadequacy of international human rights law vis-à-vis the child. *Sociological Studies of Children and Youth, 12*, 249–71.

Part 2

Legal, social and familial contexts of abuse

5 Child pornography and law in East Asia

Bernard Y. Kao, National Chung Hsing University, Taiwan

Overview

The issue of child pornography did not raise many social concerns in East Asia[1] until the mid-1990s. Child pornography prevention legislation came even later. Compared with the Western states, which began their efforts in the criminalization of child pornography in the late 1970s (Ost, 2009), this could be considered as a big lapse from child protection. The Convention on the Rights of the Child (hereafter CRC), which came into effect on 2 September 1990, played a significant role in pushing national governments to enact new legislations. Article 34(c) of the CRC states that, 'States Parties undertake to protect the child from all forms of sexual exploitation and sexual abuse. States Parties shall in particular take all appropriate national, bilateral and multilateral measures to prevent the exploitative use of children in pornographic performances and materials.' This is the first international treaty that expressly states that child pornography *is* child exploitation, and shall not be tolerated. Therefore, by concluding an international agreement, a state undertakes, if necessary, to bring its domestic legislation into line with the international commitments it has assumed (Henkin et al., 1987). It should be noted that the CRC came into effect when the Internet was still in its embryonic stage. Nevertheless, by the mid-1990s, the Internet experienced phenomenal growth. The growth rate of the Internet exceeds that of any previous technology. Measured by users and bandwidth, the Internet has been growing at a rapid rate since its conception, on a curve geometric and sometimes exponential (Joyce, 2008). Unfortunately, child pornography has grown along with it, making children even more vulnerable to paedophiles and child pornography offenders.

This chapter attempts to provide a brief analysis on the efforts of Japan, Korea and Taiwan in the fight against child pornography. These three countries in East Asia are chosen because: (1) they are all bound by the CRC;[2] (2) they have serious problems with child pornography on the Internet; (3) they are democracies and have enjoyed success both in economic and legal developments; (4) their Internet penetration rates are high (Internet World Stats, 2009);[3] and (5) historically, they are deeply influenced by the Confucian culture.

This chapter argues that, under treaty obligation and international pressures, the three East Asian democracies have transformed the international law regarding child pornography into national legislation. However, the process and results of such transformation are different due to political, economic and social variances. The wrong conception of the nature of child pornography, a huge pornography market, the inferior social status of the child, and domestic political situations have all played a role in shaping child pornography legislation. Moreover, while there is room for improvement in this legislation, it does not seem appropriate for international society to produce model legislation on child pornography. Strengthening international cooperation among national governments, international governmental and non-governmental organizations (NGO) and raising social awareness would seem to be better solutions to combating this Internet epidemic.

Legislative control of child pornography

From the international law perspective, international law is binding on all states, and every state is obliged to give effect to it. The state is responsible to assure that its government, its constitution and its laws enable it to carry out its international obligation (Henkin et al., 1987). Nevertheless, when it comes to the national level, domestic law-making is very much conditioned by political, economic, social and cultural factors. Japan, Korea and Taiwan have enacted laws to deal with child pornography since the mid-1990s. However, the process has been slow and by no means smooth. Instead of introducing the legislation generally, I shall focus on two major controversial issues regarding child pornography, namely, the punishments for child pornography, and the criminalization of mere possession, to demonstrate how these three countries respond to the problem.

Punishments for child pornography

Japan passed its Punishment for Acts Regarding Child Prostitution, Child Pornography and Protection of Child Act in 1999, five years after its ratification of the CRC, and only after numerous criticisms from non-governmental organizations,[4] the United Nations and the International Criminal Police Organization (Interpol). The main provision regarding child pornography is in Article 7, which was revised in 2004. Article 7 reads:

1. Any person who provides child pornography shall be sentenced to imprisonment with work for not more than three years or a fine of not more than three million yen. The same shall apply to a person who provides electromagnetic records or any other record which depicts the pose of a child, which falls under any of the items of paragraph 3 of Article 2, in a visible way through electric telecommunication lines.
2. Any person who produces, possesses, transports, imports to or exports from Japan child pornography for the purpose of the activities prescribed in the preceding paragraph shall be punished by the same penalty as is prescribed in the said paragraph. The same shall apply to a person who

retains the electromagnetic records prescribed in the preceding paragraph for the purpose of the same activities.

3. In addition to the preceding paragraph, any person who produces child pornography by having a child pose in any way which falls under any of the items of paragraph 3 of Article 2, depicting such poses in photographs, recording media containing electromagnetic records or any other medium shall be punished by the same penalty prescribed in paragraph 1 of this article.

4. Any person who provides child pornography to unspecified persons or a number of persons, or displays it in public shall be sentenced to imprisonment with work for not more than five years and/or a fine of not more than five million yen. The same shall apply to a person who provides electromagnetic records or any other record which depicts the pose of a child, which falls under any of the items of paragraph 3 of Article 2, to unspecified persons or a number of persons in a visible way through telecommunication lines.

5. Any person who produces, possesses, transports, imports to or exports from Japan child pornography for the purpose of the activities prescribed in the preceding paragraph shall be punished by the same penalty as is prescribed in the said paragraph. The same shall apply to a person who retains the electromagnetic records prescribed in the preceding paragraph for the purpose of the same activities.

6. Any Japanese national who imports or exports child pornography to or from a foreign country for the purpose of the activities prescribed in paragraph 4 of this article shall be punished by the same penalty prescribed in the said paragraph.

According to Article 2(1) of the same Act, the term 'child' means a person under 18 years of age. This Article 7 was revised in 2004 to include penalty for provision of child pornography to a few specific people; penalty for the production of child pornography without the purpose of providing it; and penalty for the provision of electromagnetic records and their retention for the purpose of provision (Takizawa, 2010). While this article seemed to have penalized all kinds of activities surrounding child pornography, the focus of attention lies in the definition and scope of the term child pornography. Article 3(3) of the Act states,

(t)he term 'child pornography' as used in this Act shall mean photographs, recording media containing electromagnetic records any record which is produced by electronic, magnetic or any other means unrecognizable by natural perceptive functions and is used for data processing by a computer; the same shall apply hereinafter or any other medium which depicts the pose of a child, which falls under any of the following items, in a visible way:

(i) Any pose of a child engaged in sexual intercourse or any conduct similar to sexual intercourse;

(ii) Any pose of a child having his or her genital organs touched by another person or of a child touching another person's genital organs, which arouses or stimulates the viewer's sexual desire;

(iii) Any pose of a child wholly or partially naked, which arouses or stimulates the viewer's sexual desire.

Accordingly, this article limits child pornography to visual representations of a real child. The Japanese Supreme Court has held that the term 'which arouses or stimulates the viewer's sexual desire' was not vague and over-broad, and therefore survived the constitutionality test (Supreme Court Judgment of Japan, 2002). There is one important reason why the law does not include pseudo-child pornography (digitally manipulated images that sexualize real children) and virtual child pornography (text and images that are imaginary and fictional). Japan has a huge pornography market especially in manga (Japanese graphic novels or comics), and other kinds of animation, which attract millions of readers of different ages and gender. For instance, a popular literary genre *Yaoi*, which comprises manga, illustrated stories and poetry dedicated to highly sexualized depictions of male homosexual relationships between good-looking young men and boys, has a core readership of about half a million, mostly female (McLelland and Yoo, 2007). Needless to say, the pornography industry would be badly hit if the Act included them. Therefore, the argument that virtual child pornography was an evil in and of itself (Burke, 1997) did not seem to have a market in Japan. Instead, freedom of speech prevailed.

Unlike Japan, Korean law does not use the term child pornography. Instead, it uses the term 'obscene material using children and juveniles', which, according to Article 2 para. 5 of the Juvenile Sexual Protection Act of 2000 means, 'the image or picture(video) through film, video, game or computer and other means of telecommunication media which express contents containing any activity described in Article 2 para. 4 above or other sexual activities engaged by children and juveniles'. Here, a juvenile is defined as being below 19 years of age. As to the term 'obscene material', the Supreme Court of Korea defined it generally as 'whatever damages sexual morality by arousing the sexual desire and shame of ordinary people' (Moon, 2003). This 'definition' of child pornography has been subject to criticisms simply because it does not match the definition of the Optional Protocol to the Convention on the Rights of the Child on the Sale of Children, Child Prostitution and Child Pornography (hereinafter Optional Protocol), of which Korea is a Contracting State.[5] It simply treats child pornography as another kind of pornography, and fails to realize its exploitative nature. Regarding the punishments, the revised Article 8 of the same Act states:

Art. 8 (Producing and disseminating obscene materials using child and juvenile)

1. Those who produce, import or export obscene materials using children and juveniles can be imprisoned for more than 5 years but for a limited term.

2. Those who sell, rent or distribute obscene materials using children and juveniles for profit, or for this purpose, those who own or deliver, or exhibit or show the materials can be imprisoned for at most 7 years.
3. Those who publicly exhibit or show the materials can be imprisoned for at most 7 years or fined at most KRW 20,000,000.
4. Those who simply possess the materials shall be fined at most KRW 20,000,000.
5. Those who introduce children and juveniles to a producer of the materials even though producing the materials is circumstantially known shall be imprisoned for more than 1 year but at most 10 years.
6. Those who attempt para. 1 can be punished.

In practice, this law prohibits any showing of the sexual organs or pubic hair of a child or juvenile. Much as is the case in Japan, this Act does not penalize pseudo-child pornography and virtual child pornography. It is therefore being criticized by NGOs as 'inadequate' and not complying with the Optional Protocol (Yonhap News Agency of Korea, 2006).

In Taiwan, under immense pressure from local NGOs (such as ECPAT-Taiwan and the Garden of Hope Foundation), the Child and Youth Sexual Transaction Prevention Act was promulgated in 1995. It should be noted that the original motive of Taiwan's legislative movement was in relation to child trafficking. Child pornography prevention did not attract much attention as it was not considered a serious problem at that time. In fact, similarly to the Korean law, it treated child pornography as a special kind of pornography, a kind that involves children. There are two main articles dealing with child pornography. Article 27 reads:

Whoever shoots or produces pictures, video tapes, films, discs, electronic signals or any other products about the sexual intercourse or obscene act of a person under the age of 18 shall be sentenced to fixed-term imprisonment of not less than six months but not more than five years and also be fined not more than NT$500,000.

Whoever commits a crime prescribed in the preceding paragraph with a purpose of profit shall be sentenced to fixed-term imprisonment of not less than one year but not more than seven years and also be fined not more than NT$5,000,000.

Whoever seduces or makes a match of or by any other means has a person under the age of 18 shot or produces pictures, video tapes, films, discs, electronic signals or any other products about sexual intercourse or an obscene act shall be sentenced to fixed-term imprisonment of not less than one year but not more than seven years and also be fined not more than NT$1,000,000.

Whoever has a person under the age of 18 shot or produces pictures, video tapes, films, discs, electronic signals or any other products about sexual intercourse or an obscene act by means of violence, menace, medicament, crook, hypnogenesis or any other ways against the will of himself or herself shall be sentenced to fixed-term imprisonment of not less than five years and shall also be fined not more than NT$3,000,000.

Whoever commits a crime prescribed in the second paragraph or in the fourth paragraph as his business shall be sentenced to fixed-term imprisonment of more than seven years and also be fined not more than NT$10,000,000.

An offender who attempts to commit a crime prescribed in the first paragraph to the fourth paragraph shall be punished.

The products prescribed in the first paragraph to the fourth paragraph shall be confiscated no matter whether they belong to the criminal or not.

In addition, Article 28 states:

Distributing, broadcasting, or selling, filming, producing photographs, movies, videos, DVDs, digital files, and other materials, displaying these materials in public, or using other methods to present them to others is not allowed. Anyone who has knowledge about this behavior will be sentenced to maximum of three years of prison and fined 5 million NT dollars at most.

Attempting to distribute, broadcast, sell, and possess the above items will be sentenced to a maximum of two years of prison, and fined 2 million NT dollars at most.

An individual who possesses the films and productions of child and teen photographs, movies, videos, DVDs, digital files, and other materials without proper reason with the first offence will be sentenced to two to ten hours' rehabilitation under the local county (city) authorities; an individual committing a second offence will be subjected to a fine of $20,000 to 200,000 NT dollars.

The three items mentioned above, no matter whether they belong to the criminal or not, are regulated to be confiscated.

On the surface, although term 'child pornography' is not actually used, it seems that these two articles cover almost all kinds of illegal activity related to child pornography involving real children and that the punishments are harsh enough. However, NGOs in Taiwan are particularly dissatisfied with the following: (1) the definition of obscenity is not clear. The Grand Justices Council of the Judicial Yuan (the highest judicial organ of Taiwan) has, by following the criteria established by the US Supreme Court in the case *Miller* v. *California* (413 US 15, 1973), held that (Judicial Yuan Interpretation No. 407, 2007) obscene material means something which can stimulate or satisfy prurient interest, generate among common people a feeling of shame or distaste, thereby offending their sense of sexual morality, and undermining societal cultural ethics, and which has no artistic, educational or medical values. However, in practice, different judges may have different interpretations of the term. (2) The Act does not include pseudo-child pornography and virtual child pornography since the articles require a real victim 'under the age of 18. (3) Although the legislation provides harsh punishments, judicial attitudes have been rather disappointing. For instance, in a 2001 case, the defendant, a primary school teacher, downloaded massive amounts of child pornography from a website called 'Chinese Paedophilia Association' (中華戀童協會) and disseminated them on the Internet. He was charged with disseminating obscene images depicting the sexual intercourse of girls under the age of 18, and soliciting girl prostitution on the Internet. The High Court of Taiwan applied Article 28(1) of the Act and rendered the guilty judgment but gave the defendant four years' probation under suspended sentence of seven months' imprisonment. The court opined that, 'after evaluating all the factors, and considering that the defendant was a primary school teacher, sending him to jail would mean an end to his wonderful future' (High Court of Taiwan, appeal case, 2001). Obviously, the court did not realize that child pornography was child sexual abuse, and that children were usually physically sexually assaulted to create these images. Instead, the court sympathized with the defendant because it was not easy to become a primary school teacher.

In sum, the laws of Japan, Korea and Taiwan regarding child pornography share some common features. First, the definition of obscenity is fluid and may be subject to different interpretations. Second, pseudo-child pornography and virtual child pornography are not penalized. Third, there is a lack of understanding of the nature and harmful effects of child pornography. Often law makers and legal professionals make no distinction between adult pornography and child pornography. When a society is fond of pornography and it is so convenient to talk about the constitutional protection of free speech, the idea that child pornography means child exploitation is unlikely to be accepted.

Criminalization of mere possession

The rationale behind the criminalization of mere possession is best seen in *Osborne* v. *Ohio* (495 US 103, 1990). In an unprecedented decision, the US Supreme Court held that the First Amendment (the guarantee of free speech) allowed states to outlaw the mere possession of child pornography. The court said that it was not a 'paternalistic interest' for a state to regulate a citizen's mind. By outlawing the possession of child pornography, the government sought to eradicate legitimate harms by diminishing the market of child pornography. These harms include the psychological damage to children – both the children depicted in the pornography, for whom the images produced serve as a permanent record of the abuse, and the children whom potential abusers might lure with such images. This market-reduction argument appears to be the most convincing presentation of the harm caused by mere possession. Criminalization of mere possession was also justified in the United Kingdom in 1988 because it would prevent adults from being enticed and corrupted to think about children in a sexual way (Ost, 2009). It seems that a transatlantic consensus on the criminalization of mere possession of child pornography has been reached. The wind soon blew to the East. International organizations and NGOs started to accuse Japan and other countries of not being able to criminalize mere possession (Tokyo Reuters, 2008; CRC Observation Report, 2008).

Indeed, the issue of mere possession deserves special attention. It is argued that the legal basis for criminalizing mere possession comes from Article 3(1c) of the 2002 Optional Protocol, which states: '(e)ach State Party shall ensure that producing, distributing, disseminating, importing, exporting, offering, selling or *possession* of child pornography are fully covered under its criminal or penal law' (emphasis added). While this provision does not mention 'mere possession', it could be interpreted to include it. Yet, it could also mean other kinds of possession, such as possession for the purpose of distributing, disseminating or selling child pornography. Accordingly, it does not necessarily follow that the Optional Protocol requires states to criminalize mere possession.

On the other hand, the 2004 Cybercrime Convention seems to provide clearer scope. Article 9 of the Cybercrime Convention states: '(e)ach Party shall adopt such legislative and other measures as may be necessary to establish as criminal offences under its domestic law, when committed intentionally and without right, the following conduct . . . (e) *possessing child pornography in a computer system or on a computer-data storage medium*' (emphasis added). This could be read as the mere possession clause. However, it should be noted that a treaty has binding force only upon contracting states, and that according to Article 14 of the Vienna Convention on the Law of Treaties, ratification is necessary to render a treaty binding. Although Japan signed the Cybercrime Convention on 23 November 2001, it has not yet ratified it. Therefore, arguably, Japan does not have the international obligation to criminalize mere possession. In other words, as far as Japan is concerned, criminalization of mere possession is not an international law, but rather, at best, an international trend. Legally speaking, the accusation on the part of the NGOs and other international organizations did not have grounds. One can only argue that, Japan, as a developed state, regretfully chose to ignore the international trend. Interestingly, when the bill of Punishment for Acts Regarding Child Prostitution, Child Pornography and Protection of Child Act was presented to the Diet in 1998, there was an Article 8 which penalized mere possession (Fujin Shinpo, 1998).[6] The bill was supposed to be a consensus reached between the ruling party and the local NGOs. Somehow, the article was abandoned.

As a response to international criticisms, the Japanese government agreed to revise its law. In June 2008, the ruling parties at the time, the Liberal Democratic Party and the New Komeito Party, submitted a bill to the Diet to revise part of the Punishment for Acts Regarding Child Prostitution, Child Pornography and Protection of Child Act to include mere possession. The amendment also included an obligation by the Internet service providers (ISPs) to make reasonable efforts to intercept child pornography images on the Internet. Unfortunately, these amendments were discarded because of the parliamentary elections held in July 2009, which resulted in the dissolution of the coalition government and the coming into power of the Democratic Party (Asahi Shimbun, 2010). Ironically, this important legislative initiative became a casualty of democratic elections. Nothing has changed since then.

As to Korea and Taiwan, although they were not even signatories to the Cybercrime Convention, their reactions to international criticisms were more positive.

Korea amended its law in 2007 to punish mere possession of child pornography. A paragraph 'against a person who possesses obscene material using children and juveniles' was added to Article 8 of the Juvenile Sexual Protection Act. In the same year, Taiwan amended its law to fine mere possession. Article 28(3) of the Child and Youth Sexual Transaction Prevention Act reads, '(a)nyone who possesses the films and productions of child and teen photographs, movies, videos, DVDs, digital files, and other materials without proper reason with the first offence shall be sentenced to two to ten hours rehabilitation under the local county (city) authorities; second offence shall be subject to a fine of NTD20,000 to 200,000 (USD650–6,500)'. The term 'without proper reason' is employed to exclude situations like possession by the police or NGOs for investigation or reporting purposes. Regrettably, to date, no one has been charged with this offence.

These amendments were successful only because of the enduring efforts of the local NGOs and international pressures. Especially in the case of Taiwan, it took more than eight years for the NGOs to convince the competent authority (namely the Child Welfare Bureau of the Ministry of the Interior) and lobby the members of the Legislative Yuan to achieve such a compromised provision.[7]

Several reasons accounted for the delay in the law-making and for the inadequacy of the laws in these East Asian countries. First of all, child pornography prevention laws threatened the huge pornography industry. In 2006, the revenue of the pornography industry worldwide was US$97.06 billion, larger than the revenues of Microsoft, Google, Amazon, eBay, Yahoo!, Apple, Netflix and Earth-Link combined. China, Korea and Japan accounted for 75.3 per cent of this revenue. Moreover, 2006 per-capita revenue data shows that Korea far outdistanced the pack at US$526.76. The next highest was Japan, with US$156.75 (Joyce, 2008). According to NGOs, Japan was the world's largest producer of child pornography, making a thousand illegal pornographic tapes each month in the late 1990s (Antaseeda, 1998). In the case of Taiwan, it should be noted that Taiwan's high-technology environment has been utilized by the Japanese pornography industry to manufacture (compress) Japanese porn CDs, and the revenue generated is incredibly large (Nownews, 2009).[8] The huge profits of the pornography industry have become a powerful disincentive to regulations curtailing child pornography. The pornography industry, especially in Japan, sought to challenge any laws which, if fully implemented, would be detrimental to its economic interests.

Second, in East Asian societies, which are deeply influenced by Confucianism, children have inferior social status. Confucianism emphasizes ordered relationships, and juniors are considered to owe their seniors reverence, while seniors only have duties of benevolent concern towards juniors. This kind of relationships has put children in the position of being dominated and therefore being granted lesser rights. The problem is not just that people did not understand the nature and the harmful effects of child pornography, but that they did not realize that in a democratic society a child protection policy should be given top priority. It can take time for a traditional society to transform into a modern one.

Third, in modern democracies, elections are used to fill offices in the legislature and sometimes the executive. In terms of making a law to prevent child pornography, this means that a change of government requires new lobbying efforts to new people in power. Repetition is time consuming. This is exactly what has happened in Japan and Taiwan.

Administrative control of child pornography on the Internet

Article 10(1) of the Optional Protocol requires states parties to:

> take all necessary steps to strengthen international cooperation by multilateral, regional and bilateral arrangements for the prevention, detection, investigation, prosecution and punishment of those responsible for acts involving the sale of children, child prostitution, *child pornography* and child sex tourism. States Parties shall also promote international cooperation and coordination between their authorities, national and international non-governmental organizations and international organizations [emphasis added].

International organizations also urge national states to strengthen enforcement by using various kinds of technology. Back in the late 1990s, Interpol proposed the establishment of a 'technically possible and economically reasonable' network to fight against child pornography on the Internet. Strengthening international police cooperation, training law enforcement officers, educating the public and using new technologies were considered to be the most useful means of achieving that end (Saint Maur, 1999). Since then, various kinds of cooperation networks, such as INHOPE,[9] Virtual Global Task Force (VGT)[10] and the Financial Coalition Against Child Pornography,[11] have been established to deal with illegal and harmful material on the Internet. New technologies and networks including filtering,[12] ratings,[13] and hotlines[14] were also developed and employed.

Regardless of the fact that child pornography legislation is still far from satisfactory, child pornography is recognized as one of the serious illegal materials on the Internet. In order to prevent minors from viewing it and to protect the 'public order and good morals' (公共秩序善良風俗) of society, the governments of Japan, Korea and Taiwan have been more than willing to use their administrative powers to intercept child pornography images on the Internet. Here it is logical to argue that the administrative measures taken by these governments are not based on the rationale that child pornography *is* child sexual abuse and that the child in the photograph is a victim. Due to a lack of understanding of the nature of child pornography and the influence of Confucianism, one is bound to conclude that what the East Asian governments are intending to protect is not really the victims in the photograph, but the general public. The purpose of controlling illegal and harmful materials on the Internet is to cultivate virtue and develop moral perfection so as to achieve a peaceful and harmonious Confucian society. As a result these measures have received considerable support from society and, consequently, in contrast with the Western world, no one has ever questioned their constitutionality.

A notable example is Taiwan government's compulsory rating scheme. Article 27(1) of the Children and Youth Welfare Act states: '(p)ublications, computer software, and the *Internet* shall be classified' (emphasis added). In fact, this is the world's first piece of legislation that makes rating compulsory on all domestic websites. A non-profit organization called Taiwan Internet Content Rating Promotion Foundation (TICRF) was established by the government in January 2005 to gather private and academic resources to plan and promote Internet content rating. Its prime objectives are to protect freedom of speech and 'to regulate user behaviour' (TICRF, 2010). The TICRF's content rating consists of only two levels: Restricted (R) and General (G). The '[d]epiction of sexual acts or sexual obscenity, or the exposure of genitals, through action, image, language, text, dialogue, sound, picture, photograph or any other form, but which does not embarrass or disgust adults in general' is rated as restricted and is not to be viewed by those below the age of 18 (Article 4(4), Internet Content Rating Regulation, 2004).[15] Child pornography belongs to the 'prohibitive provision of the law' and nobody is allowed to view it. This kind of compulsory content rating is rather exceptional in mature democracies in which the constitutional protection of free speech prevents governments from engaging in public censorship. Yet the TICRF's work seems to have received support in Taiwan. The democracies of Korea and Japan, in contrast, encourage content rating only by providing downloadable content-rating software.

Another controversial issue is the utilization of blocking techniques. A blocking system constitutes prior censorship because a blocked user is unable to access certain services and websites as a result of state policy. However, based on the rationale that no one has the right of access to child pornography and that blocking is undoubtedly an effective tool, some national governments have been prompted to use this technique. The proliferation of child pornography has pushed the government of Japan to adopt a blocking system. In July 2010, at a ministerial meeting on crime fighting, the government decided to require ISPs to block access to images found to violate the law banning child pornography. The images blocked were to be based on a list of problematic websites to be compiled by a new body (Japan Today, 2010). The measure was considered a necessity since it appeared too difficult to amend the existing legislation in the near future. As regards censorship, the government claimed that it would ensure neutrality in the operations of the body compiling the list. This, of course, was a bureaucratic response because no one could guarantee that all the blocked websites were illegal. Similarly, based on the rationale that obscene materials and child pornography are illegal, the government of Taiwan has implemented a filtering technique to block images at primary and secondary school levels on its academic network TANet (Tseng et al., 2010).[16]

Probably the most workable way to remove illegal and harmful materials, especially child pornography, from the Internet, without resorting to censorship or restriction, is to set up hotlines. When a member of the public informs the hotline of suspect material, a procedure is followed to determine whether it is illegal. If it is, information will be sent to the police for further investigation and to the ISPs for it to be removed. Legally speaking, this would not infringe the constitutional protection of free speech because illegal material (child pornography) belongs to the category of unprotected speech in every country. If child pornography reported is outside national jurisdiction, it must be processed via an international organization which facilitates and coordinates the works of different hotlines in different countries. INHOPE, co-funded by the European Union, was established for this purpose in 1999 under the EC Safer Internet Action Plan. INHOPE has been quite successful as it has been able to establish meaningful collaboration between national enforcement agencies, Interpol, the European Police Organization, the NGOs of member countries and other stakeholders such as industry. Other main functions of INHOPE include exchange expertise, supporting new hotlines, exchanging reports, and educating and informing policy makers at the international level. Recognizing its invaluable functions, the hotlines of Japan, Korea and Taiwan have joined INHOPE and became full members.[17] A side benefit has been that membership provides a very good opportunity to understand and compare the child pornography laws and enforcement in different member countries. The benefits are mutual. East Asian participation has transformed INHOPE from a European organization into an international one. In addition, as the East Asian countries share the same cultural and legal background, they have joined together and created a hotline union of their own. Today hotlines remain the most popular and least controversial means of controlling child pornography on the Internet.

Concluding thoughts

The widespread use of the Internet has exacerbated the problem of child pornography. Under treaty obligations and immense international pressure, Japan, Korea and Taiwan have made efforts to combat child pornography. Several observations can be made on the basis of their experience: (1) the transformation of international law into national legislation was a long and complicated process for two reasons. At the international level, even now, there is no standard legal framework for dealing with child pornography. The only international consensus is that child pornography should be penalized because it is exploitative. At the national level, the law in democratic societies is often conditioned by political, social, cultural and economic factors. In Asia, the huge pornography industry has become a disincentive to legislative control of child pornography. (2) Successful national legislation depends very much on full and right understanding of the issue and the philosophy behind child protection. International law only tells the world that child pornography, in the interests of child protection, should be penalized. Knowing the law is one thing; understanding the nature of child pornography is quite another. In the last decade, the problem for Japan, Korea and Taiwan in the battle against child pornography has been that they seemed to care more about making positive laws to fulfil international obligation than about comprehending the nature and the size of the problem. Failure to differentiate between adult pornography and child pornography was one reflection of their misconception. There is also a deeper problem. They do not seem to have recognized that child protection policy is not just about protecting children but also about the preservation of democracy. Quoting the words of the US Supreme Court in *New York* v. *Ferber* (458 US 747, 1982), '(a) democratic society rests, for its continuance, upon the healthy, well-rounded growth of young people into full maturity as citizens'. Only by recognizing this can East Asian countries make good child protection laws.

There have been NGOs that have urged the enactment of model legislation on child pornography in order to harmonize national legislation. For instance, the International Center for Missing and Exploited Children (ICMEC) has strongly suggested that model legislation with regard child pornography is crucial to a successful outcome in the fight against it (ICMEC, 2010). ICMEC has identified several topics to be included in the model legislation: definitions of 'child' and 'child pornography'; criminalizing mere possession of child pornography; ensuring criminal penalties for parents or legal guardians who acquiesce to their child's participation in child pornography; penalizing those who make known to others where to find child pornography; addressing the criminal liability of children involved in pornography; enhancing penalties for repeat offenders, organized-crime participants and other aggravated factors considered upon sentencing; and establishing mandatory reporting requirements for health-care and social-service professionals, teachers, law-enforcement officers, photo developers, information-technology (IT) professionals, ISPs, credit-card companies, and banks, etc. Some of these are enshrined in the CRC and the Optional Protocol, while others are new: for example, penalties for parents and guardians, and policy regarding repeat offenders.

This I would argue is neither realistic nor workable. Model legislation is in effect an effort on the part of international society to develop a legal framework (often with details) to enable national governments to initiate laws and regulations regarding the implementation of a particular policy. It is usually suggested by international organizations such as the United Nations and its institutions. To make it acceptable, model legislation must follow the widely accepted practices of international society. Yet it has no binding effect, and is bound to be hortatory in nature. On the other hand, the idea of making model legislation implies that all states should look to it in determining domestic law. On the issue of child pornography, it is already clear that national governments have too many different political, economic, social and legal concerns that yield to different national interests. Even ICMEC's research report admitted that only a few countries meet the criteria set forth by ICMEC (ICMEC, 2010). In short, there are no widely accepted practices or rules regarding child pornography. So far the only international consensus we have is that child pornography should be prohibited and that there should be certain criminal penalties. Moreover, model legislation sometimes means an imposition of values of those strong states on the weaker and smaller ones. In democratic societies deeply influenced by Confucian culture, model legislation by the current Western-dominated international society would be regarded as reflective of European and North American cultural ideologies – the last thing we want to see.

What is needed instead is a persuasive way of harmonizing national laws according to the special conditions of each state. To start with, East Asian democracies need to be informed that child pornography is not just a legal issue, but also a political and moral one. It is a political issue because it involves the distribution of national resources to protecting minors. Even Confucian culture agrees that children are our future. This should not remain a question of 'lip-service' but requires action. The idea of prioritizing child protection policy, thus injecting more money and staffing, should be taken seriously by law-makers. It is a moral issue because in a Confucian society, children are considered to owe their seniors reverence, making seniors (adults) morally obligated in their upbringing. In addition, East Asian societies need to strike a balance between freedom of speech and the maintenance of 'good morals'. There should be more public hearings, discussions and open debates on issues such as the definition, scope and even categorization of the term 'obscenity', the meaning and nature of 'child pornography', ideas about the 'sexual fantasies of the young' and self-regulation of the pornography industry, etc. However, the conservative attitude of Confucianism has barred society from engaging in meaningful discussion of issues regarding and surrounding sex. East Asian people of different classes tend to avoid this because sex and sexual intercourse are traditionally regarded as shameful matters and should not even be mentioned in public. At the same time, the pornography industry develops and flourishes under its own momentum, and under no clear rules. This is a deviation from democracy because 'the people' are not actually participating in the making of social policy. There is a need to change attitudes as well as policy. More recently, because of the penetration of the Internet, parents, teachers and the media have become more aware of the issue of child pornography. They have started to talk about monitoring or even boycotting those ISPs which disseminate illegal and harmful, especially pornographic, information.[18] This is a good sign if the monitoring can be carried out in accordance with the democratic process. There may be no way for a government to eradicate child pornography, but it is definitely possible for a society to minimize the harm it causes the younger generation.

In a nutshell, there is no need for model legislation. International law has given national states clear direction and the basic principles to deal with child pornography. The problem is not that we do not have adequate international law, but that in reality, at the national level, law-making is conditioned by political, economic, social and cultural factors. In other words, the process of shaping domestic law matters more. What is important is to raise the social awareness of child pornography, its relationships with child protection and the preservation of our democracy. Having said this, international cooperation and collaboration are nonetheless necessary and should be further strengthened. The efforts of Interpol, INHOPE and other international governmental and NGOs have proved that international cooperation and collaboration are extremely useful and effective, not only in cracking down on paedophilia rings and saving child victims worldwide, but also in acting as a constant reminder to national governments of the problem of child pornography. We certainly need more wisdom, resources and action to fight against it.

Notes

1 The term East Asia covers six countries, namely the People's Republic of China (including Hong Kong and Macau), Japan, Mongolia, North Korea, South Korea and Taiwan (the Republic of China). The region is one the world's most populated places, with a population of 1.5 billion people spread over an area 15 per cent larger than Europe.

2 Japan signed the CRC on 21 September 1990 and ratified it on 22 April 1994. South Korea signed the CRC on 25 September 1990 and ratified it on 20 November 1991 (see http://treaties.un.org). For international political reasons Taiwan was not able to become a state party of the CRC, but in 1995 the Taiwanese government announced its willingness to be bound by the CRC.

3 These three countries have over 150 million Internet users, constituting some 78 per cent of their population.

4 It must be emphasized that among numerous NGOs, ECPAT/STOP Japan played a significant role in the making of this Act. ECPAT/STOP Japan (Stop Child Prostitution Action) was inaugurated in 1992 as an unofficial organization affiliated with ECPAT-International (End Child Prostitution, Child Pornography and Trafficking in Children for Sexual Purposes) to carry out work in Japan. In accordance with Article 34 of the CRC, ECPAT/STOP Japan takes action against child pornography by lobbying the Diet (the Japanese parliament) in relation to bills, studying the situation of child pornography, organizing lectures and meetings, translating books and publications, and issuing newsletters.

5 Korea ratified the Optional Protocol on 24 September 2004. (See United Nations Treaty Collection, Optional Protocol to the Convention on the Rights of the Child on the Sale of Children, Child Prostitution and Child Pornography, http://treaties.un.org/pages/ ViewDetails.aspx?src=IND&mtdsg_no=IV-11-c&chapter=4&lang=en.)

6 Article 8 of the draft bill states, '(n)o one can possess child pornography for the purpose of fulfilling his own sexual curiosity'.

7 The lobbying effort has been initiated by ECPAT-Taiwan since 1998. The author was the chair of the organization. Much as in Japan, the presidential election of 2000, which resulted in a change in government, meant lobbying efforts must start anew. Since it was the first time the Democratic Progressive Party was in government, the focus of attention was on 'big' political issues such as abandoning the building of the fourth nuclear power plant, and Taiwan–China relations, etc. Politicians simply did not care much about child welfare issues.

8 In March 2009 a FedEx plane flying from Taiwan to Japan crashed at Japan's Narita Airport. The rescue team found 50,000 Japanese porn CDs to a market value of US$1.6 million. The plane crash caused a three-day delay in the distribution of certain new porn CDs.

9 Funded by the European Commission, INHOPE was established in 1999. Its mission is to support and enhance the performance of Internet hotlines around the world, ensuring swift action is taken in responding to reports of illegal content, making the Internet a safer place. In 2010, INHOPE included forty-one member hotlines from twenty-nine countries, and its network continues to expand (see https://www.inhope.org/).

10 The Virtual Global Taskforce (VGT) is made up of law enforcement agencies from around the world, working together to fight child abuse online. The aim of the VGT is to build an effective, international partnership of law enforcement agencies that helps to protect children from online child abuse (see http://www.virtualglobaltask force.com/).

11 The Financial Coalition Against Child Pornography brings together eighteen organizations including the Bank of America, American Express, MasterCard, AOL, Yahoo and Microsoft. The group shares information about websites that sell child pornography and stops payments passing to them. The group aims to make it impossible

to profit from selling child porn (see http://news.bbc.co.uk/2/hi/technology/4812962. stm).

12 Filtering is a censorship technique that censors use to prevent Internet users from accessing particular content or services. Filtering involves using software to look at what users are attempting to do and to interfere with activities that the operator considers forbidden by law. There are several kinds of filtering, such as URL filtering, DNS filtering, IP filtering and Port blocking (see http://www.sesawe.net/Filtering-Techniques.html).

13 Internet content ratings use content control software to restrict material delivered over the web. The aim is to prevent users from viewing content which the owners or government authorities may consider objectionable. An international non-profit organization called Internet Content Rating Association (ICRA) was established to promote rating systems and act as a forum through which both policy and technical infrastructure are defined to help shape the way that the world wide web and content distribution channels work (see http://www.fosi.org/icra/).

14 The hotlines are a service specifically for reporting child pornography. The service provides an environment where the public can anonymously report Internet material they suspect to be illegal. The reports can be made by email or by phone (see http://www.inhope.org/en/facts/facts.html).

15 The Internet Content Rating Regulation was promulgated by the Government Information office of Taiwan on 26 April 2004.

16 In Taiwan, there are three major Internet service providers: TANet, HiNet and Seednet. TANet was set up by the Ministry of Education's Computer Center (MOECC) and some national universities in July 1990 to establish a common national academic network infrastructure and to support research and academic institutes in Taiwan. Because of its open strategy using transmission control protocol/Internet protocol (TCP/IP), the number of networking users among campuses is growing rapidly. The topology of TANet is basically a ring/mesh using intelligent routers to interconnect high-speed leased circuits/local area networks (LANs) where a high-speed T1 (1.544 Mbps) link is installed among regional network centres. At present, there are eleven regional network service centres, which are run by eleven national universities.

17 The Japanese hotline is run by the Internet Association of Japan, a non-profit and industry-based organization. It became a full member of INHOPE in March 2007. The Korean hotline is run by the Korea Communications Standard Commission (KCSC), an independent government body. KCSC became a member of INHOPE in October 2003. The Taiwanese hotline is run by ECPAT-Taiwan, an NGO funded by the government. ECPAT-Taiwan became a full member of INHOPE in May 2005.

18 For instance, ECPAT-Taiwan issues regular announcements about ISPs which have been reported to have disseminated obscene materials and have refused to remove them. Sometimes it asks the public to boycott them until they comply. ISPs normally bow to such pressure fearing that they will suffer a decline in industry advertising.

References

Antaseeda, P. (1998). Expert urges global law to end child pornography on the Internet. *Bangkok Post*, 3 June, p. 3

Asahi Shimbun [朝日新聞社] (2010). Editorial: Child porn on the Internet. Asahi Shumbun, 26 May. Available online at http://www.asahi.com/english/TKY201005250419.html.

Burke, D. (1997). The criminalization of virtual child pornography: A constitutional question. *Harvard Journal on Legislation, 34*, 439–72 .

CRC (2008). CRC Observation Report. CRC/C/OPSC/KOR/1, available online at http://www2.ohchr.org/english/bodies/crc/docs/co/CRC.C.OPSC.KOR.CO.1.pdf.

Fujin Shinpo [婦人新報] (1998). W.C.T.U. No.1176, 2.

Henkin, L., Pugh R.C., Schachter, O. and Smit, H. (1987). *International Law, Cases and Materials*. St Paul, MN: West Publishing Co.

High Court of Taiwan, appeal case, No. 2176 (2001). 台灣高等法院90年度上訴字第2176號判決。

ICMEC (2010). Child pornography: Model legislation and global review, available online at http://polis.osce.org/portals/cseci/index/details?doc_id=3721&lang_tag=&qs=.

Internet World Stats. (2010). Internet usage in Asia – Internet users and population for 35 countries and regions in Asia. Available online at http://www.internetworldstats.com/stats3.htm.

Japan Today (2010). Government to have Internet providers block access to child porn images. Japan Today. Available online at http://www.japantoday.com/category/national/view/govt-team-oks-plan-to-get-isps-to-block-access-to-child-porn-images.

Joyce, R. (2008). Pornography and the Internet. *IEEE Internet Computing, 12*(4), 74–7.

Judicial Yuan Interpretation No. 407 (2007). The Republic of China Constitutional Court Reporter, 104–11.

McLelland, M. and Yoo, S. (2007). The international yaoi boy's love fandom and the regulation of virtual child pornography: The implications of current legislation. *Sexuality Research and Social Policy, Journal of NSRC, 4*, 93–104.

Miller v. *California* (1973) 413 US 15.

Moon, J. (2003). Obscenity laws in a paternalistic country: The Korean experience. *Washington University Global Studies Law Review, 2*, 353–90.

New York v. *Ferber* (1982) 458 US 747.

Nownews (2009). Eighty percent of Japanese porn CDs made in Taiwan, Nownews. Retrieved from *http://www.nownews.com/2009/05/11/10844–447906.htm*

Osborne v. *Ohio* (1990) 495 US 103.

Ost, S. (2009). *Child Pornography and Sexual Grooming: Legal and Societal Responses*. Cambridge: Cambridge University Press.

Saint Maur, A.F. (1999). Sexual abuse of children on the internet: A new challenge for INTERPOL. *Expert Meeting on Sexual Abuse of Children, Child Pornography and Pedophilia on the Internet: An international challenge*. Paris: UNESCO.

Supreme Court Judgment of Japan (2002), No. 281, p.577. (最判平成14年6月17日刑集281号577頁).

Takizawa, Y. (2010). Efforts against the commercial sexual exploitation of children in Japan. *Ninth Seminar on Commercial Exploitation of Children in South East Asia*, 1–3.

TICRF (2010). TICRF objectives. Available at http://www.ticrf.org.tw/english/ticrf-objective.htm.

Tokyo Reuters (2011). UNICEF says Japan failing to control child porn. 11 March, available online at http://uk.reuters.com/article/idUKT20430220080311.

Tseng, S.S., Su, L.S. and Chao, E.H. (2010). TANet: Taiwan Academic Network. Available at http://www.isoc.org/inet96/proceedings/c6/c6_4.htm.

Yonhap News Agency of Korea (2006). NGO report says Korea 'inadequate' on child pornography laws. Yonhap News Agency, 7 April. Available online at http://dlib.eastview.com/browse/doc/9292863.

6 The social dimension of the online trade of child sexual exploitation material

Angela Carr, Queensland Crime and Misconduct Commission

Overview

The current chapter will explore the potential impact that social relationships may have on the offence behaviour of individuals who use the Internet to access child pornography (otherwise referred to as child exploitation material). In particular, it will examine how the online and offline relationships of child pornography offenders may increase or reduce the likelihood that they also commit contact child sexual offences. Despite a long history of criminological theory identifying social interaction and social ties as significant in predicting or preventing offence behaviour, very little research has considered the impact of these variables on child sexual offence behaviour. Therefore, before considering that impact, the current chapter will provide a brief overview of what is currently known about the relationship between accessing child pornography and committing contact child sexual offences, including the similarities and differences between child pornography and contact child sexual offenders. That review will demonstrate the salient nature of social relationships in the lives of child pornography offenders and lead into further discussion regarding the possible implications of those relationships.

Child pornography and contact child sexual offending

In recent years the relationship between Internet access to child pornography (otherwise referred to as child exploitation material) and involvement in the commission of contact sexual offences against children has received significant public, media and academic attention. Given the apparent interest that individuals who access child pornography demonstrate in the sexualization of children, together with the fact that they are repeatedly exposed to material that reinforces that interest, a direct association between child pornography and contact child sexual offending is commonly assumed.

Despite those assumptions, however, the results of research investigating the criminal histories and trajectories of child pornography offenders suggest that relatively few individuals who use the Internet to access child pornography also commit child sexual offences and those that do often begin contact offending before they begin accessing child pornography. For example, Seto et al.'s (2011) meta-analysis of twenty-four samples involving 4,697 Internet child pornography offenders revealed that only 17 per cent of those offenders were known to have committed a contact sexual offence prior to the index child pornography offence. Furthermore, they also found that between 1.5 and 6 years following detection for a child pornography offence only 2 per cent of 2,630 child pornography offenders identified from nine independent samples had committed a contact sexual offence.

Other studies not included in Seto et al.'s (2011) meta-analysis suggest even lower rates of contact child sexual offending amongst Internet child pornography offenders. For example, Carr (2006) found that only 8 per cent of a New Zealand sample of 137 individuals who had been identified by law enforcement as accessing child pornography (including offenders who were not prosecuted for these offences because they were either too young or unable to participate in the prosecution process) were found to have also committed a contact sexual offence against a child. Another 4 per cent had been investigated for contact child sexual offences, but not convicted (either because the investigation was still continuing, or because of insufficient evidence or withdrawal of allegations resulting in warning). Similarly, Finkelhor and Ormrod (2004) found that only 8 per cent of individuals identified by police in the USA as having committed child pornography offences had also committed a contact child sexual offence against an identifiable victim.

Research that has reported higher rates of contact child sexual offending amongst child pornography offenders[1] (e.g. Bourke and Hernandez, 2009; Seto et al., 2006) tend to be limited by their reliance on clinical and correctional samples. These samples generally include only a small minority of Internet child pornography offenders identified by law enforcement agencies (and it is likely that law enforcement agencies only identify a small sample of all child pornography offenders). Given specific entry requirements associated with many clinical programmes (e.g. admission of guilt, commitment to change) and the impact that contact offence history may have on correctional outcomes, it is unlikely that clinical and correctional samples are representative of law enforcement samples or the wider child pornography offender population.

The similarities and differences between child pornography and contact child sexual offenders

Psychosocial variables

In light of the relatively low levels of contact offences identified amongst child pornography offenders, researchers have begun to consider a range of additional factors and offender characteristics that may influence and/or mediate the relationship between Internet-based (online) access to child pornography and offline contact offending against children. These factors include individual personality traits and psychological characteristics, offline social and situational variables and life events, and sexual preferences and paraphilias. However, the results of these studies appear to suggest more similarities between child pornography and contact offenders than differences. For example, Middleton et al. (2006)

found that more than half of a sample of seventy-two British child pornography offenders demonstrated psychometric scores consistent with at least one of the five psychosocial pathways identified by Ward and Siegert (2002) as predictive of contact child sexual offending:

1. Intimacy and social skill deficits
2. Distorted sexual scripts
3. Emotional dysregulation
4. Antisocial cognitions/cognitive distortions
5. Multiple dysfunctional mechanism.[2]

In particular, Middleton et al. (2006) noted high levels of emotional loneliness and impulsivity amongst these offenders. Their finding is consistent with the results of research undertaken by Bates and Metcalf (2007) that showed higher levels of emotional loneliness amongst child pornography offenders than contact child sexual offenders. Bates and Metcalf (2007) commented that the high levels of emotional loneliness demonstrated by child pornography offenders was particularly concerning because emotional loneliness has been identified as a salient predictor of recidivism amongst contact child sexual offenders.

Bates and Metcalf (2007) also noted that child pornography offenders demonstrated higher than average levels of *deviance*[3] when assessed using a range of other socio-affective assessment instruments commonly used by the UK National Probation Service to determine contact offenders' treatment needs. In particular, these offenders demonstrated relatively high levels of under-assertiveness and personal distress. According to Ward and Siegert's (2002) Pathways Model of child sexual offending, many individuals who are predisposed to committing sexual offences against children will only do so if they suffer emotional arousal as a result of personal distress or feel emotionally rejected in adult relationships.

Other research has shown that child pornography offenders demonstrate greater levels of physical arousal to visual and auditory stimuli portraying nude children than contact child sexual offenders. For example, Seto et al. (2006) compared the phallometric responses of child pornography offenders (including child pornography-only offenders and child pornography offenders who had also committed contact offences) to visual and auditory stimuli depicting nude children, nude adults and landscapes against the phallometric responses of contact only child sexual offenders, contact only offenders who had offended against adults, and general sexology patients (who had no history of charges for child pornography or contact sexual offenses). They found that 61 per cent of child pornography offenders demonstrated significantly greater levels of arousal to stimuli depicting nude children than to other stimuli. In contrast, only 35 per cent contact only child sexual offenders, 13 per cent of sexual offenders with adult victims and 22 per cent of general sexology patients demonstrated this preference.

Seto et al. (2006) concluded that accessing child pornography could be considered a valid indicator of paedophilia. That is, not all child pornography offenders are paedophiles, but child pornography offenders are more likely to be paedophiles than other members of the general population. In line with Seto et al.'s (2006) conclusions, Howitt and Sheldon (2007) have shown that child pornography offenders are more likely than contact child sexual offenders to agree with statements suggesting children's willingness to engage in sexual activity with adults. Examples of these types of statement include: 'sometimes children don't say no to sexual activity with adults because they are curious about sex or enjoy it'; 'some children are mature enough to enjoy sexual activities with, and for, adults; and some children are willing and eager to be involved in sexual activities that are with, and for, adults'.

Other variables

Notably, the most salient differences between child pornography and contact offenders tend to be demographically related or related to factors that are not obviously connected to their interest in child pornography. For example, research has consistently found that child pornography offenders tend to be significantly younger (Webb et al., 2007), better educated (Bates and Metcalf, 2007; Howitt and Sheldon, 2007; Tomak et al., 2009), more intelligent (Burke et al., 2002), more likely to be employed (Bates and Metcalf, 2007; Burke et al., 2002) and more predominantly Caucasian (e.g. fewer offenders are of non-Caucasian ethnicity) than contact child sexual offenders (Webb et al., 2007; Tomak et al., 2009). In addition, some studies have shown that child pornography-only offenders are more likely to be married or in a relationship at the time of their offence (Burke et al., 2002; Tomak et al, 2009).

Research by Bates and Metcalf (2007) also suggests that child pornography offenders may be more concerned with presenting a positive social image than contact child sexual offenders. In their psychometric comparison of child pornography only and contact offenders, Bates and Metcalf (2007) found that the largest difference between the two offender groups concerned their scores on the Paulhus Balanced Inventory of Desirable Responding (BIDR) Impression Management (IM) subscale. Impression management scales are commonly used in psychometric research to test the validity of subjects' responses to other psycho-metric instruments. Specifically, they allow assessment of whether subjects are responding truthfully or are tailoring their responses to 'present themselves in an unduly optimistic light, specifically towards other people' (Paulhus, 1998, cited in Bates and Metcalf, 2007: 15). This phenomenon is described by Bates and Metcalf (2007: 18) as 'faking good'.

Typically, high impression management scores lead to exclusion of the subject's results from the research analysis. In Bates and Metcalf's (2007) research, however, the majority (61.8 per cent) of child pornography offenders scored significantly above the general population norm for impression management. In contrast, only 39.5 per cent of contact offenders scored above the impression management norm. Bates and Metcalf (2007: 18) concluded that child pornography offenders 'are not only more likely to give unrealistically positive responses about themselves than the general population, but also at a higher rate than other sex offenders'.

Notably, Bates and Metcalf (2007) also compared child pornography and contact offenders on the BIDR self-deception (SD) subscale. In contrast to the impression management subscale, the self-deception subscale measures the degree to which 'the individual is likely to be overly positive in assessing their own qualities and attributes' (Paulhus, 1998, cited in Bates and Metcalf, 2007: 15): in other words, the degree to which the individual actually believes the unrealistically positive assessment that they present for themselves. Bates and Metcalf (2007) found that child pornography offenders (11.8 per cent) actually scored lower on this subscale than contact offenders (18.4 per cent).

Bates and Metcalf's (2007) findings clearly demonstrate child pornography offenders desire to present themselves well to others, despite knowing that the presentation is a farce and despite having already been convicted of a child pornography offence at the time they participated in the research. Given these findings, it is noteworthy that Bates and Metcalf's (2007) results showed no significant difference between the overall psychometric deviancy rating of child pornography and contact child sexual offenders.

Child pornography offenders who are also contact offenders

Included in Bates and Metcalf's (2007) sample of child pornography offenders were some who had also committed contact child sexual offences. Howitt and Sheldon (2007) also sampled both child pornography-only offenders and child pornography contact offenders. In Howitt and Sheldon's (2007) research, within-groups comparisons suggest more demographic, socio-affective and offence-predictive similarities between child pornography offenders who commit contact offences and child pornography offenders who do not, than between child pornography offenders who commit contact offences and contact-only offenders. They also suggest that child pornography offenders who commit contact offences differ from contact-only offenders in terms of the types of victim they select. For example, Howitt and Sheldon (2007) found that mixed (child pornography and contact) offenders were more likely to offend against non-familial children whilst contact-only offenders were more likely to offend against intra-familial children.

However, child pornography offenders who commit contact offences do demonstrate some notable differences from child pornography-only offenders. Like contact only offenders, they are more likely than child pornography-only offenders to have a criminal history including both sexual and non-sexual offences (Seto and Eke, 2005) and more likely to report having been personally sexually victimized (Sheldon and Howitt, 2008).

In addition, in contrast to both contact-only offenders and child pornography-only offenders, McCarthy (2010) found that child pornography contact offenders were more likely to communicate both online and in person with others who shared their sexual interest in children and child pornography.

So why don't more child pornography offenders commit contact offences?

As demonstrated above, child pornography offenders appear to demonstrate as many if not more psychosocial attributes and beliefs conducive to contact child sexual offending as contact offenders. What differentiates these offenders most from contact-only offenders is their socio-demographic characteristics, desire for social acceptance and, in the event that they do also commit contact offences, online social behaviours and their choice of victim. Notably, many of the differences that distinguish child pornography and contact offenders concern child pornography offenders' social ties to other individuals and pro-social institutions and desire for ongoing social interaction and acceptance.

Criminological theories of social control have long argued that the extent of an individual's social ties to his or her immediate environment may be critical in preventing criminal offending. These theories differ from other criminological and psychological theories in that they assume that rule breaking and criminality are inherent rather than aberrant to human nature. Therefore, instead of attempting to answer the question of why some individuals commit criminal offences, they begin with the question of why more do not (Hirschi, 1969). Clearly, this question is of particular relevance to the current chapter.

The earliest theory of social control was developed by Travis Hirschi in the late 1960s. Hirschi (1969) argues that as individuals develop they form bonds to other members of society and institutions within society. These bonds are identified as (1) attachment to others and respect for their opinion (social and familial ties and affection); (2) commitment to conventional lines of action (getting a good job, a good education and being successful); (3) involvement in conventional activities (the more activities an individual is involved in the less time they will have to get into trouble); and (4) belief in conventional values (such as those relating to being a law abiding citizen). Hirschi's theory of social control states that the formation of bonds to society facilitates the internalization of societal norms and criminal activity is deterred by the threat that social attachments may be lost if societal norms are not adhered to. Criminal and delinquent behaviour is said to occur when an individual's bonds to society are weakened or broken by poor socialization practices (Greenberg, 1999).

Despite significant academic support for Hirschi's theory of social control, it has been widely criticized for its linearity and for positing the roots of criminal offending in early life experiences. Since Hirschi first developed his theory, researchers have demonstrated that the level of involvement that individuals demonstrate in criminal offending and analogous behaviours often changes over time (Geis, 2000; Loeber and LeBlanc, 1990). They have also shown that most children who demonstrate antisocial tendencies during childhood do not actually become antisocial adults (Gove, 1985), and that many crimes are committed by adults who have no prior record of criminal offending, deviancy or analogous behaviours (Eggleston and Laub, 2002). Recent research has also shown that many child sex offenders begin offending relatively late in life (Lussier et al., 2010).

In response to these criticisms, Sampson and Laub developed a second, *age-graded* theory of social control (1993). Sampson and Laub's theory attempts to account for changes in criminal involvement across an individual's life span. In line with classic social control theory, it posits social aspects of an individual's life as important in preventing criminal involvement. However, in contrast to Hirschi's conceptualization of social ties, the age-graded theory of social control identifies informal pro-social relationships to others in society, rather than to society itself, as the source of prevention. Furthermore, the strength and nature of these relationships is said to change over time, often in relation to external factors in an individual's environment.

The concepts underpinning the age-graded theory of social control are supported by research showing that individual changes in offence behaviour are frequently associated with changes in relationships to family, peers and professional colleagues. For instance, early offending and delinquency may decrease following establishment of a romantic relationship, marriage, beginning a new job, etc. (Sampson and Laub, 1993; 1990; Wright et al., 2001). Indeed, the evidence suggests that the development of informal pro-social ties during adulthood may be as important in preventing crime and analogous behaviour as their development during childhood, if not more so (Andrews and Bonta, 1994; Sampson and Laub, 1993; 1990).

Sampson and Laub (1993) suggest that the pro-social relationships that are most likely to prevent criminal involvement are those that provide individuals with social capital and, in turn, demand social investment. The more a relationship is characterized by interdependence, and the more social and economic opportunities that participation in that relationship provides the individual, the greater its preventive value. In other words, the greater the sense of interdependence associated with a pro-social relationship, the more likely those involved will demonstrate behaviour that reflects mutually shared, pro-social values. As such, the age-graded theory of social control specifies opportunities created through pro-social bonds, or the lack thereof, as a motivating force in the commission or non-commission of criminal acts. Conversely, the weaker an individual's bonds to pro-social others, the fewer social and economic opportunities will be available to him or her, and the greater is the likelihood that they will seek to satisfy personal goals through involvement in criminal activities and relationships.

In line with Sampson and Laub's conclusions, current theories that specifically concern child sexual offending also emphasize the importance of external factors in constraining offence behaviour amongst predisposed individuals. For example, Ward and Siegert (2002: 339) state that: 'the predisposition to sexually abuse children is hypothesised to only be translated into offending behaviour under certain circumstances. These will include the presence of a victim (i.e., opportunity to offend) and the absence of any conflicting goals'.

Ward and Siegert (2002) identify a number of factors as predisposing individuals to child sexual offending, including many of the socio-affective and offence specific difficulties identified as common to child pornography offenders in the preceding section. These include: social loneliness (intimacy and social skills deficits), impulse control (emotional dysregulation), distorted sexual scripts and antisocial cognitions. Notably, with the exception of those who demonstrate antisocial cognitions, Ward and Siegert (2002) hypothesize that predisposed individuals will only offend if they experience rejection or 'blockages' in peer (adult) relationships or if they experience strong emotional arousal due to stress in some other area of their lives.

Given the evidence that child pornography offenders are more likely than contact offenders to demonstrate economic and social ties to pro-social relationships and institutions, it seems reasonable to assume that as long as these ties continue to provide emotional and tangible benefits to child pornography offenders, they will serve to constrain offending behaviour and reduce the likelihood that they will commit contact offences against children. However, if these relationships fail, the likelihood of offending may increase.

The dark side of social control

Sampson and Laub (1993) suggest that an absence or reduction in pro-social ties is sufficient to promote criminal (antisocial) behaviour. Notably, a range of studies has provided results suggesting relatively high rates of separation, divorce and/or single marital status amongst child pornography offenders (Carr, 2006; McCarthy, 2010; Webb et al., 2007; Wolak et al., 2005). In addition, Webb et al. (2007) found that child pornography offenders reported experiencing more psychological difficulties in adulthood and more contact with adult mental health services than contact offenders. It would be interesting to establish whether changes in offender marital status and periods of psychological distress coincided with the onset of child pornography offending for these individuals. It would also be useful to consider the degree to which changes in the benefits that individuals associate with their pro-social relationships are associated with changes in their offence behaviour. Unfortunately, few such studies have been undertaken.

It is known, however, that many individuals who use the Internet to access child pornography state that they do so as a means of escaping, avoiding or gaining relief from pressures in their offline world (Quayle and Taylor, 2002; 2003; Sheldon and Howitt, 2008; Surjadi et al., 2010; Taylor and Quayle, 2003). Although associated research has not explicitly considered the nature of the pressures that child pornography offenders are trying to escape, it is reasonable to assume that at least some of them may be related to the inherent conflict between having a sexual interest in children and having a strong desire for social acceptance in mainstream society and pro-social relationships. Furthermore, Quayle and Taylor (2003) showed that when accompanied by masturbation to child pornography, individuals who used the Internet in this way reported an increased sense of control over their lives, thus reinforcing further online activity and increased arousal to child pornography. In turn, many individuals who use the Internet to access child pornography as a means to escape unpleasant life events develop an almost compulsive orientation to the collection of child pornography, seeking more and more images with which to distract themselves and from which to gain pleasure (Quayle and

Taylor, 2002; 2003; Taylor and Quayle, 2003). In the Internet environment, one of the most effective ways to access increasing numbers of images is through online involvement in networks of other individuals who also share an interest in child pornography and actively trade that material through these networks (Quayle and Taylor, 2001; Taylor and Quayle, 2003). Like offline social networks, these online networks have the potential significantly to influence offenders' behaviours.

In addition to assisting child pornography offenders to gain increased access to child pornography, online networks may also provide these individuals with a range of other benefits. Although many such networks exist purely for the purpose of exchanging child pornography, others actively encourage discussion of that material, including associated offender interests, feelings and fantasies. Research demonstrates the strong sense of social support and reinforcement that child pornography offenders may experience as a result of their involvement in online networks of other individuals who demonstrate an interest in the sexualization of children (Quayle and Taylor, 2001; Quayle and Taylor, 2002; 2003; Taylor and Quayle, 2003). Child pornography offenders who engage online with others who share their interest in the sexualization of children commonly report feeling vindicated, accepted and encouraged regarding their sexual attraction to children, feeling part of a social group and sharing a sense of social belonging with other group members, feeling valued and important, feeling like they have friends, and feeling like they have a sense of purpose. Furthermore, Quayle and Taylor's (2002; 2003) research demonstrates that offender experiences of these networks may significantly change their orientations towards child pornography and motivations for associated Internet use.

Quayle and Taylor (2002) and Quayle and Taylor (2003) describe a number of cases in which child pornography offenders report a decline in the time and energy that they invest in accessing child pornography once they establish a personal 'sense of belonging to an on-line community'. Once that sense of belonging is established, child pornography offenders tend to limit their online involvement to trading child pornography between members of their online social network. In such cases, new child pornography is only accessed if it precisely fits the offender's favoured child sexual abuse fantasy or if the offender anticipates that it would be of value to an online associate. In turn, well-established networks of 'seasoned' child pornography offenders become insular and exclusive, offering only limited access to new members and encouraging current members to maintain their affiliation by providing highly specific material that fulfils other members' child sexual abuse fantasies and engaging in online discussion regarding that material. Quayle and Taylor (2002) also note that individuals who belong to established groups of child pornography offenders often organize their collections of child pornography to facilitate easier access by online associates.

The reduced time that members of child pornography networks invest in accessing child pornography does not, however, equate to increased time spent away from the Internet. Rather, the pattern of offending demonstrated by child pornography offenders who regularly engage in online interaction with other child pornography offenders suggests as great a focus on social networking activities as on the acquisition of material depicting the sexualization of children. Indeed, research undertaken by Quayle and Taylor (2002) suggests that many individuals' decisions to engage in online interaction with other child pornography offenders may have as much to do with their desire to belong to a social group as it has to do with the benefits that these networks provide in terms of access to child pornography. As stated by one of the child pornography offenders interviewed as part of that research: 'if you wanted to be a member of a group . . . you just popped into the channel and started trading and if you traded correctly . . . and you didn't abuse other users . . . and you didn't trade crap basically . . . and you didn't trade snuff or anything that showed kids actively being hurt' (Quayle and Taylor, 2002: 346).

In addition to indicating that an individual may 'enter' channels through which child pornography is traded to become 'a member of a group' (as opposed to entering for the purpose of trading child pornography), the above quotation shows that the decision to become part of an online network may actually curb the type of child pornography that individuals are able to access. It also suggests that participation in online networks may influence child pornography offenders' perceptions of the desirability of some (arguably more serious) types of child pornography. These conclusions infer that, like offline networks, online networks may exert social control over network members and contribute to the development of new social identities.

Sampson and Laub (1993) contend that where involvement in criminal activity brings an individual in contact with others who reinforce (or provide them with means to enhance the outcomes of) their involvement in that activity, the individual will attempt to maintain that contact by investing increased time and energy in associated activities and shared interests. In turn, they have less time and energy to invest in contact with non-criminal (pro-social) associates. Thus, Sampson and Laub's (1993) age-graded theory of social control infers that, just as pro-social ties and relationships can be important in controlling criminal behaviour, antisocial ties and relationships can be instrumental in undermining pro-social ties and in promoting criminal behaviour.

In line with Sampson and Laub's (1993) hypotheses, a number of researchers have demonstrated the negative impact that involvement in online relationships can have on offline relationships. Although not explicitly concerned with the trade of child pornography, those researchers have empirically demonstrated that as the amount of time and energy that an individual invests in online activities increases, the amount of time and energy available for other relationships and activities decreases, and the quality and quantity of these relationships suffer (Kraut et al., 1998; 2002). Furthermore, where individuals explicitly use the Internet to access social support or to distract themselves from offline stressors, they tend to spend more time online than individuals who demonstrate other, more instrumental motives for Internet use (Papacharissi and Rubin, 2000). It is unclear whether Internet use for the dual purposes of social support and distraction leads to increased negative impacts on non-Internet-based relationships. However, such an effect would seem likely. Given that few individuals who use the Internet to access child pornography as a means of distracting them from unpleasant life events are likely to receive social support for their sexual interest in children outside of the Internet environment, it would also seem likely that they will invest more time in these activities than most.

Once pro-social ties are undermined, Sampson and Laub (1993) argue that the importance an individual places on antisocial associations will necessarily increase. For individuals who engage in antisocial associations as a result of accessing child pornography, this increase is likely to be particularly pronounced. As discussed earlier, Bates and Metcalf (2007) have shown that child pornography offenders demonstrate a particularly strong desire for social acceptance and favourable social assessment in the offline world. Research undertaken by Quayle and Taylor (2002) suggests, however, that they also have a strong desire for social acceptance and favourable social assessment in the offline world. The child pornography offenders interviewed by Quayle and Taylor (2002) reported a strong sense of attachment to online child pornography associates and a sense of belonging in associated networks. In line with Bates and Metcalf's (2007) description of child pornography offenders 'faking good', when tested against offline pro-social norms, Quayle and Taylor (2002; 2003) report that child pornography offenders often also go to significant lengths to present themselves well to online associates. However, in those cases the norms that they aspire to conform to are definitely not pro-social. For example, child pornography offenders reported collecting material that they did not find particularly gratifying but that they thought would be valued by online associates, and engaging in activities that enabled social alignment with individuals who were perceived to have significant social status in the online world. Child pornography offenders in Quayle and Taylor's (2002) sample explained that in the online world, social status and recognition were commonly tied to the provision of rare, novel or difficult-to-access examples of child pornography. They also noted that the rarest, and therefore most socially influential, examples of child pornography were those that were personally produced by online associates and shared with a very limited group of like-minded others.

Given the evidence that some child pornography offenders will go out of their way to acquire images for others with whom they share strong online relationships, and that rare or personally produced child pornography imbues social status and recognition within online networks of child pornography offenders, it is not unreasonable to assume that some offenders' desire to maintain these relationships, and gain online social status, could motivate them to produce child pornography that specifically meets the needs of online associates. In turn, child pornography offenders' motivation to produce child pornography could lead them to commit contact sexual offences against children. As such, child pornography offenders' online social ties may have as much, if not more, influence on their motivation to commit contact offences as their sexual interest in children.

The new relationship between media consumption and contact offending

For years, researchers have searched for and failed to find a direct association between exposure to pornographic material and commission of acts depicted in that material (Bauserman, 1996; Davis and Bauserman, 1993; Freedman, 2002; Graham, 2001; Savage, 2004; Vine, 1997). That research has consistently found that pre-existing propensities such as antisocial cognitions are better predictors of offence behaviour following pornographic consumption than mere exposure (Freedman, 2002; Gunter, 1994; Huesmann and Bacharach, 1988; Vine, 1997). The propensities that predict offence behaviour following pornographic consumption have also been found to predict pornography consumption (e.g. Anderson et al., 2003; Bushman, 1995; Freedman, 2002; Lopez and George, 1995; Malamuth et al., 2000; Seto et al., 2001). Research considering the effects of media consumption on behaviour has also demonstrated that most such propensities develop within the context of relationships with other similarly predisposed individuals. Furthermore, shared consumption of violent or pornographic material both reinforces a shared social identity between predisposed individuals and increases positive orientations to the content of that material (Casas, 1998; Nathanson, 2001; Suess et al., 1998).

Until recently, however, most exposure to child pornography has tended to occur within a social vacuum. Prior to the widespread use of the Internet, police intelligence reports suggest that most such material was produced either as hard copy photographs or on video, and distributed via 'underground' networks of interested consumers (Lanning, 1992; Taylor and Quayle, 2003). Given the social stigma and legal ramifications associated with individuals demonstrating an interest in the sexual exploitation of children, such networks rarely advertised their presence and associated social interaction was probably very limited. Furthermore, the tangibility of hard copy child pornography reduced the possibility that individuals found in its possession could argue their way out of associated charges and therefore also probably reduced the likelihood that many individuals would risk forming the networks needed to access it.

The advent of the Internet, however, has increased the ease of child pornography distribution. It has also increased the ease of connecting with others who share an interest in such material. The vast, fluid and relatively unregulated size of the Internet makes it very difficult for law enforcement to police it. In addition, given the generally higher levels of education and intelligence associated with child pornography offenders, these individuals demonstrate the capacity to quickly take advantage of new applications and strategies designed to prevent law enforcement access to areas of cyberspace in which they commonly 'meet'. For example, law enforcement experience has shown that many online networks take advantage of legislation preventing police from distributing child pornography by requiring provision of child pornography as a means of entering chat rooms and forums used by their network (personal communication, 2009).[4] Therefore, the risks associated with doing so are reduced.

In turn, more and more individuals who may previously have demonstrated an interest in the sexualization of children but been prevented from acting on that interest by the perceived risk associated with doing so, are likely to be in a position to take advantage of these opportunities. Once online, the ties they form to others who share their interest have the potential to weaken the ties they have to offline associates. The weakening of offline social ties is likely to cause significant distress for many of these individuals and this may lead to them spending increasing amounts of time escaping to the Internet. In addition, given child pornography offenders' strong desire for social acceptance (Bates and Metcalf, 2007), they may feel inclined to strengthen their ties to online associates. The evidence suggests that the best way to do this is to provide new and rare examples of child pornography, particularly examples that are personally produced. As such, these individuals may be compelled to commit contact offences as much out of their desire to record those offences for online distribution as out of a desire for sexual involvement with children. The fact that both desires are satisfied, however, means that the act of doing so is likely to be even more reinforcing for them than if it were solely motivated by their sexual interest in children.

Clearly, the behavioural transitions hypothesized in the preceding paragraph require empirical testing and research support before the theoretical link between involvement in online networks of child pornography offenders and child pornography contact offending is established. However, some support for that link is provided in the results of McCarthy's (2010) research, which showed that child pornography offenders who committed contact offences were more likely to associate online with other offenders than child pornography offenders who did not. Similarly, Carr (2006) also demonstrated that offenders who chose to use socially facilitative Internet applications during the process of accessing child pornography tended to demonstrate a greater number of offence-related behaviours than those who did not. Those behaviours included actively acquiring larger, better organized collections of child pornography; acquiring large numbers of images of non-familial children that could not be defined as child pornography; actively engaging in voluntary activities that put them in contact with non-familial children; and producing child pornography. Notably, McCarthy (2010) also observed that child pornography contact offenders were significantly more likely than child pornography-only offenders to access non-pornographic websites showing child models.

Carr (2006) also observed that offenders who demonstrated stronger pro-social ties in the offline environment were most likely to make use of socially facilitative applications when accessing child pornography. Drawing on narrative theory (McAdams, 1994; 1995; 1996), Carr (2006) hypothesized that when confronted with a new environment, whether during the commission of a crime or in other day-to-day activities, individuals will navigate that environment using strategies with which they have gained familiarity in other environments. Thus, individuals who are comfortable interacting with others offline will choose to interact with others online, whereas those who are less comfortable in social situations will tend to avoid them regardless of the medium. Similarly, individuals who use social relationships to gain assistance and direction in their offline lives will be more likely to seek out online social contacts for this purpose. In turn, offenders who demonstrate offline social ties will be more likely than those who do not to become involved in online social interaction and to be influenced by social reinforcement resulting from this interaction to invest increased time and energy in their offence behaviour.

In light of these findings Carr (2006) proposed the existence of two distinct types of child pornography offenders (see Fig. 6.1). Specifically, she identified socially independent child pornography offenders who are socially isolated offline and unlikely to either seek out or be influenced by relationships formed in the online environment. Given the impact of offline social ties in constraining the offence behaviour of individuals who demonstrate an interest in the sexualization of children, these socially independent offenders are likely to include individuals who have already committed a sexual offence against a child prior to accessing child pornography. Carr (2006) describes the other type of child pornography offender as socially interdependent. Socially interdependent offenders demonstrate strong offline social ties that are likely to have prevented their involvement in contact offending prior to involvement in the Internet. However, once online, their awareness of the benefits associated with social networks means that they are most likely to seek out and engage with others who also share their interest. In the event that their offline ties to pro-social networks become compromised, either as a result of external pressures or because of their increasing involvement in online activities, they are also most likely to seek social reinforcement and acceptance from online associates. As described above, that search may result in their involvement in activities such as contact child sexual offending as a means of producing material to increase their status in online relationships.

Further research is recommended to test the model presented in Fig. 6.1. That research could benefit from social network analyses of the communication patterns of different types of child pornography offenders.

Summary and conclusions

The research reviewed in this chapter suggests that relatively few individuals who are identified as using the Internet to access child pornography also commit contact child sexual offences. Given evidence suggesting that individuals who access child pornography demonstrate many socio-affective similarities to contact child sexual offenders, and appear more attracted to children and accepting of cognitive distortions regarding children as sexual partners, these findings are surprising. However, socio-demographic comparisons between individuals who access child pornography and contact child sexual offenders differ, revealing that individuals who access child pornography tend to have stronger pro-social ties to mainstream relationships and institutions and a greater desire for social acceptance than contact child sexual offenders. Therefore, it is hypothesized that these factors play a significant role in preventing individuals who access child pornography from also committing contact child sexual offences. This conclusion is supported by criminological theories of social control.

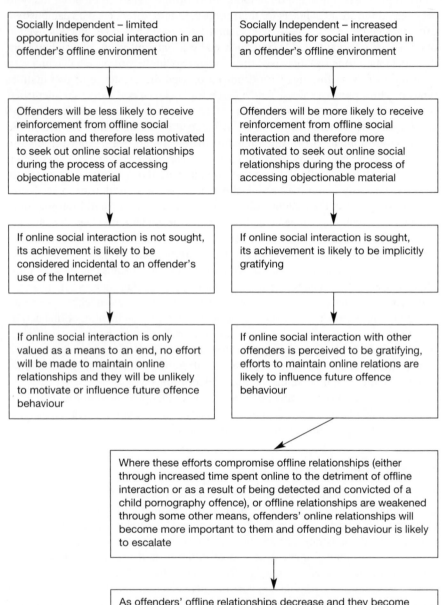

Figure 6.1
Carr's (2006)
model of the
social dimensions
of child
pornography
offending

Socially Independent – limited opportunities for social interaction in an offender's offline environment

Socially Independent – increased opportunities for social interaction in an offender's offline environment

Offenders will be less likely to receive reinforcement from offline social interaction and therefore less motivated to seek out online social relationships during the process of accessing objectionable material

Offenders will be more likely to receive reinforcement from offline social interaction and therefore more motivated to seek out online social relationships during the process of accessing objectionable material

If online social interaction is not sought, its achievement is likely to be considered incidental to an offender's use of the Internet

If online social interaction is sought, its achievement is likely to be implicitly gratifying

If online social interaction is only valued as a means to an end, no effort will be made to maintain online relationships and they will be unlikely to motivate or influence future offence behaviour

If online social interaction with other offenders is perceived to be gratifying, efforts to maintain online relations are likely to influence future offence behaviour

Where these efforts compromise offline relationships (either through increased time spent online to the detriment of offline interaction or as a result of being detected and convicted of a child pornography offence), or offline relationships are weakened through some other means, offenders' online relationships will become more important to them and offending behaviour is likely to escalate

As offenders' offline relationships decrease and they become increasingly dependent on online associates for social support, their desire to please online associates will lead to increasing efforts to share new and rare examples of child pornography with those associates. In turn, they will be more likely to participate in the production of child pornography and associated contact offences

While the existence of pro-social ties may prevent many individuals who use the Internet to access child pornography from also committing contact child sexual offences, the review presented in this chapter suggests that if these ties are compromised, the risk of contact child sexual offending may increase. Furthermore, the research considered as part of that review suggests that online contact with other offenders during the process of accessing child pornography may increase the pressures on offline social ties. Specifically, individuals who access child pornography by way of the Internet may find online ties more rewarding than offline ties. In turn, they may invest increasing amounts of time in maintaining online ties and seeking acceptance from online associates, to the detriment of time for maintaining offline ties and acceptance by offline associates. Investment of time in the maintenance of online ties to others who share an interest in child pornography has also been shown to change child pornography offenders' orientations towards their Internet use and involvement in accessing child pornography. As child pornography offenders gain an increased sense of belonging in online networks of individuals who share their interest in child pornography, their behaviour typically becomes less focused on the collection of child pornography for their own purposes and more focused on providing child pornography for the purpose of building social status and acceptance within their online network. Child pornography offenders report that within online networks, social status is achieved through the provision of new, rare or personally produced material depicting the sexualization of children. Therefore, it is hypothesized that some offenders may feel compelled to commit contact child sexual offences as much as a part of producing such material as for their own sexual pleasure. Although this hypothesis requires testing, research has demonstrated that child pornography offenders who commit contact offences and who personally produce child pornography are more likely to be actively involved in online networks than those who do not.

Notably, research also suggests that child pornography offenders who demonstrate the greatest level of experience with offline social networks are most likely to seek out and become involved in online social networks. This finding is supported by narrative theories of psychology. Narrative theories suggest that when confronted with a new environment, individuals will navigate that environment using strategies that they have gained familiarity with in other environments. It also suggests that associated offenders perceive significant personal benefit in both the online and offline relationships that they develop. Assuming that involvement in online child pornography networks has the potential to increase the likelihood of contact child sexual offences, an understanding of the motives that lead individuals to engage in these networks could have significant law enforcement and therapeutic implications. For example, if it is established that in some cases online networks come to replace offline networks because the benefits associated with the former are perceived to outweigh the benefits associated with the latter, interventions aimed at restrengthening offender ties to offline networks and increasing associated benefits could have a significant impact on the likelihood of future contact child sexual offences. Similarly, given the potential for criminal conviction to undermine pro-social ties, these findings may also suggest the need to increase support for child pornography offenders' non-offending friends and family during the prosecution process and involve them in the offender treatment process.

Notes

1   Including a number of the studies included in Seto et al.'s (2011) meta-analysis.
2   Distorted sexual scripts together with flaws in all the other primary psychological mechanisms associated with pathways 1 to 4.
3   Difference in terms of relevant attitudes and beliefs from a non-offending sample.
4   Detective Inspector Jonathan Rouse, Taskforce Argos, Queensland Police Service, personal communication, 23 January 2009; Detective Inspector Lance Vercoe, Taskforce Cerberus, Queensland Police Service, personal communication, 23 January 2009; Federal Agent George Feifers, child protection operations, high tech crime operations, Australian Federal Police, personal communication, 2 October 2008.

References

American Psychological Society. (2006). *Diagnostic and Statistical Manual of Mental Disorders DSM-IV TR (Text Revision)*. Arlington, VA, USA: American Psychiatric Publishing, Inc.

Anderson, C.A., Berkowitz, L., Donnerstein, E., Huesmann, L.R., Johnson, J.D., Linz, D., Malamuth, N.M. and Wartella, E. (2003). The influence of media violence on youth. *Psychological Science in the Public Interest, 4*, 81–110.

Andrews, D.A. and Bonta, J. (1994). *The Psychology of Criminal Conduct*. Cincinnati, OH: Anderson Publishing Company.

Bates, A. and Metcalf, C. (2007). A psychometric comparison of internet and non-Internet sex offenders from a community treatment sample. *Journal of Sexual Aggression, 13*, 11–20.

Bauserman, R. (1996). Sexual aggression and pornography: A review of correlational research. *Basic and Applied Social Psychology, 18*, 405–27.

Bourke, M. L., and Hernandez, A. E. (2009). The 'Butner Study' redux: A report of the incidence of hands-on child victimization by child pornography offenders. *Journal of Family Violence, 24*, 183–91.

Burke, A., Sowerbutts, S., Blundell, B. and Sherry, M. (2002). Child pornography and the Internet: Policing and treatment issues. *Psychiatry, Psychology and Law, 9*, 79–84.

Bushman, B.J. (1995). Moderating role of trait aggressiveness in the effects of violent media on aggression. *Journal of Personality and Social Psychology, 69*, 950–60.

Carr, A. (2006). *Internet Censorship Offending: A Preliminary Analysis of the Social and Behavioural Patterns of Offenders*. Unpublished thesis submitted to Bond University in fulfilment of the requirement for the degree of Doctor of Philosophy.

Casas, F., (1998). *Children, Media and the Relational Planet: Some Reflections from the European Context*. Speech presented at 'Cultural Ecology' seminar in Tokyo, Japan.

Davis, K.E., and Bauserman, R. (1993). Exposure to sexually explicit materials: An attitude change perspective. *Annual Review of Sex Research, 4*, 121–209.

Eggleston, E.P., and Laub, J.H. (2002). The onset of adult offending: A neglected dimension of the criminal career. *Journal of Criminal Justice, 30*, 603–22.

Finkelhor, D. and Ormrod, R. (2004). *Child Pornography: Patterns from the NIBRS*. Washington, DC: US Department of Justice, Office of Justice Programs, Office of

Juvenile Justice and Delinquency Prevention, available online at http://www.ncjrs.gov/pdffiles1/ojjdp/204911.pdf.

Freedman, J.L. (2002). *Media Violence and Its Effect on Aggression: Assessing the Scientific Evidence*. Toronto, ON: University of Ontario Press.

Geis, G. (2000). On the absence of self-control as the basis for a general theory of crime: A critique. *Theoretical Criminology, 4*, 35–53.

Gove, W.R. (1985). The effect of age and gender on deviant behaviour: A biopsychosocial perspective. In A.S. Rossi (ed.), *Gender and the Life Course*. New York, NY: Aldine, pp. 115–44).

Graham, I. (2001). *A Candle in the Dark: A Report on 'Evidence' Submitted to the Australian Senate NVE Inquiry in March 2000*, available online at http://libertus.net/censor/rdocs/candle.html.

Greenberg, D.F. (1999). The weak strength of social control theory. *Crime and Delinquency, 45*, 66–81.

Gunter, B. (1994). The question of media violence. In J. Bryant and D. Zillman (eds), *Media Effects: Advances in Theory and Research*. Hillsdale, NJ: Lawrence Erlbaum Associates, pp. 163–211.

Hirschi, T. (1969). *Causes of Delinquency*. Berkeley, CA: University of California Press.

Howitt, D. and Sheldon, K. (2007). The role of cognitive distortions in paedophilic offending: Internet and contact offenders compared. *Psychology, Crime and Law, 13*, 469–86

Huesmann, L.R. and Bachrach, R.S. (1988). Differential effects of television violence in kibbutz and city children. In R. Patterson and P. Drummond (eds), *Television and Its Audience: International Research Perspectives* London: BFI Publishing, pp. 154–76.

Kraut, R., Kiesler, S., Boneva, B., Cummings, J., Helgeson, V. and Crawford, A. (2002). Internet paradox revisited. *Journal of Social Issues, 58*, 49–74

Kraut, R., Patterson, M., Lundmark, V., Kiesler, S., Mukopadhyay, T. and Scherlis, W. (1998). Internet paradox: A social technology that reduces social involvement and psychological well-being? *American Psychologist, 53*, 1017–31.

Lanning, K.V. (1992). *Child Molesters: A Behavioural Analysis*. Quantico, VA: National Center for Missing and Exploited Children, Behavioural Science Unit, U.S. Federal Bureau of Investigation, available online at http://www.ccoso.org/library articles/Lanning-molester behavior analysis.pdf.

Loeber, R. and LeBlanc, M. (1990). Toward a developmental criminology. In M. Tonry and N. Morris (eds), *Crime and Justice*. Chicago: University of Chicago Press, vol. 12, pp. 375–437.

Lopez, P. and George, W. (1995). Men's enjoyment of explicit erotica. *The Journal of Sex Research, 32*, 275–88.

Lussier, P., Tzoumakis, S., Cale, J. and Amirault, J. (2010). Criminal trajectories of adult sex offenders and the age effect: Examining the dynamic aspect of offending in adulthood. *International Criminal Justice Review, 20*, 147–68.

McAdams, D.P. (1994). A psychology of the stranger. *Psychological Inquiry, 5*, 145–49.

—— (1995). What do we know when we know a person? *Journal of Personality, 63*, 365–96.

—— (1996). Personality, modernity and the storied self: A contemporary framework for studying persons. *Psychological Inquiry, 7*, 295–321.

McCarthy, J.A. (2010). Internet sexual activity: A comparison between contact and non-contact child pornography offenders. *Journal of Sexual Aggression, 16*, 181–95.

Malamuth, N.M., Addison, T. and Koss, M. (2000). Pornography and sexual aggression: Are there reliable effects and can we understand them? *Annual Review of Sex Research, 11*, 26–91.

Middleton, D., Elliott, I.A., Mandeville-Norden, R. and Beech, A.R. (2006). An investigation into the applicability of the Ward and Siegert Pathways Model of child sexual abuse with Internet offenders. *Psychology, Crime and Law, 12*, 589–603.

Nathanson, A.I. (2001). Parents versus peers: Exploring the significance of peer mediation of antisocial television. *Communication Research, 28*, 251–74.

Papacharissi, Z. and Rubin, A.M., (2000). Predictors of Internet use. *Journal of Broadcasting and Electronic Media, 44*, 175–96.

Quayle, E. and Taylor, M. (2001). Child seduction and self representation on the Internet. *Cyberpsychology and Behaviour, 4*, 597–604.

—— (2002). Child pornography and the Internet: Perpetuating a cycle of abuse. *Deviant Behaviour, 23*, 331–62.

—— (2003). Model of problematic Internet use in people with a sexual interest in children. *Cyberpsychology and Behaviour, 6*, 93–106.

Sampson, R.J. and Laub, J.H. (1990). Crime and deviance over the life course: The salience of adult social bonds. *American Sociological Review 55*, 609–27.

—— (1993). *Crime in the Making: Pathways and Turning Points through Life.* Cambridge, MA: Harvard University Press.

Savage, J. (2004). Does viewing violent media really cause criminal violence? A methodological review. *Aggression and Violent Behavior, 10*, 99–128.

Seto, M.C. and Eke, A.W. (2005). The criminal histories and later offending of child pornography offenders. *Sexual Abuse: A Journal of Research and Treatment, 17*, 201–10.

Seto, M.C., Cantor, J.M. and Blanchard, R. (2006). Child pornography offenses are a valid diagnostic indicator of pedophilia. *Journal of Abnormal Psychology, 115*, 610–15.

Seto, M.C., Hanson, R.K. and Babchishin, K.M. (2011). Contact sexual offending by men with online sexual offenses. *Sexual Abuse: A Journal of Research and Treatment, 23*, 124–45.

Seto, M.C., Maric, A. and Barbaree, H.E. (2001). The role of pornography in the etiology of sexual aggression. *Aggression and Violent Behavior, 6*, 35–53.

Sheldon, K. and Howitt, D. (2008). Sexual fantasy in paedophile offenders: Can any model explain satisfactorily new findings from a study of Internet and contact sexual offenders? *Legal and Criminological Psychology, 13*, 137–58.

Suess, D., Suoninen, A., Garitaonandia, C., Juaristi, P., Koikkalainen, R. and Oleaga, J.A. (1998). Media use and the relationships of children and teenagers with their peer groups. *European Journal of Communication, 13*, 521–38.

Surjadi, B., Bullens, R., van Horn, J. and Bogaerts, S. (2010). Internet offending: Sexual and non-sexual functions within a Dutch sample. *Journal of Sexual Aggression, 16*, 47–58.

Taylor, M. and Quayle, E. (2003). *Child Pornography: An Internet Crime.* Hove, UK: Brunner-Routledge.

Tomak, S., Weschler, F.S., Ghahramanlou-Holloway, M., Virden, T. and Nademin, M.E. (2009). An empirical study of the personality characteristics of internet sex offenders. *Journal of Sexual Aggression, 15*, 139–48.

Vine, I. (1997). The dangerous psycho-logic of media 'effects'. In M. Barker and J. Petley (eds), *Ill Effects: The Media/Violence Debate.* London, UK: Routledge, pp. 125–46.

Ward, T. and Siegert, R. J. (2002). Toward a comprehensive theory of child sexual abuse: A theory knitting perspective. Psychology. *Crime and Law, 8*, 319–51.

Webb, L., Craissati, J. and Keen, S. (2007). Characteristics of Internet child pornography offenders: A comparison with child molesters. *Sexual Abuse: A Journal of Research and Treatment, 19,* 449–65.

Wolak, J., Finkelhor, D. and Mitchell, K. J. (2005). *Child Pornography Possessors Arrested in Internet-Related Crimes: Findings from the National Juvenile Online Victimization Study.* National Center for Missing and Exploited Children, available online at http://www.unh.edu/ccrc/pdf/jvq/CV81.pdf.

Wright, B., Caspi, A., Moffit, T. and Silva, P. (2001). The effects of social ties on crime vary by criminal propensity: A life-course model of interdependence. *Criminology, 39,* 321–48.

7 Online child pornography, paedophilia and the sexualized child

Mediated myths and moral panics

Yvonne Jewkes, University of Leicester, UK

Overview

In recent years there have been numerous media stories concerning the dangers that may face children when they use computers, the Internet and social networking sites. These narratives serve to reinforce confusion surrounding childhood sexuality, employ a language that implies loss of parental control, and have oriented political and public concerns away from 'real world' crimes against children. In other words, building on and exacerbating existing concerns about 'stranger danger' and applying technologically deterministic characteristics to the Internet, the media have positioned both the 'paedophile'[1] and pornography involving child victims in virtual rather than real space and orchestrated a moral panic linking children, sexual abuse and the Internet. This chapter aims to demonstrate that such discourses not only fail to protect children, but work to maintain widespread cultural tolerance towards the fetishizing of children. The chapter interrogates the hypocrisy surrounding societal attitudes to children, both historically and contemporaneously and, in the process, explores and explodes five common myths regarding computer-facilitated child sexual abuse (CSA):

1. Sexual attraction to children is a problem of late-modern, technologically advanced nations.
2. CSA is an offence carried out by strangers and children are protected within the home.
3. CSA is less pervasive within societies with strong family structures.
4. Paedophilia is an individual pathology.
5. Children are always 'innocent' victims.

It should be stated at the outset that this chapter is not arguing that culturally constructed myths surrounding CSA mean that it is not a real and serious problem; as other chapters in this volume demonstrate, the myths discussed here are frequently underpinned by highly abusive content, often constituting very serious offences. What this chapter *is* arguing is that the relationship between child pornography and child abuse is sometimes more complex that the popular media suggests.

Myth 1: sexual attraction to children is a problem of late-modern, technologically advanced nations

'Paedophiles' and 'paedophilia' are terms that have only been in common usage in the 'Anglo' world since the mid-1990s. The relatively recent introduction of these words in the common lexicon – and the particular meanings they convey – may be a partial explanation for the tendency of contemporary media to present stories concerning the sexual exploitation of children by adults as a uniquely modern concern. Public anxiety has further escalated since computers, the Internet and the World Wide Web have been implicated in CSA. Despite the fact that, in the UK, the Protection of Children Act 1978 prohibited the production and distribution of indecent images of children years before these technologies came into existence, online child pornography and the grooming of children in chat rooms by predatory adults are never far from the top of the news agenda.

In fact it is well established that the origins of almost all contemporary moral panics go back a considerable length of time and the sexual abuse of children certainly pre-dates the Internet. In the Victorian era, erotic images of children in both art and the new medium of photography were relatively common among collectors (typically, aristocrats and professional men) and there was far less public censure regarding the sexualization of children (Pearsall, 1993). Famous children's writers of the time J.M. Barrie (creator of *Peter Pan*) and Lewis Carroll (author of *Alice in Wonderland*) are among several high-profile figures who have been subjected to revisionist scrutiny questioning the morality they displayed both in their depictions of children in art and in their relationships with children in life. There was, for a few years in the late nineteenth century, a 'cult of little girls' (Sweet, 2001: 166) during which the use of naked children by the growing advertising industry and on other commercial products such as Christmas cards might be regarded as a logical – if somewhat sentimental – consequence of the newly privileged status of children and childhood (ibid.). Alternatively, given the preponderance of images of 'childhood innocence . . . erotically framed against visible signs of immoral sexuality such as exposed genitalia or the depraved stare' (Mort, 2000: 65), the cult of little girls might more accurately be regarded as evidence of a (barely) repressed paedophilia.

In short, Victorian ideas about children and sexuality were as confused and as polarized as our own:

> The romanticised images of children which enjoyed such a vogue in the mid- and late-nineteenth century might now appear creepy and saccharine: Dodgson's four surviving child nudes; the Pears Soap child – half-boy, half-Bambi . . . Put these side by side with those other familiar images of young Victorians – Thomas Barnardo's photographs of cadaverous street arabs, William Daniels's pictures of starving match girls – and they seem to articulate one of the key injustices with which the Victorians have been charged: generating a sentimental eroticism around childhood at the same time as

enjoying the fruits of child labour – idealising the young but still expecting them to deliver the coal.

(Sweet, 2001: 166)

The Victorians used a range of euphemisms for child sexual abuse, including 'molestation', 'tampering', 'ruining' and 'ravishing', but only in relation to girls; while there was a market for boy prostitutes, Victorian society judged females by their sexual reputation and girls constituted a specifically targeted social problem (Jackson, 2000). The contemporary criminological concern with the trafficking of girls and young women from Eastern Europe to the UK to work in the sex trade has parallels with the work of political activists and reformers in Victorian England who, in 1879, set up the London Committee for the Purposes of Exposure and Suppression of the Traffic in English Girls for the Purposes of Continental Prostitution (ibid). The establishment of this organization coincided with newspaper reports that English girls as young as 10 were being abducted and sold to brothel owners in Paris and Brussels for the enjoyment of wealthy clients; a story which scandalized respectable Victorian society, popularized the term 'white slave trade', and resulted in the age of consent being raised from 13 to 16 in the Criminal Law Amendment Act (1885).

Not only does CSA pre-date the Internet by several centuries but it is also a transnational problem regardless of the prevalence of new communication technologies. Put simply, the Internet is not as 'global' as is often thought (http://www.internetworldstats.com/stats.htm), but sexual abuse of children is. To give just one example, Internet users in Oceania, including Australia, number just 1.3 per cent of the world total Internet population, and the digital divide is especially marked with regard to Aboriginal communities due to geographical isolation, economic disadvantage and cultural factors. Currently, in remote indigenous communities in Australia, better telephone services are of a higher priority than Internet access (Smillie-Adjarkwa, 2005). Yet in some Aboriginal communities of Australia, there are high trends of child abuse, with children being exposed to pornography, used as prostitutes in exchange for drugs (including petrol, a substance reported to be commonly sniffed by youths in Aboriginal communities) and some as young as 5 years old testing positive for sexually transmitted diseases (http://news.bbc.co.uk/1/hi/world/asia-pacific/6756515.stm). So serious is the problem that the Northern Territory government of Australia established a Board of Inquiry which released a report in June 2007 linking alcohol and lack of education to the high rate of child sex abuse in indigenous communities in northern Australia (http://www.inquirysaac.nt.gov.au/). While the report outlines allegations of sex trades and juvenile prostitution, Federal Indigenous Affairs Minister Mal Brough went further, claiming that paedophile rings operate in indigenous communities in the Northern Territory and that in the two months prior to the report's publication, 14 per cent of this adult population had been charged 'with child sex offences against children as young as three with the main offence being penetration of a girl under 13' (http://www.abc.net.au/news/news items/200706/s1952739.htm).

While research is contradictory (see, for example, Wolak et al., 2009, who argue that in the US the number of child pornography offences is on the increase), some experts have suggested that the notion that CSA is growing as a result of the global expansion of Internet access may be wide of the mark:

> [T]he Internet Safety Technical Taskforce (2008) argue that although they are frequently reported in the media, US Internet sex crimes against minors have not overtaken the number of unmediated sex crimes against minors, nor have they contributed to a rise in such crimes. The report states that the increased popularity of the Internet in the United States has not been correlated with an overall increase in reported sexual offenses. Evidence is cited from the US that overall, sexual offenses against children have declined in the last 18 years (National Center for Missing and Exploited Children, 2006), with research indicating a dramatic reduction in reports of sexual offenses against children from 1992 to 2006.
>
> (Quayle, 2010: 366)

In support of this view, in January 2009 a 278-page document, compiled by the Berkman Center for Internet and Society at Harvard University, reported on the findings of the Internet Safety Technical Task Force, a group made up of forty-nine attorneys-general and representatives of Internet service providers (ISPs) and social networking sites. The taskforce were charged with examining the problem of sexual solicitation of children online, and their conclusion was that there is not a significant problem and that the reality of online grooming runs counter to popular perceptions of the dangers reinforced by depictions in the media. Meanwhile, decisions about the prioritization of resources to protect children are arguably skewed in favour of funding very visible organizations online such as the Internet Watch Foundation. This means that money is directed away from initiatives such as police child protection units with the result, some maintain, of actually putting children in the community at risk (Cullen, 2003). Yet as this section, and the one that follows, show, children may be at most danger from members of their immediate families and communities.

Myth 2: CSA is an offence carried out by strangers and children are protected within the home

The media persist in peddling the myth that children are most at risk from strangers (sometimes strangers who live at considerable distance from their victims), and atypical but highly newsworthy cases of abductions and sexual assault on young, white, attractive girls from middle-class families continue to dominate the news agenda. Yet most academic researchers and support services underline the heightened risk for children from family members and estimate that 95 per cent of child victims of sexual and physical abuse know their abuser (see, for example, ChildLine, 2002; Grubin, 1998; Thomas, 2005). Once again, it has *always* been the case that most sexual abuse of children has taken place within the home and the family. In England, there was no law against incest until 1908 (in 2003 the crime of incest was replaced with a new offence of familial sexual abuse to cover not just assaults by blood relatives but also foster and adoptive parents and live-in partners), and in many societies in earlier times sexual relations between adult males and pubescent girls was considered perfectly acceptable.

In the mid- to late 1990s there were a number of catalysts for a sudden eruption of media coverage of CSA involving offenders unknown to their victims and for the rapid adoption by the popular media of the terms 'paedophile' and 'stranger danger'. The British press revealed that several care homes operating as halfway houses to accommodate individuals released from prison after serving sentences for sexual offences against children were situated within close proximity of schools and children's play areas. At the same time, cases came to light of child sexual abuse in residential childcare homes and other institutions where children were supposed to be protected, and (predominantly in Northern Ireland and, latterly, in Italy) several priests were accused of sexual offences against children which fuelled accusations of high-level cover-ups within the Catholic Church. In the autumn of 1996 a released paedophile was charged with a series of child murders in Belgium and, once again, there were accusations of a high-level cover-up, this time involving politicians, the police and civil servants. A campaign began in the UK for a sex offenders' register, which was made legal by the 1997 Sex Offenders Act and was given added impetus by the creation of 'Megan's Law' in the US a year earlier, which gave parents access to information on paedophiles living in their local area, following the rape and murder of 7-year-old Megan Kanka by a twice-convicted sex offender who lived in the same street in New Jersey.[2] Stories also emerged involving 'paedophile celebrities', e.g. former pop-star Gary Glitter who, in 1999, was cleared of underage sex charges but convicted of downloading images of sexual abuse of children from the world wide web. Despite his acquittal of the 1999 sex charges,[3] the press still found ways of labelling him a paedophile, with headlines such as 'Beast raped me aged 8' (*News of the World*, 14 November 1999) and 'Monster masquerading under the mask of glam rock' (*Daily Mail*, 18 November 1999).

By the start of the new millennium, then, missing children, abduction and assault narratives had become recurring themes in news and television drama, and public debate focused on the need for stringent police checks on those working with children, the risks posed by releasing convicted child sex offenders into the community, and the perceived dangerousness of public spaces. One of the conse-quences of these issues becoming prominent in the public imagination was a reorganization of the childhood and adolescent experience as pleasure and leisure became privatized. The increasing tendency for parents to accompany their chil-dren in all public spheres coincided with the rapid emergence of the Internet and, together, these new social trends constituted a profound change in the way that young people's identities were shaped and their social skills learned. By 2005, 91 per cent of the UK's 16–21-year-olds had access to mobile phones, the Internet and email (Haste, 2005), and 94 per cent of young people go online from home, with most having multiple points of access, including from their mobile phones

(Molloy, n.d.). According to media regulator Ofcom, by 2008, 35 per cent of children aged 12–15 and 16 per cent of children aged between 8 and 11 had Internet access in their bedrooms – up from 20 per cent and 9 per cent respectively in 2007 (*The Telegraph*, 6 October 2009). Social networking sites such as Bebo, MySpace, Twitter and Facebook have led the revolution in how young people communicate and interact with each other, with five out of six regularly using at least one social networking site. Facebook is particularly popular. By 2009 it was being used by 72 per cent of 11–15-year-olds, 80 per cent of 17–25-year-olds, and 83 per cent of those at or who have been to university, according to a survey conducted by research consultants NfpSynergy (http://www.prweek.com/news/). Its growing ubiquity is also demonstrated by reports that, having celebrated its 250 millionth user in July 2009, by February of the following year that figure had risen to 400 million users (http://blog.facebook.com/blog.php?post=287542162130). As these forces came together – that is, the growing fear of predatory paedophiles, the privatization of social interaction and the growing ubiquity of mobile digital communications – a common media discourse linking the predatory stranger with the Internet as a danger to children emerged, accompanied by powerful headlines such as 'Twisted secrets of the web' (*The Sun*, 13 November 1999) and 'Who is policing the Internet?' (*The Mirror*, 13 November 1999). In a typically hysterical editorial, *Daily Mail* columnist Lynda Lee-Potter claimed:

> Paedophiles are cunning, devious, ruthless and incurable . . . There are large paedophile rings in every town. There are paedophile killers living in safe houses at the expense of the state. Police officers and social workers are forced to protect men who only want to defile unformed bodies. Our prisons are overcrowded and overburdened with perverts who are a danger to the outside world. Through the Internet, their numbers are growing and their sick desires are being inflamed. They're arrogant, vile and believe they are above the law.
>
> (cited in Critcher, 2002: 531)

These events combined not only to embed the word 'paedophile' in the public consciousness and to reinforce the theme of 'stranger danger', but also resulted in the routine use of labels including 'sicko', 'evil', 'paedo', 'pervert' and 'monster', moving child sex abuse outside of any framework linked to adult male hetero-sexuality and the family (Kitzinger, 1996). This was despite reports in the broad-sheet press claiming that 'restricted Scotland Yard documents' showed that Britain's child abusers are usually 'white males aged between 36 to 45 and in a long-term relationship, married or have children' (*The Observer*, 9 September 2007). By way of illustration, in 2007 the Child Exploitation and Online Protection Centre (CEOP) successfully arrested and prosecuted Timothy Cox, who was running a paedophile ring from his parents' home in Suffolk. The operation allowed abusers to share real-time films of their crimes. Cox's own hard drive contained 75,960 images of child abuse and, in addition, he had disseminated 11,491 images to other site users. Among them were clips of fathers abusing their children, and fifteen children were identified and rescued in the UK (thirty-one worldwide), many from their own homes. As one journalist put it, 'The grim truth is that many of those abused will be related to their attackers' (http://www.thisislondon.co.uk/news/ article-23401088-15-children-saved-from-uks-biggest-paedophile-ring.do), underlining the rather obvious fact that abusers tend to be individuals who have easy access to children. Nonetheless, the media's inclination to deal in binary oppositions (good/evil, folk heroes/folk devils, black/white, guilty/innocent, 'normal'/'sick', and so on) means that parents are not easily cast as potential paedophiles and they persist in preserving the image of the ideal family and underplaying or ignoring the fact that sexual abuse of children is more likely to occur within the family than at the hands of a stranger.

Myth 3: child sexual abuse is less pervasive within societies with strong family structures

As with all events that might be described as moral panics, the tone of much reporting of CSA implies that it is indicative of a wider malaise; specifically, in this case, yet another symptom of the breakdown of families and societies in which lower-class children are neglected by their unfit parents. The distinctly class-edged bias of much reporting is somewhat balanced by the scare stories aimed at middle-class parents who allow their children to have computers in their bedrooms, but whether it is children of dysfunctional, 'underclass' families or the offspring of middle-class parents who are too busy to supervise their children's leisure activities who are, according to journalists, more likely to become victims of pae-dophiles, the implication is that sexual abuse does not occur within cultures and communities that have strong family structures. However, this assumption is not supported by research; indeed, given the high prevalence of family abuse already discussed, it is unsurprising that familial structures which embody an allocentric group orientation and place great emphasis on religion, culture, patriarchy and age-associated status not only nurture dependency along those lines (Segal, 1999), but can also foster secrecy around socially taboo practices. The traditional family system in many areas of southern Europe is the joint and/or extended family. To take Greece as an example, citizen journalism site Spero News (http://www.spero forum.com) claims that 200 new child pornography images are posted daily, and one in seven Greek children has received an online sexual solicitation. It also reports that 35 per cent of offenders are parents, while 10 per cent are other close relatives (Spero News, 28 March 2008).

In recent years the incidence and impact of child sexual abuse have also been increasingly recognized in Asian communities, especially those originating from Pakistan, India and Bangladesh (Gilligan and Akhtar, 2005; 2006). This research has challenged suggestions that sexual abuse is only a 'Western' problem or a phenomenon which results primarily from 'the unIslamic sexual norms of the West' (Rivzi, 2000). For example, a UK clinical study of sexual abuse of Asian children examined thirty-seven cases where definite or probable sexual abuse had been referred to two hospitals in Leeds over an eight-year period (1985–93). Perpetrators were identified in sixteen of the cases; all were male; all but three were of Asian origin. The majority of the perpetrators were known to their victims: father (7), mother's partner (3), uncle (1), grandfather (1), and brother (1); three were strangers (Moghal et al., 1995). These findings reflect research conducted in countries in Asia; for example, Sahil (an organization established in 1996 in Pakistan that works exclusively on the issue of child sexual abuse and exploitation) reports that 78 per cent of abusers are known to victims (http://www.sahil.org). While it underlines similar links to those found in aboriginal communities in Australia (i.e. connections between CSA, child prostitution, drug abuse, etc.), Indian charity RAHI highlights that sexual abuse also occurs in middle-class families (http://www.rahifoundation.org). Dealing specifically with female victims of incest, RAHI reports that 2 per cent of victims were abused when they were under 4 years, 17 per cent when under 8 years, 28 per cent aged 8–12 years, 35 per cent aged 12–16 years and 15 per cent when over 16 years (RAHI, 1999). A point that all these organizations make is that in many Asian communities (including those based in the UK) the 'taboo' or 'hidden' nature of the issue is even more salient than in other communities; indeed not only is there a general unwillingness to discuss CSA and an absence of understanding, but there is also a lack of appropriate vocabulary in Asian languages. 'Sexual abuse' remains a concept, constructed through (predominantly English) academic, professional and clinical discourses and explored through the experiences of white children in North America, Western Europe and Australasia.

Paedophilia also occurs in close community environments which support (albeit sometimes unorthodox) family structures such as religious or pseudo-religious organizations and cults. Not only do established religions such as the Catholic Church provide abusers with the authority to cover up their activities and protect them from public exposure, but non-traditional religions and cults have also frequently involved sexual abuse of children. There are numerous examples of paedophile cult leaders who invent theological justifications for their sexual desires, including Dwight York, leader of a cult called the United Nuwaubian Nation of Moors, who was convicted of 197 offences in Georgia in 2002, including the sexual molestation of thirteen children aged between 4 and 14 (Wilson, 2000). In recent years, the most infamous cult leader was probably David Koresh, founder of the Branch Davidian cult in Waco, Texas. Rumours about Koresh's alleged practice of having sex with girls as young as 12 and 'wives' in their mid-teens were used as partial justification for an official raid on the cult's headquarters which led to a 51-day standoff and, ultimately, the deaths of Koresh and seventy-five of his followers when federal agents stormed the building in what the media commonly refer to as the 'Waco massacre' (http://www.independent.co.uk/news/uk/waco-massacre-victims-buried-1503476.html).

Myth 4: paedophilia is an individual pathology

Given the examples of privatization of leisure and social retreat already discussed, it follows that forms of social discourse and interaction have also changed. Adventure is for many children now a virtual pleasure; competitiveness is honed at the games console rather than on the sports field; and sexual development occurs in chat rooms, on social networking sites and via mobile phones. In the UK, police report that children as young as 10 are posing as predatory 'paedophiles' on Internet networking sites to frighten other children they have fallen out with (*The Guardian*, 10 April 2008), and there have been numerous reported cases of sexual assaults by school-aged children which have been filmed and distributed via mobile phones. It is impossible to assess to what extent these cases are isolated or atypical but their very existence counters the dominant understanding of offender behaviour from clinical psychology, which suggests a model of Internet use as an illness or pathology and relegates it to an extreme end of a continuum of behaviour (Taylor and Quayle, 2003). In fact, research from clinical psychology has over-whelmingly found that offenders (both of child pornography offences and groom-ing and contact offences) are in most respects a diverse and heterogeneous group (Wolak et al., 2005).

By routinely attaching emotive and derogatory labels to offenders, the media reinforce the belief that paedophiles are a separate species, a breed apart, and the agenda on child protection is still largely dominated by a view of the child sex offender that is laden with very specific ideas and assumptions. Thus, even though the scale of abuse perpetrated on an institutional scale by priests, teachers, local authority employed carers, police officers and other 'upstanding' members of the community has, in recent years, had to be acknowledged by the media and other social institutions, it is muted in comparison to the coverage given to individuals who fit the archetype of the 'dirty old man' or social misfit. For example, news reports linking individuals to the disappearance of 4-year-old British girl, Madeleine McCann from a Portuguese holiday resort have described suspects in terms which underline the inherent tendency of the UK press to fall back on xenophobic stereotypes linking heinous crimes to 'outsiders' or 'others'. *The Telegraph* (28 January 2008) carried a photograph of a 'Spanish loner' who, with 'his thick moustache, dark, straggly hair and protruding teeth', admits 'he resembles a sketch of a "scruffy" suspect' wanted for questioning. Another sus-pect, described by witnesses as a 'very ugly' man with 'pitted skin and a large nose' (*The Independent*, 7 May 2009), was identified by tabloids as a 'convicted paedophile' who led a nomadic existence and had a 'desperate hand-to-mouth lifestyle' (*Daily Record*, 22 May 2009).

Research also indicates that a small but significant number of offenders are women, adolescents and children (including children who have themselves been abused), although it is impossible to estimate with any accuracy the numbers involved, due partly to the probable under-reporting (to police) of female-perpetrated and child-on-child offences (Taylor and Quayle, 2003). CSA crimes perpetrated by women pose a dilemma for the popular media as they run counter to the dominant 'dirty old man' stereotype. So, in line with reporting of serious crimes by women more generally, it is the offences which most undermine the press's dominant conservative moral ideology, and the offenders who can most easily be ridiculed and demonized, that come to occupy a particularly symbolic place in the collective psyche. For example, reports of the arrest of Plymouth nursery worker Vanessa George, charged in June 2009 with four counts of sexually assaulting children, and three of making, possessing and distributing indecent images of children, appeared to tap into, and magnify, deepseated public fears about deviant women (Jewkes, 2010). The press portrayed her as an overweight, sexually voracious monster who neglected her family and craved the attention of her co-accused, Colin Blanchard, who called her 'Daddy's little princess' (*The Times*, 16 December 2009). She received an indefinite prison sentence and was told by the judge that she may never be released. At the same time, the press reported another case of a woman charged with sexual activity with a minor in ways which also supported their dominant news values, yet offered support and sympathy to the woman in question. Helen Goddard was a 26-year-old public school music teacher who pleaded guilty to six charges of sexual activity with a 15-year-old pupil in August 2009. According to the *Daily Mail* (22 August 2009) the teacher 'looked like a teenager' and was a 'devout Christian with a glittering career ahead of her' as an 'exceptionally gifted musician'. The 'victim', meanwhile, was not only a willing and complicit partner who expressed her wish to continue the relationship when she reached 16, but had the support of her parents in doing so. The story was constructed, then, as one which, in many senses, *upholds* a conservative moral ideology. As the *Mail* put it: 'Her best hope is that she is treated, not as a paedophile, but as someone who has made an inexcusably stupid mistake' (22 August 2009).

The media's characterization of paedophilia as an individual pathology, and their construction of abusers as sub-human, abnormal and not of society, sits uncomfortably within a culture which, in other arenas (such as fashion, beauty and art) fetishizes youthful bodies. Fashion for adult women is perennially suggestive of a sexual construction of childhood. For example, some of the spring/summer 2004 collections created by the fashion houses of Paris and Milan were explicitly themed around Nabokov's novel *Lolita*, the story of a middle-aged man's quest to seduce a 12-year-old-girl. Commenting on the designs of John Galliano, one newspaper summed up the 'look' under the headline, 'Lolita knocks our socks off again': 'This designer's models came down the catwalk in quite the most fluffy baby-doll dresses the world has ever seen. These were paired with bright white bobby socks . . . and matching silk Mary-Jane shoes' (*The Independent*, Review section, 22 April 2004: 14, cited in Greer and Jewkes, 2005). Women in the pop music industry (and their management teams) are similarly cognizant of the fact that connotations of prepubescent sex sell. In the Spice Girls' heyday, 'Baby Spice' Emma Bunton was regularly photographed in baby-doll dresses, white socks or stockings, and with a lollipop in her mouth, while Britney Spears' first global chart-topper combined dubious lyrics ('hit me baby one more time') with a provocative dance routine by the 17-year-old dressed in school uniform. A similar, overtly sexual schoolgirl look was adopted by members of pop group Girls Aloud when they appeared in a 2007 re-make of the film *St Trinian's*.

Just as adult women are frequently persuaded by the fashion and music industries to dress like children and adolescents, so children are frequently, and, many argue, inappropriately, encouraged to look and behave like adults. The sexualization of children by commercial outfits, or 'corporate paedophilia' as it has been termed (Rush and La Nauze, 2006), is pervasive in Western nations where images of partially clothed children imitating adults and adults emulating children are routinely used to sell products and aspirations. An image promoting Armani's Junior range of children's clothes in 2004, sparked seventy-four complaints to the Advertising Standards Authority (ASA) on the grounds that it sexualized a child, encouraged the adoption of adult poses and made the model's gender ambiguous (*The Independent*, 12 May 2004). The advert was withdrawn before the ASA made its decision but, in another case the ASA ruled that images in the catalogues of clothing company Jack Wills (a brand aimed at 18- to 24-year-olds, according to the company, and therefore very likely to appeal to lower age groups) were neither offensive nor overtly sexual. The images, which might justifiably be described as soft pornography, included one of a young-looking girl lying on a bed wearing only knickers and with one of her breasts visible (http://news.bbc.co.uk/1/hi/england/devon/8069531.stm).

In 2010 the sexualization of children became a political issue. Following the publication of a Labour government 'fact-finding review' led by TV psychologist Dr Linda Papadopoulos, which uncovered a contradictory and inconclusive picture (though was reported by the media in typically hyperbolic style), the Conservative party leader announced in January that it was inappropriate for children to be treated like adults, and promised that, if brought to power, he would pass laws outlawing 'premature sexualization' and 'excessive commercialization' targeted at young people. True to his word, when elected prime minister, David Cameron commissioned another review paving the way for new laws to be put in place to allow companies who issue adverts, images or clothing sexualizing children to be prosecuted. This move followed media reports of a number of high-profile retail outlets selling goods that were aimed precisely at sexualizing children. For example, in February 2009, the Chief Executive of Consumer Focus, a watchdog organization, reported that he had successfully lobbied for the withdrawal of Playboy-themed merchandise for schoolgirls from the shelves of high-street retailer WH Smith, but remained concerned that T-shirts with slogans such as 'sex kitten' and 'flirt!' were still being marketed to girls as young as 6 (*Daily Mail*, 10 February 2009).

Similar causes for concern included a Bratz doll with heavy make-up, a short skirt and stockings, aimed at children as young as 5; a pink and black lingerie set, including push-up bra aimed at girls from age 9 and sold by Asda; and T-shirts sold by the clothes chain Next to girls from age 6 with slogans such as 'So many boys, so little time'. In April 2010, David Cameron, branded as 'disgraceful' the decision by retail giant Primark to sell padded bikinis to girls aged 7 and 8, a product which was subsequently withdrawn from stores (*The Telegraph*, 15 April 2010). Perhaps most blatantly symptomatic of the premature sexualization and commodification of little girls' bodies, however, was the '£50 pole-dancing kit' being sold in the toy department of the biggest UK retailer Tesco which was marketed with the caption: 'Unleash the sex kitten inside . . . extend the Peekaboo pole inside the tube, slip on the sexy tunes and away you go! Soon you'll be flaunting it to the world and earning a fortune in Peekaboo Dance Dollars' (*Daily Mail*, 24 October 2006). The kit – eventually withdrawn by Tesco in the face of public condemnation and political pressure – comprised a chrome pole extendible to 8ft 6in, a 'sexy dance garter' and a DVD demonstrating suggestive dance moves.

However, despite the fact that the Prime Minister may have genuine concerns (not least because he is the father of three young children), not everyone is happy that the government has intervened in this issue. Describing Cameron's campaign – backed by influential Internet forum Mumsnet – as a 'curious synthesis of feminist concerns with more traditional moral panic', an editorial in *The Guardian* (26 February 2010) says that a more precise definition of 'sexualization' needs to be determined and then a link established between sexualization and other social problems such as poor academic achievement and eating disorders (http://www. guardian.co.uk/commentisfree/2010/feb/26/sexualisation-children-parental-guidance-editorial). In the meantime, mediated public opinion seems to be divided between those who would rather see commercial companies and retail stores voluntarily take a stance and parents exercise free choice when buying goods for their offspring, and those who support the introduction of legislation and feel that parents need this kind of help from governments. Interestingly, the same *Guardian* editorial notes that research undertaken for a Scottish parliament inquiry found that it is predominantly parents, not children, who are concerned and that it is the sexualization not of their own but of other people's children that worries them. This may be because there remains a persistent belief that allowing young people free access to the net equates to bad parenting; as a headline in the *Telegraph* (12 November 2009) stated, the 'Internet [is] "as dangerous as letting children go out into the street", according to Professor Tanya Byron'. Meanwhile, children themselves, interviewed for the same research, were found to be media savvy from a young age and far more likely to be influenced by peer pressure than the Internet (ibid).

Myth 5: children are 'innocent' victims

The fact that the companies manufacturing the products and pop stars described above have identified a market for them further underlines the confusion over children's sexual awareness and sexuality. Moreover, as adults we may be guilty of over-protecting children and adopting a somewhat hypocritical attitude, given that many of us will have memories of ourselves as youths that counter our ideals of children as precious innocents, protected from the sordid and the spoiled. No wonder that out of such incongruities, when children commit sexual offences, or knowingly expose themselves to risk of victimization of sexual offences, or simply assert their sexual agency, a deep and pervasive cultural unease is borne.

Ironically, for children and young adults, denied many of the freedoms enjoyed by their parents and grandparents in their own youth, the Internet as a form of social retreat provides certain freedoms – freedom of thought, freedom of expression, freedom to present an identity or indeed a multitude of identities, a *freedom of being* – quite unlike anything they have at their disposal in the physical world. Part of this freedom indisputably concerns sexual freedom. In cyberspace identity is not fixed but is an ephemeral, fluid entity, open to constant negotiation, change and manipulation. Disentanglement from the body allows the self to break free from the usual constraints of corporeality which, in the physical world, may prevent individuals from displaying aspects of their identities that would be discredited or disapproved of by others (Jewkes and Sharp, 2003). This may be regarded as a positive characteristic of cyberspace: it liberates people from the shackles that bind them in the physical world. But at the same time, it may encourage users, including children and young people, to put themselves at risk of victimization and engage in more 'extreme' behaviours than they would in the 'real' world. For example, Kent police report that predatory adults are taking advantage of the willingness of young people to experiment with their sexuality over the net by engaging in sexually explicit chat and by exposing their bodies in front of a webcam (Molloy, n.d.). In addition, 22 per cent of students report having their own webcam (ibid.).

A related phenomenon is 'sexting', where an individual sends nude or suggestive photos of themselves over their mobile phone. This new application of technology came to public attention in 2008, when 18-year-old Jessica Logan committed suicide following months of taunting and bullying after nude images of herself that she had sent to her boyfriend were circulated, first across her Cincinnati high school and subsequently far beyond. In the United States, a survey carried out by the National Campaign to Prevent Teen and Unplanned Pregnancy (2009) found that one in five teenagers had sent or posted online nude or semi-nude pictures of themselves and 39 per cent had sent or posted sexually suggestive messages. So widely reported has 'sexting' since become (including stories of young celebrities who have found their 'private' photos posted online) that Australia's state government of New South Wales launched an education campaign in May 2009 to try to educate young people about the dangers of the practice and warn them of the consequences which can include bullying, harassment, sexual assault and, in the case of Jessica Logan, suicide.

The apparent willingness of children to take risks with their online activities, in part because of the restrictions imposed on their outdoor freedoms, is highlighted with alarming frequency in the popular media. Psychologist and *Times* columnist Tanya Byron was asked for help by a reader in a letter that began:

> For the past two years my 14-year-old daughter has been using the Internet to communicate with men in an illicitly sexual fashion. When this first came to my attention I got the police involved. They spoke to my daughter about the dangers and left it at that. She is now not allowed on the computer unless I am present. Earlier this year she bought herself an Internet-enabled mobile phone from which she has access to instant messaging. I recently caught her having the same type of conversation again.
>
> (http://women.timesonline.co.uk/tol/life_and_style/
> women/families/article5547354.ece)

In another case, police investigating a sexual assault on a 13-year-old girl in Nuneaton said they were exploring whether there was a connection between the attack and the fact that she described herself on her webpage as a 'Bebo whore' (*Sunday Mercury*, 14 April 2008).

Of course, children have always bullied, and their sexual experimentation has always, on occasion, had a dark side. Perhaps social networking sites and mobile phones simply offer a new means and a new lexicon with which to explore their identities, including their psycho-socio-sexual make-up, and exert power over their peers. The *Sunday Mercury* article perceptively notes that, for young people, the virtual realm represents a space for teenage rebellion: 'children see MySpace literally as their own space away from parents' (*Sunday Mercury*, 14 April 2008). Despite the age restrictions imposed on social networking sites (Bebo and Facebook state that users must be 13 or older, while MySpace users must be 14 years old) many children simply lie about their age to gain access and girls, in particular, use the net to flaunt their emerging sexuality:

> A trawl of social network sites revealed the shocking, highly personal content youngsters are uploading for all to see. They include a 15 year-old girl whose profile picture, which can be viewed by anyone, focuses on her breasts. Another 15 year-old is pictured sitting provocatively, exposing her breasts and bare legs up to her thigh. And we found one 16 year-old girl who is seen posing in her underwear in dozens of photographs.
>
> (*Sunday Mercury*, 14 April 2008)

The pervasiveness of images of young women asserting their sexual agency on networking sites and on YouTube may be unsettling but it is arguable that they are simply using a new channel to express what is essentially 'normal' adolescent behaviour, especially in a culture which increasingly attaches less stigma to nudity, confessional and explicit material in published diaries and blogs, and open displays of sexuality.

Of course, the inherent properties of the Internet – its anonymity, immediacy and global reach – make it a rather different prospect from, for example, writing to a penfriend, but perhaps it is not quite as novel, unusual or exploitative as media reporting sometimes suggests. What we can confidently state is that victimization is not as random as the media would have us believe. In 2009 police in the UK appealed for sightings of a 15-year-old girl from the north of England who had disappeared with a 49-year-old man with whom she had been communicating on Facebook for six months. The couple were tracked down by police in France and the offender, Robert Williams, admitted having sex with the victim and another girl aged 16. Williams was arrested, convicted and sentenced to five years' imprisonment. This case was simply the latest in a long line of high-profile examples of girls disappearing 'on holiday' or going away to 'start a new life' with older men they had met in chat rooms, including the 12-year-old who disappeared to Europe with a 31-year-old American marine in 2003 and, in the same year, the 14-year-old who went on holiday with a 46-year-old 'family friend'. That there may be common risk factors is underlined by the fact that the girls in these cases were routinely described in court and by the media as 'vulnerable', 'naïve', 'besotted', 'depressed' and 'lacking confidence' (*BBC News*, 11 June 2009). The fact that they were all under the age of consent makes the media construction of them as victims understandable. Nonetheless, there has been little media discussion of the fact that they were all willing partners who left their families under no coercion. For Finkelhor (2009), these are not generally violent sex crimes but are criminal seductions that take advantage of common teenage vulnerabilities and should be characterized as statutory rape. In 73 per cent of cases the victim meets the offender on multiple occasions for sexual encounters and in around half of the cases investigators describe the victim as being in love with or experiencing a close friendship with the offender (ibid.) But the complex issues of morality that underpin such offences (what do the male perpetrators offer these girls that was otherwise missing from their lives? How would these cases be treated in countries where the age of consent for girls is lower?) tends to be elided in favour of the simple explanation that they were the passive victims of male manipulators who tricked them into leaving the safety of their loving families (Jewkes, 2010).

Concluding thoughts

Concerns about the potential of the Internet for crimes such as identity theft and terrorism have also increased noticeably in recent years, but it is sex, technology and crimes against children that have become particularly entwined in media accounts. This chapter has highlighted several impacts arising from the mixed attitudes surrounding both (late) modern childhood sexuality and the ubiquity of the Internet and social networking sites, including concerns about policy and legal discourses which imply a loss of parental control and a shift of political and public concerns away from 'real world' crimes against children to those that occur in virtual space. The chapter has interrogated the cultural hypocrisy surrounding attitudes to children and has discussed five common myths regarding computer-facilitated child sexual abuse.

The chapter has also demonstrated that the focus on Internet safety masks the reality that children are, and always have been, in more danger from those close to them than from strangers. 'Ordinary' abuse challenges consensual ideas of the family, fathers, male heterosexuality and childhood (Wykes and Welsh, 2009) and is therefore not commonly reported by the media, which continues to peddle the myth that danger resides in 'others' and strikes randomly. The media's recon-struction of the child sexual abuser from the stranger in dangerous places to the cyber-paedophile in virtual space has multiple outcomes. It makes the topic less uncomfortable as it feeds into a familiar stereotype and enables the public to disassociate themselves from the individual described, while simultaneously maintaining the horror of the unknown predator (Ashenden, 2002). It therefore also avoids any real risk to the essential structures of society. Those who look for alternative explanations are silenced or condemned as wet liberals seeking to make excuses for the worst examples of human depravity. Not only does this close down further aetiological inquiry, but it also allows the community to remain intact emotionally and physically. The reluctance on the part of journalists, and the wider public for whom they write, to acknowledge the reality of abuse by men or women within the family – which accounts for more incidents and is arguably more damaging in the long term than assaults by strangers – reflects a powerful emotional and intellectual block. Incest is, quite simply, 'a crime too far' (Greer, 2003: 188).

At one and the same time, then, moral panics over the paedophile and the Internet have perpetuated the notion that attraction to children, even within a culture that celebrates and fetishizes youthful bodies, is a sexual perversion that resides in strangers and is facilitated by new communications technologies. But have our fears of crime and concerns for personal safety – especially the safety of our children – been exaggerated and exacerbated by media hyperbole? And are the consequences of society's fears detrimental to the late-modern experience of childhood?

Notes

1   Throughout this chapter the terms 'paedophile' and 'paedophilia' are used because of their popular, cultural currency in the media and more generally. It is acknowledged, however, that in clinical usage the terms are used differently. The American Psychological Association (APA) *Diagnostic and Statistical Manual of Mental Disorders* (4th edn) defines paedophilia as an erotic preference for prepubescent children – that is, those under 11 years of age. In common currency 'paedophile' refers to adults who are sexually attracted to children of any age, including pubescents of 12 years or older. In psychology these individuals are more accurately described as 'hebephiles' (Blanchard et al., 2009). A further point worth making at the outset is that, while the popular press frequently refers to offenders as 'convicted paedophiles', no such offence exists in law.
2   At the time of writing, a similar scheme in the UK – known as 'Sarah's Law', following the sexually motivated murder of 8-year-old Sarah Payne by convicted paedophile Roy Whiting in 2000 – is being rolled out nationally after being trialled in four police forces.
3   Glitter returned to the UK after his release from a Vietnamese jail in 2008, having served a three-year sentence for actual sexual offences against young girls.

References

Ashenden, S. (2002). Policing perversion: The contemporary governance of paedophilia. *Cultural Values, 6*(1&2): 197–222.

ChildLine (2002). How common is child abuse?, available online at http://www.childline. org.uk/Howcommonischildabuse.asp.

Critcher, C. (2002). Media, government and moral panic: The politics of paedophilia in Britain 2000–1. *Journalism Studies, 3*(4): 521–35.

Cullen, D. (2003). Typical child porn user is white male IT pro. *The Register*, 22 October, available online at http://www.theregister.co.uk/2003/10/22/typical_child_porn_user/.

Finkelhor D. (2009). Future of children, available online at http://www.futureofchildren.org/ futureofchildren/index.xml.

Gilligan, P. and Akhtar, S. (2005). Child sexual abuse among Asian communities: Developing materials to raise awareness in Bradford. *Practice, 17*(4): 267–84.

—— (2006). Cultural barriers to the disclosure of child sexual abuse in Asian communities. *British Journal of Social Work, 36*, 1361–77.

Greer, C. (2003). *Sex Crime and the Media: Sex Offending and the Press in a Divided Society*. Cullompton: Willan.

Greer, C. and Jewkes, Y. (2005). Images and processes of social exclusion. *Social Justice* special edition, *32*(1). 20–31.

Grubin D. (1998). *Sex Offending against Children: Understanding the Risk*. Police Research series paper 99. London: Home Office.

Haste, H. (2005). Joined-up texting: Mobile phones and young people. *Young Consumers: Insight and Ideas for Responsible Marketers, 6*(3), 56–67.

Jackson, L.A. (2000). *Child Sexual Abuse in Victorian England*. London: Routledge.

Jewkes, Y. (2010). *Media and Crime*. 2nd edn. London: Sage.

Jewkes, Y. and Sharp, K. (2003). Crime, deviance and the disembodied self: Transcending the dangers of corporeality. In Y. Jewkes (ed.). *Dot.cons: Criminal and Deviant Identities on the Internet*. Cullompton: Willan.

Kitzinger, J. (1996). Media constructions of sexual abuse risks. *Child Abuse Review, 5*(5), 319–33.

Moghal, N.E., Nota, I.K. and Hobbs, C.J. (1995). A study of sexual abuse in an Asian community. *Archives of Disease in Childhood, 72*, 346–47.

Molloy, J. (n.d.). Internet or 'cyber' bullying, available at http://www.clusterweb.org.uk/UserFiles/CW/File/Childrens_Services/Safe_Schools/ab_john.pdf.

Mort, F. (2000). *Dangerous Sexualities: Medico-Moral Politics in England Since 1830*. London: Routledge.

Pearsall, R. (1993). *The Worm in the Bud: the World of Victorian Sexuality*. London: Pimlico.

Quayle, E. (2010). Child pornography. In Y. Jewkes and M. Yar (eds), *Handbook of Internet Crime*. Cullompton: Willan.

RAHI (1999). *The RAHI Findings: Voices from the Silent Zone: Women's Experiences of Incest and Childhood Sexual Abuse*. New Delhi: RAHI.

Rivzi, S.M. (2000). *Marriage and Morals in Islam*. Scarborough, ON: Islamic Education and Information Centre.

Rush, E. and La Nauze, A. (2006). *Corporate Paedophilia: Sexualisation of Children in Australia*. Canberra: The Australia Institute.

Segal, U.A. (1999). Family violence: A focus on India. *Aggression and Violent Behaviour, 4*(2): 213–31.

Smillie-Adjarkwa, C. (2005). Is the Internet a useful resource for indigenous women living in remote communities in Canada, Australia and New Zealand to access health resources?, research paper, available online at http://research.arts.yorku.ca/nhnf/DigitalDivide.pdf.

Sweet, M. (2001). *Inventing the Victorians*. London: Faber & Faber.

Taylor, M. and Quayle, E. (2003). *Child Pornography: An Internet Crime*. Hove: Brunner Routledge.

Thomas, T. (2005). *Sex Crime: Sex Offending and Society*. 2nd edn. Cullompton: Willan.

Wilson, C. (2000). *The Devil's Party: A History of Charlatan Messiahs*. London: Virgin.

Wolak, J., Finkelhor, D. and Mitchell, K.J. (2005). Child pornography possessors arrested in Internet-related crimes: findings from the National Juvenile Online Victimization study, available online at http://www.nsvrc.org/publications/reports/child-pornography-possessors-arrested-internet-related-crimes-findings-national. Washington, DC: Centre for Missing and Exploited Children.

—— (2009). Trends in arrests of online predators. Crimes Against Children Research Center, available online at http://www.unh.edu/ccrc/pdf/cv194.pdf.

Wykes, M. and Welsh, K. (2009). *Violence, Gender and Justice*. London: Sage.

8 Sexual behaviour, adolescents and problematic content

Lars Lööf, Council of the Baltic Sea States, Expert Group for Cooperation on Children at Risk

Overview

We need a de-dramatized view of nudity and sexuality – regardless if it has to do with texts, images, cartoons or films especially in our common social networking sites. Young people's relationship with their body and with their sexuality otherwise risk becoming even more filled with pressure and hang-ups. Ignorance around sexuality will grow. Without a permitting and open discussion about sexuality it will be harder for a young person to recognize and acknowledge boundaries around what feels like OK sex and what constitutes submission to something that shouldn't have happened.

(Lindquist and Hemlin in the Swedish daily newspaper, *Svenska Dagbladet*, 15 January 2011. Translated by author)[1]

Children and young people up to the age of 18 have a special inherent right to protection from sexual abuse, sexual exploitation and violence. The age span is challenging, however. A child can be a person of 3 years of age and a young woman of 17, which has repercussions on the protection of children in the online world as well as in the offline world.

Which online behaviours constitute risk behaviours, and which behaviours will further the interest in and access to child abusive material via information and communication technologies? If behaviours that we categorize as risk behaviours are common behaviours online and not associated with harm, are they to be considered risk behaviours? If exchange of self-generated nude images between young people is a common phenomenon, how can this best be understood and how can young people best be approached regarding real dangers online and regarding abusive and exploitative behaviours they themselves may be involved in?

We need to recognize that young people will always be creators of their own contexts and will as far as possible adapt the way they interact with peers, adults and new acquaintances to the opportunities they see in a way that will enhance their feeling of competence and ability to master their lives. This makes it necessary for us all to be careful not to categorize all online exchanges around sexual matters with a young person involved as illegal or as risk taking. Should consensual access to sexual texts, images, and films and exchanging them with another youth be considered problematic or is it to be seen as a young person's private sphere? Should consensually produced sexual materials exchanged between young people who have reached the age of sexual consent be left alone?

In most countries the age of sexual consent, i.e. when a young person is considered old enough to make informed decisions about sexual relations, is between 13 and 18.[2] The age of being able to consent to sex has at times been compounded with the age at which you can consent to becoming involved in acts that are sexually exploitative such as selling sex or performing in sex shows. In European countries there is a legal difference between these. In most countries in Europe consent to participate in sexually exploitative acts cannot be given before the age of 18.

Young people will use information and communications technology (ICT) to explore their sexuality. Such use of ICT includes accessing sites with information about sexuality; accessing semi-nude, nude or pornographic images; accessing texts written for the purpose of arousing the reader sexually; sites where you can contact other persons for online exchanges on sex; shops where you can buy products manufactured to be used in sexual situations; and sites offering films with explicit sexual content. Some young people will use ICT for having online sex where technologies are used to convey image and sound. When discussing protection of children from sexual abuse and sexual exploitation the fact that young people will also themselves be sexually active agents of their own sexuality has been disregarded. We have often discussed how to protect young people from adults with an interest in meeting minors for sex without looking at how young people themselves think about their sexuality within the ICT context.

Risks and risk-taking

A number of ICT-related activities are habitually and often uncritically placed in the category of risk-taking behaviour. Risk behaviours when using ICT have come to include the following activities (Baumgartner et al., 2010; Ungar and Medier, 2010; Livingstone et al., 2010):

- using ICT to discuss sex and sexuality;
- using ICT with the purpose of meeting someone to have sex, online or offline;
- sending nude or semi-nude images of yourself to someone you only know online;
- sending your contact details to someone you only know online;
- meeting someone offline that you have met only online.

From the stories of young people that have been abused we can see that the young people have taken some or several of the above risks. However, so many of the behaviours listed are present in the online lives of so many young people we need to go further in understanding more about the behaviours and when they actually put a young person at risk.

Late 2010 in Sweden saw the emergence of a Twitter exchange called #prataomdet,[2] (translates to #talkaboutit). In this exchange of texts, women and men of all ages contributed their experiences around sexual meetings that went wrong. All stories are not about abusive sex, the majority are about inability to express wishes and describe situations leaving the persons feeling misused and misunderstood. This kind of anonymous exchange of vignettes through Twitter messages is powerful since it doesn't shy away from complexities or ambiguities. Accessing and discussing these texts online or contributing with a text of your own is quite the contrary of risk behaviour: it should if anything be seen as protective.

Discussing sex online is an activity that has been suggested to pose a severe risk to young people. The Swedish Media Council in the recent Swedish study on children's use of media sent a questionnaire via regular mail to 1,000 children aged 12–16 years. Among these, 60 per cent responded. (Another 1,000 questionnaires were sent to children aged 9–12 and also to parents with children in the above age groups.) The survey to children aged 12–16 included questions on the use of the Internet to access pornography or if the young person had been involved in discussing sexual matters online. Among the 12–16-year-olds, 29 per cent reported having discussed sex with someone on the Internet. Half of them did so with a person they already knew and had met, and half did this with online acquaintances (Ungar and Medier, 2010). In the questionnaire, those who had discussed sex with someone on the Internet were given a follow-up question regarding the result of the discussion: 13 per cent felt the conversation was exciting, 5 per cent decided to meet the person they were talking with and 3 per cent showed themselves in webcam.

An area typically considered a risk area is when young people meet online acquaintances offline. Questions on offline meetings with online friends have been prominent in surveys of use of ICT, and the percentage of young people meeting with online friends offline has been taken as a measure of how safe a specific country's young people keep themselves. Recent estimates give a figure suggesting that around 25–30 per cent of young persons have done so (Ungar and Medier, 2010; Livingstone et al., 2010; Barn og digitala medier, 2010: Suseg et al., 2008). This then seems to be quite a common way of using ICT by young people.

Who initiated the meeting? On follow-up questions young people will often reveal that they found the meetings rewarding, fun or neutral but the invitation to the meeting remains unclear. It seems obvious that if you sometimes suggest to an online friend to meet offline, you are more likely to accept a proposal from someone else to meet offline. The recent EU Kids Online study includes a chapter on offline meetings with online acquaintances, where these meetings are discussed in a neutral way, not as equal 'putting yourself at risk'. Even so, the issue of whether the young person interviewed has ever initiated such a meeting is left unanswered (Livingstone et al., 2010).

Webcam use may in many countries mean that young people find it safer to meet someone offline that they have only previously met online. A slight increase in offline meetings of online friends can be seen in some countries (Barn og digitala medier, 2010). It may be that webcams have brought a little bit more security to such meetings. The Norwegian report hypothesizes that this has to do with the increased use of webcams. If an online friend does not show her/his face live on cam, it is possibly an established warning sign that the person is not the individual they claim to be.

The child and the young person is not only a recipient of messages and requests, but sometimes they are active communicators in their world. When a Swedish survey asked 18-year-olds if they had received requests for sexual images online, almost a fifth who received such a request said that they also did indeed send such an image (Se mig, 2009). This clearly indicates that the request for a sexual image was part of a relationship and much more reciprocal, and might not necessarily be equated with attempted online abuse.

In order to assess how risky ICT use is we have often look at the prevalence of reported online solicitations. Prevalence figures vary with the methodology used and with the age of the respondents. Reports from Nordic countries generally give higher figures for online solicitations than US surveys. There are a number of possible explanations for this, including the question wording, the mode of data collection (e.g. questionnaires, telephone interviews or face-to-face interviews), but recognizing ICT as being a legitimate place for romantic meetings may play a role in how the young person reports solicitations and attempts at unwanted contacts.

The Swedish Crime Prevention board's study, in which 38 per cent of the girls (18 per cent of the boys) claimed they had in the previous 12-month period been contacted online with sexual requests, is an example of this (Brottsförebyggande rådet, 2007). This study does not differentiate between wanted or unwanted requests, but the questions ask the respondent if they think that an adult initiated the request. In the study organized by the Youth Council in 2009, 48 per cent of the girls had been contacted online with sexual requests. The age group here is older, 16 to 25, and it seems that with increasing age, sexual requests become increasingly prevalent (Se mig, 2009). This is also in line with the Dutch findings where older adolescent female respondents were contacted to a high degree by persons wanting to engage them in some form of sexual interaction (Baumgartner et al., 2010).

We are left with the question unanswered of what constitutes risk behaviours. Talking online about sex seems to happen and we cannot clearly connect it to young people coming to harm. However, several reports from young people that have suffered abuse do tell us that sex talk had been one part of the process leading up to the abuse (Wagner, 2008). In the study 'Children and sexual abuse via IT' (Jonsson et al., 2009), some of the girls that had been abused speak about the way they had interacted sexually online with the men that later abused them. To the girls in the study the sequencing of the events came naturally and their story was that the online interactions had been as much their own creation as that of the perpetrator. (See Chapter 2 for a more detailed discussion of this study.)

Adolescents have been attributed with a high level of risk taking. According to cognitive theories they will weigh risks and benefits differently than adults. There also seems to be a gender difference in that boys and men tend to be greater risk takers than girls and women. Much of this has been seen as part of the adolescent story in which they think of themselves as being invulnerable and consider that nothing really bad will ever happen to them. As years pass, this story becomes less and less dominant and most adults would be seen as weighing risks and benefits in a more conservative manner than would most adolescents

A study undertaken in the Netherlands (Baumgartner et al., 2010) to examine adolescent risk behaviours and adult risk behaviours in connection with online sex, interestingly does not show differences in these. The risk behaviours studied were four behaviours that have commonly been understood to be risky. As the authors point out, however, we cannot for certain say that these behaviours put the person at special risk since they have not been validated but some have been proven to put the person at risk in studies on offline sexual behaviours. These included: (1) searching for someone online to discuss sexual matters; (2) looking for someone to have sex; (3) sending an image or video to someone; and (4) sending your address and contact details to someone.

Surprisingly, adult men continued to engage in the same level of risk behaviours as adolescent boys. It may be that the trait that lies behind risky online behaviours is quite stable and the authors consider if this shows that an interest in sex remains over the life span. Another accepted truth that the study challenges is that male adolescents are more prone to risk behaviours than female. This proved not to be the case. The authors discuss this referring to studies saying that in liberal Western societies like the Dutch, the gender gap is quickly closing regarding how young women and men experiment with and explore their sexuality. This may then be a culturally sensitive issue where cultures with a more restricted view on adolescent sexuality would score higher on gender differences in this regard (Baumgartner et al., 2010).

Coercion, peer pressure, grooming

The phenomena called 'sexting': the seemingly consensual sending and receiving of nude or semi-nude images or the sending of sexual text messages most often using mobile devices can cause severe harm. We can estimate that in countries where mobile phone penetration is high and where the phones are camera equipped, around 50 per cent of adolescents have sexted. Young people will claim they did this in order not to lose the attention of their boy/girlfriend. Others say they did it to flirt (Lenhart, 2009). If the motivation behind each sexting case were to be carefully scrutinized we would surely see that most actions fall somewhere between being consensual and being forced by circumstances where some form of perceived pressure can be discerned even in the cases where the act is carried out by informed consent. Online sex, just like offline sex for both adults and adolescents, will involve a number of sometimes difficult decisions to make and the person closest at hand when these dilemmas arise and need to be resolved is usually a part of the dilemma. The boyfriend is the one asking the girl to send him a sexy image via text, for example, and can therefore not support the girl if she is uneasy about doing so. Parents are unfortunately not often involved in discussing these expressions of sexuality and can therefore not give advice. When discussing how young people use ICT for sex, we must not shy away from the dilemmas that arise nor simplify the solutions. Young people may imagine that it is the thing to do, that they have to do it in order to stay close to someone they love or in order to maintain a position in the hierarchy of their peers. (See Chapter 1 for further discussion about 'sexting'.)

Grooming a child online with the intention of meeting the child offline for sex may similarly be placed on a continuum where some young people may feel that they are acting voluntarily. While a 35-year-old in Massachusetts who after long online contact will meet a 16-year-old and have sex would be considered an online sex offender, the same train of events in Norway would not be seen as illegal if the 16-year-old maintains that sex was consensual. The exchange online may be similar; data and chat logs would be comparable. The young Norwegian girl may well have been coerced into the relationship as well as the young American. This again underscores the need to better understand the nature of adolescent online interaction and how parts of this can be exploited by persons wanting to meet minors for sex, without stigmatizing all sexual online interactions. The majority of cases in the National Juvenile Online Victimization Study (N-JOV) studying police records with online perpetrators in the US were classified as statutory rape cases, meaning that the perpetrator and the young person were involved in voluntary sex to which the young person was not yet old enough to consent. Many of the cases reviewed in the study would not have been criminal cases at all in a European country so the conclusions on a global level may be limited (Wolak et al., 2008). The authors in the study strongly advocate for age-appropriate information to adolescents about sexual relationships and the potential pitfalls when age differences are large. Such information should not be dependent on whether or not a specific behaviour is illegal. Young people have a right to be informed about sex and about meeting people using ICT, not necessarily to avoid any sexual content or exchange, rather for them to be able to use their own judgement and make ICT safe in their own way. In order to achieve this, education and awareness initiatives need to take account of the spectrum of sexual behaviours displayed online by adolescents (Atkinson and Newton, 2010).

It has been argued that the specific quality of ICT-mediated contacts makes informed consent to different acts a contentious issue. The immediacy and intimacy coupled with the perceived anonymity of online interactions have been presumed to give online relationships a specific texture that diffuses concerns and clouds judgements that would normally guide a young person in dilemmas like the ones involved when deciding on whether or not to send a nude image or to agree to meeting for sex offline. The speed at which online relationships sometimes develop has been taken as proof for the specific character of online communication (Palmer, 2004). Several young people will also witness how they came to rely on the online relationship that they developed since the period in their life was a specifically difficult one with relationship problems at school and at home. The need to maintain the online contact became the primary concern and the sexually abusive acts the person at the other end requested were agreed to since it was the way by which the relationship could be maintained (Wagner, 2008).

Exploitation or abuse

Young people's online behaviours can be exploited. An image can be exploited if the recipient of the image sends it on to others to make money or to boost her/his status. The image in itself and the primary exchange do not necessarily constitute exploitative acts. The exploiter, in order to exploit the act, will be hierarchically superior, at least momentarily, to the person performing the act for it to be considered exploitation.

To persuade a young person under the age of 18 to send an image may be preparation for the exploitation of the young person and of the image. On the other hand, if the question is asked by a boyfriend or girlfriend and the image is only to be used by those two, then the request may and should be seen as a legitimate private exchange. This is one example showing how the same act could be viewed as an illegal act of coercion or as a voluntary consensual exchange that is a private matter. The context of the request also says something about the possible harm the young person(s) may experience. In order to assist young people to properly discuss and integrate the harms they may encounter, the same act must be seen in the different contexts in which it may appear. This highlights the need to see what is exploitation, what is abuse and how one context may be protective and one may be conducive of exploitation.

All the considerations about consent in the online world can be translated into similar contentious issues in the offline world. Some would argue that the online world does offer some form of protection that the offline world does not. The time gap is mentioned as one possibly protective aspect by Wolak et al. (2008). Other protective factors may be the geographical distance between the potential abuser and the young person that will force the abuser either to travel or take steps so that the young person can do so in order to gain access. On the other hand ICT does include a directness and an immediacy that are conducive for different forms of abusive practices that may also quickly turn into exploitation as images and films may be uploaded upon a direct request. The lack of time to think may inhibit the regular consideration of the young person. Crimes that are entirely committed without any physical contact can then be committed. Legal practice will need to adapt in order properly to be both norm setting and protective.

Young people's sexual behaviour online and their safety when using information and communication technologies

For most adolescents in affluent parts of the world life is no longer divided into online and offline. Entering into a text exchange on a mobile phone, chatting online, talking over a landline phone or being physically present in a café will impact on the experience of the conversation, the emotions they evoke, physical sensations, psychological expressions or emotional reactions, but the young person will not see them as critically appearing in different worlds. However, interacting will presumably remain qualitatively different from consuming. Watching TV or reading a book will be an experience qualitatively different from entering into a telephone conversation or participating in an online chat exchange since the content of the latter will be of the participants' own creation. The important division is not between the different platforms or technologies used for accessing information or for interaction but between if and how the platforms will allow participants to generate content and manage the context or not. ICT platforms will in parts be highly interactive and constructed as participants join in; their specific input will change the direction of the interaction in both chats and in social networking sites. Other parts of the ICT will be there only for consumption; informative websites or the accessing of images or films to watch and consume. The interactive and creative quality and flavour of many of the technology mediated contacts is likely to explain their attraction to young people.

In a convenience sample of 1,015 young people responding to questions about their consensual online sexual experiences, the most positive aspect of engaging in online sex was that you could have a relationship at a distance. Other positive aspects mentioned were that you can test what you liked sexually, that you can remain anonymous, that you do not risk sexually transmitted diseases and that it allows you to meet people you would otherwise not have met (Olsson 2010). The respondents came from a convenience sample which most likely consisted of a group that had tested webcam sex to a higher degree: around 50 per cent of the young persons had. The questionnaire that they completed also brought up the issue of making money by selling sex via webcam as one of the first issues. This may well have even more reduced the number of young people willing to respond out of fear of being considered a prostitute. Among those that were positive towards having webcam sex, the relationship to the person they had webcam sex with was important. Only a few marked the alternative that it did not matter. The absolute majority thought it to be important that they knew the person.

Emergence of self-generated content

An increasing number of young people are actively producing nude or semi-nude images of themselves. These images are used in diverse ways; some will be uploaded to a social networking site, others will be sent privately via email or as a text message on a handheld device to a chosen recipient. Inevitably, some of these images will be of young people below the age of 18, technically making them fall under the child pornography legislation in many countries. In the US and Australia, pictures have come to the attention of law enforcement considered to be child pornography. Young persons will be in possession of child abuse images of themselves, making them both the victim and the perpetrator. Self-produced images may indeed be labelled as child pornography, thus technically making the child a sex offender. The recent Council of Europe Convention on the Protection of Children against Sexual Exploitation and Sexual Abuse gives signatories the option not to criminalize the consensual production or possession of sexualized images created by children who have reached the age of sexual consent (Council of Europe, 2007). Images taken of a consensual sexual act may however be non-consensual and also be a part of possibly harassing behaviours (Powell, 2010).

We can get some understanding of young people's considerations when they post sexual images online from Nigård's interviews with young people members of an Internet-based club where adults meet to find sex partners (Se mig, 2009). Even though you must be 18 to join the club, several of the informants interviewed had indeed started to post images when they were younger.

Both in Nigård's interviews with young people that post images of themselves on sex sites, and in the study made by Niclas Olsson on young people engaging in webcam sex, the topic of self-esteem is important (Olsson 2010). Young people posting images of themselves in highly sexualized ways believe that it boosts their self-esteem. The ways in which they choose to show themselves reflect their own opinion of when they look their best. When they then receive appreciative comments regarding how fantastic they look, they experience this as highly rewarding.

The female interviewees in Nigård's study were introduced to the sexually explicit sites by friends. These sites are overtly clear about their content and openly state they are a place for people wanting to talk openly about sex. As a member you openly signal that you are interested in sharing sexual pictures of yourself and in discussing sex with others. The interviewed women all had specific views on what they felt was acceptable to show on the images they posted. For example, it was important to them not to post 'slutty' images, but pictures that would show them at an advantageous angle – artistic images showing parts of their body they were proud of. For the men it seems that pornography had been the main reason for visiting the site, not finding friends. Some of the men showed their genitals in their private folders to which they could allow access to persons they met on the site. In these highly sexualized circumstances it is interesting to note how important it is for the participants to be in control. This group of young people were well informed on how to stay in control of their images and privacy, and had seriously considered how they wanted their pictures to be accessed and what they wanted to show in them. On sites where the context is not explicitly sexual, such considerations may be less common (Se mig, 2009).

In the survey of students in their third year of further education, at approximately 18 years of age, 18 per cent reported that a person whom they only knew via the Internet had in the last twelve months asked them to send sexual images of themselves. Experiences of this kind were significantly more common among the female respondents (23 per cent) than among the male respondents (12 per cent). Of those who had been asked to send sexual images, 17 per cent stated that they had also done so. Males had done so more often than females (Se mig, 2009). When young people are surveyed about having received such requests, they are generally not asked if the request was welcomed. With neutral questions allowing for consensual exchange of images, the respondents in this study, as in others, may well have reported more frequent use of the possibilities for exchange of sexual images.

On sites where images are central, like the specific sex sites where the interviewees quoted above were active, the assumption is made that participants take control. These are communities where the image is expected to be very private in nature. Privacy settings are primary here, since giving access to a picture folder is part of the flirting and contact process. On sites built around presumably more innocent images and where sharing text and image is in focus, like Facebook or Myspace, concerns around privacy are not as frequently discussed. Taking control over the privacy settings may not seem vital when the images you place there are of your regular life.

Young people who are same-sex attracted and knowledge about online behaviours

Wolak et al., in their analysis of online-initiated sex crime cases in the US, were struck by the fact that the 25 per cent of boys who were victims were all victimized by men, and that so many of both the boys and girls who were victimized were victims of statutory rape, i.e. non-forcible sex crimes committed against a minor who had not yet reached the legal age of sexual consent in their state. The authors claim that adolescent boys who are same-sex attracted or questioning their sexuality are specifically vulnerable as they may be on sites seeking out information or contacts (Wolak et al., 2008).

The Swedish study conducted by the Swedish Youth Council in 2009 (Se mig, 2009) included a questionnaire sent out to a representative sample of 6,000 young Swedes between 16 and 25. Out of these, 2,951 were completed, corresponding to a response rate of around 50 per cent. In the questionnaire, the group of non-heterosexual young people, the gay, lesbian, bisexual, and transgender (GLBT) group differed in their experiences of a number of online actions from those defining themselves as heterosexual:

- Almost three times as many of the GLBT group had posted sexualized images or film clips online: 18.8 per cent compared to 6.8 per cent.
- Twice as many in the GLBT group had had sexualized images or film clips of themselves distributed online without their approval: 4.5 per cent vs 2.1 per cent.
- In the GLBT group half of the respondents had experienced someone on the Internet trying to persuade them into talking about sex/sending sexy images/ do things in front of the webcam against their will. In the heterosexual group this was experienced by almost a third of the respondents: 48.5 per cent vs 29.1 per cent.
- Twice as many in the GLBT group had had sex with someone offline that they first met online compared to the heterosexual group: 31.9 per cent vs 16.3 per cent.

When comparing the responses between the GLBT group and the heterosexual group we note that ICT-mediated sex is a more frequent experience in the GLBT group. Many of the behaviours that are associated with exposure to higher risks were more than twice as frequent in the GLBT group as in the heterosexual group of young people.

Suseg et al. show similar results based on their study of a representative sample of 18–19-year-olds in Norwegian secondary schools. The group that identify themselves as homosexual or bisexual receive many more aggressive solicitations in their interactions on ICT than do young people who are attracted to the opposite sex. In the group of homosexual young people 76 per cent have been asked to meet for sex, with a corresponding figure of 45 per cent for those identifying themselves as bisexual young people. As many as 37 per cent of the homosexual young people have been offered money or gifts in exchange for sex; among bisexuals this figure is 17 per cent. This compared to a mere 4 per cent of young people in the study identifying as heterosexual (Suseg et al., 2008).

Svedin and Priebe's study in cooperation with members of the GLBT youth group in Sweden looking at experiences of online sex is consistent with the above findings. Men with a homo- or bisexual identity seem to be more sexually active on the Internet; they have more consensual sex using ICT but also more frequently experience unwanted sexual solicitations. The more you use ICT for sexual purposes, the more negative experiences you will have. Anecdotal reports from discussions with young GLBT people however will emphasize that awareness of the possibilities for mutual and consensual sex using ICT makes it easier to identify attempted online harassments and abuse at an early stage.

Lesbian young women are also over-represented in the group of young people that have negative experiences of sexual harassment over ICT, even if levels of harassment and unwanted suggestions are lower than for gay young men. Interestingly, the study found that the perceived psychological and physical health of young GLBT persons who engage in consensual sex using ICT was the same as for those without experiences of webcam sex. In the group of heterosexual young persons with webcam sex experiences there was a correlation between such experiences and anxiety and depression. Heterosexual youth with experiences of webcam sex also had lower self-esteem and a lower sense of coherence than those that had no such experience (Se mig, 2009).

Exposure to pornography/accessing pornography?

Visiting sexually explicit websites today is easier than buying sexually explicit magazines forty years ago. The anonymity aspect, the cost and certainly the availability have all changed dramatically. Cooper et al. in 1999 stressed the three factors that facilitated online sexuality. He termed this the triple A engine: Accessibility, Affordability, Anonymity (Cooper et al., 1999). A wealth of research has looked at the possible harm the 'flow' of sex may have on children and young people. A number of possible harms have been suggested but strong evidential support is lacking and experts have

> concluded that, the evidence that viewing pornography harms children remains scarce, given ethical restrictions on the research, though many experts believe it to be harmful. Other vulnerable groups have been researched, however, with some evidence that the harmful effects of violent content

especially are greater for those who are already aggressive, for children with behaviour disorders, for young offenders with a history of domestic violence and – for pornographic content – among sexual offenders.

(Quayle et al., 2008)

Research has not been able to establish whether accessing sexually explicit material adversely impacts the social development of the young person. Some studies have indicated that behaviours and attitudes are indeed influenced (Lo and Wei, 2005) but it has not been possible to see how the attitudes towards the opposite sex or the views on sexuality have been affected. There is concern expressed by many researchers that the uncontrollable access to materials that the young person does not yet understand in a meaningful way will be detrimental to their psychosocial development (Kanuga and Rosenfeld, 2004) and some would argue that accessing Sexually Explicit Internet Material (SEIM) will make the adolescent view sex as a utility more than as a relation-based activity. Similarly, there are worries that viewing SEIM may increase beliefs that what you see is true to life and is a true depiction of sex. Peter and Valkenburg (2010) tested this in a group of adolescents. They found that adolescents viewing SEIM did have a higher perception of sex as a utility, and similarly that those frequently viewing SEIM would consider it more to be depicting real-life sex than infrequent users.

In the Baltic Sea Regional Study on Adolescents' Sexuality (Mossige et al., 2007) more than 20,000 young people around the age of 18 in seven different countries answered a questionnaire in which, among other issues, they were asked to report on their habits in accessing pornography Out of the 11,528 boys and girls studied more rigorously, 93 per cent of the boys claimed that they had accessed pornography of some sort, whereas the same figure for girls was 72 per cent. These relatively high figures can be compared with much more modest reports from the USA and from Asia, where several studies will only indicate a low level of voluntary access to pornographic websites. The differences between countries and cultures may well be a true difference or we may just be measuring acceptance for viewing pornography between different cultures and sub-cultures (Braun-Courville and Rojas, 2008).

In 2006 a pan-Nordic study looked at how young persons aged 12–18 accessed pornography (n = 1,776). Out of the respondents 96 per cent of the boys and 85 per cent of the girls had watched pornography, with 61 per cent of those reporting that watching porn was exciting. The study shows that most of the young people are low-level consumers of porn and an overwhelming majority watch mainstream porn, with very few indicating ever having viewed child pornography, animal porn or violent porn. It is not known if the small number who have accessed child abuse images have done so intentionally. We do know, however, that among online offenders collecting abusive images a disturbing number are under 18 (Carr, 2004).

Most of the adolescents in the study claimed it is acceptable to watch pornography and that especially the fact that young boys access porn was a given (Sørensen and Knudsen, 2006). In the Icelandic study forming a part of the report, a group of 323 adolescents aged between 14 and 18 were asked about their experiences with pornography. The average age at which young Icelandic people accessed pornography was found to be surprisingly low, 11.4 years.

Balancing the rights of the child to explore their sexuality and the right to be protected from that which might cause harm

The older an adolescent gets, the more difficult is it to balance the right to integrity, participation and information with protection. The adolescent's agency and potential for self-generated actions interfere with many protective measures. Historically, this is in no way a new situation and all adolescents have had to negotiate a level at which their integrity and their safety can be sufficiently secured. These considerations become more pertinent when discussing how older adolescents can remain safe when using ICT.

Young people will use the information and communication technologies to express themselves sexually

Knowledge of young people's experiences of self-generated content and posting of or sharing images online give us some understanding of processes underlying these activities. As always, the struggle for self-confidence is high on the agenda for adolescents and producing images for online posting seems for some to be a way of receiving appreciation and boosting self-esteem. Young people who have engaged in consensual sexual activity using technologies as a mediator are not necessarily more at risk than others for coming to harm. It may be that young people who have been active in chat rooms and in social networks steer away from unwanted contacts more easily. Language in the online world, just as in the offline world, follows specific trails and if sex is brought into the conversation in a way that is unexpected or different, then this may be easily spotted and further contact can be avoided. The same seems to be true for young people with some form of disability. When interviewed they show a high awareness of how to avoid unpleasant and unwanted contact attempts and an awareness of how to use blocking techniques (Löfgren-Mårtenson, 2005).

Safety messages should focus on contexts that may include risk, not behaviours

European youth are risk-taking but not necessarily at risk. We need to consider how the safety we envision can be made each and every young person's private safety. If staying safe means not using the technologies to socialize or meeting with people you may not yet know, then this level of safety will be refuted by the average young person and they will make do with the safety measures they themselves think fit them. It is time to take this a little further and fully acknowledge that these behaviours are not risk-taking behaviours as such. However, there are situations, contexts that are risk-prone, in which behaviours may indeed constitute a risk of severe harm.

***Discussions about sex and sexuality are increasingly important in order
to give young people the possibility to balance for themselves the
different messages they will receive***

Discussions should take place between adults and young people as well as between peers. Online platforms for such discussions should be developed and supported. Discussing how children and young people can stay safe using ICT means looking at their way of using the techniques non-judgementally. The relationship between parents and children as the latter grow older will influence both the children's behaviour as such and what the children will tell us about experiences from different contexts, including experiences from when using ICT.

If the young person's use of the Internet follows a pattern of risk behaviour, where their life in general involves taking risks and crossing boundaries, the adolescent may also get into difficult situations on the Internet. Risks appear and knowing how to deal with them is what must be the goal. Young peoples' use of ICT to explore their sexuality should be respected, as well as the age-adequate adolescent wish to be in control, the agent of your own life.

Notes

1   http://www.svd.se/kulturnoje/mer/kulturdebatt/vi-behover-oppenhet-pa-natet_5867073. svd, accessed 15 January 2011.
2   http://prataomdet.se, accessed 15 January 2011.

References

Atkinson, C. and Newton, D: (2010) Online behaviours of adolescents: Victims, perpetrators and Web 2.0. *Journal of Sexual Aggression, 16*(1), 107–20.
Barn og digitale medier (2010). Medietilsynet, Norway, available online at http://www.medietilsynet.no/no/Selvbetjening2/Horinger-og-kunngjoringer/Medietilsynets-rapport-om-barn-og-digitale-medier/.
Baumgartner, S.E., Valkenburg, P.M. and Peter, J. (2010). Unwanted online sexual solicitation and risky sexual online behavior across the lifespan. *Journal of Applied Developmental Psychology, 31*, 439–47.
Braun-Courville, D. and Rojas, M. (2009). Exposure to sexually explicit web sites and adolescent sexual attitudes and behaviors. *Journal of Adolescent Health, 45*, 156–62.
Brottsförebyggande rådet (2007). The online sexual solicitation of children by adults in Sweden. Vuxnas kontakter med barn via Internet, report no 2007: 11. Available online at http://www.bra.se/extra/faq/?module_instance=2&action=question_show&id=409&category_id=9.
Cameron, K.A., Salazarb, L.F., Bernhardtb, J.M., Burgess-Whitman, N., Wingood, G. DiClemente, R.J. (2005). Adolescents' experience with sex on the web: Results from online focus groups: *Journal of Adolescence, 28*, 535–40.
Carr, A. (2004). *Internet Traders of Child Pornography and Other Censorship Offenders in New Zealand.* Department of Internal Affairs, New Zealand.
Cooper, A., Scherer, C.R., Sylvain, C.B. and Gordon, B.L. (1999). Sexuality on the Internet: From sexual exploration to pathological expression. *Professional Psychology: Research and Practice, 30*(2), 154–64.

Council of Europe (2007). Council of Europe Convention on the Protection of Children against Sexual Exploitation and Sexual Abuse. Council of Europe Treaty Series No. 201.

Jonsson, L. Warfvinge, C. and Banck, L. (2009). *Children and Sexual Abuse via IT.* The County Council of Östergötland, Linköping.

Kanuga, M. and Rosenfeld, W.D. (2004). Adolescent sexuality and the internet: The good, the bad, and the URL. *Journal of Pediatric and Adolescent Gynecology, 17*(2), 117–24.

Lenhart, A. (2009). *Teens and Sexting. How and Why Minor Teens are Sending Sexually Suggestive Nude or Nearly Nude Images via Text Messaging.* Washington, DC: Pew Research Center.

Livingstone, S., Haddon, L., Görzig, A., Ólafsson, K. (2010). *Risks and Safety on the Internet.* EU Kids Online. London: LSE.

Lo, V.-H. and Wei, R. (2005). Exposure to Internet pornography and Taiwanese adolescents' sexual attitudes and behaviour. *Journal of Broadcasting and Electronic Media, 49*(2), 221–37.

Löfgren-Mårtenson, L. (2005). *Kärlek.nu Om Internet och unga med utvecklingsstörning.* Lund: Studenlitteratur.

Mossige, S., Ainsaar, M. and Svedin, C.G. (2007). *The Baltic Sea Regional Study on Adolescents' Sexuality.* NOVA Rapport 18/07. NOVA. Oslo.

Olsson, N. (2010). *Handlar det om val?* (Is it about Choice?). Malmö Stad: Sociala Resursförvaltningen, Kompetenscenter prostitution.

Palmer, T. (2004). *Just One Click.* London: Barnardo's.

Peter, J. and Valkenburg, P.M. (2010). Processes underlying the effects of adolescents' use of sexually explicit Internet material: The role of perceived realism. *Communication Research, 37*, 375–99.

Powell, A. (2010). Configuring consent: Emerging technologies, unauthorised sexual images and sexual assault. *The Australian and New Zealand Journal of Criminology, 43*(1), 76–90.

Quayle, E., Lööf, L. and Palmer, T. (2008). *Child Pornography and Sexual Exploitation of Children Online.* ECPAT International.

Se mig – Unga om sex och internet. (2009). Available online at http://www.ungdomssty relsen.se/ad2/user_documents/Se_mig.pdf. Stockholm: Ungdomsstyrelsen.

Sørensen, D and Knudsen, S. (2006). *Unge køn og pornografi i Norden.* Copenhagen: Nordic Council of Ministers.

Suseg, H., Grødem, A., Valset, K. and Mossige, S. (2008). *Seksuelle krenkelser via nettet – hvor stort er problemet?* Oslo: Nova.

Ungar and Medier 2010. (2010). Available online at http://www.medieradet.se/upload/ Rapporter_pdf/Ungar per cent20och per cent20medier per cent202010 per cent20 web.pdf. Stockholm: Medierådet, Stockholm.

Wagner, K. (2008) *Alexandramannen.* Västra Frölunda: Förlags AB Weinco.

Wolak, J., Finkelhor, D., Mitchell, K.J. and Ybarra, M.L. (2008). Online 'predators' and their victims. *American Psychologist, 63*(2), 111–28.

9 Risk assessment of child pornography offenders

Applications for law enforcement

Angela W. Eke, Ontario Provincial Police

Michael C. Seto, Royal Ottawa Health Care Group[1]

Overview

There is increasing public and professional concern about Internet-related sexual offending, including the use of Internet technologies to access and distribute child pornography. This concern parallels an increase in the number of child pornography cases faced by police, other criminal justice professionals, and clinicians. The key concern for many is the likelihood that someone who accesses or collects child pornography will go on to directly sexually assault a child (also referred to as 'offline' offending). This concern is paramount for professionals who are tasked with a variety of duties including investigating these offences, providing assessments of risk for bail and sentencing, correctional intake assessments and treatment planning, and creating supervision plans for offenders on a variety of forms of conditional release (e.g. bail, probation, parole). The current chapter addresses the risk to commit a future sexual offence, focusing on risk factors that could be used within law enforcement as well as other criminal justice settings. We provide an overview of risk assessment relating to sexual offenders more generally as well as the literature specifically focused on risk for contact offending among Internet sexual offenders, especially child pornography offenders. There is evidence to suggest that criminal history variables predict contact and child pornography recidivism. In addition, we examine how other variables such as characteristics relating to offender collections (e.g. gender of the children in the images) and other sexual interests may relate to the risk of future offending for both dual offenders (online as well as offline sex offenders) and online-only sex offenders. We will discuss the limitations of the current research and suggest future directions. Implications for policy and practice are also discussed.

The scope of the problem

The Internet sexual exploitation of children and youth, including the production and sharing of child pornography, occurs in myriad ways. Offenders may be in contact with children through online chat rooms and bulletin boards, as well as other communication technologies such as Internet-compatible mobile phones, text-messaging devices, webcams, and Voice over Internet Protocol (VOIP). Similar services also may be used by individuals to converse with others who support adult sex with children and justify their sexual attraction to children, often attempting to normalize child–adult sex and minimize beliefs about harm to the child (Beech et al., 2008; O'Halloran and Quayle, 2010).

The Internet has dramatically changed the way child pornography is produced and shared. Although it is not a new type of offence or one that only emerged with the advent of the Internet, child pornography offending is enabled by Internet technology such as photo-sharing sites as well as other related advances, including the relatively low-cost availability of digital cameras and scanners. In comparison to previous methods used to obtain child pornography, which often required specific knowledge and contacts to obtain the material (in the physical exchange of magazines, books, or photos and videos), the Internet provides greater access to all forms of pornography, with greater perceived anonymity and greater affordability (see Cooper, 1998; Cooper et al., 2000). In the current context of child pornography offending, not only can offenders immediately upload and share images and video they have created, they can also use webcams to stream sexual abuse content to others in real time.

Because of the widespread impacts of the Internet on pornography use and sexual behaviour, there is increasing public and professional concern about Internet-related child sexual exploitation, paralleling a rapid increase in the number of child pornography cases faced by police, other criminal justice professionals and clinicians (Bates and Metcalf, 2007; Motivans and Kyckelhahn, 2007; Wolak et al., 2009). Child pornography has been described as a global problem (McCarthy, 2010); these offences account for the greatest number of reported Internet sexual offences involving children (majority of online tips, Canadian Centre for Child Protection, 2009; most convictions, Sheldon and Howitt, 2007). The development of specialist centres – such as the Child Exploitation and Online Protection Centre in the United Kingdom, the National Child Exploitation Coordination Centre in Canada, and the National Center for Missing and Exploited Children in the United States – that coordinate, assist and support public awareness, public reporting and criminal justice responses, has contributed to the increase in charges and convictions for Internet sexual offences. But despite the increase in numbers of investigations and substantial increases in law enforcement resources, the greater worldwide access to the Internet and potential number of offenders accessing and sharing child pornography may be larger than the investigative capacity of police services and available government or private funding. In a demonstration of recently developed specialized software that can identify computers involved in the exchange of child pornography material (through the identification of internet protocol or IP addresses), thousands of such computers were identified in the Canadian province of Ontario alone (Canwest News Service, 2008). Police services in the United Kingdom are also using such software; it allows them to identify users, target the most prolific traders, and assess for evidence of users abusing children, which would make them a top priority for further investigation (Watts, 2009).

With increasing case loads, it becomes even more imperative to understand how most effectively to allocate law enforcement, other criminal justice and clinical resources. Offending can be examined on two fronts. The first is the severity of the offence; those convicted of child pornography are in part sentenced based on the type of child pornography offence(s) committed (e.g. possessing vs distributing or making illegal images) as well as the content of the child exploitation material. For example, those who possess more violent child pornography content may be sentenced more severely, as with the five-level sentencing scale used in England, modified from the COPINE scale (Taylor et al., 2001) or federal sentencing guidelines in the United States, which includes certain aspects of the material as aggravating factors (Akdeniz, 2008). When sentences were examined in a Canadian sample, offenders with multiple child pornography offences (e.g. three possession charges or charges for different types of child pornography offences such as one making and two possession charges) received significantly greater sentences such as lengthier incarceration (Eke et al., 2011). The second front is the risk posed by an individual to continue to offend; with particular interest in the risk of future violence, including contact sexual assaults against a child (also referred to as 'offline' offending), especially among offenders with no reported history of contact offending. This concern is paramount for many professionals, including law enforcement who are involved in these cases in multiple ways and for whom risk information may be important for various tasks from initial investigations to offender monitoring in the community.

The present chapter

The current chapter addresses the risk (probability or likelihood) of a charged or convicted adult male child pornography offender committing a future sexual offence, including child pornography offences, child luring (solicitation) or contact sexual offending. We focus on adult men because adult women are rarely present in child pornography offender samples (e.g. see Seigfried-Spellar and Rogers, 2010; Seto and Eke, 2005), and there is little research focusing on adolescent offenders (see Moultrie, 2006, for a description of seven adolescents convicted of possession or distribution of child abuse images). We focus on risk factors that can be assessed by professionals working within law enforcement, particularly factors that will be known or evident prior to any full clinical assessments that might occur later in the criminal justice process. Such information may also be of use to other criminal justice partners (e.g. correctional officials) and clinical professionals who subsequently deal with offenders involved in the criminal justice system. As part of this chapter, we integrate information on risk assessment relating to sexual offenders in general, as this literature informs the work on risk among child pornography offenders. We then examine the small number of studies that focus on the risk of recidivism posed by child pornography offenders and predictors of recidivism. We conclude with a discussion of the limitations of the research to date and suggest future directions for inquiry. We begin by defining some of our terms.

Definitions

While other terms have been proposed and used in the research literature, we use the common legal term *child pornography* in this chapter to refer to the possession, production (making), distribution or accessing of sexually explicit visual or auditory depictions of children.[2] Another term we sometimes use is *child exploitation images*, as we believe it reflects the exploitation of children in the production of pornographic images and can also encompass child images used by offenders for a sexual (e.g. masturbation stimulus) or other (e.g. grooming a potential victim) purpose, even those images that do not meet legal definitions of child pornography.

Some offenders commit multiple types of offence. Those who are involved with child pornography with no evidence of other offences (e.g. criminal charges) will be referred to as *online-only* offenders if they have no known *offline* (contact sexual) offences. Some of these offenders are undetected offline offenders (e.g. see Eke et al., 2011; Seto et al., 2011); however this information is often not known until post-conviction, such as during treatment. Other offenders are officially known to have committed both online and offline offences and will be referred to as *dual offenders*.

Risk assessment within law enforcement

Law enforcement routinely uses risk-based information in carrying out various duties. As the point of entry into the criminal justice system, police officers provide one of the first opportunities for risk assessment. Depending on local jurisdiction and criminal justice policies, law enforcement officers are also involved in bail applications, sentencing recommendations, offender management, offender registration, community notification and threat assessment. So there are a variety of circumstances under which police are concerned with the potential risk posed by a suspect or convicted offender. Police may need to prioritize their investigations, given the number of cases that may be open at any particular time or that may be distributed to them from coordinating centres.

Police may also require risk-related information when preparing search warrants or bail recommendations. Some law enforcement agencies provide threat assessments to assist in bail and sentencing hearings or special court order proceedings, including hearings for special conditions or legal designations to be applied to the offender (e.g. the *dangerous offender* designation in Canada). In Canada, high-risk offender units and threat analysts use formal risk assessments as part of their comprehensive assessment of released offenders to assist in creating effective management strategies, to increase compliance with release conditions and reduce recidivism.

The type and amount of risk-related information that is available to police is likely to be limited at the beginning of an investigation, when little is known about a suspect (especially those with no prior offences), as compared to the time of sentencing, when police will have obtained much more information about personal history, including suspect interviews, possible interviews with family members and others, and when clinical assessments may have been completed. In the following sections, we focus on information that we expect will be available to law enforcement officials during the course of their investigations, without requiring clinical professional input.

Risk assessment of child pornography offenders

Based on several decades of research on risk factors for recidivism among contact (offline) sexual offenders, meta-analytic reviews have identified a variety of risk factors that may also be of relevance with online or child pornography offenders (Hanson and Bussière, 1998; Hanson and Morton-Bourgon, 2005). The risk domains for adult male contact sexual offenders are summarized by Hanson and Babchishin (2009) and include the following: young offender age, sexual deviance, antisocial orientation, problems with secure adult attachment, and negative social influences. Individual risk factors can be organized under each of these domains; for example, sexual deviance includes having male child victims, being sexually preoccupied, having a sexual preference for prepubescent children (paedophilia), and being sexually aroused by depictions of sexual violence. Some of these factors have now been examined in research with child pornography offenders, with much of the initial work focusing on sexual deviance; we discuss this domain first.

There is evidence that many child pornography offenders are sexually aroused by the child pornography content they access. This evidence includes self-admissions: when interviewed by police, one-third to one-half of child pornography offenders admitted they were sexually interested in children or in viewing child pornography (Eke and Seto, 2011; Seto et al., 2010). One study showed that, when asked, half admitted to masturbating to child pornography (Webb et al., 2007) and another study found that a majority showed greater sexual arousal to children than to adults when assessed in the laboratory (phallometric assessment; Seto et al., 2006). Indeed, a recent meta-analysis by Babchishin et al. (2011) found that Internet offenders (mostly child pornography offenders) scored higher on measures of sexual deviance than contact sexual offenders in the three studies that compared them on relevant measures. Child pornography use is being considered for use as a diagnostic consideration for paedophilia in the next version of the *Diagnostic and Statistical Manual of Mental Disorders* (see Seto, 2010).

Given that many child pornography offenders are likely to be sexually interested in children, it is understandable that there is concern about the likelihood that child pornography offenders will act upon these interests by sexually offending against children directly. Among contact sexual offenders, indicators of paedophilia such as sexual arousal to children in the laboratory are significant predictors of sexual recidivism (Hanson and Bussière, 1998; Hanson and Morton-Bourgon, 2005). However, not all individuals with paedophilia will sexually offend against children, and not all sexual offenders against children are paedophiles (see Seto, 2008). This indicates that other factors in addition to sexual interest in children contribute to the likelihood of directly offending against children. Referring back to risk factors relevant for offline offenders, both theory and empirical evidence suggest that indicators of *antisociality*, such as criminal history, substance abuse, and antisocial attitudes and beliefs are important (Hanson and Morton-Bourgon, 2005; Seto, 2008).

Drawing on extensive knowledge about these two major dimensions of risk – *sexual deviance* and *antisociality* – a number of risk measures have been developed and validated for adult male contact sexual offenders. For example, the Static-99 consists of ten items related to these two dimensions (Hanson and Thornton, 2000): offender age upon release from custody or anticipated opportunity to re-offend in the community; number of prior charges or convictions for sexual offences; number of prior sentencing dates; any non-sexually violent offences concurrent to the index sexual offence; ever married or lived common-law for two or more years; any stranger victims; any male victims; any unrelated victims. This measure is currently the most cross-validated of existing sexual offender risk measures by independent research teams, and has a good degree of accuracy in predicting sexual recidivism.

We do not yet know, however, whether these established risk measures are valid for child pornography offenders, although there is some emerging research (to be discussed later) that some factors on these measures apply to this population as well. To address this question, several other questions need to be addressed: (1) How many child pornography offenders have no history of contact sexual offending? Those who already are known to have committed contact sexual offences can be assessed using established measures such as the Static-99. (2) How similar or different are child pornography offenders from contact sexual offenders? Evidence that the two groups are highly similar, especially on risk-relevant characteristics (e.g. sexual preoccupation, impulsivity), would support the application of existing risk measures to child pornography offenders. (3) What are the risk factors for sexual recidivism among child pornography offenders? Evidence that recidivism risk factors are similar to those identified in the contact sexual offender research, and with similar predictive relationships, would again support the generalization of existing risk measures. If factors specific to child pornography offending (e.g. based on the content of images accessed or other online behaviour such as communicating with minors) are identified as predictive of future sexual offending among online offenders, this would support the potential modification of existing measures (e.g. the addition of relevant child pornography related factors) or the development of a new, offence-specific measure. In the following sections, we address each of these three more fundamental questions.

Contact offending histories

Seto and colleagues (2011) conducted a meta-analysis of twenty-one samples of online offenders regarding their contact sexual offending histories; the majority of samples were of child pornography only offenders, with luring offenders comprising a small minority of the remaining samples where the composition of the groups was known. Approximately one in eight online offenders had an officially known history of contact sexual offending. One of the studies included in this meta-analysis was a sample of 541 convicted child pornography offenders that we conducted (Eke et al., 2011); when criminal history and offending concurrent to the child pornography offence was examined, 30 per cent of offenders had an officially documented contact sex offence against a child. In the subset of six samples where self-reported data were available in Seto et al.'s meta-analysis, approximately half of the online offenders acknowledged having committed a contact sexual offence.

Two of these six studies included information gathered after a polygraph: 39 per cent of a sample of twenty-seven registered child pornography offenders admitted to contact sexual offences after a polygraph, despite denying these offences during a clinical interview (Wood et al., 2009) and 85 per cent of a group of 155 child pornography offenders admitted contact sexual offences while participating in treatment, with approximately half undergoing polygraph testing (Bourke and Hernandez, 2009). Though the Bourke and Hernandez study was a statistical outlier in the meta-analysis, both these studies illustrate the gap between detected and undetected offences. Seto et al.'s results also suggest that not all online offenders have committed contact sexual offences, although exact proportions are unknown as some offenders who denied contact sexual offending may have lied. As mentioned earlier, established risk measures can be used for those with a known contact sex offence history, generally one that involves a charge or conviction. Seto et al.'s meta-analysis suggests there is a large proportion of online (child pornography) offenders who have no officially known history and for whom these measures can therefore not be immediately applied.

Comparisons of child pornography and contact offenders

Babchishin and colleagues (2011) conducted a meta-analysis of twenty-seven studies reporting on the characteristics of online offenders, many of whom were child pornography offenders. Of particular relevance here are the nine direct comparisons of online and contact offenders they identified (with a minimum of three studies for each variable they examined). Online offenders scored higher in victim empathy, higher in sexual deviance, and lower in impression management (a tendency to present oneself in an unrealistically positive light) when compared to contact offenders. Unfortunately, however, we are unable specifically to discuss those online or child pornography offenders with no known contact offences, as these offenders were not always differentiated across samples.

Individual studies suggest that child pornography offenders (again, undifferentiated for prior offending) are less likely to engage in antisocial behaviour or abuse substances, score lower on impulsivity, and are more accepting of personal responsibility than contact offenders (Elliot et al., 2009; Webb et al., 2007). These results suggest that some online offenders may have more self-control than contact offenders and thus exhibit fewer antisocial behaviours associated with committing future sexual offences.

Individual studies also suggest that online offenders are higher in intelligence and better educated than offline offenders (Blanchard et al., 2007). This result may be attributed to a selection effect; offenders convicted of online offences used computers to commit their crimes, and thus are possibly more intelligent or better educated, on average, than individuals who commit their crimes directly against children. These differences may disappear as computers become more ubiquitous and easier to use. Online offenders are also less likely to have ever been married or lived with a common-law partner (Eke and Seto, 2011; Webb et al., 2007). This may reflect the fact that online offenders have more difficulties with interpersonal relationships, and that these interpersonal deficits make online involvement more attractive. Another plausible explanation is that online offenders are more likely to have a sexual interest in children and are therefore perhaps less likely to be interested in relationships with adult peers. Regardless, problems with adult attachments and intimate relationships have been associated with risk for future sexual offending in the contact sex offender literature.

In summary, there appear to be risk-relevant factors that pertain to online or child pornography offenders as a group (i.e. some who have committed contact sexual offences and some who have not). What is important next is to understand the recidivism of these offenders. Although child pornography offenders as a group are more likely to be preferentially sexually interested in children than offline offenders, how many go on to commit reported additional offences, are there any within-group differences in recidivism rates, and could established risk measures still apply?

Recidivism of child pornography offenders

Research on the recidivism rates and predictors of recidivism among child pornography offenders is just beginning to emerge, and therefore many studies are as yet unpublished. For recidivism rates, Seto et al. (2011) conducted a second meta-analysis of nine samples of online offenders (again, mostly child pornography offenders) followed for 1.5 to 6 years. Across samples, a total of 2 per cent committed a detected new contact sexual offence during the follow-up period and 5 per cent committed a new sexual offence of some kind, which included new child pornography offences.

As mentioned, one of the samples included in Seto et al.'s meta-analysis was our follow-up study (average time at risk of 4.1 years) of 541 adult men convicted of child pornography offences (Eke et al., 2011). We found that a third (32 per cent) had a documented re-offence of any kind, with 4 per cent charged with a new contact sexual offence and 2.4 per cent charged for a sexual offence they had committed in the past (e.g. a past contact sexual assault victim coming forward following publicity about the child pornography conviction). A total of 11 per cent of the sample had a documented sexual re-offence of some kind, which includes both contact and non-contact offences.

Both our study and the meta-analysis suggest that child pornography offenders as a group (i.e. undifferentiated based on prior contact sexual offending) are unlikely to be reported for new sexual offences, especially when compared to the average contact sex recidivism rate (13 per cent) from large meta-analyses of follow-up studies conducted on contact sexual offenders followed for four to five years of opportunity (Hanson and Bussière, 1998; Hanson and Morton-Bourgon, 2005). However, this does not mean that child pornography offenders are all at low risk to re-offend. In our study, we found that child pornography offenders with a prior or concurrent violent or contact sexual offence were significantly more likely to be subsequently reported for a sexual re-offence (Eke et al., 2011). Offenders are heterogeneous with regard to risk; an important task is to identify those who pose a relatively high risk to re-offend.

Risk factors

Applying traditional risk factors to child pornography offenders

We had information on offender age and criminal history for the offenders followed in the Eke et al. (2011) study. We found that, as expected from much research on offenders in general and contact sexual offenders, younger offender age at the time of first arrest or conviction and criminal history were significant predictors of future detected offending, including contact sexual offending. Overall, offenders with a prior violent (including sexual) criminal history re-offended most often, including sexual re-offences. As mentioned earlier, established risk measures were developed for use with offenders with a known history of violence and/or sexual offending, and thus can be applied to child pornography offenders who have this history.

For this chapter, we also examined offenders who had no prior violent offending, as this is the group many criminal justice professionals and clinicians have the most difficulty with in risk assessment. We again found that younger age at first offence significantly predicted any re-offence, failure on conditional release, and non-violent offending; any prior or index non-violent offending significantly predicted violent re-offending; and any recorded failure on conditional release significantly predicted non-contact sexual recidivism (e.g. invitation to sexual touching), non-violent recidivism, and additional release failures.

In another as yet unpublished study of 286 convicted adult male child pornography offenders followed for an average of 5.5 years (three-quarter overlap with Eke et al., 2011), we also found that younger offender age at time of first arrest, criminal history and failures on conditions of release associated with future reported contact sexual offending as well as any new sex recidivism (e.g. child pornography offences, non-contact sex offences; Eke and Seto, 2011). In addition, substance use problems and self-reported sexual interest in children were significantly associated with of sexual recidivism. Additional analyses are being conducted with this sample, including assessing for potential recidivism risk factors for online-only offenders.

Faust et al. (2009) followed a large sample of 870 child pornography offenders released from federal custody in the United States between 2002 and 2005, resulting in an average follow-up time of 3.8 years. Significant predictors of sexual recidivism were the following: low education, a history of prior treatment for sexual offending (which may be a proxy for prior sexual offending rather than evidence that treatment increases risk) and being single.

Table 9.1 summarizes these research findings in relation to risk factors for future offending. Similar variables have also been found to discriminate contact from non-contact offenders. McCarthy (2010) compared two groups of child pornography offenders: fifty-six non-contact sex offenders and fifty-one known to have committed contact sexual offences; drug use, a criminal history and deviant sexual interest in children significantly discriminated the contact and non-contact groups.

Existing measures

Other studies suggest that risk factors included in existing measures are useful when assessing child pornography offenders. Wakeling et al. (2011) examined the ability of a modified version of the Risk Matrix 2000, a risk measure commonly used in the United Kingdom, to predict contact sexual recidivism across different groups of sex offenders, including online (child pornography) offenders. The measure had to be modified for online-only offenders because one item had no variance (non-contact offending, as all offenders scored positively on this item) and another item was not applicable (having stranger victims). The data available to Wakeling et al. did not include relationship history or the gender of children depicted in child pornography. Online offenders could still be scored on the basis of age at release; number of court appearances for sexual crimes; and number of court appearances for any crimes. Over a two-year follow-up, the child pornography offenders had a low sexual (including Internet sexual offences) reconviction rate (3.1 per cent). Nonetheless, scores on this modified version of the Risk Matrix 2000 were a significant predictor of sexual recidivism among online offenders.

Webb et al. (2007) examined the use of the Risk Matrix 2000 and Stable-2000 with a relatively small sample of child pornography offenders followed for a short period of time and found the low base rates of re-offending made it difficult to conduct a useful statistical examination of specific outcomes. However, they did find that Stable-2000 scores were significant predictors of 'sexually risky behaviors', which included continuing to access Internet pornography. This again suggests that some of our knowledge of sexual offenders in general applies to child pornography offenders.

With a sample of seventy-three adult male child pornography offenders, Osborn et al. (2010) examined short-term prediction of the Static-99, the Risk Matrix 2000 as well as a revised Risk Matrix 2000, a version specifically modified for use with Internet offenders (factors relating to *stranger victims* and *non-contact offences* were removed in the revision; see Thornton, 2007). None of the offenders were reported for a new offence during the follow-up time (1.5 to 4 years) so no analyses could be carried out regarding the predictive accuracy of the measures. However, based on the risk categorizations using the original Risk Matrix 2000 and Static-99, the authors suggest both overestimate risk for these Internet offenders because the majority were categorized as moderate to high risk (and none re-offended). They

Table 9.1 Summary of traditional risk factors empirically demonstrated for use with child pornography offenders as a group

Risk factor	Outcome predicted	Sources
Traditional risk factors		
Age at first offence (including a specific category of 24 years of age or younger)	Any re-offence, conditional release failure, violent re-offence (including contact sexual), contact sexual re-offence, non-contact sexual re-offence, child pornography re-offence	Eke et al. (2011)
Criminal history		
Any prior criminal history	Any re-offence, conditional release failure, violent re-offence (including contact sexual), contact sexual re-offence, non-contact sexual re-offence, child pornography re-offence	Eke et al. (2011)
Pre or index conditional release failure	Any re-offence, conditional release failure, violent re-offence (including contact sexual), non-contact sexual re-offence, child pornography re-offence	Eke et al. (2011)
Prior non-violent history	Any re-offence, conditional release failure, violent re-offence (including contact sexual), non-contact sexual re-offence, child pornography re-offence	Eke et al. (2011)
Prior violent history	Any re-offence, conditional release failure, violent re-offence (including contact sexual), contact sexual re-offence, non-contact sexual re-offence, child pornography re-offence	Eke et al. (2011)
Number of prior non-violent offences	Any re-offence, conditional release failure, non-contact sexual re-offence, child pornography re-offence	Eke et al. (2011)
Number of prior violent offences	Any re-offence, conditional release failure, violent re-offence (including contact sexual), contact sexual re-offence, non-contact sexual re-offence, child pornography re-offence	Eke et al. (2011)
Number of prior contact sexual offences	Any re-offence, conditional release failure, violent re-offence (including contact sexual), contact sexual re-offence	Eke et al. (2011)

History of treatment for sexual offending (possibly a proxy for prior offending)	Contact sexual re-offence	Faust et al. (2009)
Low education	Sexual recidivism	Faust et al. (2009)
Single	Sexual recidivism	Faust et al. (2009)
Sexual interest in children (self-reported)	Any new sexual recidivism	Eke and Seto (2011)
Substance use problems (use has led to problems at work, school, with family, or with the law)	Contact sexual re-offences Any new sexual recidivism	Eke and Seto (2011)
Ratio of males to females in CP images	Any new sexual recidivism	Eke and Seto (2011)
Existing measures		
RM2000 (modified use)	Sexual re-offences	Wakeling et al. (2011)
Stable-2000 (total score)	'Sexually risky behaviors' such as accessing Internet pornography	Webb et al. (2007)

Note: These variables relate to child pornography offenders as a group, as the majority of follow-up research has not separately examined or compared contact, non-contact, and dual offenders. These variables predicted specific outcome in individual studies. How they might work together, for example the weight of any item or the redundancy of items, is currently unknown. The follow-up period for each study was under five years; longer follow-up could lead to additional variables being identified as base rates of re-offending increase over time.

found the revised Risk Matrix 2000 was more conservative, categorizing the majority of the offenders as low risk.

Whether modified versions of existing tools will be useful for assessing risk among child pornography offenders remains to be seen. Another possibility is the development and validation of a new measure that encompasses both traditional risk factors for sexual offending and offence-specific factors that can be scored from collections or other information that relate specifically to child pornography offending.

Risk factors specific to child pornography

In our follow-up study of 286 offenders, we were able to collect data on variables such as the gender and age of children depicted in the images or videos that offenders were viewing or collecting (Eke and Seto, 2011). Some factors show promise for predicting future sexual offending (contact or child pornography offences), including whether the offender has more child pornography content depicting boys relative to girls. Additional factors are being analysed from this work, including the relationship between the age and gender of the children in the images offenders collect and any children they have directly victimized. Faust et al.'s study (2009) also identified two collection-specific predictors of sexual recidivism: possession of sexual material depicting children in the 13–15 year age range, and possession of non-Internet child pornography (magazines, photographs, etc.).

Development of an offence-specific risk measure?

An offence-specific risk measure would most likely include established factors associated with risk, especially offender age and criminal history, while also including some offence-specific variables. A possible complication for the identification of offence-specific variables is the evolving nature of child pornography offending. For example, the availability of digital child pornography content and a tendency to prefer digital over non-digital content among young adults may result in possession of non-Internet child pornography no longer being a significant predictor of sexual recidivism in newer follow-up studies (see Faust et al., 2009). Another potential complication in the identification of offence-specific variables is the availability of sufficient details about child pornography collections for those conducting risk or pre-treatment assessments (Glasgow, 2010; see Glasgow, Chapter 10, this volume). Knowing only that someone has been convicted of child pornography offences may be less informative for risk assessment and management than knowing that the offender had a large collection of images emphasizing a certain gender or age of the children. Providing more details about the size and nature of child pornography collections seized by police, from police, prosecution or court documents, would help professionals involved in risk assessment, management or treatment.

We suspect it would also be helpful to know about legal pornography content as well, as other pornography content can also shed light on the individual's sexual interests. For example, in our police case file study, analysis of computer hard drives and other media revealed that some child pornography offenders also possessed pornography depicting paraphilic content such as fetishism or voyeurism (Seto and Eke, 2008). Police may not describe this content because it is legal (depending on jurisdiction) and not the focus of the criminal proceedings, but knowing about the full range of pornographic content may assist with risk assessment or management. Law enforcement is the best source for a variety of potentially risk-relevant information such as child pornography content, presence of other pornography, and online behaviour (e.g. did the offender attempt to contact children, did they participate in online forums intended for paedophiles, create their own written stories about sex with children).

Failures on conditional release

Of additional specific interest to law enforcement are failures on conditional release (e.g. failure to appear in court, violation of probation conditions), given the decisions that criminal justice officials have to make about release on bail, probation or parole. For example, a common condition of release in child pornography cases includes restricting access to computers with Internet access. Home computers and connections are the most likely to be used in online child exploitation but some offenders also use equipment from their workplace (e.g. Mitchell et al., 2005); almost half of child pornography offenders in one of our studies were willing to use non-private computers (e.g. computers they shared with others, work or school computers, Internet café computers) when accessing this content (Seto and Eke, 2008).

A quarter of the offenders followed by Eke et al. (2011) had officially recorded failures on conditional release. Just over half of the failures involved being around children unsupervised by a responsible adult, contacting children using Internet technologies or accessing child pornography again. Predictors of failures included younger age at first offence, prior criminal history and prior or index failures. To illustrate, 11 per cent of those known to be child pornography-only offenders had a failure on conditional release, whereas 34 per cent of child pornography offenders with any other kind of offending in their history failed.

Research limitations

Some of the research reviewed in this chapter examines samples of online offenders, which may include individuals who have committed Internet-facilitated offences other than child pornography. Though the majority of samples are comprised of specifically child pornography offenders, and non-child pornography offenders comprise only a small minority of online offender samples, differences between child pornography and other online offenders may obscure group differences and relationships found (Wood et al., 2009). Our main research projects (Eke et al., 2011; Eke and Seto, 2011; and Seto and Eke, 2008) examined child pornography offenders exclusively.

A related issue is that varying proportions of child pornography offenders have already committed contact sexual offences (Seto et al., 2011) and these dual offenders may differ in meaningful ways from child pornography only offenders or contact only offenders on personal characteristics or on risk to re-offend. One could theorize that those who have committed both online and offline offences are more likely to be sexually interested in children, though Seto et al. (2006) found no difference between dual and child pornography only offenders in their relative sexual arousal to children. Dual offenders recidivate more frequently than online-only child pornography offenders, but it is not clear how they compare to contact only offenders. Similarly, some ostensibly contact only offenders may in fact have committed undetected online offences, and their inclusion in comparison studies may attenuate group differences that might exist. Future research that can carefully compare online-only with offline-only and dual offenders would shed more light on the strength (and direction) of group differences.

A general limitation of all recidivism research is that it usually relies on official records. Official records are an underestimate of true offending and are influenced by reporting rates, police actions, prosecution decisions and trial outcomes. Non-reporting is a particular concern; in Canada in 2009, 88 per cent of self-reported sexual victimization was not reported to police (Statistics Canada, 2010). Non-reporting may be even more problematic among children who may delay reporting until adulthood; those who do report in childhood generally must first disclose the sexual abuse to an adult such as a parent or teacher, who in turn must make the decision to contact police or child protection authorities. The reporting bias in official data affects our ability to identify predictors of all new offending; instead, what is being predicted is the likelihood of an offender being detected and reported for a new offence.

Summary and implications for law enforcement

As discussed earlier, risk assessment is common within law enforcement, where it is used for both suspected and convicted offenders, starting with initial investigations through to threat assessments for court and risk management of released offenders. The information available to police will vary over the course of an investigation, with potentially less information available at the start of an investigation and more risk-relevant information accumulating over time.

Research is beginning to address questions about the characteristics, offence histories and risk of recidivism of child pornography offenders. Risk factors identified in this emerging research include established criminological variables such as offender age at first arrest and criminal history. There is also evidence to suggest that factors such as substance use and indicators of sexual interest in children (e.g. self-reported sexual interests) are relevant. Evidence that modified versions of existing measures have predictive accuracy supports the idea that some factors that help predict recidivism among contact sexual offenders will also work with child pornography offenders. Offender age and prior history are also pre-dictors of failure on conditional release among child pornography offenders and should be considered when making recommendations regarding bail. Our analysis of conditional release failures suggests that many child pornography offenders (half of those who failed) may put themselves in risky situations with children (e.g. by being around children unsupervised or by contacting children online) or continue to access (child) pornography; this is an important consideration for post-arrest or post-conviction supervision.

While more research is clearly needed, other readily accessible variables may also be important to consider, such as offender contact with, or access to, children. Most children who are sexually molested are victimized by someone already known to them such as a family member or acquaintance (Snyder and Sickmund, 2006) and this is also evident among child victims of dual child pornography/contact sex offenders (Eke et al., 2011).

Initial warrant information prepared by law enforcement could include empirically gathered group-based information about child pornography offenders and offending (e.g. general characteristics, information about sexual interests). Once the warrant is executed, additional information about the offender and the material they accessed will assist in more specific assessments of risk relating to re-offending. Well-validated risk measures are already available for child pornography suspects who have a known history of contact sexual offending. Some are well suited for use by law enforcement because they do not require clinical diagnosis or the use of specialized mental health assessments such as for psychopathy (e.g. the Static-99 or Risk Matrix 2000). Further research may support the use of risk factors on existing risk measures for child pornography offenders without any known contact offending history. Findings from recent research, including our recent examination of police case files, support the possibility of identifying a set of offence-specific risk factors for child pornography offenders.

Future directions for research

As mentioned earlier, studies that carefully distinguish online-only offenders from offline- (contact) only offenders and dual offenders would clarify the nature and magnitude of group differences. Longer follow-up studies of larger samples of child pornography offenders, particularly those with no known history of contact sexual offending, would allow us to identify risk factors that may pertain to this particular subgroup. To date, the longest published follow-up time is just under seven years (see offender sub-sample in Eke et al., 2011). Distinguishing between pseudo-recidivism involving historical offences (offences committed in the past that were not reported and prosecuted until after the child pornography conviction) and true recidivism involving new offences would clarify true recidivism rates, predictors of true recidivism, as well as provide insight into originally undetected sexual offending (Eke et al., 2011). Studies with non-clinical and non-correctional samples of individuals accessing child pornography (e.g. anonymous self-report surveys conducted on the Internet; Ray et al., 2010; Seigfried et al., 2008) would shed light on child pornography offending among individuals who are not already known to the criminal justice or mental health systems.

The majority of the follow-up work in the area of online and child pornography offending has focused on sexual recidivism and predicting these new offences. It is important for future research also to examine violent recidivism, including contact sexual offending, because the risk for any type of subsequent violent offending is a key concern among criminal justice professionals, clinicians and the public. An additional benefit to examining violent recidivism as an outcome is that some sexually motivated crimes may result in criminal charges and convictions for non-sexual offences (e.g. a sexual assault pled as an assault) and this broader variable would include these cases (see Rice et al., 2006).

Recidivism research has focused on the persistence of offending (new child pornography offences) or escalation in offending (committing contact sexual offences with no history of such) after a formal sanction for a child pornography offence. Research examining factors that predict the *onset* of child pornography offending would contribute greatly to prevention efforts. The importance of questions such as why offenders begin accessing child exploitation images, why they continue to access it and the effect this material has on the likelihood of contact offending is evident in recent theory and research, including work published in recent special journal issues (*Journal of Sexual Aggression* and *Sexual Abuse: Journal of Research and Treatment*).

Final comments

Along with an offender's potential for directly abusing a child or committing additional child pornography offences, law enforcement agencies are also concerned with the potential negative impact working in this area may have on their employees. The exploitative and sexually abusive material that offenders find sexually exciting or interesting can also be psychologically harmful to those responsible for investigating and trying these offences (Burns et al., 2008; Krause, 2009; Perez et al., 2010; Wolak and Mitchell, 2009). Employee stress will also be a concern as case loads continue to increase. Additional research in the area of investigator well-being is important and needed. Protecting the well-being of individuals working in the field of child exploitation should be a priority, starting with the selection of staff, the use of ongoing psychological assessments and staff wellness programmes, and post-appointment or exit assessments; an example of a specialized employee programme is the Safeguard programme of the Ontario Provincial Police.

One goal of completing a risk assessment is to assign the finite resources available to those offenders who pose the greatest risk of continuing to harm society as well as related considerations such as addressing risk among young offenders with whom early intervention may reduce the likelihood of future offending. By identifying specific factors associated with an individual's risk (e.g. substance abuse issues) specific management strategies can be developed to reduce their potential for offending. As research in the area of child pornography offending continues to develop, our ability to effectively assess risk and thereby better protect children will also continue to improve.

Notes

1   We thank Grant Harris, Debra Heaton, Zoe Hilton, Tina Maier, Scott Naylor and Glenn Sheil for their helpful comments on an earlier draft.
2   Children are defined as individuals under the age of 18. The modal child pornography image is of a prepubescent girl (e.g. Quayle and Jones, 2011); images of teenagers are more difficult to classify as child pornography because of the difficulty in establishing the age of the depicted persons. Images of prepubescent or pubescent children, however, clearly meet legal definitions. In some countries, legal definitions of child pornography offences can also include shared written material depicting, advocating or counselling sex with minors, and computer-generated images of children (e.g. Canada).

References

Akdeniz, Y. (2008). *Internet Child Pornography and the Law: National and International Responses*. Aldershot: Ashgate.

Babchishin, K.M., Hanson, R.K. and Hermann, C.A. (2011). The characteristics of online sex offenders: A meta-analysis. *Sexual Abuse: A Journal of Research and Treatment, 23*, 92–123.

Bates, A. and Metcalf, C. (2007). A psychometric comparison of Internet and non-Internet sex offenders from a community treatment sample. *Journal of Sexual Aggression, 13*, 11–20.

Beech, A.R., Elliot, I.A., Birgden, A. and Findlater, D. (2008). The Internet and child sexual offending: A criminological review. *Aggression and Violent Behaviour, 13*, 216–28.

Blanchard, R., Kolla, N.J., Cantor, J.M., Klassen, P.E., Dickey, R., Kuban, M.E. and Blak, T. (2007). IQ, handedness, and pedophilia in adult male patients stratified by referral. *Sexual Abuse: A Journal of Research and Treatment, 19*, 285–309.

Bourke, M.L. and Hernandez, A.E. (2009). The 'Butner Study' redux: A report of the incidence of hands-on child victimization by child pornography offenders. *Journal of Family Violence, 24*, 183–91.

Burns, C.M., Morley, J., Bradshaw, R. and Domene, J. (2008). The emotional impact on and coping strategies employed by police teams investigating Internet child exploitation. *Traumatology, 14*, 20–31.

Canadian Centre for Child Protection (2009). Child Sexual Abuse Images: An Analysis of Websites by Cybertip! Available online at http://www.cyberaide.ca/pdfs/Cybertip_researchreport.pdf.

Canwest News Service (2008). Ontario police crack down on child pornography, available online at http://www.canada.com/ottawacitizen/news/story.html?id=392a7d0f-e5dc–4e5b-b163-ef34711a9994&k=79268.

Cooper, A. (1998). Sexuality and the internet: Surfing into the new millennium. *Cyber Psychology and Behaviour, 1*, 187–93.

Cooper, A., McLoughlin, I.P. and Campbell, K.M. (2000). Sexuality in cyberspace: Update for the 21st century. *CyberPsychology and Behaviour, 3*, 521–36.

Eke. A.W. and Seto, M.C. (2011). Identifying recidivism risk factors for child pornography offenders from police files. Paper presented at the 4th International Congress on Psychology and Law and the 2011 American Psychology and Law Society Annual Meeting, Miami, Florida.

Eke, A.W., Seto., M.C. and Williams, J. (2011). Examining the criminal history and future offending of child pornography offenders: An extended prospective follow-up study. *Law and Human Behaviour, 35*, 466–78.

Elliot, I.A., Beech, R.B., Mandeville-Norden, R. and Hayes, E. (2009). Psychological profiles of Internet sexual offenders: Comparisons with contact sex offenders. *Sexual Abuse: A Journal of Research and Treatment, 21*, 76–92.

Faust, E., Renaud, C. and Bickart, W. (2009). Predictors of re-offence among a sample of federally convicted child pornography offenders. Paper presented at the 28th Annual Conference of the Association for the Treatment of Sexual Abusers, Dallas, Texas.

Glasgow, D. (2010). The potential of digital evidence to contribute to risk assessment of Internet offenders. *Journal of Sexual Aggression, 16*, 87–106.

Hanson, R.K. and Babchishin, K.M. (2009). How should we advance our knowledge of risk assessment for Internet sexual offenders? Paper presented at the global symposium for examining relationship between online and offline offences and preventing the sexual exploitation of children. Chapel Hill, North Carolina, April 6–7. Available online at http://www.iprc.unc.edu/G8/Karl_Hanson_3.6.09.doc.

Hanson, R.K. and Bussière, M.T. (1998). Predicting relapse: A meta-analysis of sexual offender recidivism studies. *Journal of Consulting and Clinical Psychology, 66*, 348–62.

Hanson, R. K. and Morton-Bourgon, K. (2005). The characteristics of persistent sexual offenders: A meta-analysis of recidivism studies. *Journal of Consulting and Clinical Psychology, 73*, 1154–63.

Hanson, R.K. and Thornton, D. (2000). Improving risk assessments for sex offenders: A comparison of three actuarial scales. *Law and Human Behavior, 24*, 119–36.

Krause, M. (2009). Identifying and managing stress in child pornography and child exploitation investigators. *Journal of Police and Criminal Psychology, 24*, 22–29.

McCarthy, J.A. (2010). Internet sexual activity: A comparison between contact and non-contact child pornography offenders. *Journal of Sexual Aggression, 16*, 181–95.

Mitchell, K.J., Wolak, J. and Finkelhor, D. (2005). Police posing as juveniles to catch sex offenders: Is it working? *Sexual Abuse: A Journal of Research and Treatment, 17*, 242–67.

Motivans, M. and Kyckelhahn, T. (2007). Federal prosecution of child sex exploitation offenders, 2006. *Bureau of Justice Statistics Bulletin* (Report No. NCJ 219412). Washington, DC: Bureau of Justice Statistics. Available online at http://bjs.ojp.usdoj.gov/index.cfm?ty=pbdetail&iid=886.

Moultrie, D. (2006). Adolescents convicted of possession of abuse images of children: A new type of adolescent sex offender? *Journal of Sexual Aggression, 12*, 165–74.

O'Halloran, E. and Quayle, E. (2010). A content analysis of a 'boy-love' support forum: Revisiting Durkin and Bryant. *Journal of Sexual Aggression, 16*, 71–85.

Osborn, J., Elliott, I.A., Middleton, D. and Beech, A.R. (2010). The use of actuarial risk assessment measures with UK internet child pornography offenders. *Journal of Aggression, Conflict and Peace Research, 2*, 16–24.

Perez, L.M., Jones, J., Englert, D.R. and Sachau, D. (2010). Secondary trauma, stress, and burnout among law enforcement investigators exposed to disturbing media images. *Journal of Police and Criminal Psychology, 25*, 113–24.

Quayle, E. and Jones, T. (2011). Sexualized images of children on the Internet. *Sexual Abuse: A Journal of Research and Treatment, 23*, 7–21.

Ray, J., Kimonis, E. and Donoghue, C. (2010). Legal, ethical, and methodological considerations in the Internet-based study of child pornography offenders. *Behavioral Sciences and the Law, 28*, 84–105.

Rice, M.E., Harris, G.T., Lang, C. and Cormier, C.A. (2006). Violent sex offenses: How are they best measured from official records? *Law and Human Behavior, 30*, 525–41.

Seto, M.C. (2008). *Pedophilia and sexual offending against children: Theory, assessment, and intervention*. Washington, DC: American Psychological Association.

—— (2010). Child pornography use and Internet solicitation in the diagnosis of pedophilia. *Archives of Sexual Behaviour, 39*, 591–93.

Seto, M.C. and Eke, A.W. (2005). The criminal histories and later offending of child pornography offenders. *Sexual Abuse: A Journal of Research and Treatment, 17*, 201–10.

—— (2008). Predicting new offences committed by child pornography offenders. Paper presented at the 27th Annual Conference of the Association for the Treatment of Sexual Abusers, Atlanta, GA.

Seto, M. C., Cantor, J. M., and Blanchard, R. (2006). Child pornography offences are a valid diagnostic indicator of pedophilia. *Journal of Abnormal Psychology, 115*, 610–15.

Seto, M.C., Hanson, R.K. and Babchishin, K.M. (2011). Contact sexual offending by men with online sexual offenses. *Sexual Abuse: A Journal of Research and Treatment, 23*, 124–45.

Seto, M. C., Reeves, L. and Jung, S. (2010). Motives for child pornography offending: The explanations given by the offenders. *Journal of Sexual Aggression, 16*, 169–80.

Sheldon, K. and Howitt., D. (2007). *Sex Offenders and the Internet*. West Sussex: Wiley.

Seigfried, K., Lovely, R. and Rogers, M. (2008). Self-reported consumers of internet child pornography: A psychological analysis. *International Journal of Cyber Criminology, 2*, 286–97.

Seigfried-Spellar, K.C. and Rogers, M.K. (2010). Low neuroticism and high hedonistic traits for female internet child pornography consumers. *Cyberpsychology, Behavior, and Social Networking, 13*, 629–35.

Snyder, H. and Sickmund, M. (2006). *Juvenile Offenders and Victims: 2006 National Report*. Washington, DC: Office of Juvenile Justice and Delinquency Prevention.

Statistics Canada (2010). *Criminal Victimization in Canada, 2009*, available online at http://www.statcan.gc.ca/pub/85–002-x/2010002/article/11340-eng.htm#a3.

Taylor, M., Holland, G. and Quayle, E. (2001). Typology of paedophile picture collections. *The Police Journal, 74*, 97–107.

Thornton, D. (2007). Scorring Guide for the Risk Matrix 2000.9/SVC. Available online at http://www.cfcp.bham.ac.uk/Extras/SCORING per cent20GUIDE per cent20FORper cent20RISK per cent20MATRIX per cent202000.9- per cent20SVC per cent20- per cent20(ver. per cent20Feb per cent202007).pdf.

Wakeling, H.C., Howard, P. and Barnett, G. (2011). Comparing the validity of the RM2000 Scales and OGRS3 for predicting recidivism by internet sexual offenders. *Sexual Abuse: A Journal of Research and Treatment, 23*, 146–68.

Watts, A. (2009). *Spy software helps net child porn offenders*. Sky News, available online at http://news.sky.com/skynews/Home/UK-News/Child-Porn-Police-Using-New-Spy-Software-Arrest-Dozens-Of-Offenders/Article/200910215402894.

Webb, L., Craisatti, J. and Keen, S. (2007). Characteristics of Internet child pornography: A comparison with child molesters. *Sexual Abuse: A Journal of Research and Treatment, 19*, 449–65.

Wolak, J. and Mitchell, K.J. (2009). *Work Exposure to Child Pornography in ICAC Task Forces and Affiliates*. Crimes Against Children Research Center University of New Hampshire, available online at http://www.unh.edu/ccrc/pdf/Law%20Enforcement%20Work%20Exposure%20to%20CP.pdf.

Wolak, J., Finkelhor, D. and Mitchell, K. (2009). *Trends in arrests of 'online predators'*. Crimes Against Children Research Center, available online at http://www.unh.edu/ccrc/pdf/cv194.pdf.

Wood, M. K., Seto, M. C., Flynn, S., Wilson-Cotton, S. and Dedmon, P. (2009). Is it 'just' pictures? The use of polygraph with Internet offenders who deny abusive sexual contact. Poster presented at the 28th Annual Conference of the Association for the Treatment of Sexual Abusers, Dallas, Texas.

Part 3

Prevention and harm reduction

10 The importance of digital evidence in Internet sex offending

David Glasgow, Carlton Glasgow Partnership

Overview

Although definitions of illegal material, laws and practice within the criminal justice system (CJS) of various countries differ quite significantly, there is increasingly compelling evidence that only a minority of those found to be in possession of illegal images are likely to have been previously convicted for contact sexual offences (see Chapter 9 for further discussion). One possible explanation for this is that these offenders were arrested at an early stage in a process of escalation of deviant interest and behaviour which would probably, or even inevitably, result in a contact offence against a child or children. This belief has some face validity, and it is often implicit in the representation of Internet offenders in the media and in the accounts of some professionals. The assumption is that even in the absence of evidence for contact offending, consumers of child pornography present an inevitable, if not immediate, direct risk to children. It is very difficult to identify the processes implicit in the assumptions of risk, often because they are assumed to be self-evident. One possibility is that the accessing of sexually explicit material (SEM) reflects a covert planning process to engage in the behaviour depicted. Alternatively, it may be felt that SEMs are so toxic that they will inevitably drive an interaction between sexual fantasy and behaviour such that contact offending becomes inevitable, or at least highly likely.

However, whatever hypothetical processes are being implied, there is precious little evidence that the possession of SEM alone presages contact offending. In fact, it is not the first time in the field of working with offenders that assumptions have been made in relation to risk related trajectories in human behaviour. In a number of instances these assumptions have proved at least over-simplistic and often ill-founded. For example, public policy and case management in relation to juvenile offenders, including sexual offenders, was substantially influenced by the belief that juvenile crime inevitably presaged adult offending (Vizard, 2007). Although debate raged with respect to the best way to intervene (punishment, retraining, therapy; see Lipsey, 2009) the debate itself was predicated on the assumption that intervention was required to divert the individual from recidivism throughout adulthood. Both with respect to non-sexual and sexual offending, the empirical evidence did not support the assumption made. Taken overall, neither group was likely to persist in offending, with very young sexual offenders pre-senting a particularly low rate of recidivism (Lussier et al., 2010).

Similarly, there was once an assumption that the experience of sexual victimiza-tion, particularly in males, would lead to becoming a sexual offender in adulthood (Romano and De Luca, 1997). Fortunately, research evidence has confirmed a much more optimistic picture, with the majority of individuals developing into adults who do not display offending behaviour (Jespersen et al., 2009). The formulation of the relationship between sexual victimization and sexual offending is now much more sophisticated than it once was.

The early signs are that those individuals convicted of Internet only offending also have a surprisingly low rate of recidivism (with respect to further Internet-only offending) and, perhaps more significantly, exhibit a low rate of subsequent conviction for contact offending (Eke et al., 2010). It would be premature to be very specific with respect to the likely percentage of escalation to contact offending, particularly in the absence of meta-analytic studies. However, research emerging for a number of countries strongly suggests that using established measures of recidivism, Internet-only offenders should be regarded as relatively low risk (Eke et al., 2010; Endrass et al., 2009).

On the face of it this is good news. It seems that considered as a group, those found in possession of sexually explicit images of children (and having committed no other offences previously) are unlikely to present a grave or immediate danger of sexually abusing children. However, as is often the case in the field of risk assessment, what appears on the face of it to be simple evidence leading to straightforward conclusions, is actually rather more complex and controversial in practice.

For the sake of argument, if one supposes that approximately10 per cent of Internet-only offenders will escalate to commit a contact sexual offence, a number of issues arise. The first is that it is clearly quite wrong to support the presumption of risk which underlies prevailing lay attitudes towards Internet-only offenders (see Chapter 7). These attitudes are strongly held and vociferously expressed, and it is likely that professionals making the case for informed risk assessment and management, or even simply publicly reporting the empirical evidence, may find themselves suffering undeserved opprobrium. It is utterly unsurprising that politi-cians and policy makers typically avoid contradicting public perceptions. With varying degrees of commitment, politicians tend to focus on punitive and coercive responses preferred by the electorate (desistance, rather than those informed by the evidence). This is not simply an issue of social justice, but one of developing informed and effective risk assessment and management. The prevailing Zeitgeist in the lay public domain, as evidenced by sexual crime reports in the press, is perhaps more at odds with that of professionals working to assess and manage sex offender risk than it has ever been (see for example the Good Lives Model of clinical and community rehabilitation by by Siegert et al., 2007). Lam et al. (2010) examined university students' perceptions of the offence of possession of child pornography. In the study 492 participants rated perceived offence severity, appropriate sentence, probability of child pornography re-offence, probability of past and future sexual contact with a minor, and probability that the offender is a paedophile. One of a number of findings from this study was that the belief that 'Mr. Smith is a paedophile' was correlated with the perceived probabilities of past or future sexual contact with a minor. The authors conclude that, 'While it has been established that people tend to strongly support "child saving", which generally manifests as encouraging the rehabilitation of youthful offenders and the use of early intervention programs . . . this tendency might manifest differently in child pornography cases, such that the public provides support for harsher penalties against these offenders in order to "save the children"'. (p. 194).

A consideration of empirical evidence relating to factors or mechanisms that might be hypothesized as being implicated in a trajectory from consumption of online child pornography to contact offending is of value. Pornography consumption itself has over many years and on many occasions been hypothesized to cause expressed sexual behaviour to be more likely to be coercive or deviant (see Bensimon, 2007 for a review of this subject). Such a process has proved remarkably elusive and difficult to demonstrate. Many research studies failed to find a harmful effect of pornography on the consumer of the material, although a number of more recent studies appear to be converging on what appears to be an interaction between personality characteristics and in particular, consumption of violent pornography. Different studies define the personality characteristics in different terms, such as 'hypermasculinity' (Beesley and McGuire, 2009), the 'dark triad' (Jonason and Tost, 2010) and 'subclinical psychopathy' (Williams et al., 2009). The general finding is that those individuals who already engage in or endorse social behaviour characterized by hostility and coercion, who also consume pornography (particularly violent pornography), are more likely to exhibit or endorse sexually exploitative behaviour (Seto et al., 2001).

In contrast to this finding, the rapid growth in the availability of sexually explicit images, and the apparent escalation in the prevalence of pornography consumption, does not appear to have triggered a corresponding increase in coercive sexual behaviour as measured by crime statistics. It therefore seems that for the majority of individuals, exposure to pornographic material does not trigger an escalation from fantasy to exploitative sexual behaviour. Perhaps these findings are echoed among men who consume specifically child pornography. Those who exhibit personality traits associated with coercive hostility, impulsivity, manipulation and poor self-regulation may be much more likely to become involved with the CJS as 'mixed' offenders, whose consumption of SEM involving children is adjunctive to contact offending. There is certainly initial evidence that Internet-only offenders are different to other offenders in a number of respects and lack the characteristics that seem to interact in the genesis of sexually motivated violence, and in particular sexually motivated murder (Maniglio, 2010). Babchishin et al. (2010) in their meta-analysis of twenty-seven distinct samples found that online offenders were more likely to be Caucasian and were slightly younger than offline offenders. In relation to psychological variables, online offenders demonstrated greater victim empathy, greater sexual deviancy and lower impression management than offline offenders. This indirectly also supports Lussier et al. (2010), who demonstrated two distinct developmental pathways of sexual deviance. The first involved sexual interest in non-violent sexual stimuli involving children, and the second sexual interest for violent sexual stimuli involving children.

Another strand of research of relevance is that relating to sexual fantasy. Many studies have revealed that both men and women are likely to have numerous sexual fantasies, very few of which are likely to be realized (King et al., 2009). In fact, it seems that they are often experienced as quite clearly disconnected from real sexual behaviour. This was debated quite vigorously in relation to the discovery that a substantial minority of women generate fantasies of being coerced into sexual activity (Bivona and Critelli, 2009). The interpretation of this is not that these women would in fact wish to be sexually assaulted or raped, but the fantasy itself serves a function quite independent of actual sexual behaviour. Similarly, a significant proportion of men generate, but apparently do not act upon, sexual fantasies in which they coerce a partner into sexual activity (Zurbriggen and Yost, 2004). Finally, an often referenced study reported that a significant proportion of male college students were prepared to acknowledge not only sexual interests in children, but a probability that they would engage in actual sexual behaviour if they could expect no consequences for their actions (Briere and Runtz, 1989).

Risk assessment and Internet offenders

The specific circumstances in which investigations into sexually explicit images of children held on digital equipment are triggered vary. Sometimes investigation follows a chance discovery by a third party of potentially illegal images or other files on equipment owned or accessed by the suspect. In other cases it can be evidence emerging from file servers supplying illegal images to computers owned by or accessed by the suspect. Sometimes unlawful images are uncovered during an investigation for other offences, including child sexual abuse. In this particular circumstance, the digital evidence will be of significance, but the existence of evidence for concurrent contact offences may somewhat reduce the significance of digital images in any later risk assessment process.

Whatever the trigger for an investigation, once an individual is subjected to an investigation relating to the possession of unlawful sexually explicit digital images, it signals the beginning of a complex and often lengthy process, likely to substantially transform the life of the alleged offender, and also the lives of his family. A simplified timeline with respect to the CJS would move through a number of stages: investigation; prosecution; conviction and sentencing, to management. From beginning to end, the process is very unlikely to take less than many months, and more probably will take several years to complete. The relative duration of each phase in any one case depends on the complexity of the evidence and the seriousness of the charges. So, for example, the process of preparing and bringing a prosecution may well involve the synthesis and evaluation of a great deal of evidence taken from computer equipment, perhaps involving a number of individuals in geographically distant locations. Similarly, post-sentence management in relatively minor, straightforward cases might last only a matter of months.

However, in some cases, supervision may last many years, even a lifetime. This might be as a result of the sentence of the court, or, alternatively, as a result of a risk assessment undertaken by a community risk assessment and management agency. In the UK this role is taken by a multi-agency risk assessment panel (MAPPA).

At several points in the process, a risk assessment will be undertaken. The precise purpose and nature of this varies very significantly, although the shared goal at all points is the anticipation and minimization of potential harm, very often towards children. The first risk assessment, undertaken at stage 1, is the evaluation of the possibility of direct harm to children with whom the suspected offender has been, or is, in contact. This might include members of the immediate and extended family, neighbours and the children of friends or acquaintances. If it is concluded that there has been or may be a future risk, it is likely that child protection services will be involved in the investigation.

The requirements of guidance to police officers conducting an investigation are that 'investigators will undertake a risk assessment at the earliest opportunity'. No recommendations are made with respect to how this outcome should be achieved, and one might argue that it might constitute little more than an 'on-the-hoof' judgement as to whether direct harm can be anticipated. However, more recently training courses have been offered in the United Kingdom by CEOP (the Child Exploitation and Online Protection Centre) for police officers involved in investigating Internet offences, and these are based on established risk assessment procedures, albeit those for sex offenders generally. The proportion of initial risk assessments that are structured in this way is unknown. Risk is also considered at later points in the process, including at the sentencing stage. The 'seriousness' of a crime, and, as a result, the severity of the sentence, is significantly and explicitly influenced by the perceived harm caused historically, and the expectations of the severity of future harm.

Finally, Internet offenders may be supervised in the community post-sentence in a process led by the probation service. This might be as a result of the sentence of the court, or, alternatively, as a result of a risk assessment undertaken (in the UK) by a MAPPA. This process is very often informed by detailed structured or actuarial risk assessment procedures, and involves regular discussions and reviews in order to monitor progress and to detect any changes in the level of perceived risk.

> In essence, MAPPAs are meant to concentrate on the 'critical few' in order to subject them to greater scrutiny and more intensive management ... The critical few is an operational term, and relates to very high-risk offenders (as defined by the Probation Service risk assessment tool OASys), and those deemed to require very intensive risk management at level 3 of MAPPA.
>
> (Kemshall and Wood, 2008: 617)

However, as these authors point out, correct detection of the 'critical' few has proved quite problematic.

Thus, the assessment of historical and future risk is an important consideration throughout the criminal justice process. However, this chapter is focused not on the criminal justice process, but on risk assessment conducted within the community, typically after an individual has left the CJS. Sometimes such risk assessments are triggered in anticipation of an individual exiting the CJS, either following completion of a sentence, or much earlier triggered by the collapse of a criminal trial or the decision not to proceed with a prosecution. Whatever the specific trigger, what is anticipated when an alleged or convicted Internet offender's circumstances might bring or have brought him into contact with children? It may come as a surprise to some that this happens at all, although logically, even if a convicted offender is sentenced to a lengthy period in custody, he is thereafter likely to return to the community, and will attempt to rebuild as fulfilling a personal life as possible. It is inevitable that this will involve the renewal of old relationships or the establishment of new relationships, and at least some of these are likely to involve contact with children.

It is therefore possible to elaborate on our simple stage model, to form Fig. 10.1, displaying a number of routes through which an individual investigated for the possession of SEM involving children can exit the CJS.

In later stages, and therefore necessarily in cases involving a conviction, the process of transition from CJS into the community can itself be associated with, or even determined by, a risk assessment process. However, this is often restricted to a simple categorization of perceived risk in order to determine a binary decision-making process: i.e. to release or not to release, to subject to restrictions or not, and so on.

Risk assessments undertaken in the community after an individual has exited the CJS (at whatever stage) and has returned to the community are complicated and challenging. In the UK they are also often conducted within the family courts,

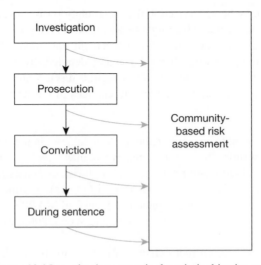

Figure 10.1 Investigation routes in the criminal justice system

and accordingly the standard of proof is 'on the balance of probability' rather than 'beyond reasonable doubt'. This means that in many cases in which the prosecution is abandoned after the investigatory stage because it is anticipated that the evidence will not be sufficient to secure a conviction, the same evidence can be acted upon to protect children within civil proceedings. The importance and prevalence of these cases is often overlooked in the risk assessment literature and their role in risk assessment and management is underestimated.

In part this may be because the proceedings are not in the UK currently held in public. Further, there is a widely held misconception that risk management by the CJS is the primary child protection system in relation to sex offenders. There is an assumption that a vaguely envisaged but robust process of 'supervision', 'registration' or 'notification' will act as a prophylactic, and prevent any risk of harm to children (Logan, 2008). The reality is that many general procedures intended to manage risk in the community cannot be other than rather modest in effect, and are likely to have a similarly modest risk reduction effect. Some have even argued that they may paradoxically increase risk. Logan (2008: 14) has suggested that, 'over-broad notification might enhance the prospects of recidivism among otherwise law-abiding ex-offenders. While researchers have not yet provided conclusive evidence of the anti-therapeutic effects of community notification, a considerable body of evidence highlights that notification negatively affects various lifestyle considerations shown to lessen the chances of recidivism (e.g., employment, steady residence, and social relationships)'. Further, post-sentence Internet-only offenders are unlikely to be identified as high risk, and few will be supervised by a MAPPA. Not only does research evidence suggests that this is probably justified, almost by definition existing risk assessment tools are likely determine the risk to be low, because they rely upon discriminating between the presence and absence of historical antisocial behaviour. Nevertheless, amongst Internet-only offenders, a small minority are at risk of escalating to contact offending. The pressing question is how might that minority be identified prior to such escalation?

Candidate measures for risk assessment

Personality traits

The significance of antisocial personality traits has long been recognized, both in risk assessment generally, and in the literature referred to above, in relation to the consumption of pornography and offending. Traditionally, in risk assessment, antisocial traits are assessed using measures referenced to the general population. The threshold for psychopathology or categorization as high risk are generally set quite high in order to capture those individuals who are most psychologically deviant, and presenting the highest risk.

With respect to Internet only offenders it may be necessary to 'retune' the sensitivity of assessment tools, or at the least modify the threshold for risk to be rather lower than it is amongst general offenders. Osborn et al. (2010), in a study of two actuarial measures, Risk Matrix 2000 and Static-99, with individuals con-victed of downloading child pornography on the Internet, found that both measures overestimated the risk levels posed by these offenders and that an adapted version of Risk Matrix 2000 provide a more realistic estimate. The rationale for this is the evidence from the pornography literature that risk only emerges through an interaction between what might be described as 'subclinical' psychopathology and pornography consumption. We know that Internet only offenders consume pornog-raphy, but we also know that the majority appear to defy the risk that deviant sexual interest appears to confer on general sexual offenders. Perhaps the minority of Internet-only offenders who escalate to contact offending are those who exhibit poor self-regulation, hostility, coercive traits, poor planning, impulsivity and so on relative to other Internet-only offenders.

However such personality traits are measured, the proposition that there is likely to be an interaction between the expression of sexual deviance and such traits is scarcely novel. However, research undertaken with respect to associating psycho-logical characteristics and risk of escalation to contact offending might miss such an association if assessment measures are only norm referenced, and not refer-enced to the relevant population.

Sexual deviance and sexual preoccupation

Since the pioneering work of Kurt Freund (e.g. Freund and Blanchard, 1989), an enormous investment has been made in attempting to develop valid and reliable measures of deviant sexual interest. For many years the dominant methods were phallometry and traditional psychometrics, but more recently a number of very promising cognitive measures have been developed (e.g. Price and Hanson, 2007; Gress, 2005). It is of course important to investigate Internet offenders and Internet offending using whatever measures of sexual deviance are available. However, whereas with respect to personality traits Internet-only offenders present with a relatively low base rate of antisocial traits, the reverse is true with respect to sexual deviance. By definition, all Internet-only offenders have exhibited deviant sexual interest and it is no surprise that assessed by phallometry, many prove to be very responsive to images of children, and 'more paedophile' than contact sexual offenders (Seto et al., 2006). The question therefore arises as to whether there are any patterns of response that predict escalation to contact offending. Whether or not any association between patterns of sexual deviance and escalation can be established, understanding patterns of interest can be of great assistance when attempting to manage risk in the community.

Sexual preoccupation is the extent to which all facets of sexual behaviour and interest dominate an individual's life. Of course, this may fluctuate over time, rendering it rather difficult to measure and ascribe a fixed value. Attempts have been made to incorporate sexual preoccupation in psychometric tools (e.g. Lee and Forbey, 2010) but typically judgements are made following interview assess-ment. Whilst fluctuation in sexual preoccupation means it is a very poor static measure, it follows that accurate and reliable measurement of sexual preoccupation would offer an important measure of acute changes in risk (Hanson and Harris, 2000).

Risk factors and digital evidence

The recurrence of risk assessment throughout an investigation and possible prosecution of an individual found to be in possession of SEM on their computer (or mobile device) has already been described. Further, the digital evidence is subjected to a great deal of analysis in consideration of or preparation for a prosecution. This is achieved using extremely powerful and sophisticated forensic software tools. These are designed to analyse (without modifying) the content of digital storage devices. The process is a semi-automatic one, which means that investigators can focus their attention on material (whether text, video or images) most likely to reflect illegal activity. The software intelligently explores all of the locations in which information may be stored, whether that is intended or unintended by the user. Even material that has been deleted, encrypted or intentionally hidden can often be recovered and produced as evidence of possession or production of illegal material (Casey, 2002).

It might therefore be surprising to learn that only in the most evidently risky cases does the evidence emerging during the investigation process directly inform risk assessment and management once the individual has returned to the community. In the UK it is rare for professionals undertaking community risk assessments to receive documentation including risk assessment, and even more rare to have direct access to the digital evidence emerging during an investigation. The implicit assumption appears to be that the evidence relating to the offence and any risk assessment undertaken during transition through the CJS serve decision making within the CJS, but not child protection thereafter. This is directly contradictory to the prevailing guidance published by the UK government in Working Together to Safeguard Children (2010). If community based risk assessment were to be relatively straightforward, then the lack of continuity and liaison between criminal justice and child protection services would not be a particularly serious problem. However, as has been indicated, the means of assessing Internet only offenders are in the early stages of development, and professionals undertaking risk assessment in the community face very considerable challenges.

One such problem is simply knowing whether the individual being assessed or managed is honestly describing his historical behaviour with respect to SEM and the Internet, or indeed his own psychological processes underlying the behaviour. Buschman et al. (2010) have indicated in their study of Internet offenders that there were differences between the number of disclosed behaviours related to child sexual abuse images made between self-report and the use of the polygraph. This alone strongly suggests that a definitive description of the pattern and nature of Internet activity should be generated at the earliest opportunity, preserved and made available to all professionals thereafter involved in child protection. However, an even stronger case can be made for a more detailed analysis of the digital evidence in forming risk assessment. Glasgow (2010) argued in favour of multiple convergent measures of Internet offenders, including a detailed analysis of the digital evidence. Although such an analysis presents technical and systemic challenges, the potential for the digital record of online and offline activity in relation to SEM and other behaviour is considerable. Contained on the computer is a remarkably detailed record of what was accessed, downloaded, created, modified, browsed and deleted. The illegal activity can be placed in the context of legal but related activity, such as accessing legal pornography of various types, or undertaking searches for deviant and also non-deviant material.

To those investigating alleged offenders, legally held pornographic material is of very little interest. The process of analysis tends to be focused on identifying the presence of illegal material and attempting to associate that with provable activity of the individual under investigation. So, for example, if illegal online activity in a workplace only occurs when a specific employee is present, and ceases when he is absent through sickness or annual leave, this will have a forensic significance. Thus, the onset, frequency and duration of illegal behaviour is often analysed in some detail, because it may well have forensic significance with respect to establishing the link between the suspect and the activity. However, at the investigation stage there is understandably very little interest in associating patterns of activity or a trajectory of deviance with respect to the possibility of this reflecting relative risk of escalation to contact offending. The concepts of 'escalation' and 'trajectory' imply changes in activity that might reflect a number of factors critical to risk assessment. Changes in the pattern of Internet use might reflect dispositional instability or emotional dysregulation which may best be considered as 'within person' characteristics of relevance to risk assessment. Alternatively, or possibly concurrently, changes in the pattern of Internet use might reflect relational changes attributable to environmental or interpersonal triggers. If these triggers can be identified they might be hypothesized to be setting conditions for Internet offending and potential measures in risk mitigation and monitoring.

Another possibility is that escalation of the diversity and deviance of material sought by the individual can be detected. This is sometimes reported by Internet offenders post hoc, that is to say that they describe feeling the need to access and possess increasingly diverse or extreme material. Finally, there may be specific content elements that increase in prevalence over time, which might reflect an increasing salience of instrumental behaviour; that is the mechanisms and actions by which direct contact with a child might be achieved. This could either be in the form of written accounts of abuse, or in images that depict coercion, restraint or abuse-related contexts rather than simply sexual activity with a child. The converse of the above patterns would be a stable pattern of modest Internet use involving no escalation of instrumental behaviour, no instability of deviant focus and a few depictions of coercion, or restraint.

Whether such hypotheses about trajectory are supported by evidence remains to be seen. However, the hypotheses are relatively straightforward and eminently testable. In fact, assuming that trajectory in pattern or content can be satisfactorily operationalized, it would be quite straightforward to test these hypotheses using retrospective methodology. In other words, the data that would prove or disprove them already exist. The digital evidence in Internet offender cases is preserved and, if necessary, the original or additional analyses can be applied to the data. Somewhat ironically, the greatest challenge might be finding a sufficiently large sample of Internet-only offenders who have escalated to contact offending with whom non-escalators could be compared.

One of the most promising methods of quantitatively and qualitatively analysing both images and text is criterion-based content analysis (Glasgow et al., 2003). In fact, perhaps without being aware of it, investigators routinely used this methodology on digital evidence when they apply the COPINE scale (Taylor et al., 2001) to digital evidence. This is a 10-point scale that can be used to categorize SEM. It is essentially an atheoretical procedure, although the general characteristics are an escalating measure of 'seriousness' and deviance towards the higher end of the scale. This has been hugely influential both in structuring academic thought and also in the legal domain. So, for example, level 1 is 'Non-erotic and non-sexualised pictures showing children in their underwear, swimming costumes, etc. from either commercial sources or family albums; pictures of children playing in normal settings, in which the context or organisation of pictures by the collector indicates inappropriateness'. Level 5 is defined as 'Deliberately posed pictures of fully, partially clothed or naked children in sexualised or provocative poses', and level 9 as 'Grossly obscene pictures of sexual assault, involving penetrative sex, masturbation or oral sex involving an adult' (see Chapter 1 for a further discussion of the scale).

Unfortunately, research on the risk-related significance of the co-pilot scale has been seriously impaired by the fact that in the Court of Appeal decision of *R* v *Oliver* (Sentencing Advisory Panel 2002, *R* v *Oliver* (2003) Crim LR 127), it was held that images in categories of indicative, nudist or erotica material (i.e. COPINE categories 1-5) should not be used within the criminal definition of child pornography for the UK. As a result, for the purposes of criminal investigations/proceedings the COPINE scale is truncated and categories 6–10 are renumbered 1–5. These 'Oliver' categories are unfortunately also sometimes continue to be referred to as COPINE categories so that it is very easy for significant misunderstanding to arise in community risk assessments, where the foundation of the content analysis and numerical scale might not be made explicit. For the sake of absolute clarity the correspondence between COPINE and *Oliver* is represented in Table 10.1.

Routinely, in criminal proceedings and in the public reports of the same, an account is given of the frequencies of sexually explicit content at the various levels of the *Oliver* scale. So for example, in one case there might be seven images deemed to be at *Oliver* level 5, and in another case twelve determined to be at *Oliver* level 5. For the purposes of criminal proceedings that may well be satisfactory, because the heart of the issue is the presence or absence of illegal material. However, for the purposes of a risk assessment it is obviously important to place the highly deviant material within the context of non-deviant material sought and downloaded. Thus, to continue the example given above, if the seven images at *Oliver* level 5 arise within the context of only fifty or sixty images, this may have

Table 10.1 The correspondence between the COPINE scale and the *Oliver* ruling

COPINE	1	2	3	4	5	6	7	8	9	10
Oliver	Unused					1	2	3	4	5

completely different implications from twelve images excerpted from a corpus of 5,000. This would be particularly true if the profile of the corpus was skewed towards the lower end of the co-pilot scale, and some or all of the twelve deviant images had never actually been viewed. Although the pattern of images within an *Oliver* content analysis is often taken into account by a criminal court, it does not determine whether or not an offence has been committed.

The importance of the nature and intensity of sexual deviance in determining risk of recidivism in non-Internet offenders is well established. Content analysis of SEM possessed by an Internet offender offers the promise of an extremely direct measure of numerous preference expressions captured over weeks, months or even years. There are no psychometric or behavioural measures currently in use that can offer the prospect of anything approaching such fine-grained, repeated measures, free from response bias (although see Mokros et al., 2010). Further, the possibility of a new and independent measure of sexual deviance based on content analysis could offer a valuable corroboration of physiological, self-report and cognitive measures. Over a decade ago Laws et al. demonstrated the potential of convergent measures of sexual interest, although it remains rare for direct measures of interest to be used at all (Laws et al., 2000).

The sheer volume of downloaded material in some cases can render criterion-based content analysis a rather daunting proposition. However, the quantity of material offers the opportunity to treat it as a sample frame from which to draw material which is preferred by the individual being assessed, rather than having been downloaded and never viewed, or only accessed once, or even simply left in a compressed archive. Based on these principles, Glasgow (2010) describes the Internet Sex Offender Profiling System (ISOPS), along with how to identify material likely to be preferred by the system user. The overriding principle is to focus on the files that have been operated on either to camouflage them or to make them easier to access on a regular basis. For example, those that are encrypted or copied to external drives, those that are camouflaged by being placed in obscure sub-directories or given deceptive names, and those that are represented in a favourites folder or equivalent. This selection process requires some technical knowledge, but would represent only a very small additional burden to the detailed analyses already undertaken.

Once a sample of material likely to represent preferred stimuli is identified, it can be subjected to a content analysis addressing the erotic focus of the material by age, gender and sexual activity. It follows that a simple tally can be obtained and summarized in a table, the categories of which correspond to both self-report categories and those of convergent measures of paedophile interest. So for example, Table 10.2 would strongly suggest heterosexual hebephilia (a sexual

Table 10.2 Content analysis of materials suggesting
heterosexual hebephilia.

	Male	*Female*
Adult	2	25
Juvenile	2	53
Pre-juvenile	3	9
Small-child	2	1
Unspecified-child	6	7

preference for pubertal children between the ages of, approximately, 11 to 14 years of age), which could be corroborated (or otherwise) by comparison with other measures of sexual interest (e.g. the Affinity procedure which is explained in detail in Glasgow et al., 2003 and Worling, 2006). (Inter-rater reliability of the Affinity category system is of significance here, and as yet untested, largely because the Affinity system is itself an appositive procedure.) However, the developmental categories specified and used within ISOPS are clear, and are supported with estimated age ranges, and illustrative archetypes. The categorization task using ISOPS is certainly much easier than categorizing according to Tanner scales (Marshall and Tanner, 1969), where categories are skewed towards pubertal and post-pubertal figures, and also require rather nuanced distinctions based on primary and secondary sexual characteristics.

A similar analysis can be applied to text images and video, and the same procedure adopted to determine whether coercive or sadistic activity is a significant feature in the individual sexual interest or fantasies. Of course, the presence of sadomasochistic material, or that including coercion, restraint, representation of abduction does not imply that contact offending involving these features will necessarily follow. (Determining the association between sadomasochistic material and behaviour is an empirical question which again could be answered quite readily by appropriately informed research). However, the value of these assessments can often lie in the reassuring absence of any evidence of sadistic traits.

By way of illustration, it might be helpful to refer to a real case example. A man (N) who had been convicted of child pornography offences four years previously formed a relationship with a woman who had a 10-year-old son who suffered from Down's syndrome. N was no longer subject to any statutory supervision, so social services commenced child protection proceedings, for which a risk assessment was commissioned. Relationships between N, the child and the child's mother appeared positive. The offence had not been kept a secret, and in fact the initiative for contacting social services was taken by N.

Routine psychometric assessment of personality revealed no significant concerns, and on any static risk assessment tool, N would be deemed to present a low risk of offending. Cognitive and self-report measures of sexual interest suggested sexual interests focusing on both adults and adolescent females. However, as is often the case, it proved remarkably difficult to obtain information regarding the digital evidence relating to N's conviction, or even summary statistics on the SEM found on his computer equipment. It was recorded that among the evidence were three images at *Oliver* level 2 (COPINE 6, 'Involves touching, mutual and self-masturbation, oral sex and intercourse by child, not involving an adult') and two at *Oliver* 3 (COPINE 7, 'Pictures of children being subject to a sexual assault, involving digital touching, involving an adult'). Aside from this, very little information was available. It seemed there was the possibility that a decision about whether to remove the child into care would have to be made without a systematic analysis of the digital evidence.

Fortunately, the digital evidence was eventually released, and subjected to criteria-based content analysis using the ISOPS system. The key findings were as follows:

- All the images upon which the conviction was based had been deleted by N. There was no evidence that this was in anticipation of arrest.
- Other images had been retained for repeated access.
- Search terms he used related to sexually explicit images of adults, or pubertal females.
- There was no evidence of preference for material featuring coercion, sado-masochism or restraint.
- He had never created or acquired material supportive of adult–child sexual behaviour.
- He had the opportunity to offend for many months prior to the commencement of downloading SEM, but apparently had not done so.
- The offences were committed over a period of several weeks coinciding with an episode of depression and deterioration of his then sexual relationship.
- There was evidence of an escalation in use of the Internet and during this time, suggesting increased sexual preoccupation.
- It was not possible to specify when the illegal material was downloaded (because it had been deleted, and therefore was no longer associated with the date that the file was created).
- There was no evidence that N had exhibited any 'digital' instrumental behaviour, relating to contacting or attempting to contact any adult of child via the Internet.
- He had only one online persona and this was an honest one. That is, it had not been used to misrepresent himself, or deceive others.
- A content analysis revealed a profile of preferred images consisting of adult and pubertal females. The profile closely matched that arising from self-report and cognitive assessment.
- There was no evidence of dominant paedophile interests, and no evidence of homosexual interests.

The convergence of the digital evidence and that arising from assessment and interview was very clear. Had there been any discrepancies, these could have been exploited in further investigation and interview in order to make an informed decision in this case. As it was, the decision was made that Mr N was unlikely to present a significant risk of sexual harm to his prospective stepson. The family therefore remained intact, although a degree of monitoring continued thereafter for some time.

Informing community risk assessments

This example illustrates how many of the dilemmas surrounding the assessment of sexually criminal behaviour which relate to the Internet may be managed. To date, assessments of Internet sex offenders often rely on self-report information and official reports of prior offending, and make little reference to the nature of the images downloaded outside of the fact that they are illegal. Glasgow (2010) has argued that Internet offenders constitute a heterogeneous group, some of whom may present a significant risk of future contact offending, but many of whom, perhaps a majority, do not. It is essential that risk assessment procedures are developed which can discriminate reliably between relatively high-risk and low-risk groups. The sheer volume, complexity and inaccessibility of digital evidence has deterred a systematic analysis of the relationship between downloaded material and potential risk. However, rather than being regarded as an impenetrable confusion of information, it is possible to regard downloaded material as a golden opportunity to analyse unequivocal evidence of sexual and possibly also personality deviance known to be associated with risk. It also offers the potential of informing and validating other assessment procedures, including interviews.

References

Babchishin, K.M., Hanson, R.K. and Hermann, C.A. (2010). The characteristics of online sex offenders: A meta-analysis. *Sexual Abuse: A Journal of Research and Treatment, 23*(1), 92–23.

Beesley, F. and McGuire, J. (2009) Gender-role identity and hypermasculinity in violent offending. *Psychology, Crime and Law, 15*(2&3), 251–68.

Bensimon, P. (2007). The role of pornography in sexual offending. *Sexual Addiction and Compulsivity, 14*, 95–117.

Bivona, J. and Critelli, J. (2009). The nature of women's rape fantasies: An analysis of prevalence, frequency, and contents. *Journal of Sex Research, 46*(1), 33–45.

Briere, J. and Runtz, M. (1989). University males' sexual interest in children: Predicting potential indices of 'pedophilia' in a nonforensic sample. *Child Abuse and Neglect, 13*, 65–5.

Buschman, J., Bogaerts, S., Foulger, S., Wilcox, D., Sosnowski, D. and Cushman, B. (2010). Sexual history disclosure polygraph examinations with cybercrime offences: A first Dutch explorative study. *International Journal of Offender Therapy and Comparative Criminology, 54*, 395–11.

Casey, E. (2002). Practical approaches to recovering encrypted digital evidence. *International Journal of Digital Evidence, 1*(3), available online at http://www.ijde.org.

Eke, A.W., Seto., M.C. and Williams, J. (in press). Examining the criminal history and future offending of child pornography offenders: An extended prospective follow-up study. *Law and Human Behaviour, 1–3.*

Endrass, J., Urbaniok, F., Hammermeister, L.C., Benz, C., Elbert, T., Laubacher, A and Rossegger, A. (2009). The consumption of Internet child pornography and violent and sex offending. *BMC Psychiatry, 9*, 43–9.

Freund, K. and Blanchard, R. (1989). Phallometric diagnosis of pedophilia. *Journal of Consulting and Clinical Psychology, 57*(1), 100–105.

Glasgow, D. (2010). The potential of digital evidence to contribute to risk assessment of internet offenders. *Journal of Sexual Aggression, 16*(1), 223–37.

Glasgow, D.V., Osborne, A. and Croxen, J. (2003). An assessment tool for investigating paedophile sexual interest using viewing time: An application of single case methodology. *British Journal of Learning Disabilities, 31*(2), 96–102.

Gress, C.L.Z. (2005). Viewing time measures and sexual interest: Another piece of the puzzle. *Journal of Sexual Aggression, 11*(2), 117–25.

Hanson, R.K., and Harris, A.J.R. (2000). Where should we intervene? Dynamic predictors of sexual offense recidivism. *Criminal Justice and Behavior, 27*, 6–35.

Jespersen, A.F., Lalumière, M.L. and Seto, M.C. (2009). Sexual abuse history among adult sex offenders and non-sex offenders: A meta-analysis. *Child Abuse and Neglect, 33*(3), 179–2.

Jonason, P.K. and Tost, J. (2010). I just cannot control myself: the dark triad and self-control. *Personality and Individual Differences, 49*, 606–10.

Kemshall, H. and Wood, J. (2008). Risk and public protection: Responding to involuntary and 'taboo' risk. *Social Policy &Administration, 42*(6), 611–29.

King, D.B., DeCicco, T.L. and Humphreys, T.P. (2009). Investigating sexual dream imagery in relation to daytime sexual behaviours and fantasies among Canadian university students. *Canadian Journal of Human Sexuality, 18*(3), 135–46.

Lam, A, Mitchell, J. and Seto, M.C. (2010). Lay perceptions of child pornography offenders. *Canadian Journal of Criminology and Criminal Justice, 52*, 173–201.

Laws, D.R., Hanson, R.K., Osborn, C.A. and Greenbaum, C.E. (2000). Classification of child molesters by plethysmographic assessment of sexual arousal and a self-report measure of sexual preference. *Journal of Interpersonal Violence, 15*(12), 1297–312.

Lee, T. and Forbey, J.D. (2010). MMPI– correlates of sexual preoccupation as measured by the sexuality scale in a college setting. *Sexual Addiction and Compulsivity, 17*(3), 219–35.

Lipsey, M.W. (2009). The primary factors that characterize effective interventions with juvenile offenders: A meta-analytic overview. *Victims and Offenders, 4*, 124–47.

Logan, W.A. (2008). Sex offender registration and community notification: Past, present, and future. *Criminal and Civil Confinement, 34*, 3–6.

Lussier, P., Tzoumakis, S., Cale, J. and Amirault, J. (2010). Criminal trajectories of adult sex offenders and the age effect: Examining the dynamic aspect of offending in adulthood. *International Criminal Justice Review, 20*, 147–68.

Maniglio, R. (2010). The role of deviant sexual fantasy in the etiopathogenesis of sexual homicide: A systematic review. *Aggression and Violent Behavior, 15*(4), 294–302.

Marshall, W.A. and Tanner, J.M. (1969). Variations in pattern of pubertal changes in girls. *Archives of Diseases of Childhood, 44* (235), 291–303.

Mokros, A., Dombert, B., Osterheider, M., Zappalà, A. and Santtila, P. (2010). Assessment of pedophilic sexual interest with an attentional choice reaction time task. *Archives of Sexual Behavior, 39*(5), 1081–90.

Osborn, J., Elliott, I.A. and Beech, A.R. (2010). The use of actuarial risk assessment measures with UK internet child pornography offenders. *Journal of Aggression, Conflict and Peace Research, 2*(3), 16–24.

Price, S.A. and Hanson, K.A. (2007). A modified Stroop task with sexual offenders: Replication of a study. *Journal of Sexual Aggression, 13*(3), 203–16.

Romano, E. and De Luca, R.V. (1997). Exploring the relationship between childhood sexual abuse and adult sexual perpetration. *Journal of Family Violence, 12*(1), 85–8.

Seto, M.C., Maric, A. and Barbaree, H.C. (2001). The role of pornography in the etiology of sexual aggression. *Aggression and Violent Behavior*, 6(1), 35–3.

Seto, M.C., Cantor, J.M. and Blanchard, R. (2006). Child pornography offences are a valid diagnostic indicator of pedophilia. *Journal of Abnormal Psychology*, *115*, 610–15.

Siegert, R.J., Ward, T., Levack, W.E. and McPherson, K.M. (2007). A good lives model of clinical and community rehabilitation. *Disability and Rehabilitation, 29*(20–1), 1604–15.

Taylor, M., Holland, G. and Quayle, E. (2001). Typology of paedophile picture collections. *The Police Journal, 74*(2), 97–107.

Vizard, E. (2007). Adolescent sexual offenders. *Psychiatry*, 6(10), 433–7.

Williams, K.M., Cooper, B.S., Howell, T.M., Yuille, J.C. and Paulhus, D.L. (2009). Inferring sexually deviant behavior from corresponding fantasies: The role of personality and pornography consumption. *Criminal Justice and Behavior, 36*, 198–22.

Working Together to Safeguard Children: A guide to inter-agency working to safeguard and promote the welfare of children (2010). Department of Education: United Kingdom. Available online at https://www.education.gov.uk/publications/standard/publication detail/page1/DCSF-00305–010.

Worling, J.R. (2006). Assessing sexual arousal with adolescent males who have offended sexually: Self-report and unobtrusively measured viewing time. **Sexual Abuse, 18**, 383–400.

Zurbriggen, E.L. and Yost, M.R. (2004). Power, desire, and pleasure in sexual fantasies. *The Journal of Sex Research, 41*(3), 288–300.

11 Situational prevention of child abuse in the new technologies

Richard Wortley, Jill Dando Institute of Security and Crime Science, University College London

Overview

Situational prevention shifts attention from the psychological characteristics of the individual performing behaviour to the facilitating role played by the immediate environment in which the behaviour occurs. Applied to the problem of Internet child pornography, the situational approach emphasizes the role of opportunity in driving consumption. It is argued that under the right environmental conditions the potential to view children as sexual objects is more widespread than sexual deviance models suggest. The Internet allows individuals to satisfy their secret desires conveniently, cheaply and relatively risk-free. Situational prevention of Internet child pornography requires strategies that reduce the opportunities for accessing child abuse images by making the activity less rewarding, more difficult and riskier.

Introduction

In April 1982, the US General Accounting Office reported to the Sub Committee on Juvenile Justice of the House Committee on Education and Labor that:

> discussions with Federal, State and local officials indicated that commercially produced (child) pornography has declined. The factors responsible for this decline were (1) the Protection of Children Against Sexual Exploitation Act of 1977, (2) tougher State laws covering child pornography, (3) stricter enforcement of obscenity laws involving child pornography, (4) media attention, (5) the tendency of juries to convict child pornographers more readily than adult pornographers, and (6) the banning in 1979 of child pornography in Sweden and Denmark, which had been the major overseas supplier of child pornography. As a result of the decline in commercial child pornography, the principal Federal agencies responsible for enforcing laws covering the distribution of child pornography – the U.S. Customs Service and the U.S. Postal Service – do not consider child pornography a high priority.
>
> (Ahart, 1982: 7)

On 1 January 1983 the first standardized protocols for the Internet were implemented and everything changed. While it is impossible accurately to estimate the amount of child pornography currently available via the Internet, or the number of individuals who now access child exploitation images, all commentators agree that the problem has increased exponentially since the 1980s (Carr, 2004; Ferraro and Casey, 2003; Jenkins, 2001). Prior to the Internet, images were scarce, locally produced, of poor quality, expensive and difficult to obtain, traded furtively in hard-copy form among small, closely knit networks of dedicated consumers. The Internet has dramatically escalated the child pornography problem by increasing the amount of material that is available, the efficiency of its distribution, and the ease by which it can be accessed. It has made vast quantities of technically high-quality images instantly available, at any time, and with (apparent) anonymity. Alone and in the comfort of their own home, individuals are able to satisfy their secret curiosities and desires conveniently, cheaply and relatively risk free (Calder, 2004; Wortley and Smallbone, 2006a).

The argument to be made in this chapter is that the growth of the child pornography problem in the Internet age is a classic example of supply-led demand. The treatment of children as sexual objects is as old as humanity, and there is a long history of erotic literature, drawings and (since the mid-nineteenth century) photographs involving children (Bullough, 2004; Linz and Imrich, 2001; O'Donnell and Milner, 2007). However, the extent to which child pornography has been a social problem has been limited by the supply of pornographic material. What has changed since 1982 is the easy availability of images with which latent sexual interest in children can be satisfied. The prevention of Internet child pornography cannot be approached simply as a problem of individual sexual deviancy. The recent surge in child pornography usage is a product of the Internet, and any attempts to reduce levels of child pornography use that do not include reducing the opportunities provided by the Internet to access images are bound to be inadequate.

Theoretical orientation: the person–situation interaction

The role that opportunity has played in increasing the problem of child sexual exploitation derives from the principle that all behaviour is the product of a person–situation interaction (e.g. Mischel, 1968). The immediate environment is more than an incidental backdrop to behaviour; it plays a fundamental role in initiating behaviour and shaping its course. While this principle is fundamental in psychology, its full significance is widely overlooked by psychologists in their theorizing and practice. The causes of behaviour – particularly in the clinical field – are typically construed in person-centred terms. Explanatory models of aberrant behaviour focus on the historical processes by which an individual is assumed to have become deviant or disordered. Once a particular behavioural propensity has been acquired, the behaviour is assumed inevitably to follow and the job of explaining it is complete. A person behaves in deviant ways because he/she has a deviant disposition. Accordingly, the way of preventing unwanted behaviour is seen to be through treatments that are designed to alter these underlying aberrant propensities.

Psychologists have recognized the tendency for human beings to construe causation in person-centred terms and to ignore or downplay the role of situational factors. This cognitive bias is referred to as fundamental attribution error (Jones, 1979; Ross, 1977). Even when someone's actions are unambiguously forced upon them by circumstances beyond their control, observers typically underestimate the role of these outside pressures and construct causal explanations that assume personal agency on the part of the actor. Fundamental attribution error is accompanied by an exaggerated belief in the stability of the personal characteristics of others and overconfidence that their behaviour is therefore constant from one situation to the next. It is thought that the tendency to categorize others in terms of predictable dispositions has evolved as an efficient information processing strategy that helps people deal with the complexity of the world around them. However, this ingrained faith in personal control makes it difficult for people to accept that situational factors play anything other than a trivial role in behaviour. There is perhaps some irony in the fact that, by focusing on the intrapsychic causes of deviant behaviour, many psychologists seem as prone to fundamental attribution error as is the general population.

The role played by situational factors in behaviour is consistent with the so-called control perspective on criminal behaviour (Gottfredson and Hirshi, 1990). The usual question in criminology and forensic psychology is to ask: how do individuals come to behave in antisocial ways? Most theories of crime are theories of the acquisition of behaviour. They begin from the assumption that individuals are born in a criminally neutral state, and that antisocial behaviours are learned via cultural and developmental experiences. Control theories turn this question around and ask: how do individuals come to behave in pro-social ways? Control theories begin with the assumption that the tendency to act impulsively and selfishly is the natural human condition and does not need to be explained. What needs to be explained is the process by which these natural impulses are brought under control. Control theorists ask you to imagine the case of a child raised without any constraints being placed on his/her behaviour. The result would be an individual who satisfies his/her urges indiscriminately. Socialization involves learning to curb these self-satisfying urges. 'Deviant' and 'non-deviant' individuals differ not so much in the nature of their self-serving motivations but in their capacity to control those motivations. However, even individuals with high levels of self-control are not always successful in controlling self-gratifying impulses and may from time to time succumb to temptation.

The desire for sexual gratification is a powerful and universal motivator. Consider the inventive study carried out by Demetriou and Silke (2003). They established a website that contained links to legal sites, offering shareware and soft pornography, as well as purported links (that did not work) to illegal or obscene sites, offering commercial games, commercial software, hardcore pornography and stolen passwords. People were directed to the website if they searched for 'shareware', 'freeware', 'free', 'free games' and 'free software', although some search engines accessed other terms contained on the site itself. Tracking the key words used to arrive at the site, Demetriou and Silke found that of 803 visitors, only 26 were specifically looking for pornography. Nevertheless, the hard-core pornography link was by far the most popular of all the links, clicked by 483 visitors, while the soft-core pornography link, with 358 clicks, was the second most popular. Legal shareware, the reason most people visited the site in the first place, was the least popular link with only 268 clicks. Demetriou and Silke interpreted their findings in terms of the psychological construct of deindividuation. Deindividuation is the reduced capacity of individuals to self-regulate their behaviour under conditions of anonymity. Disinhibition is produced not just by a perceived freedom from the censure of others, but more fundamentally by freedom from self-censure. Freed from the personal and social controls that might otherwise have inhibited them from viewing hard-core pornography, the majority of visitors to the site chose to satisfy their sexual curiosities.

Viewing hard-core pornography is one thing, but what about clearly deviant inclinations such as sexual attraction to children? The problem with the sexual deviancy model is that no one has adequately defined sexual normalcy against which deviancy can be measured. The human sexual response is extraordinarily versatile. The control approach suggests that the potential to view children as sexual objects is common (perhaps universal) in humans. Human males in particular – and the overwhelming majority of child sexual offenders are male – are evolutionarily designed for a sexual preference for youthful partners (Thornhill and Thornhill, 1987; 1992). In Victorian Britain it was legal to have sex with a girl as young as 10 years of age (raised to 12 by the Offences Against the Person Act, 1861), while there are still countries in the world in which the age of consent for girls is as low as 12 years (Avert, n.d.). In fact, all of us have probably experienced being sexually attracted to a child when we ourselves were children. Thankfully, for most of us, our sexual preferences have remained age appropriate as we have aged. Any latent sexual attraction to children is controlled by our personal values and inhibitions, social pressures and expectations, cultural taboos and legal sanctions, and physical deterrents and barriers. However, where these controls break down, many men may take advantage of available opportunities for sexual gratification involving children. While clearly ethically problematic, it is intriguing to ponder what Demetriou and Silke (2003) might have found if they had included a purported link to a child pornography site in their Internet study.

There is an understandable reluctance about openly discussing the widespread potential for sexual attraction to children. Few people are comfortable admitting that they may have dark thoughts buried deep in the private recesses of their minds. Moreover, it may be feared that talking about sexual attraction to youthful partners as an evolutionary-endowed component of human nature is tantamount to excusing the sexual exploitation of children. Let me make it clear that whether or not men are designed to prefer youthful partners has no bearing on the moral or legal status of the sexual exploitation of children. If one accepted the logic of a link, then it could be equally argued that assault and murder ought to be legalized because human beings are naturally aggressive. There are very good reasons for making the sexual exploitation of children illegal. Indeed, it can be argued that treating the sexual exploitation of children as a legal rather than a psychological issue makes the moral culpability of the offender clearer, not less clear. Sexual exploitation of children is illegal because we have chosen to make it illegal; as a society we have declared that we find such behaviour unacceptable and we want to stamp it out. Pretending that the world is neatly divided into paedophiles and non-paedophiles may be comforting but it is unhelpful when formulating strategies to control the sexual exploitation of children.

I should also emphasize that I am not arguing that all men are equally vulnerable to exhibiting sexually exploitive behaviour towards children and that dispositions do not matter. Most men reading this chapter will (quite rightly) deny any adult experiences of sexual attraction to children. The concept of a person–situation interaction, in fact, depends upon this being the case. By definition, a person–situation interaction occurs when different individuals react differently to the same situation, with some people more dispositionally susceptible to respond to particular situational cues than others (see Wortley, 2011). Thus, the effect of the situation on behaviour depends upon (interacts with) the characteristics of the person; the stronger the individual's propensity to perform a given behaviour, the weaker the situational pressures required for that behaviour to occur, and vice versa. Undoubtedly, there is a relatively small core of men who are strongly predisposed to exploit children sexually. They need little in the way of situational encouragement and will actively and determinedly seek out opportunities to satisfy their sexual urges. Most men are not preferentially attracted to children. However, to varying degrees according to their dispositional characteristics, they may be tempted or induced to engage in sexually exploitative behaviour given the 'right' situational conditions (Smallbone et al., 2008; Wortley and Smallbone, 2006b). Of course, for most, these 'right' circumstances will never eventuate.

The person–situation interaction provides an explanation for why the introduction of the Internet has resulted in such a dramatic escalation of the child pornography problem. It has exacerbated the problem in two ways: increasing both the amount of available pornography and the number of individuals accessing it. First, for those individuals with an active interest in child pornography the Internet has greatly facilitated their access to the images that they crave. Had these individuals lived in the pre-Internet era, many may have sought out hard-copy child pornography images. However, the task would have been much more difficult, the choice much more restricted, and the collection of images that they would have managed to accumulate much smaller. It is not uncommon for offenders to be arrested with child pornography collections exceeding half a million images (Carr, 2004).

Second, while no one has accurate figures comparing the number of people using child pornography pre- and post-Internet, there seems little doubt that the Internet has allowed many individuals who otherwise would not have used child pornography now to do so. Jenkins (2001) reported that a single child pornography site received over one million hits in a one-month period. In the pre-Internet era, many of these new users would have lacked the know-how and/or dedicated sexual interest in children that was required to hunt down hard-copy images. By making it easier for people to view child pornography, the Internet has provided individuals with the opportunity to explore their perhaps casual and vaguely formed sexual attraction to children. Conventionally, we tend to think of deviant sexual behaviour as resulting from deviant sexual motivations. However, it is possible that for many users of child pornography the order of causation is reversed; the act of viewing child pornography ignites and strengthens their sexual interest in children. Initially curious, over time the individual may become increasingly interested in child pornography, become attracted to images of increasing severity, and become desensitized to the harms that victims experience. It is noteworthy that attempts to profile Internet child pornography offenders have identified few distinguishing psychological and socio-demographic characteristics, and they share few features with contact child sex offenders (Elliott et al., 2009; Sheldon and Howitt, 2007; Webb et al., 2007). Most Internet pornography offenders are likely to be male, to be between the ages of 26 and 39 years, to be white, to be in a relationship, to be employed, to have above average IQ, to be college educated, and not to have a criminal record (Blundell, et al., 2002; Schwartz and Southern, 2000; Wolak et al., 2005; Wolak et al., 2003). Those arrested for online pornography crimes have come from all walks of life, and include judges, soldiers, dentists, teachers, academics and police officers (Calder, 2004). It is the ordinariness, not the deviance, of many online child pornography users that is striking.

Situational prevention

Just as psychologists typically think about the causes of behaviour in person-centred terms, so too do they tend to think about prevention of behaviour in person-centred terms. Prevention of criminal behaviour is seen to require fundamental changes to the individual's disposition. This might be achieved via developmental interventions aimed at altering the early risk factors for criminality, or more commonly through the treatment of individuals once they have exhibited unwanted behaviours. However, if behaviour is the product of a person–situation interaction, then attempting to change it by addressing the situational side of the equation is at least as valid as is the traditional focus on attempting to change the individual's dispositions.

Clinicians will be familiar with environmental interventions in the form of behaviour therapies such as relapse prevention and stimulus control. In these treatments, clients are instructed to identify and avoid situations that might trigger unwanted behavioural patterns. For example, a person on a diet might ensure that food is put away in cupboards, and a convicted child sex offender might avoid walking past schools. However, developed originally in criminology (Clarke, 1997; 2008; Cornish and Clarke, 2003), situational prevention has more in common with the public health primary and secondary prevention models than with the clinical treatment model. Situational interventions are designed to prevent behaviour before it occurs. Moreover, they are not formulated for a single client in the manner of behaviour therapy, but are directed at specific environments that might facilitate the unwanted behaviour of many individuals. It is the crime event rather than the individual that is the object of analysis. By carefully analysing the situational characteristics of crime events, the prevention practitioner is in a position to develop environmental counter-strategies. The object of situation interventions is to inhibit unwanted behaviour in specific contexts, not to cure individuals.

The most common model of situational prevention is opportunity reduction (Clarke, 2008; Cornish and Clarke, 2003; 2008). In line with the control perspective on behaviour, individuals are assumed to act in ways that will deliver them benefits. Opportunity reduction involves manipulating the immediate environmental contingencies so as to increase the perceived costs of offending. Reducing the opportunities for crime can significantly slow down prolific offenders, and may deter completely those less determined offenders. In this section, three opportunity-reduction strategies are examined and applied to the problem of Internet child pornography – reducing perceived rewards, increasing the perceived effort, and increasing the perceived risks.[1]

Reducing perceived rewards

According to the opportunity thesis, offenders commit crimes because they are seeking to benefit in some way from the outcome of the crime. In the case of Internet child pornography, the primary benefit is the acquisition of images from which the offender derives sexual gratification. Reducing the rewards of Internet child pornography essentially involves removing or denying access to the child pornography images that are targeted by offenders.

Internet Service Provider (ISPs) have a central role to play in reducing the number of child pornography images available on the Internet. The legal obligations of ISPs vary among jurisdictions. By and large they are not required actively to seek out and remove illegal sites (Klain et al., 2001; Stanley, 2001) although they may be required to report sites of which they become aware (McCabe, 2008). The policing of child pornography on servers therefore usually depends upon industry self-regulation. A number of ISP associations have drafted formal codes of practice that explicitly bind members not knowingly to accept illegal content on their sites and to removing such sites when they become aware of their existence. Service agreement contracts with clients will often set out expected standards that apply to site content, including explicit proscription of the uploading of child pornography. Large ISPs may have active cyber patrols that search for illegal sites. In addition, some ISP associations have set up Internet sites or hotlines that allow users to report illegal practices (Stewart, 1997). ISPs may also be notified by police Internet child exploitations (ICE) investigators about illegal child pornography hosted on their servers.

ISPs can apply filters to the browsers and search engines their customers use to locate websites (Carr, 2004; Jenkins, 2001; Linz and Imrich, 2001). There are numerous filtering methods. For example, filters can effectively treat certain keywords as if they do not exist, so that using these words in a search will be fruitless (Thornburgh and Lin, 2002; Lee et al., 2003). Additionally, some search engines display a warning message advising the searcher when he/she may be about to enter an illegal site. Software that can identify pornographic images is also being developed (Thompson, 2009).

There are two competing commercial forces acting on ISPs with respect to self-regulation. On the one hand, if an ISP restricts access to child pornography on its server, it may lose out financially to other ISPs who do not. Therefore, it will always be possible for offenders to find ISPs who will store or provide access to child pornography sites. On the other hand, ISPs also have their commercial reputation to protect, and it is often in their best interests to cooperate with law enforcement agencies. Most major ISPs have shown a commitment to tackling the problem of child pornography, partly motivated by the desire to protect the reputation of their brand name. In some cases direct economic pressure may be applied to service providers to encourage them to monitor illegal content. In one example of this, major brands have withdrawn advertising from networks that carry child pornography (Adegoke, 2003).

The success of reducing rewards as a prevention strategy has had mixed results. Calder (2004) estimated that ISPs have removed over 20,000 pornographic images of children from the Internet over the previous eight years. However, removing all child pornography from the Internet is an enormous, and frankly impossible, task. Arguably there has been considerable success in reducing the volume of child pornography in open areas of the Internet such as the World Wide Web (www).[2] Many researchers believe that because of the vigilance of ISPs and the police in tracking down and closing child pornography websites, it is unlikely that a normal web search using keywords such as 'childporn' would reveal much in the way of genuine child pornography (Forde and Patterson, 1998; Jenkins, 2001; Lesce, 1999). Instead, at most, searchers are likely to find legal pornography websites with adults purporting to be minors, and they may encounter police sting operations or vigilante sites.[3] One consequence has been to drive dedicated offenders to deeper levels of the Internet where they trade images in specific child pornography chat rooms and newsgroups. While most commercial servers block access to such sites they are much more difficult to regulate. Equally, they are also more difficult for offenders to access. Offenders require knowledge of where to locate child pornography sites and the technical skill to access them. Many child pornography chat rooms and newsgroups are secured sites, that is, a password is required in order to gain access to them. Passwords, in turn, can be difficult to obtain. Because of the risk that these sites will be infiltrated by undercover police, potential users are carefully vetted before being allowed to join. Thus, the movement of child pornography activity to these hidden areas of the Internet has at least increased the effort that offenders must expend in order to locate child pornography images, and as described in the following section, effort is a deterrent.

Increasing the perceived effort

All things being equal, offenders will select crimes that are easy to commit, and they may impulsively commit crimes just because they require so little effort. Even where increased effort does not prevent crime it may reduce the number of offences that can be committed by a given offender. At a trivial level, we can observe the effect of effort on our own behaviour when we decide that we cannot be bothered to get up from the couch to make ourselves a cup of coffee. However, effort plays a significant role in even deeply motivated behaviour. Consider the classic study by Clarke and Mayhew (1988) on suicide patterns in the UK. Traditionally, up to 40 per cent of suicide cases involved the use of domestic coal gas, which is toxic. However, from 1958 to 1977 the UK progressively switched from coal gas to non-toxic natural gas. As the changeover occurred, suicide rates fell from 5,298 to 3,944, a reduction that was almost entirely accounted for by the drop in suicide by gassing, which fell from 2,637 to two. Gassing is a relatively convenient and easy method of suicide, requiring little in the way of skill or planning. Many potential suicide victims who might have selected gassing as their method of choice, abandoned their suicide attempt when that option was denied rather than seek out other less convenient methods.

In the context of Internet child pornography, increasing the perceived effort involves making it more difficult for offenders to access child pornography images. As noted in the previous section, removing easily accessed child pornography from the Internet has the effect of forcing offenders to expend greater effort in order to obtain images, an effort that many cannot or will not make. Other suggestions to increase effort include making it more difficult to get Internet access, to send and receive child pornography, and to pay for child pornography.

One way to increase the effort required to gain Internet access is for ISPs to verify the identities of people who open Internet accounts. Currently, in most jurisdictions accounts may be opened using false names and addresses, and this makes it difficult to trace individuals who engage in illegal Internet activity. In addition, without verifying users' ages, there is no way of knowing if children are operating Internet accounts without adult supervision. This problem of Internet anonymity has increased as accessing the Internet via mobile phones has become commonplace, and both ISPs and mobile phone networks need to strengthen procedures for user verification (Carr, 2004).

Internet child pornography images must be traded electronically. At present there are a number of relatively simple strategies that offenders can employ to send and receive images safely. One technique is to trade via peer-to-peer (P2P) networks, in which computers connect directly to one another's hard drive without the need for a central server. There have been repeated calls for tighter regulation of P2P networks, and police agencies are increasingly targeting P2P networks in crackdowns on child pornography (GAO, 2004; Lemos, 2008; Lyman, 2004). Another strategy is to send files via anonymous remailers. Remailers are servers that forward emails after stripping them of sender identification. It has been argued that much tighter regulation of remailers is necessary. Some have advocated making remailer administrators legally responsible for knowingly forwarding illegal material, while others have called for a complete ban on remailers (Mostyn, 2000). In the language of situational crime prevention, targeting the use by offenders of P2P networks and remailers is an example of controlling the tools that aid the commission of crime (Cornish and Clarke, 2003).

Finally, in many cases child pornography has to be paid for, and this is most easily done via credit card transactions. It has been argued that credit card companies have a duty not to contribute knowingly to illegal acts (Taylor and Quayle, 2006). A number of credit card companies now block payments for child pornography (Sutton and Jones, 2004). A similar strategy has been applied to block the illegal sale of cigarettes over the Internet. Ribisl et al. (2011) showed that banning credit card payments for illegal cigarette sales resulted in a 3.5-fold decline in traffic to the most popular Internet cigarette vendor sites.

Increasing the perceived risks

Most major police jurisdictions have dedicated units devoted to scanning the Internet for ICE images and infiltrating ICE newsgroups. However, law enforcement personnel are under no illusions that they will be able to make a serious dent in the number of illegal sites or to arrest significant numbers of offenders. This is not because it is too difficult to find offenders but because it is too easy. The sheer volume of traffic in child pornography makes the task of prosecuting all offenders impossible and in truth the chances of an Internet child pornography offender being arrested are very small (Jewkes and Andrews, 2005). In the US, for example, around 1,000 people per year are arrested for possessing Internet child pornography (Wolak et al., 2003), while a major sting operation can result in fewer than 100 arrests worldwide (Federal Bureau of Investigation, 2002). While no one knows exactly how many offenders are accessing child pornography, these figures most certainly represent a drop in the ocean.

However, risk and perceived risk are two different things. As the previously cited study by Demetriou and Silke (2003) suggests, a crucial factor that governs Internet behaviour is the perception of anonymity. People can behave very differently on the Internet than they do in other areas of their life and interacting anonymously with a computer in the safety of one's own home is a disinhibiting experience and encourages people to express hidden thoughts and desires (Quayle and Taylor, 2001). One of the chief purposes of policing the Internet is not so much to catch offenders as it is to create the impression that the Internet is an unsafe environment in which to access child pornography images.

Police can create uncertainty about the safety of the Internet in a number of ways. Law enforcement agents may enter paedophile newsgroups, chat rooms or P2P networks posing as paedophiles and request emailed child pornography images from others in the group (US Department of Justice, 2004). Alternatively, they may enter child or teen groups posing as children and engage predatory paedophiles lurking in the group who may send pornography or suggest a meeting. Wolak et al. (2009) report increasing use of this strategy by law enforcement personnel, with 3,100 US arrests in 2006 for solicitation of undercover investigators posing as minors, a 381 per cent increase over the previous six years. A variation of the sting operation is to place ads on the Internet offering child pornography for sale and to wait for replies (Lesce, 1999). Police may also set up 'honey trap' sites. These sites purport to contain child pornography but in fact are designed to capture the IP or credit card details of visitors trying to download images. Rather than keep these operations secret in order to maximize the number of arrests, police may do just the opposite and widely publicize crackdowns on Internet child pornography. This is a case where general deterrence takes precedence over specific deterrence. Coverage of crackdowns in the mass media increases the perception among potential offenders that the Internet is an unsafe environment; they can never be entirely sure that site they have accessed is real or bogus.

A classic example of the use of a honey trap to increase the perception of risk is Operation Pin (BBC News, 2003). The operation was started in 2003 by West Midlands (UK) police and was expanded to include the FBI, the Australian Federal Police, the Royal Canadian Mounties, and Interpol. Far from being a covert operation, it was officially launched with media releases by the relevant police forces. A website purporting to contain child pornography was set up. Visitors to the site were required to go through a series of web pages, which appeared to be identical to real web porn sites, searching for the image they wanted. At each point it was reinforced that they were in a child pornography site, and they were given the option to exit. When they did try to access an image they were told they had committed a crime. They were tracked down via their credit card details, which they were required to provide to login. The operation resulted in numerous arrests, although the precise numbers are not available. However, the main purpose of the operation was to make searchers of child pornography on the Internet uncertain that they can do so anonymously.

Increasing the perceived risk of searching for child pornography online can be achieved without the setting up of elaborate stings. Police and other law enforcement personnel routinely scan the Internet, monitoring the traffic to servers known to contain child pornography. Theoretically, many of the individuals attempting to access these sites could be traced and, if they are operating in a region that falls within the jurisdiction of the ICE unit, they could be arrested. However, the cost and effort that would be required to trace each individual and to mount a conviction is far too great to make that course of action feasible. Nevertheless, in addition to blocking access to the offending site, ICE personnel could send a message to the potential users warning them that their attempt to access the site has been intercepted by law enforcement officials and that their online activity is now being monitored (see Williams, 2005).

Conclusion

The scale of the child pornography problem has increased dramatically with the introduction and rapid growth of the Internet. While statistics about Internet use are notoriously unreliable and often little more than guesses, there are undoubtedly many more child pornography images available now, and many more individuals accessing those images, than would have been the case had the Internet not existed. The Internet is not just an alternative platform that dedicated paedophiles happen to use to view child pornography; the Internet is a *cause* of child pornography. Relying solely on traditional models of individually focused tertiary prevention – arrest and rehabilitation – is not a viable solution to the problem of Internet child pornography. Certainly, offenders – especially those at the more serious end of the spectrum involved in producing and distributing child pornography – ought to be targeted by law enforcement personnel and arrested where possible. But there are many more people accessing child pornography via the Internet than can ever be arrested, and the impact of treating those few who are arrested – even with very good rehabilitation programmes – is negligible in the overall scheme of things. If, as I have argued, the proliferation of child pornography is a function of increased opportunity, then tackling the child pornography problem must be centred on reducing that opportunity.

Admittedly, the task is not a simple one. The structure of the Internet makes the control of child pornography very difficult (Wortley and Smallbone, 2006a). The Internet is an international communication tool that crosses jurisdictional boundaries. Offenders may access child pornography images that were produced and/or are stored on another continent. This raises jurisdictional problems for law enforcement officers and makes necessary international cooperation. Moreover, the Internet is a decentralized system with no single controlling agency or storage facility, making it difficult to enforce legislation or to screen content electronically even when there is agreement between jurisdictions. Because it is a network of networks, even if one pathway is blocked there are many alternative pathways that can be taken to reach the same destination. Technological developments such as P2P networks, remailers and file encryption only exacerbate the control problem (Burke et al., 2002; Ferraro and Casey, 2003; Jewkes and Andrews, 2005).

Because of the difficulties of policing the Internet, it is easy to be pessimistic about the prospects of controlling Internet child pornography. There is especially the danger of interpreting partial success as complete failure. Undoubtedly none of the situational strategies that have been discussed in this chapter work perfectly. Offenders vary considerably in the strength of their attraction to child pornography and the technological sophistication they are able to employ to access images and to avoid detection. Whatever we do, there will a core of dedicated offenders who possess both the determination and technical skills to thwart prevention attempts (Jewkes and Andrews, 2005). But to get the issue into perspective, let us turn the question around. Imagine that we did nothing to inhibit access to child pornography on the Internet; that there were no efforts to take down child pornography sites, no search filters, no police stings, and so on. Would there be more child pornography on the Internet, and more offenders accessing that pornography? Of course, it is impossible to know the answer for certain, but common sense suggests that if child pornography was freely available on the Internet, then the problem would be significantly greater than is currently the case. The battle to prevent Internet child pornography is not one that can ever be won once and for all. Rather it is an ongoing arms race characterized by a cycle involving the deployment of prevention strategies, the adaptation of offenders to those strategies, and the deployment of new prevention strategies to counter offender adaptation.

Notes

1   Clarke's (2008; Cornish and Clarke, 2003) latest model of situational prevention involves five general strategies. Two are not discussed here – reducing provocations and removing excuses – since they are not strictly methods of opportunity reduction. They target the offender's motivation to offend.
2   While the terms Internet and the World Wide Web (www) are often used interchangeably, the web specifically refers to the worldwide collection of electronic documents and other files stored as web pages and websites throughout the Internet. In addition to the www, the Internet enables a number of other forms of communication. These services include email, newsgroups, bulletin boards, chat rooms and instant messaging. They permit a user to have direct contact with other individuals, as well as to share electronic files.
3   As a researcher in this field, I regularly conduct online searches using search terms such as 'child pornography' and have only ever been directed to websites and scholarly articles concerned with the control of child pornography.

References

Adegoke, Y. (2003). Top brands start to pull ads from P2P networks. *New Media Age*, 24 April, 1.

Ahart, G.J. (1982). Sexual exploitation of children – a problem of unknown magnitude. *Report to the Chairman, Subcommittee on Select Education, House Committee on Education and Labor*. Gaithersburg, MD: US General Accounting Office.

Avert (n.d.). World wide ages of consent, available online at http://www.avert.org/age-of-consent.htm.

BBC News (2003). Police trap online paedophiles, 18 December, available online at http://news.bbc.co.uk/1/hi/uk/3329567.stm.

Blundell, B., Sherry, M., Burke, A. and Sowerbutts, S. (2002). Child pornography and the Internet: Accessibility and policing. *Australian Police Journal, 56*(1), 59–65.

Bullough, V.L. (2004). Children and adolescents as sexual beings: A historical overview. *Child and Adolescent Psychiatric Clinics of North America, 13*, 447–59.

Burke, A., Sowerbutts, S., Blundell, B. and Sherry, M. (2002). Child pornography and the Internet: Policing and treatment issues. *Psychiatry, Psychology and Law, 9*(1), 79–4.

Calder, M.C. (2004). The Internet: Potential, problems and pathways to hands-on sexual offending. In M.C. Calder (ed.). *Child Sexual Abuse and the Internet: Tackling the New Frontier*. Lyme Regis: Russell House Publishing.

Carr, J. (2004). *Child Abuse, Child Pornography and the Internet*. London: NCH.

Clarke, R.V. (1997). Introduction. In R.V. Clarke (ed.), *Situational Crime Prevention: Successful Case Studies*. 2nd edn. Albany NY, Harrow and Heston, pp. 2–43.

—— (2008). Situational crime prevention. In R. Wortley and L. Mazerolle (eds), *Environmental Criminology and Crime Analysis*. Cullompton: Willan.

Clarke, R.V. and Mayhew, P. (1988). The British gas suicide story and its criminological implications. In M. Tonry and N. Morris (eds), *Crime and Justice*, vol 10. Chicago: University of Chicago Press.

Cornish, D.B. and Clarke, R.V. (2003). Opportunities, precipitators and criminal dispositions: A reply to Wortley's critique of situational crime prevention. In M.J. Smith and D.B. Cornish (eds), *Theory for Practice in Situational Crime Prevention. Crime Prevention Studies*, vol. 16. Monsey, NJ: Criminal Justice Press.

—— (2008). Rational choice perspective. In R. Wortley and L. Mazerolle (eds), *Environmental Criminology and Crime Analysis*. Cullompton: Willan.

Demetriou, C. and Silke, A. (2003). A criminological Internet 'sting': Experimental evidence of illegal and deviant visits to a website trap. *British Journal of Criminology, 43*, 213–22.

Elliott, I.A., Beech, A.R., Manderville-Norden, R. and Hayes, E. (2009). Psychological profiles of Internet sexual offenders: Comparison with contact sexual offenders. *Sexual Abuse: A Journal of Research and Treatment, 21*, 76–92.

Federal Bureau of Investigation (2002). Operation Candyman, available online at http://www.fbi.gov/news/pressrel/press-releases/operation-candyman.

Ferraro, M.M. and Casey, E. (2005). *Investigating Child Exploitation and Pornography: The Internet, the Law and Forensic Science*. San Diego: Elsevier.

Forde, P. and A. Patterson (1998). Paedophile Internet activity. Trends and issues in crime and criminal justice, No. 97. Canberra: Australian Institute of Criminology, available online at http://www.aic.gov.au/documents/8/D/C/%7B8DC57715-E250-43B1-91BD-D04752499CA8%7Dti97.pdf.

GAO (2004). File sharing programs: Users of peer-to-peer networks can readily access child pornography. *Testimony before the Subcommittee on Commerce, Trade, and Consumer Protection, Committee on Energy and Commerce, House of Representatives*. Washington, DC: United States General Accounting Office.

Gottfredson, M.R. and Hirschi, T. (1990). *A General Theory of Crime*. Stanford, CA: Stanford University Press.

Jenkins, P. (2001). *Beyond Tolerance: Child Pornography on the Internet*. New York: New York University Press.

Jewkes, Y. and C. Andrews (2005). Policing the filth: The problems of investigating online child pornography in England and Wales. *Policing and Society, 15*, 42–62.

Jones, E.E. (1979). The rocky road from acts to dispositions. *American Psychologist, 34*, 107–17.

Klain, E., Davies, H. and Hicks, M. (2001). *Child Pornography: The Criminal Justice System Response*. Washington, DC: National Center for Missing and Exploited Children, available online at https://www.ncjrs.gov/App/publications/Abstract.aspx?id=201355.

Lee, P., Hui, S. and Fong, A. (2003). A structural and content-based analysis for web filtering. *Internet Research: Electronic Networking Applications and Policy, 13*(1), 27–37.

Lemos, R (2008). P2P investigation leads to child-porn busts. *Security Focus*, available online at http://www.securityfocus.com/brief/801.

Lesce, T. (1999). Pedophiles on the Internet: Law enforcement investigates abuse. *Law and Order, 47*(5), 74–78.

Linz, D. and Imrich, D. (2001). Child pornography. In S. White (ed.), *Handbook of Youth Justice*. New York: Kluwer Academic Press.

Lyman, J. (2004). Feds crack down on P2P child porn. *TechNewsWorld*, available online at http://www.technewsworld.com/story/technology/33836.html.

McCabe, K.A. (2008). The role of Internet service providers in cases of child pornography and child prostitution. *Social Science Computer Review, 26*, 247–51.

Mischel, W. (1968). *Personality and Assessment*. New York: Wiley.

Mostyn, M. (2000). The need for regulating anonymous remailers. *International Review of Law, Computers and Technology, 14*(1), 79–88.

O'Donnell, I. and Milner, C. (2007). *Child Pornography: Crime, Computers and Society*. Cullompton: Willan.

Offences Against the Person Act (1861). Available online at http://www.legislation.gov.uk/ukpga/1861/100/pdfs/ukpga_18610100_en.pdf.

Quayle, E. and Taylor, M. (2001). Child seduction and self-representation on the Internet: A case study. *Cyber Psychology and Behavior, 4*, 597–609.

Ribisl, K.M., Williams, R., Gizlice, Z. and Herring, A.H. (2011). Effectiveness of state and federal government agreements with major credit card and shipping companies to block illegal Internet cigarette sales. *PLoS One, 6*(2), e16745.

Ross, L. (1977). The intuitive psychologist and his shortcomings: Distortions in the attribution process. In L. Berkowitz (ed.), *Advances in Experimental Psychology*, vol. 10. New York: Academic Press.

Schwartz, M.F. and Southern, S. (2000). Compulsive cybersex. In A. Cooper (ed.), *Cybersex: The Dark Side of the Force*. New York: Brunner/Mazel.

Sheldon, K. and Howitt, D. (2007). *Sex Offenders and the Internet*. Chichester: John Wiley.

Smallbone, S., Marshall, W.L. and Wortley, R. (2008). *Preventing Child Sexual Abuse: Evidence, Policy and Practice*. Cullompton: Willan.

Stanley, J. (2001). *Child Abuse and the Internet*. National Child Protection Clearinghouse No. 15. Melbourne: Australian Institute of Family Studies, available online at http://www.aifs.org.au/nch.

Stewart, J. (1997). If this is the global community, we must be on the bad side of town: International policing of child pornography on the Internet. *Houston Journal of International Law, 20*, 205–46.

Sutton, D. and V. Jones (2004). *Position Paper on Child Pornography and Internet-related Sexual Exploitation of Children*. Save the Children, available online at http://ec.europa.eu/justice_home/daphnetoolkit/files/projects/2002_004/int_position_paper_on_child_pornography.pdf.

Taylor, M. and Quayle, E. (2006). The Internet and abuse images of children: Search, precriminal situations and opportunity. In R. Wortley and S. Smallbone (eds), *Situational Prevention of Child Sexual Abuse. Crime Prevention Studies*, vol. 19. Monsey, NY: Criminal Justice Press.

Thompson, G. (2009). Automatic detection of child pornography. Proceedings of the 7th Australian Digital Forensics Conference, Edith Cowan University, Perth, Western Australia, 3 December 2009.

Thornburgh, D. and Lin, H. (2002). *Youth, Pornography, and the Internet*. Washington, DC: National Academy Press.

Thornhill, R. and Thornhill, N. (1987). Human rape: The strengths of the evolutionary perspective. In C. Crawford, M. Smith and D. Krebbs (eds), *Sociobiology and Psychology: Ideas, Issues, and Applications*. Hillsdale, NJ: Lawrence Erlbaum.

—— (1992). The evolutionary psychology of men's coercive sexuality. *Behavioral and Brain Sciences, 15*, 363–75.

US Department of Justice (2004). *Department of Justice, Homeland Security Announce Child Pornography File-sharing Crackdown: Law Enforcement Initiative Targets Child Pornography over Peer-to-peer Networks*, available online at http://www.fbi.gov/news/pressrel/press-releases/departments-of-justice-homeland-security-announce-child-pornography-file-sharing-crackdown.

Webb, L., Craissati, J. and Keen, S. (2007). Characteristics of Internet child pornography offenders: A comparison with child molesters. *Sexual Abuse: A Journal of Research and Treatment, 19*, 449–65.

Williams, K.S. (2005). Facilitating safer choices: Use of warnings to dissuade viewing of pornography on the Internet, *Child Abuse Review, 14*, 415–29.

Wolak, J., Finkelhor, D. and Mitchell, K.J. (2005). *Child Pornography Possessors Arrested in Internet-related Crimes*. Alexandria, VA: Department of Justice, National Center for Missing and Exploited Children.

Wolak, J., Finkelhor, D. and Mitchell, K.J. (2009). *Trends in Arrests of 'On-line Predators'*. Durham, NH: Crime Against Children Research Center.

Wolak, J., Mitchell, K. and Finkelhor, D. (2003). *Internet Sex Crimes against Minors: The Response*. Alexandria, VA: Crime Against Children Research Center, University of New Hampshire.

Wortley, R. (2011) Exploring the person–situation interaction in situational crime prevention. In N. Tilley and G. Farrell (eds), *The Reasoning Criminologist: Essays in Honour of Ronald V. Clarke*. London: Routledge.

Wortley, R. and Smallbone, S. (2006a). *Child Pornography on the Internet. Problem-oriented Guides for Police Series*. Washington, DC: US Department of Justice.

—— (2006b). Applying situational principles to sexual offending against children. In R. Wortley and S. Smallbone (eds), *Situational Prevention of Child Sexual Abuse. Crime Prevention Studies*, vol. 19. Monsey, NY: Criminal Justice.

12 Proactive strategies to prevent the use of child abusive images

The Dunkelfeld Project

Klaus M. Beier and Janina Neutze, Institute of Sexology and Sexual Medicine, Charité – Universitätsmedizin, Berlin

Overview

This chapter describes a proactive approach that aims at improving preventive strategies to protect children from sexual exploitation by online offences such as the consumption or distribution of child abusive images (incorrectly called child pornography) and offline contact or non-contact child sexual abuse offences. Prevention strategies include research on individuals at risk of committing first or persistent sexual offences against children, as well as offering preventive assessment and treatment. As it is acknowledged that many offenders against children remain undetected by legal authorities in the 'Dunkelfeld' (literally 'dark field') and are therefore not included in any official statistics, this chapter focuses on those who have a long-standing sexual interest in prepubescent and/or pubescent children and (1) admit online sexual and/or offline offending behaviour against children, but are unknown to the legal authorities, and (2) never offended. All individuals seek help in order to prevent initial or persistent sexual offences against children.

The authors argue that non-offending paedophiles and hebephiles, as potential or real offenders in the Dunkelfeld, should be targeted in order to improve prevention of child sexual exploitation, because sexual deviant interests have been identified as a major risk factor for sexual re-offending against children. Moreover, in line with Seto (2009), it is argued that to date there is no evidence to suggest that a sexual preference for children will ever change – neither clinically nor empirically (Beier 1998).

This is the reason why inclined individuals suffer from their feelings, fantasies and impulses and experience distress for a lifetime, even worsening with increasing age. Public health services have a real chance of encouraging such individuals to seek professional help before sexual offences against children are carried out.

'Dunkelfeld': offences that go undetected

According to police crime statistics, in recent years some 15,000 cases of sexual abuse of children have been reported annually to the German authorities (and approximately 3,000 offenders were convicted). In contrast, results of representative surveys within the general public in Germany (Wetzels, 1997), suggest that approximately 60,000 child sexual abuse offences are committed every year. Thus, child sexual abuse offending remains an extremely underreported phenomenon. Incidents recorded in police crime statistics – i.e. the number of reported cases – seem to represent the tip of the iceberg whereas the number of undetected cases is significantly higher. Finkelhor (1984) concluded that for every reported case of contact or non-contact child sexual abuse at least five remained unreported. Similarly, in one American study 91 per cent of victims of child sexual abuse had not reported their abuse (Henry and McMahon, 2000). The majority of actual incidences involving the sexual abuse of children is therefore never reported to the police, is not registered by the judiciary and criminal prosecution authorities, and remains in the Dunkelfeld.

The same presumably holds true for online sexual offences against children, for example using Internet technologies to access and distribute child pornography (a belittling term for child abusive behaviour which has nothing to do with pornography). According to the German annual police report (PCS, 2007; 2008), in 2008 a rise of 14.5 per cent (n = 18,264) of registered cases of distribution of child pornography compared to 2007 occurred. The number of detected cases of child pornography offences in 2008 was ten times as high as in the year 1996 (PCS, 1996; 2008). In 2007, 15.7 per cent of all reported sex offences were criminal acts concerning images depicting children and juveniles exposing their uncovered genital or anal areas and/or engaged in sexual activities among themselves or with an adult (PCS, 2007). The prevalence of undetected child pornography offences is difficult to assess, because estimations are reliant on data derived from convictions, but a proportion of child pornography offenders operate within private Internet networks, which are inaccessible to monitoring. According to the Internet Watch Foundation (IWF, 2007), it is assumed that websites with depictions of child pornographic content are accessed daily about 300,000 to 450,000 times. There are approximately 5 million pictures depicting child abuse images in circulation, whereupon an estimated additional 10,000 pictures are presumably added weekly. During 2010 an average of fifty-nine web pages with child sexual abuse content were added to a web page blocking list and IWF took action regarding 16,739 instances of child sexual abuse content on different web pages around the world (IWF, 2010).

Various factors may explain the phenomenon of undetected offline or online sexual offences against children. The victims themselves are likely not to report the abuse, particularly to the authorities, because of their own feelings of responsibility for what happened as well as fear, shame and guilt. As far as the offenders are concerned, many obviously have no interest at all in being discovered. However, others might not report their behaviour because of their fear of legal consequences and social alienation as well as their own feelings of shame and guilt (Feelgood and Schaefer, 2011).

Offender factors (amongst others) most likely also hinder contact with researchers and clinicians. Thus, the under-reporting of incidents has resulted in the fact that most research on child pornography and child sexual abuse offenders is based on forensic mental health or correctional samples. To date there have been only few studies that have involved or focused on Dunkelfeld offenders and may provide information about individuals committing undetected child sexual abuse and/or child pornography offences (Bernard, 1975; Durkin and Bryant, 1999; Lautmann, 1994; Malesky and Ennis, 2004; Neutze, Seto et al., 2011; Riegel, 2004; Rossman, 1976; Wilson and Cox, 1983). Results indicate that Dunkelfeld offenders are well educated, display high levels of child pornography use and fantasizing about children, and may also be more likely to report the awareness of their sexual interest in children having occurred before the age of 20 (for a critical overview see Schaefer et al., 2010).

In summary, the majority of child pornography and child sexual abuse offences are never detected and detection rarely results in conviction. Thus, studies investigating child pornography and child sexual abuse offenders are based on forensic mental health or correctional samples. As a consequence, the previously applied approach could have distorted theoretical development and led to biased empirical findings. At present it is not known if Dunkelfeld offenders differ in a systematic way from detected offenders and it remains unclear whether previous findings on risk factors and treatment needs can be generalized to the Dunkelfeld. From a public health perspective investigating undetected sexual offenders against children may raise important issues for empirically based improvement of prevention strategies such as risk assessment and treatment.

Sexual preference for children: paedophilia and hebephilia

There are intuitive and empirical links between paedophilia (defined as sexual attraction to prepubescent children) and hebephilia (defined as sexual attraction to pubescent children),[1] and child sexual abuse or child pornography offences committed by adults.

Offenders who commit child sexual abuse differ from other men—sex offenders with adult victims, non-sex offenders and non-offending volunteers—in their sexual responses to stimuli depicting prepubescent or pubescent children in the laboratory (e.g. Blanchard et al., 2001; Blanchard et al., 2006). In addition, indicators of sexual interest in children are strong predictors for sexual recidivism among identified sex offenders in clinical or correctional samples (Hanson and Morton-Bourgon, 2005). For example, the rate of recidivism in the case of paedophilically inclined offenders has been shown to be between 50 and 80 per cent (Beier, 1998).

With respect to child pornography offences, most self-identified paedophiles report that child pornography is sexually arousing and many acknowledge using child pornography at some point in their life (Neutze, Seto et al., 2011; Quayle and Taylor, 2002; Riegel, 2004). In addition, detected child pornography offenders show paedophilic patterns of sexual arousal. By comparing the phallometric test results of 100 child pornography offenders with those of 178 sex offenders with child victims, a group of child pornography offenders showed significantly greater sexual arousal to children than a group of offenders against children. Overall, 61 per cent of the child pornography offenders showed a preference for depictions of children over depictions of adults (Seto et al., 2006). Thus, child pornography offending seems to be a valid indicator of paedophilia, because men often choose to view pornography corresponding to their sexual interests.

On the other hand, the diagnosis of paedophilia is not applicable to all child sexual abuse or child pornography offenders (Seto, 2008). Approximately 60 per cent of men detained for sexual abuse of children cannot be diagnosed as having a preference disorder in the sense of paedophilia. Offences are also committed as a substitute activity for sexual interaction with desired adult partners who are not available for various reasons (e.g. a personality disorder or low intelligence level). By contrast, approximately 40 per cent of men sentenced for child sexual abuse fulfil the diagnostic criteria for paedophilia (Beier, 1998). Paedophilia and child pornography offending against children are also not synonymous. Several typologies of online offenders who are not sexually motivated have been suggested in the literature. For example, some online offenders are suggested to access child pornography out of curiosity, by accident, or in order to shock people, without a specific sexual arousal function. Others create and distribute child pornography solely for financial gain (Krone, 2004; Lanning, 2001). Most recently, Surjadi and colleagues (Surjadi et al., 2010) studied different functions regarding Internet offending in a small Dutch sample of forty-three Internet offenders: sexual arousal, facilitating social relationships, collecting behaviour and avoiding real life. Besides sexual arousal, however, offenders not sexually motivated (participants who reported that they have never masturbated while watching child pornography) scored only lower on avoidance than those who reported masturbation (sexually motivated). Finally, because most research on paedophilia is based on forensic mental health or correctional samples of sex offenders, little is known about paedophiles who are not formally involved with the criminal justice system, and even less is known about the factors that distinguish those who act upon their sexual interest in prepubescent or pubescent children from those who do not.

However, as paedophiles have been found to be at greater risk of recommitting child sexual abuse and child pornography offences, particularly at an early age (Eke et al., 2010), these individuals must be assumed also to have a greater lifetime risk for initial offending, and therefore they are considered to be an important target group for prevention approaches.

The relevance of sexual preference for children concerning sexual offending behaviour is all the more worrying considering data from the general population, which revealed that one-fifth of university males reported some sexual attraction to small children, and one-tenth had fantasized about having sex with children (Briere and Runtz, 1989). Using phallometry, researchers have found that non-paedophilic men also show penile response to pictures of pubescent and pre-pubescent images of children (Quinsey et al., 1975). Over a quarter of community participants in another study indicated paedophilic interests via self-reporting or phallometric response (Hall et al., 1995). Most recently, Lykins and colleagues studied sexual arousal in a clinical and forensic sample of 214 men sexually attracted to females. Participants (no child sexual abuse and/or child pornography offenders) showed physiological arousal to pubescent and prepubescent girls as measured by phallometric testing. Arousal to prepubescent girls was greater than to neutral stimuli (Lykins et al., 2010). Recent epidemiological data state that the prevalence of a paedophilic inclination is between 0.37 and 6 per cent of the male population (Ahlers et al., 2009). In comparison: 1 per cent is the prevalence of Parkinson's disease in the German male population. While many people may know someone who is suffering from Parkinson's disease, only few will be consciously aware of knowing a paedophilic person: paedophilia cannot be (visibly) identified and those affected do not admit to it for fear of social discrimination; not even when they have never offended against children.

It is important to acknowledge that no one can 'choose' his sexual preference – it is a matter of 'fate not choice' – which is why it would be wrong to pass moral judgement on it. Moral judgement is only permitted – and then by all means – when someone acts on his sexual interest in children, thereby damaging the individuality and integrity of a child. Moreover, clinical experience suggests that sexual age and gender preference manifest at a young age as part of sexual identity and remain unchanged over a lifespan (APA, 2000; Beier, 1998; Wille, 1968). Thus, from their late teens or early twenties on, individuals sexually interested in children have to cope with the ramifications of their unusual sexual preference (Schaefer et al., 2010). Facing these challenges time and time again, the development of distress at some point is not surprising. Additionally, the occurrence of preference-related distress finds validation in both the DSM-IV-TR (APA, 2000) and the ICD-10 (WHO, 1992), both of which explicitly list distress as a diagnostic criterion for paedophilia. Thus, non-offending paedophiles and paedophilic offenders in the Dunkelfeld appear to be ideal target groups for prevention of sexual offending against children: they are at-risk individuals, some of whom are motivated for treatment due to distress and therefore reachable (Beier, Neutze et al., 2009; Schaefer et al., 2010).

Primary and secondary prevention efforts

Conventionally, primary prevention efforts focus on children, families, teachers, youth service workers and others who may be in a position to intervene. Educational programmes have been most successfully delivered through schools and have recently also been adopted by other organizations (Finkelhor, 2009). The main goal is to teach the difference between acceptable and unacceptable touching and how to disclose to a trusted adult if sexual touching occurs. Evaluation data suggest that school-based programmes increase knowledge about sexual abuse and protection strategies and that participants are more likely to report experiencing sexual abuse (Gibson and Leitenberg, 2000; Rispens et al., 1997). A more recent meta-analysis on studies evaluating school-based programmes in North America found improvements in knowledge and protective behaviours in simulated at-risk situations among children asked a short time after participating, but also revealed increased anxiety (Zwi et al., 2007). Regarding prevention of child pornography or additional online offences against children (e.g. grooming), approaches such as the ThinkuKnow (TUK) programme provide Internet safety advice to children aged between 5 and 16 years, parents and professionals. However, first evaluation data on a non-stratified sample of 1,718 children (aged 11–16) do not suggest a decrease in risk-taking Internet behaviour after participating in TUK (e.g. interaction and sharing personal information with strangers). In addition, more than half of the programme participants report difficulties in recalling the safety messages accurately or over time, and even if they did remember them, did not always act on the advice (Davidson et al., 2009). Thus, educational approaches addressing prevention of Internet offences need to be expanded with appropriate quality management including evaluation.

In fact, primary prevention can be also focused on at-risk individuals, including persons who are pedophilically or hebephilically inclined and who have not yet sexually offended against children. That is why the rationale of primary prevention is to prevent the offence itself, no matter how. Therefore targeting paedophiles at risk to commit initial offences could also be seen as a proactive primary prevention approach, given that strategies provide successfully preventive treatment to these individuals (Beier, Neutze et al., 2009). There are few clinical data suggesting that men sexually interested in children may be reached for prevention offers, before initial child sexual offending behaviour occurs. For example, a Canadian outpatient clinic for men with paraphilic sexual disorders was contacted by twenty-six victimless and self-referred paedophiles (Fedoroff et al., 2001). Arguably, these patients, as well as some self-referred patients in another study (Bogaert et al., 1997), sought professional help because they experienced distress related to their sexual preference for minors. Regardless of whether these patients were distressed due to fear of society, or due to a sense of being sick or dangerous to society, their distress was clearly related to their sexual preference (Schaefer et al., 2010).

Despite this, some authors are defining preventive work with at-risk (not yet offending) individuals as secondary (Seto, 2008). In fact, secondary prevention means to prevent a relapse if an offence has already occurred – even if it has not been detected and took place in the Dunkelfeld. One approach dealing with at-risk individuals in a primary and a secondary preventive way, is the 'Stop It Now! Campaign', which uses social marketing strategies to reach persons who are at risk of committing sexual offences against children in order to convince them to seek treatment and to encourage non-offending adults to intervene if they suspect child sexual abuse may be occurring. With numbers of up to 1,960 self-identified potential (n = 313) or Dunkelfeld (n = 249) offenders voluntarily contacting the campaign-bureau within a four-year period, and 34 per cent of all calls addressing child pornography or other Internet offences, the results of the 'Stop it Now!' campaign indicate a similar demand to comparable prevention approaches (Stop it Now!, 2009).

Other strategies try to mobilize third parties (family members, friends and colleagues of either victims or offenders) to detect situations where abuse is actually or potentially occurring and to intervene or report the situation. Some surveys have shown that overall community knowledge and attitudes about sexual abuse can shift in the wake of advertising campaigns (Chasan-Taber and Tabachnick, 1999).

However, a fundamental problem with the hotline and self-referral strategy for potential offenders is that in the current statutory and retributive environment of most countries, it is hard to promise or persuade an offender that he will receive confidential help.

Legal framework conditions in Germany

In Germany, all those working in community-based treatment programmes are subject to the requirement of confidentiality (section 203 of the Criminal Code: 'Violation of private secrets' – imprisonment for not more than one year or a fine), which also includes information regarding sexual abuse (the only explicit exception is the treatment of previously convicted offenders in the context of so-called supervision of conduct, section 68a(8) of the Criminal Code).

The requirement of confidentiality also applies to possible future child sexual abuse, since it is not listed in section 138 of the Criminal Code ('Failure to report planned crimes') – in contrast to, among others, serious trafficking in human beings, murder, manslaughter or other crimes against personal liberty (in which case the failure to report would constitute a punishable offence).

However, with reference to section 34 of the Criminal Code ('Necessity as justification'), medical confidentiality can be broken and the case reported to the police if the therapist is convinced, in the context of a community-based treatment relationship, that a patient will commit a sex offence. The clinician can then invoke the fact that, upon weighing up the conflicting interests, the protected interest that is in danger (abuse of a child) substantially outweighs the one interfered with (the requirement of confidentiality). Nevertheless, under the Criminal Code this only applies to the extent that reporting the matter 'is a proportionate means to avert the danger'. That is questionable, since the person reported will deny any motivation whatsoever to commit the offence when official investigations are instituted, and permanent deprivation of liberty cannot be justified on this basis. In addition, one must remember in the context of self-referred paedophiles who seek self-motivated professional help, these individuals want to prevent anything happening, which is the experience in the Prevention Project Dunkelfeld (PPD) (see below): a conflict could only arise if different assessments are made of the risk that the impulse can no longer be controlled and the participant does not act on the means of averting the danger recommended by the therapist. But even in such a case (which has not arisen in the PPD to date), the participant would not reveal his inner life to the authorities if he were reported and he would no longer be accessible for interventions.

For that reason, the legal situation in Germany must be regarded as an extremely favourable starting point for prevention work in this field, because it enables a protective framework, which leads to potential offenders or real undetected offenders being prepared to accept help in the first place. Since, however, these offenders certainly do exist and the probability that they would commit their first or further sexual offences or use child pornography is much greater if they do not accept help, it is definitely better to have the opportunity to begin an intervention than not to gain any access to this target group at all.

With regard to prevention work, Germany is in a privileged position compared to other countries, since in other countries therapists working in community projects are subject to the requirement of disclosure if they become aware of acts of child sexual abuse or the use of child pornography, or they have reason for suspecting that their patient will commit such acts. An ethical debate on this matter would raise the question of whether utilitarian principles (choice of the lesser evil) in view of the benefit achieved (being able to prevent offences against sexual self-determination) permit a procedure obligated more to protecting children than a strictly normative orientation (duty to report cases on account of the interest being in danger), which is also linked to the restriction of civil liberties (lifting of the requirement of confidentiality).

The Berlin Prevention Project Dunkelfeld

The Berlin Prevention Project Dunkelfeld (PPD) is an innovative example of a combined primary and secondary prevention approach. The ongoing research project was initially funded by the Volkswagen Foundation and from 2008 also – on the particular initiative of the former Federal Ministry of Justice – from federal funds. It was also supported by the child protection organization Hänsel + Gretel Foundation, as well as by the international media group Scholz and Friends.

The prevention project – established in 2004 – was designed as a preliminary treatment evaluation study, intending to establish treatment for individuals within the community who seek help to prevent initial offending (i.e. primary prevention) or persisting sexual offences (i.e. secondary prevention) against children. Thus, the project aims at both improving child protection by preventing child sexual abuse and offering treatment to a neglected group of patients suffering from a sexual preference disorder. Thereby the target group was specified as individuals living in the community who (1) are troubled by their sexual preference or behaviour involving prepubescent and/or pubescent minors and searching for help in coming to terms with their sexuality, and/or (2) fear they may act out sexually with children (again), and if applicable (3) are currently not involved with legal authorities for respective offences.

In order to reach the target group, a media campaign was developed. Findings of a small pilot study suggested the necessity of an empathic, non-judgemental, non-discriminating, non-medicalizing, non-criminalizing and anonymity-assuring approach (Feelgood et al., 2002), resulting in the following message: 'You are not guilty because of your sexual desire, but you are responsible for your sexual behaviour. There is help! Don't become an offender!' (see Fig. 12.1).

The campaign text translates as: 'Do you like children in ways you shouldn't? There is help free of charge and confidential. Charité – Institute of Sexology and Sexual Medicine.' The TV spot is available from www.dont-offend.org

Anyone interested in further assessment and treatment undergoes a multi-stage, multi-method intake procedure, which comprises (1) a computer-assisted tele-phone interview (CATI); (2) a 90-minute semi-structured clinical interview; and (3) a number of questionnaires. The CATI is intended to be a low-threat means of

Figure 12.1 Image from the Berlin Prevention Project Dunkelfeld's media campaign

contact and thus offered the most favourable conditions to facilitate the participation of respondents highly fearful of being identified as paedophiles. Individuals are screened by trained interviewers with respect to basic socio-demographic data, sexual interests, criminal history, use of sexually non-explicit and explicit materials for sexual arousal as well as data on current and lifetime involvement with the authorities related to sexual offending behaviour (Beier, Ahlers et al., 2009). In addition, appointments for information on treatment and further assessments was offered. The clinical interview serves primarily to assess aspects of psychosexual development and criminological data, to verify the presence of paedophilia or hebephilia, and to determine the absence of treatment exclusion criteria (see below).

Questionnaires are administered in order to assess previously identified risk factors including offence supportive attitudes, empathy deficits, loneliness, intimacy deficits, coping strategies, sexual and general self-regulation, and personality measures as well as self-reported psychopathy, perceived self-efficacy to control problematic behaviour and attitudes towards child pornography offending (Neutze, Seto et al., 2011). In addition, questionnaires were administered to investigate an individual's motivation for starting treatment and to establish the preconditions for an evaluation of the treatment results.

Finally, decisions regarding the inclusion of an individual into the treatment evaluation study were made following a clinical case conference. Individuals with acute drug or alcohol problems, psychotic disorders, or developmental disabilities were excluded from the treatment programme, as resources for appropriate treatment or management of their special needs were not available. Volunteers who were currently involved with the legal authorities (e.g. being investigated for sexual crime, under parole) were also excluded.

First results from the Berlin Prevention Project Dunkelfeld

By July 2010, 1,085 men had contacted the project hotline. Of these potential participants 505 were interviewed, 406 had completed the diagnostic procedure and 244 were offered a treatment place. Those fulfilling intake criteria had travelled on average more than 138 km to take part in the study. These men had an average age of 37.5 years (range 17–66) when they joined the project, came from all levels of society, with half of them having attended school for more than ten years. The majority was employed (70 per cent) and one-third had a partner at the time of assessment. More than half had already tried to get therapeutic help elsewhere.

With respect to paedophilia 30.7 per cent self-reported a sexual interest in prepubescent boys, 32.4 per cent in prepubescent girls and 4.5 per cent in prepubescent girls and boys. With respect to hebephilia 11.5 per cent self-reported a sexual interest in pubescent boys, 18 per cent in prepubescent girls and 2.9 per cent in prepubescent girls and boys. Most men were aware of their sexual disposition on average since the age of 22 and many displayed other psychological symptoms (see Beier, Neutze et al., 2009).

Regarding self-reported offence history, 13.5 per cent had never committed any sexual offence against children, 29.5 admitted child pornography-only offences, 18.4 per cent child sexual abuse-only offences, and 38.5 per cent admitted both child sexual abuse and child pornography offences at some point in their life (mixed offender).[2] Only 6.9 per cent of the child pornography, 22.2 per cent of the child sexual abuse only and 25.5 per cent of the mixed offenders had been previously detected by the criminal justice system. Finally, 46.3 per cent of those men included in the project rejected the treatment place because of the distance to Berlin, 8.6 per cent are on the waiting list, 32.4 per cent completed or are still undergoing treatment and 12.7 dropped out for various reasons.

With respect to the fifty-seven participants who completed the treatment programme, a significant reduction in cognitive distortion as well as a significant increase in victim empathy was noted, and therefore a positive impact on a major risk factor for performing child sexual abuse can be assumed. Around one-fifth of the participants treated in the PPD or who were still undergoing treatment decided to take antiandrogens in order to increase their impulse control through supplementary medication. In comparison to the other patients, these were significantly more likely to perceive risks and had committed sexual offences more often in the six months prior to the start of treatment (Beier et al., 2010).

Treatment efficacy with respect to various risk factors and offence behaviour is currently being evaluated. Further results pertaining to the various stages of the project and comparisons of different groups have been reported elsewhere (Ahlers et al., 2006; Beier, Neutze, et al., 2009; Mundt et al., 2009; Schaefer et al., 2008).

Special focus on child pornography offences

Empirical evidence supports both similarities and differences between child pornography and child sexual abuse offenders. Seto et al. (2010) found that approximately one in eight online offenders admitted having had an official history of hands-on sexual offences, suggesting that at least some online offenders may have similar characteristics to offline offenders. However, other studies have also found differences between child pornography and child sexual abuse offenders (Babchishin et al., 2010; Bates and Metcalf, 2007; Elliott et al., 2009; Webb et al., 2007).

Data from the PPD show that close to 70 per cent of undetected paedophiles and hebephiles had already been child pornography offenders at some point in their life. About one-third exclusively used child abusive images and tended to be less aware of their problem in this regard than child sexual abuse offenders. Results of group comparisons by offence history reveal that non-offenders and child pornography-only offenders were younger, scored lower on offence supportive attitudes as measured by the Bumby MOLEST scale and scored higher on a measure of sexual preoccupation (Neutze, Grundmann, et al., 2010; Neutze, Seto et al., 2011). In addition, comparing child pornography only with mixed offenders, the latter scored higher on self-reported psychopathy and offence-supportive attitudes. Also additional paraphilic interests were found to be an indicator of a broad spectrum of sexually deviant interests in child pornography offenders (Grundmann et al., 2010). Recent (past six months) users of child abusive images differed from recent mixed offenders on offence-supportive attitudes, sexual preoccupation, frequent use of depictions of explicitly erotic posing and sexual activities amongst children and approaching feelings after material use (Kuhle et al., 2010).

In summary, data indicate that child pornography offending is common in undetected paedophiles and hebephiles. With the increasing age of the participants the probability that one had committed a child pornography offence (or both offences) seems to increase. Furthermore, paedophilic child pornography-only offenders seem to have more problems with sexual self-regulation and additional paraphilias, although they in general seem to be less conspicuous with respect to known risk factors, suggesting a distinct subgroup of online offenders showing a low risk of also committing offline offences.

Based on current empirical data and the preliminary results of the PPD in 2009 the Prevention Project Dunkelfeld was extended to include potential and unde-tected child pornography offenders. This new project also receives, among others, funding from the federal budget – supported by the Federal Ministry for Family Affairs. The project extension aims in particular at preventing initial and persisting child pornography offences as child pornography depicts exactly those types of sexual offence that the PPD aims to prevent. It is assumed that paedophiles can be reached proactively before they start to look for child abusive images matching their sexual fantasies. Thus, the target population consists of (1) men who, as yet, have neither committed child sexual abuse nor child pornography offences but fear they may do so (i.e. potential child pornography offenders); (2) men who have never committed child sexual abuse but undetected child pornography offences in the Dunkelfeld and fear to continue child pornography offending; and (3) men with a criminal record of child pornography offences only, who fear re-offending, providing they are no longer under the supervision of the justice system.

As data suggest that paedophilic child pornography offenders are part of various social networks and have a family or a partner, the new project also aims to provide general information on the problem of child pornography and on the special connection to users who on account of their sexual interest in children need to resist impulses to store, download, collect or swap child abusive images. Thus, the project aims at including third parties (family members, friends) in diagnostics and treatment, to provide targeted information, to cope with new situations, and to support and motivate the (potential) child pornography offenders to take part in treatment.

In order to reach the target group of the extended project via TV and Internet banner adverts, a new media campaign was designed. The basic message is comparable to the PPD media campaign, namely that no one is to blame for their sexual desires, except when their fantasies lead them to commit acts that are harmful to others: 'Child pornography is sexual abuse. You are not to blame for your sexual responsiveness to child pornography, but you are responsible for your behaviour, that is whether you click on it or not. Help is available! Don't become an offender. Not even on the web!' (see Fig. 12.2).

In the campaign concerning child pornography offences, the text translates as: 'Don't offend, not even online. There is help free of charge and confidential.

Figure 12.2 Image from the Berlin Prevention Project Dunkelfeld's second media campaign

Charité – Institute of Sexology and Sexual Medicine.' The TV spot is available from www.dont-offend.org

By July 2010, 175 men had contacted the project hotline. Of these potential participants 59 were interviewed, 53 had completed the diagnostic procedure and 33 were offered a treatment place. Those fulfilling intake criteria had travelled on average more than 220 km to take part in the study. These men who came were aged on average 35 years (range 22–57) when they joined the project, came from all levels of society, with two-thirds of them having attended school for more than ten years. The vast majority was employed (88 per cent) and 61 per cent were involved in a relationship at the time of assessment. With respect to paedophilia, 3 per cent reported a sexual interest in prepubescent boys, 33 per cent in prepubescent girls and 3 per cent in prepubescent girls and boys. With respect to hebephilia, 3 per cent reported a sexual interest in pubescent boys, 48 per cent in pubescent girls and 9 per cent in pubescent girls and boys. Regarding self-reported offence history, all participants admitted child pornography only offences, at some point in their life. Twenty-seven had been previously detected by the criminal justice system. Finally, 42 per cent of those men included in the project were not able to participate in the treatment programme because of the distance to Berlin.

The treatment

Even if a paedophilic sexual preference represents an important motivation for sexual offending, biological, psychological and social factors are influential when someone acts upon this sexual motivation. These factors have previously been described as dynamic risk factors because they are assumed to be associated with the likelihood of re-offending and potentially responsive to treatment and supervision. Thus, dynamic risk factors are considered to be important treatment targets (see Andrews and Bonta, 2006; Marshall et al., 2006) and many are included in contemporary theories of sexual offending against children or pathological Internet use (Davis, 2001; Finkelhor, 1994; Hall and Hirschman, 1992; Marshall and Barbaree, 1990; Ward and Beech, 2006; Ward and Siegert, 2002; Quayle and Taylor, 2003).

According to the integrated theory of sexual offending, a need for a multi-dimensional treatment approach comprising biomedical (pharmacological), psychological (cognitive behavioural therapy) and sexological (partnership counselling including the sexual relationship) intervention strategies are relevant in order to prevent child sexual offending behaviour in paedophiles and hebephiles (Ward and Beech, 2006). The Berlin Dissexuality Therapy (BEDIT), therefore, is a treatment programme based on a broader cognitive behavioural approach which additionally incorporates interventions based on sexual medicine, including pharmacological treatment options (Beier and Loewit, 2011). Interventions are based on a cognitive behavioral model as well as aspects of the relapse prevention, the self-regulation and good lives models (Pithers, 1990; Ward and Gannon, 2006; Ward and Hudson, 1998; Ward et al., 1998). Thus the BEDIT is a treatment approach in line with current practice in the US and Canada, where most treatment providers for detected sex offenders identify themselves with a broader cognitive behavioural approach (McGrath et al., 2010). However, adaptations of previously existing treatment approaches were required in order to meet basic assumptions derived from years of clinical experience gained at the Berlin outpatient clinic in individual treatment of clients suffering from sexual preference disorders. These basic assumptions are (Beier et al., 2005):

1. The sexual (body) age and gender preference as well as additional paraphilia-associated sexual arousal patterns are unchangeable components of an individual's personality. An individual is not responsible for the existence of a preference but for the behavioural consequences thereof. Thus, dealing with inappropriate sexual impulses directed at prepubescent or pubescent children is linked to lifelong demands on sexual self-regulation and behavioural control.
2. Due to sexual fantasies being genuinely integrated into an individual's personality structure there is a constant confrontation of being sexually directed at children and/or adolescents, which undermines self-esteem, leading to personal devaluation, which impedes the development of a socially adequate coping strategy for dealing with one's sexual impulses.
3. Based on a multidimensional understanding of sexuality (dimension of desire, reproduction and attachment) we must take into account that paedophilically inclined individuals try to achieve fulfilment within the dimension of attachment (focusing on the bio-psychosocial needs for acceptance, security and warmth) with a child as a partner. Therefore, it is necessary to establish other relationships in order to receive these emotionally stabilizing factors, even if those persons are not attractive on the level of sexual desire according to sexual preference structure.

Treatment setting and manual construction

The programme is designed to be delivered in a group format comprising forty-five to fifty three-hour sessions, broken into several modules which can be allocated to each treatment target. All participants are assessed prior to and after the treatment using the standard psychometric assessment battery (Neutze, Seto et al., 2011), and a monthly aftercare service is provided for the following two years. For individual treatment, identical content is being used, but with an adjustment of time structure (forty-five sessions at 50 minutes) and the modification of specific exercises relating to group dynamics (role play, intensified use of imagination, exercises regarding victim empathy). Following the risk, need and responsivity principles, groups are matched by offence history (child sexual abuse/mixed offenders vs non-offenders/child pornography-only offenders).

A manual formally serves as a guide to the treatment contents (including graphical material and worksheets), processes and objectives, the primary objective of which is to maintain or increase sexual behaviour control. A sequential administration of the modules may be chosen just as well as the basic cluster structure may be used to customize the degree of structuring and sequencing of modules according to the individual needs and circumstances of the group (Allam et al., 1997).

Treatment targets

Previous research with detected child sexual abuse offenders suggests – next to sexual deviance – four major types of risk dimension that influence acting upon sexual motivation: offence-supportive attitudes, sexual and general self-regulation deficits, and emotional or intimacy deficits (Hanson et al., 2007). Selected factors, such as empathy deficits, could not be empirically supported, although clinical experts consider them to be a key factor in sex offender treatment (McGrath et al., 2010). However, the extent to which identified recidivism risk factors and associated treatment targets are applicable to paedophiles at risk of initial offence and undetected paedophile offenders has not been established yet (Duff and Willis, 2006).

Basically the BEDIT programme aims at an increase of motivation, an improvement of self-efficacy and self-monitoring (including sexual fantasies and interests), a reduction in sexual arousal and sexualized coping by an increase of adequate coping strategies, emotional and sexual self-regulation, an increase in social functioning (focusing on the attachment dimension of sexuality, see above), a decrease in offence supportive attitudes and behaviours, an increase in empathic response to children involved in sexual acts with an adult or depicted in child abusive images, and finally the development of appropriate relapse prevention strategies and goals.

With respect to a self-regulation model the programme begins with a number of exercises designed to increase motivation by enhancing group cohesion, identifying positive and negative outcome expectancies that are believed to be important for behavioural change, and to focus on goal-setting. At the same time active self-monitoring – an individual's ability to be aware of and manage his internal processes – is encouraged. Recognition and management of thoughts, attitudes, feelings and situations involving children should also serve to raise patients' awareness of their sexual interest and arousal, including needs and impulses.

Recognition of sexual fantasies also involves asking clients to describe and accept responsibility for their sexually deviant interests. Thus, BEDIT gives increased attention to the acceptance of fantasizing about sexual activities with children and in some cases additional paraphilia-associated contents (e.g. sadism, masochism, fetishism, etc.). It is argued that (1) those paedophiles and hebephiles who have never acted on their sexual fantasies can only describe their desired sexual acts with children; (2) describing sexual fantasies increases problem or risk awareness; and (3) awareness of sexual interests raises responsibility for future behaviour. Content of sexual fantasies is never morally judged by the therapists, but rather its impact on the client's life and the necessity of responsibility is emphasized. The acceptance of the inconvertibility of one's sexual preference structure enables unambiguous distinction between fantasy and behaviour. Active self-monitoring, self-evaluation and self-consequence in socially controlled everyday situations are also essential for the acquirement and/or stabilization of effective behavioural self-control regarding the use of sexually explicit and non-explicit material (including child pornography) and/or sexually motivated contact with children. In doing so, the importance of volitional conditions, external conditions and the initiative, or rather the onset of self-control, are considered stronger than in existing treatment approaches (Karoly 1993; Locke 1996). These are aspects that in part do not apply in detention institutions. In contrast, however, they become more important in the case of successful self-motivated self-control.

Behavioural self-control is strongly associated with sexual arousal control. In contrast to behavioural sexual arousal control techniques, such as covert sensitization or minimal arousal conditioning, which are typically used in programmes in the United States and Canada (McGrath et al., 2010), sexual preoccupation and sexual arousal control problems in potential and undetected offenders against children are treated with medication such as serotonin reuptake inhibitors or antiandrogens like cyproteronacetate or GnRH-analogues (Beier et al., 2010). The indicator required for a differential diagnosis for various groups of medications is in particular dependent on the extent to which the affected person's actual control at the behavioural level is possibly at risk, since these represent the primary goal of the treatment efforts. With respect to sexual and general self-regulation BEDIT additionally gives a high priority to the improvement of emotional regulation. The goal is to help clients recognize, monitor, understand, and appropriately cope with emotions and needs. Interventions in this regard are experience-orientated (confrontation, imagination exercises, role play regarding real or fantasized offences, role reversal offender–victim, etc.) and encourage the use of emotions explicitly in order to internalize changes in behaviour and attitudes. Striking deficits in handling emotions (perception, consciousness, communication and regulation) are not addressed merely in the context of victim empathy but repeatedly receive explicit feedback by the therapist. In following concepts of controlled information processing, ineffective attempts at problem solving are blocked systematically and alternatives are consciously stimulated (Shiffrin and Schneider, 1984). By means of acquiring new skills precisely within the context of one's personal learning history (i.e. during therapy vs autobiographical self-report) a step-by-step correction of emotional schema should be additionally made possible (Nichols and Efran, 1985; Linehan, 1996).

At the same time the acquirement of emotional skills is closely linked to an enhancement of social skills. Paedophiles often have a variety of social skills deficits, such as impairment in the areas of conflict resolution, conversational skills, parenting and use of leisure time. Besides treating sexual preoccupation, enhancement of social skills is particularly important in child pornography offenders. Strongly associated are problems in developing and maintaining satisfying relationships with friends of a similar age. However, the meaning and necessity of fulfilment of basic psychosocial needs for closeness, acceptance, and a sense of safety, security and protection in interpersonal relationships are emphasized more strongly than before (Drapeau, 2006). From a sexological perspective this actively counteracts the vulnerability that induces feelings of emotional loneliness and lack of attachment (Beier et al., 2005). Intimacy deficits, attachment problems and sexual dysfunctions may also affect a sense of closeness and sexuality in couples of non-exclusive-type paedophiles and hebephiles. For this purpose the patients' partners are involved and both sexual dissatisfaction within the relationship and sexual dysfunctions are taken into consideration, so that salutogenetic aspects of sexuality may be integrated into self-regulation. Also, contacts with friends and other confidants, which are characterized by openly communicating one's sexual preference structure, are purposefully encouraged. An informed network of family and friends is suggested to provide positive social support that helps to reduce risk, reinforce pro-social attitudes, and help to avoid and cope with high-risk situations.

Finally, several exercises seek to develop the offenders' level of victim awareness by teaching them to see situations from the perspective of another person, and about the effects of sexual victimization by contact and online offences. However, research has not identified poor victim empathy as a risk factor. In contrast, those who display high levels of offence-supportive attitudes (rationalizing or justifying cognitions) have increased rates of sexual re-offending. These exercises in particular have been found to be important in (potential) child pornography offenders in order to understand the link between the production of child sexual abusive images and the depictions that are used for sexual purposes.

In summary, the BEDIT treatment programme is based on three pillars that represent the bio-psychosocial nature of the preventive approach: sexological interventions help participants to accept their sexual interest by integrating their fantasies into their self-concept in order to take responsibility for sexual behaviours; cognitive behavioral therapy improves participants' general and sexual self-regulation by restructuring attitudes towards sexuality and increasing coping and social skills. With the aid of pharmacotherapy additionally sexual impulses and fantasies can be reduced (Beier et al., 2010). While there are many similarities between BEDIT and other Sex Offender Treatment Programmes such as the Core SOTP or i-SOTP (i. e. modules, treatment targets, group sessions), differences exist in particular with respect to the selection of participants and the focus on sexual deviancy. The i-SOTP, for example, is designed for offenders convicted of an Internet-related offence (Middleton et al., 2009), whereas participants of BEDIT will be excluded from the programme for as long as they are involved with legal authorities for such offences. Undetected offenders are assumed to show more problem awareness, motivation to change and responsivity to intervention. In addition, as Middleton and colleagues consider 'high deviance' offenders unsuitable for the i-SOTP, because they are assumed to demonstrate more criminogenic needs, BEDIT particularly addresses paedophiles and hebephiles who are usually described by a high deviance cluster. Moreover, inclusion criteria reasonably affect the importance and weighting of treatment targets such as the self-monitoring of sexual fantasies and paraphilic interests as well as the control of sexual arousal and impulses. Thus, any intervention addressing social skills, intimacy or attachment deficits or dysfunctional coping is strongly connected to the impact of sexual preference as the underlying determining trait. Thereby, sexual preference always determines which pattern of intimate relationship could be expected as a functional treatment goal. For example, establishing an adequate intimate relationship with an adult partner is suggested to be a dysfunctional treatment goal in exclusive type paedophiles or hebephiles within the BEDIT programme.

Outlook and new challenges

Paedophiles and hebephiles have been found to be at greater risk for persistent child sexual abuse and child pornography offences. As these individuals must be assumed to also have a greater lifetime risk for initial offending behaviours, they are considered to be an important target group of prevention approaches, particularly at early stages (juveniles). However, little is known of the risk factors of child sexual abuse and child pornography offences in paedophiles or hebephiles not formally involved with the criminal justice system, and even less of those who never acted upon their sexual interest in children. Of particular interest would be knowledge about factors distinguishing those who act upon their sexual preference by use of child abuse images from those who do not offend against children. In addition, which factors lead to sexual contact offences against children in child pornography offenders and what is the connection between child sexual abuse and child pornography offences, if any? (See Chapter 9 for further discussion.)

Research on help-seeking non-offending and undetected paedophiles and hebephiles from the community, it is suggested, may provide data on sexual deviance and behaviour, which will less likely be jeopardized by deliberate faking in order to avoid legal consequences, is common in forensic contexts. The accessibility of this sample has been shown by results from the ongoing Berlin Prevention Project Dunkelfeld. Future research on this target group should focus on specifying the applicability of risk factors and risk assessment established in detected sex offenders to this target group. Further, an improvement of the assessment of sexual preference by comparing direct and indirect approaches (such as penis plethysmography and neuro-imaging techniques like f-MRI), an elaboration of risk management by developing new tools assessing sexual deviancy and empathy, and the evaluation of pharmaceutical support seem necessary. Exploitation of the results may add to an ongoing debate on specific treatment targets (e.g. empathy, drugs) and improve primary and secondary prevention approaches by granting valid and reliable tools assessing risk and treatment efficacy. Moreover, results will provide clinicians, who aim at proactive intervention in paedophilic and hebephilic patients, with information about treatment targets, the benefit, risks and efficacy of treatment in this population.

Nevertheless, on account of the fact that a paedophilic sexual preference is inconvertible, it must be seen as a chronic lifelong disorder. The consequence is that programmes for the chronically impaired need to be established within a frame of meaningful proactive prevention work. That is why those who have completed the treatment programme also need to have a point of contact (in the sense of a community-based centre for sexual medicine) with access to the necessary treatment options (including medication to modulate sexual arousal processes) so that help can be provided immediately in situations in which those affected are at risk of committing an offence. As a matter of fact, this is a genuine challenge specifically for the healthcare system rather than for forensic services.

Of course, for that purpose an adequate legal framework is needed to guarantee the pledge of confidentiality. In countries with a strictly normative orientation and mandatory reporting laws, intelligent alternatives need to be developed in order to enable the relevant people to dare to seek help, perhaps as a double-blind assessment and treatment concept.

The prevention project at the Charité in Berlin has been able to show that in the Dunkelfeld it is possible actually to prevent child sexual abuse and child pornography offences, where in the past nothing was done at all. This opportunity should be taken in other countries as well.

Notes

1   As the onset of puberty is well below 14 for both sexes, the classification of hebephilia as a sexual preference disorder is useful with respect to risk assessment and prevention of child sexual exploitation, though still a matter of discussion (see Green, 2010a; 2010b).
2   Child sexual abuse offences include non-contact offences such as exhibitionistic or voyeuristic offences.

References

Ahlers, C.J., Feelgood, S., Schaefer, G.A. and Beier, K.M. (2006). Media campaign: Prevention of child sexual abuse in the Dunkelfeld. Paper (poster) presented at the 9th International Conference of the International Association for the Treatment of Sexual Offenders (IATSO), 6–9 September. Hamburg.

Ahlers, C.J., Schaefer, G.A., Mundt, I.A., Roll, S., Englert, H., Willich, S. and Beier, K.M. (2009). How unusual are the contents of paraphilias – prevalence of paraphilia-associated sexual arousal patterns (PASAPs) in a community-based Sample of Men. *Journal of Sexual Medicine*, doi: 10.1111/j.1743–6109.2009.01597.

Allam J.M., Middleton, D. and Browne, K.D. (1997). Different clients, different needs? Practice issues in community-based treatment for sex offenders. *Criminal Behaviour and Mental Health, 7*, 69–84.

American Psychiatric Association (APA) (2000). *Diagnostic and Statistical Manual of Mental Disorders. DSM-IV-TR*. 4th rev. edn. Arlington VA: American Psychiatric Association.

Andrews, D.A. and Bonta, J. (2006). *The Psychology of Criminal Conduct*. 4th edn. Cincinnati, OH: Anderson.

Babchishin, K.M., Hanson, K.R. and Hermann, C.A. (2010). The characteristics of online sex offenders: A meta-analysis. *Sexual Abuse: A Journal of Research and Treatment*, doi: 10.1177/1079063210370708.

Bates, A. and Metcalf, C. (2007). A psychometric comparison of internet and non-Internet sex offenders from a community treatment sample. *Journal of Sexual Aggression, 13*, 11–20.

Beier, K.M. (1998). Differential typology and prognosis for dissexual behaviour – a follow-up study of previously expert-appraised child molesters. *International Journal of Legal Medicine, 111*, 133–41.

Beier, K.M. and Loewit, K. (2011). *Praxisleitfaden Sexualmedizin*, Heidelberg: Springer

Beier, K.M., Amelung, T. and Pauls, A. (2010). Antiandrogene Therapie als Teil der Prävention von sexuellem Kindesmissbrauch im Dunkelfeld. *Forens Psychiatr Psychol Kriminol, 4*, 49–57.

Beier, K.M., Bosinski, H.A.G. and Loewit, K. (2005). *Sexualmedizin*, 2nd edn. München: Elsevier Urban and Fischer.

Beier, K.M., Neutze, J., Mundt, I.A., Ahlers, C.J., Goecker, D. and Konrad, A. (2009). Encouraging self-identified pedophiles and hebephiles to seek professional help: First results of the Berlin Prevention Project Dunkelfeld (PPD). *Child Abuse and Neglect, 33*, 545–9.

Beier, K. M., Ahlers, C.J., Goecker, D., Neutze, J., Mundt, I.A., Hupp, E. and Schaefer, G. A. (2009). Can pedophiles be reached for primary prevention of child sexual abuse? First results of the Berlin Prevention Project Dunkelfeld (PPD). *Journal of Forensic Psychiatry and Psychology, 20*, 51–67.

Bernard, J.S. (1975). *Adolescence and Socialization for Motherhood*. In S.E. Dragastin and G.H. Elder, Jr (eds), *Adolescence in the Life Cycle, Psychological Change and Social Context*. Washington, DC: Hemisphere.

Blanchard, R., Klassen, P., Dickey, R., Kuban, M.E. and Blak, T. (2001). Sensitivity and specificity of the phallometric test for pedophilia in nonadmitting sex offenders. *Psychological Assessment, 13*, 118–26.

Blanchard, R., Kuban, M.E., Blak, T., Cantor, J.M., Klassen, P. and Dickey, R. (2006). Phallometric comparison of pedophilic interest in nonadmitting sexual offenders against stepdaughters, biological daughters, other biologically related girls, and unrelated girls. *Sexual Abuse: Journal of Research and Treatment, 18(1)*, 1–14.

Bogaert, A.F., Bezeau, S., Kuban, M. and Blanchard, R. (1997). Pedophilia, sexual orientation, and birth order. *Journal of Abnormal Psychology, 106(2)*, 331–5.

Briere J. and Runtz, M. (1989). University males' sexual interest in children: Predicting potential indices of 'pedophilia' in a nonforensic sample. *Child Abuse and Neglect, 113*, 65–75.

Chasan-Taber, L. and Tabachnick, J. (1999). Evaluation of a child sexual abuse prevention program. *Sexual Abuse: A Journal of Research and Treatment, 11*, 279–92.

Davidson, J., Martellozzo, E. and Lorent. M. (2009). Evaluation of CEOP ThinkuKnow Internet safety programme and exploration of young people's Internet safety knowledge. Available online at http://www.cats-rp.org.uk/pdf%20files/Internet%20safety%20report%204-2010.pdf/

Davis, R.A. (2001). A cognitive-behavioral model of pathological Internet use. *Computers in Human Behavior, 17*, 187–95.

Drapeau, M. (2006). Repetition or reparation? An exploratory study of the relationship schemas of child molesters in treatment. *Journal of Interpersonal Violence, 21(9)*, 1224–33.

Duff, S. and Willis, A. (2006). At the precipice: Assessing a non-offending client's potential to sexually offend. *Journal of Sexual Aggression, 12*, 43–51.

Durkin, K.F. and Bryant, C.D. (1999). Propagandizing pederasty: A thematic analysis of the on-line exculpatory accounts of unrepentant pedophiles. *Deviant Behavior, 20*, 103–27.

Eke, A.W., Seto, M.C. and Williams, J. (2010). Examining the criminal history and future offending of child pornography offenders: An extended prospective follow-up study. *Law and Human Behavior*, doi: 10.1007/s10979-010-9252-2.

Elliott, I.A., Beech, A.R., Mandeville-Norden, R. and Hayes, E. (2009). Psychological profiles of Internet sexual offenders: Comparisons with contact sexual offenders. *Sexual Abuse: A Journal of Research and Treatment, 21,* 76–92.

Fedoroff, J.P., Smolewska, K., Selhi, Z., Ng, E. and Bradford, J.M.W. (2001). Victimless pedophiles. Paper presented at the Annual Meeting of the International Academy of Sex Research (IASR), 11–14 July. Montreal, Quebec, Canada.

Feelgood, S. and Schaefer, G. A. (2011). Dealing with missing data: The promise of Dunkelfeld research with sexual offenders against minors. In D.P. Boer, R. Eher, L. Craig, M. Miner and F. Pfafflin (eds), *International Perspectives on the Assessment and Treatment of Sexual Offenders: Theory, Practice and Research*, Hoboken, NJ: John Wiley and Sons.

Feelgood, S., Ahlers, C.J., Schaefer, G.A. and Ferrier, A. (2002). Generation of concrete ideas for a media campaign to motivate undetected sexual offenders to seek treatment using the Marketing Psychology approach. 7th International Conference of the International Association for the Treatment of Sexual Offenders (IATSO). Vienna, Austria.

Finkelhor, D. (1984). *Child Sexual Abuse: New Theory and Research.* New York: Free Press.

—— (1994). The international epidemiology of child sexual abuse. *Child Abuse and Neglect, 18,* 409–17.

—— (2009). The prevention of childhood sexual abuse. *The Future of Children, 19,* 169–94.

German Criminal Code (2009). Available online at http://bundesrecht.juris.de/englisch_stgb/englisch_stgb.html#StGB_000P34; http://bundesrecht.juris.de/englisch_stgb/englisch_stgb.html#StGB_000P68; http://bundesrecht.juris.de/englisch_stgb/englisch_stgb.html#StGB_000P138; http://bundesrecht.juris.de/englisch_stgb/englisch_stgb.html#StGB_000P203.

Gibson, L.E. and Leitenberg , H. (2000). Child sexual abuse prevention programs: Do they decrease the occurrence of child sexual abuse? *Child Abuse and Neglect, 24,* 115–25.

Green, R. (2010a). Sexual preference for 14-year-olds as a mental disorder: You can't be serious! *Archives of Sexual Behavior, 39*(3), 585–6.

—— (2010b). Hebephila is a mental disorder? *Sexual Offender Treatment, 5,* 1–7.

Grundmann, D., Neutze, J. and Beier, K.M. (2010). Psychopathic characteristics and sexual deviancy in pedophilic and hebephilic child pornography offenders. Paper presented at the 11th International Conference of the International Association for the Treatment of Sexual Offenders (IATSO), 1–4 September 2010. Oslo, Norway.

Hall, G.C.N. and Hirschman, R. (1992). Sexual aggression against children: A conceptual perspective of etiology. *Criminal Justice and Behavior, 19,* 8–23.

Hall, G.C.N., Hirschman, R. and Oliver, L.L. (1995). Sexual arousal and arousability to pedophilic stimuli in a community sample of normal men. *Behavioral Therapy, 26,* 681.

Hanson, R.K and Morton-Bourgon, K.E. (2005). The characteristics of persistent sexual offenders: A meta-analysis of recidivism studies. *Journal of Consulting and Clinical Psychology, 73,* 1154–63.

Hanson, R.K., Harris, A.J.R., Scott, T.-L., and Helmus, L. (2007). *Assessing the Risk of Sexual Offenders on Community Supervision: The Dynamic Supervision Project* (User Report 2007–05). Ottawa: Public Safety Canada.

Henry, F. and McMahon, P. (2000). What survivors of child sexual abuse told us about the people who abused them. Paper presented at the National Sexual Violence Prevention Conference. Dallas, Texas.

IWF (2007). Internet Watch Foundation. Annual and Charity Report. Available online at http://www.iwf.org.uk/accountability/annual-reports/2007-annual-report.

—— (2010). Internet Watch Foundation. Annual and Charity Report. Available online at http://www.iwf.org.uk/accountability/annual-reports/2010-annual-report.

Karoly, P. (1993). Goal systems: An organizing framework for clinical assessment and treatment planning. *Psychological Assessment, 5*, 273–80.

Krone, T. (2004). Typology of online child pornography offending. *Trends and Issues in Crime and Criminal Justice, 279*, 1–6. Available online at http://aic.gov.au/documents/4/F/8/percent7B4F8B4249–7BEE–4F57-B9ED–993479D9196Dpercent7Dtandi279.pdf.

Kuhle, L., Neutze, J. and Beier, K.M. (2010). Use of sexually explicit and non-explicit images of children and associated risk factors for child sexual abuse. Paper presented at the 11th International Conference of the International Association for the Treatment of Sexual Offenders (IATSO), 1–4 September 2010. Oslo, Norway.

Lanning, K.V. (2001). Child molesters: A behavioral analysis. 4th edn. Available online at http://www.missingkids.com/en_US/publications/NC70.pdf.

Lautmann, R. (1994). Die Lust am Kind. Portrait des Paedophilen [The desire for children. Portrait of the paedophile]. Hamburg: Ingrid Klein.

Linehan, M. (1996). *Dialektisch-Behaviorale Therapie der Borderline-Persönlichkeitsstörung.* München: Cip-Medien.

Locke, E.A. (1996). Motivation through conscious goal setting. *Applied and Preventive Psychology, 5*, 117–26.

Lykins, A.D., Cantor, J.M., Kuban, M.E., Blak, T., Dickey, E., Klassen, P.E. and Blanchard, R. (2010). Sexual arousal to female children in gynephilic men. *Sexual Abuse: Journal of Research and Treatment, 22*, 279–89.

McGrath, R., Cumming, G., Burchard, B., Zeoli, S. and Ellerby, L. (2010). *Current Practices and Emerging Trends in Sexual Abuser Management: The Safer Society 2009 North American Survey.* Brandon, VT: Safer Society Press. Available at http://www.safersociety.org/surveydownload.php.

Malesky, L.A. and Ennis, L. (2004). Supportive distortions: An analysis of posts on a pedophile Internet message board. *Journal of Addictions and Offender Counseling, 24*, 92–100.

Marshall, W.L. and Barbaree, H.E. (1990). Integrated theory of the etiology of sexual offending. In W.L. Marshall, H.E., Barbaree and D.R. Laws (eds), *Handbook of Sexual Assault: Issues, Theories, and Treatment of the Offender.* New York: Plenum, pp. 257–75.

Marshall, W.L., Marshall, L.E. and Serran, G.A. (2006). Strategies in the treatment of paraphilias: A critical review. *Annual Review of Sex Research, 17*, 162–82.

Middleton, D., Mandeville-Norden, R. and Hayes, E. (2009). Does treatment work with Internet sex offenders? Emerging findings from the internet sex offender treatment programme (i-SOTP). *Journal of Sexual Aggression, 15*, 5–19.

Mundt, I.A., Schaefer, G.A., Neutze, J. and Beier, K.M. (2009). Paraphilia associated sexual arousal patterns of help-seeking CSA offenders from the community. *Paper presented at the 28th Annual ATSA Conference*, Dallas, Texas.

Neutze, J., Grundmann, D., Schaefer, G.A. and Beier, K.M. (2010). Dynamic risk factors in undetected help seeking pedophiles and hebephiles. *Paper presented at the 11th International Conference of the International Association for the Treatment of Sexual Offenders (IATSO)*, 1–4 September 2010. Oslo, Norway.

Neutze, J., Seto, M., Schaefer, G.A. and Beier, K.M. (2011). Predictors of child pornography offences and child sexual abuse in a community sample of pedophiles and hebephiles. *Sexual Abuse: A Journal of Research and Treatment, 22*, 1–31.

Nichols, M.P. and Efran, J.S. (1985). Catharsis in psychotherapy. *Psychotherapy, 22*, 46–58.

Pithers, W.D. (1990). Relapse prevention with sexual aggressors: A method of maintaining therapeutic gain and enhancing external supervision. In W.L. Marshall, D.R. Laws and H.E. Barbaree (eds), *Handbook of Sexual Assault: Issues, Theories and Treatment of the Offender*. New York: Plenum, pp. 343–61.

Police Crime Statistic (2007, 2008). Retrieved 13 February 2011 from Federal Criminal Police Office Website, http://www.bka.de/profil/englisch.html.

Quayle, E. and Taylor, M. (2002). Paedophiles, pornography and the internet: Assessment issues. *British Journal of Social Work, 32*, 863–75.

—— (2003). Model of problematic Internet use in people with a sexual interest in children. *Cyber Psychology and Behavior, 6*, 93–106.

Quinsey, V.L., Steinman, C.M., Bergersen, S.G. and Holmes, T.F. (1975). Penile circumference, skin conductance, and ranking responses of child molesters and 'normals' to sexual and nonsexual visual stimuli. *Behavioral Therapy, 6*, 213–16.

Riegel, D.L. (2004). Effects on boy-attracted pedosexual males of viewing boy erotica [Letter to the editor]. *Archives of Sexual Behavior, 33*, 321–23.

Rispens, J., Aleman, A. and Goudena, P.P. (1997). Prevention of child sexual abuse victimization: A meta-analysis of school programs. *Child Abuse and Neglect, 21*, 975–87.

Rossman, P. (1976). *Sexual Experience between Men and Boys. Exploring the Pederast Underground*. New York: Association Press.

Schaefer, G.A., Neutze, J., Mundt, I.A., Goecker, D. and Beier, K.M. (2008). Pedophiles and hebephiles in the community – findings from the Berlin Prevention Project Dunkelfeld (PPD). Paper presented at the 27th Annual Research and Treatment Conference of the Association for the Treatment of Sexual Abusers (ATSA), 22–5 October, Atlanta, Georgia, USA.

Schaefer, G.A., Mundt, I.A., Feelgood, S., Hupp, E., Neutze, J., Ahlers, C.J., Goecker, D. and Beier, K.M. (2010). Potential and Dunkelfeld offenders: Two neglected target groups for prevention of child sexual abuse. *International Journal of Law and Psychiatry, 33*(3), 154–63.

Seto, M.C. (2008). *Pedophilia and Sexual Offending against Children: Theory, Assessment, and Intervention*. Washington, DC: US: American Psychological Association.

—— (2009). Pedophilia. *Annual Review of Clinical Psychology, 5*, 391–407.

Seto, M.C., Cantor, J.M. and Blanchard, R. (2006). Child pornography offences are a valid diagnostic indicator of pedophilia. *Journal of Abnormal Psychology, 115*, 610–15.

Seto, M.C., Hanson, R.K. and Babchishin, K.M. (in press). Contact sexual offending by men arrested for online sexual offences. *Sexual Abuse: A Journal of Research and Treatment*.

Shiffrin, R.M. and Schneider, W. (1984). Automatic and controlled processing revisited. *Psychological Review, 914*, 269–79.

Stop it Now! (2009). Helpline Report 2005–2009. Available online at http://www.stop itnow.org.uk/Helpline per cent20Report.pdf.

Surjadi, B., Bullens, R., van Horn, J. and Bogaerts, S. (2010). Internet offending: Sexual and non-sexual functions within a Dutch sample. *Journal of Sexual Aggression, 16*, 47–58.

Ward, T. and Beech, A. (2006). An integrated theory of sexual offending. *Aggression and Violent Behavior, 11*, 44–63.

Ward, T. and Gannon, T.A. (2006). Rehabilitation, etiology, and self-regulation: The good Lives Model of sexual offender treatment. *Aggression and Violent Behavior, 11*, 77–94.

Ward, T. and Hudson, S.M. (1998). A self-regulation model of the relapse process in sexual offenders. *Journal of Interpersonal Violence, 13*, 700–725.

Ward, T. and Siegert, R.J. (2002). Toward a comprehensive theory of child sexual abuse: A theory knitting perspective. *Psychology, Crime, and Law, 8*, 319–51.

Ward, T., Hudson, S.M., and Keenan, T. (1998). A self-regulation model of the sexual offence process. *Sexual Abuse: A Journal of Research and Treatment, 10*, 141–57.

Webb, L., Craissati, J. and Keen, S. (2007). Characteristics of internet child pornography offenders: A comparison with child molesters. *Sexual Abuse: A Journal of Research and Treatment, 19*, 249–65.

Wetzels, P. (1997). Prävalenz und familiäre Hintergründe sexuellen Kindesmißbrauchs i Deutschland: Ergebnisse einer repräsentativen Befragung. *Sexuologi, 4*(2), 89–107.

WHO (1992). *International Statistical Classification of Diseases and Related Health Problems*, 10th revn. Geneva: WHO.

Wille, R. (1968). Die forensisch-psychopathologische Beurteilung der Exhibitionisten, Pädophilen, Inzest- und Notzuchttäter. Postdoctorial thesis, Universität Kiel.

Wilson, G.D. and Cox, D.N. (1983). *The Child-Lovers: A Study of Paedophiles in Society*. London: Peter Owen.

Zwi, K., Woolfenden, S. Wheeler, D.M., O'Brien, T., Tait, P. and Williams, K.J. (2007). School-based education programmes for the prevention of child sexual abuse. *Cochrane Database of Systematic Reviews, 3*, 1–36.

13 Technological solutions to offending

Awais Rashid, Phil Greenwood,
James Walkerdine, Alistair Baron and Paul Rayson,
School of Computing and Communications,
Infolab21, Lancaster University

Overview

Technological solutions have often been proposed as a possible means for online child protection through the use of filtering software and, more recently, the use of software to detect problematic use by offenders in the context of illegal images. However, filtering technologies currently in use are often easy to bypass and more advanced solutions, such as the Child Protection System (CPS) from TLO, though effective, pose significant resourcing challenges for law enforcement agencies. More recent research seeks to develop tools to enable police officers to combat predators in online social networks by automating various resource-intensive analysis tasks as well as identifying the stylistic footprints of offenders to enhance the investigators' understanding of behavioural patterns and tactics. First, this chapter examines the key challenges that technological solutions must overcome both from the perspective of offender tactics and typical constraints that govern investigative practices. This is followed by a discussion of recent research breakthroughs in technical solutions to overcome some of the aforementioned challenges. The chapter culminates with a roadmap for key technological advances and shifts in investigative practices that are needed to ensure that protective strategies can keep pace with the increasingly sophisticated tactics being employed by offenders.

Introduction

The proliferation of the Internet has led to a number of innovative media that enable people from around the world and various walks of life to come together and share materials and experiences. Examples of these mediums include: peer-to-peer file-sharing networks (Gnutella, BitTorrent and eDonkey), chat applications (Skype, IRC and MSN), social networking sites (Facebook, Myspace, and Twitter), online virtual worlds (SecondLife) and massive multi-player online games (World of Warcraft). Children actively participate in social interactions using such forums and web-based communities. These innovative mediums, however, also enable child sex offenders to have direct and easy access to potential victims for grooming and sexual exploitation purposes, potentially twenty-four hours a day, as these mediums are now not only available via computers but also through mobile phones. Sex offenders can use these mediums to predate on children or facilitate networking with like-minded offenders in the proliferation of abusive imagery. This is high-lighted by high-profile cases such as that of Lee Costi (2006), who was arrested after arranging to meet his third victim following grooming in chat rooms (subsequent investigation found over 300 chat logs on his computer containing conversations with young girls, mostly detailing his interest in underage sex); Wayne Baker (2010), who used various tactics, including masquerading as a young person in chat rooms and promises of modelling contracts, to lure his victims for sex, subsequently blackmailing them into child prostitution; and Michael Williams (2010), who groomed and abused hundreds, potentially thousands, of children via social networking sites. These media have also been used by offenders for planning their activities, illustrated by the conviction of those using such systems to plan child abuse or engage in deviant fantasies, for instance, 'Wonderland', the secret children's playground used by child sex offenders in SecondLife.

While there is scientific debate (Middleton, 2009) on whether the online child sex offender is a new type of offender (Quayle et al., 2000) or if those with a predisposition to offend are responding to the opportunities afforded by the new forms of social media (Cooper, 1998), empirical evidence points to the problem of Internet-based child sex abuse as endemic. Hughes et al. (2006a) found that 1.6 per cent of searches and 2.4 per cent of responses on the Gnutella peer-to-peer network alone related to illegal sexual content (e.g. rape, bestiality, child abuse). Given the system's scale, these results suggest that, on the Gnutella network alone, hundreds of searches for illegal images occur each second. The study also found that, of those users sharing illegal sexual content, 57 per cent were solely devoted to such distribution while half of the material shared by another 17 per cent involved such content. With tens of peer-to-peer networks in use, the scale of this activity on these networks alone can be estimated to be in the tens of thousands of searches, if not hundreds of thousands per day. This is corroborated by Middleton (2009), who reports that in June 2004 British Telecom (BT) blocked 10,000 hits a day to websites sharing indecent images of children (the list was supplied by the Internet Watch Foundation, IWF). Eighteen months later, in February 2006, there were 35,000 attempts per day to access the material. He goes on to extrapolate the total volume to 100,000 hits per day based on UK broadband market share of BT.

Similar trends can be observed in data from the criminal justice system. Middleton (2009) reports that for England and Wales in 1999 there were 238 convictions for the publication, possession or distribution of obscene matter and indecent photographs of children, which by 2005 had increased to 1,296. This indicated that such offences accounted for almost one-third of all sexual convictions. A study by Henry et al. (2010) with the UK Probation Service identified 633 men who had been convicted of Internet sexual offences between 2005 and 2007. Data from the FBI indicates that between 1996 and 2006 there was a 1,789 per cent increase in the number of open cases, a 2,174 per cent increase in arrests and summons, and a 1,397 per cent increase in convictions for such crimes on the Internet; showing that this trend appears to be reflected in the US.

Our research within the Isis project (http://www.comp.lancs.ac.uk/isis) over the last three years indicates that Internet-based child sex offenders are often highly technology-savvy, using a range of tactics to groom victims and to mask the trail of their activities, such as:

• masquerading as young persons to gain trust of potential victims;
• use of multiple online personas so that several offenders in a group may share the personas and groom a victim at different times;
• use of a specialized vocabulary to share child abuse materials, which evolves as the keywords come to the attention of law enforcement agencies and organizations such as the IWF; and
• use of encryption and anonymization technologies or private networks which are harder to monitor and police.

In fact, offenders tend to stay ahead of the efforts of law enforcement agents, as evidenced by the recent surge in a move of such activity to other file-sharing networks that support greater anonymization and privacy following crackdowns by the FBI and Interpol on several well-known peer-to-peer networks.

The question that naturally follows is the following: what role can technological solutions play in aiding those with a vested interest in protecting children (e.g. law enforcement agents, children's services, parents, schools) in the face of the increasingly sophisticated technology base utilized by offenders? Surely we can engineer technological solutions that counter different threat vectors arising from offender tactics. Unfortunately, the answer is neither that simple nor that straight-forward. The Internet is an open medium. While this openness brings a great deal of freedom and opportunities for innovation, it also poses new challenges in that traditional lock-down approaches to security and safety become ineffective. This openness, coupled with constantly evolving offender tactics and a growing number of heterogeneous online social interaction media accessible to both offenders and victims, means that one needs to look beyond contemporary gate-keeping and forensics software. Technologies are required that are able to cope with the open nature of the Internet as well as the evolving nature of threat patterns that arise when aiming to protect potential victims or apprehending the offenders.

Current technological landscape

The rapid rise in the number of children using the Internet has resulted in a grow-ing research community and software industry dedicated to developing tech-nologies to help keep children safe online. Specifically, the types of technology can be split into two camps: filtering (or gate-keeping) software that seeks to block activities that are deemed to put a child at risk, and forensics software intended to help investigators identify, track and examine online offender activities.

Filtering software

Filtering software for the purpose of online child protection seeks to provide real-time analysis and, when necessary, functionality to restrict or block a given data source (for example, instant messenger communications). This type of software is most commonly used in the home or in schools and as a consequence a large commercial industry has now been built around developing filtering software solutions.

From a chat-filtering perspective, the level of analysis that can be performed by such software can vary. The more common and simplest approach is to use keyword-based analysis, where the software examines a data stream in real time for a set of specified words or phrases. Should they appear or reach a given threshold, then the software can censor/block the communication or alert an interested party (i.e. the parent or teacher). Numerous products exist that use these techniques including NetNanny (http://www.netnanny.com), PureSightPC (http://www.puresight.com), Spector Pro (http://www.spectorsoft.com) and SpyAgent (http://www.spytech-web.com). The main limitation of these systems is their reliance on keyword lists that may be defined by child protection organizations such as the IWF, or by the users themselves. Although they can help identify when certain words are used, the approach does not scale, allowing it to be bypassed (or more importantly, an offender to bypass it) if a word deviates slightly (for example, 'fck', 'f**k', etc.). In addition, the language used by individuals online is continually evolving (Crystal, 2006) meaning that these lists need to be constantly updated to maintain relevance. This kind of language evaluation is discussed in Thelwall (2008) where the variations in the spelling of swear words were examined. Such updates pose a significant challenge, as offenders often disguise the words and terminology they use, and the online chat language that children use varies depending on their age, cultural, regional and social backgrounds.

More sophisticated systems use pattern analysis techniques that build upon keyword matching so that word sequences and word collocations are considered. Pattern-analysis-based approaches can be more successful in identifying risky behaviour as they can extract additional content information from a communication and analyse a range of factors before flagging up a concern. Solutions provided by Crisp Thinking (http://www.crispthinking.com) make use of these types of approach and claim a high accuracy in identifying risk behaviour such as grooming and cyber-bullying.

However, in both keyword- and pattern-based approaches, the analysis is only performed at the word level, with the stylistic context and meaning of a communication not taken into account. This can lead to misinterpretation; for example in 'what sex is your dog?', sex refers to gender rather than the sexual act. In addition, the nature of the participants and the context of the interaction is not considered, which can result in situations such as 'normal' youth sexual behaviour being wrongly categorized. By extension, these systems tend to be developed to monitor a predator stereotype (middle-aged adult male), which does not reflect patterns of Internet-based sexual predation of children and young people. According to Finkelhor et al. (2000), in a significant number of cases it is young people who make aggressive sexual advances towards other young people.

Although gate-keeping software has predominantly focused on the filtering of online chat, techniques and technologies have also been developed to filter inappropriate websites and pornographic images that may be found on the Internet. Organizations such as the IWF maintain blacklists of websites that are deemed to contain criminal online content (such as child abuse or illegal pornography), and make these available to Internet service providers and the filtering industry so that access to such sites can be blocked. The use of blacklists has proven to be very effective in transparently 'removing' criminal content from the Internet. However, such an approach is reactive, requiring the lists to be kept constantly up to date as perpetrators inevitably move their content around the Internet.

Products like NetNanny and PureSightPC build on the use of blacklists by also providing keyword-based analysis functionality to examine the content of Internet artefacts such as websites, emails and the names of files that are shared on peer-to-peer networks. This can be effective for filtering some sources, but suffers from the limitations of keyword analysis highlighted above. In addition, such systems only focus on textual content and hence illegal image content can be hidden behind legitimate keywords. Being able accurately to identify and filter nudity in images is still a sizeable challenge, although recent developments have started to see effective solutions being released that can be used in home and school environments (http://www.patrick-wied.at/static/nudejs/).

Forensic software

Forensic software is an established area with new technologies and products being released for use by law enforcement and forensics experts on a regular basis. They reflect the growing challenge that investigators face – namely being able to analyse efficiently the vast amounts of digital data that can be collected during an ongoing investigation. From an online child protection perspective, the forensic software that exists can be classified from the standpoint of whether it provides real-time data capture and analysis or only support for analysing pre-captured data.

Real-time forensic software

Forensic software that operates in a real-time fashion requires the use of monitoring technologies to capture the data first. This in itself introduces a number of challenges not only in terms of building the technologies to capture the required data, but also ensuring that such data can be legally monitored and held, and that the amount of captured data does not result in an overload of information that can inhibit the investigative process.

A key area in which this type of software is utilized is in the monitoring of peer-to-peer (P2P) networks for the distribution of child abuse media. The global popularity of using P2P technologies as a mechanism for sharing illegal content (e.g. music and films protected by copyright, illegal sexual content) has conversely resulted in an interest in developing solutions that can monitor such activity. To an extent, this has been led by the entertainment industry, seeking to clamp down on the distribution of material protected by copyright. However, monitoring approaches have also been developed to help identify child abuse content. The challenge faced when monitoring P2P systems is that numerous communication protocols exist with new ones being developed on a regular basis. The differing nature of these protocols means that no single standard monitoring approach can be built, but instead monitoring technology needs to be developed for each P2P protocol. A discussion of the types of P2P monitoring approaches that can be used was provided by Hughes et al. (2006b).

In terms of identifying child abuse media on P2P systems, the system used by many law enforcement agencies around the world is CPC (previously known as Peer Precision). Developed by law enforcement in the US, this system is able to monitor a variety of P2P protocols and compare content against a database of known child abuse media based on the use of hash-values in files. In this context, a hash-value is a unique numerical representation of a file generated from its contents. Employing hash-values allows identical files to be reliably found rather than depending on other editable file descriptors (e.g. their filename). By utilizing this system, investigators are not only able to determine who is sharing child abuse media on the various P2P networks but also extract information that can help them identify the perpetrator in the physical world, such as their IP address and geo-graphical location (on a worldwide level). Elsewhere, within the MAPAP Safer Internet project (http://antipaedo.lip6.fr/) monitors have been built for identifying child abuse media on the eDonkey P2P network and also the identification of child abuse terminology within queries. The project has also undertaken trend analysis in currently running P2P systems, including an evaluation of the number of files/users involved, the identification of various kinds of files/users, and their evolution over time. Within the Isis project at Lancaster University, we have also developed our own P2P-monitoring technologies that have been adapted to identify the distribution of child abuse media. These operate over a number of P2P networks including Gnutella, OpenNap and Bittorrent, as well as for file sharing over IRC.

Although these monitoring tools are able successfully to identify child abuse media, they are unable to adequately filter or prioritize the thousands of results they find. Nor are they able to automatically verify the existence of new child abuse media or identify child abuse media that is not on record. As a consequence, the only current way to identify new and previously unknown media is through manual analysis by law enforcement personnel. However, such a manual approach is difficult to resource given the large number of files that need to be reviewed individually and the limited resources law enforcement agencies possess. As a result, in some cases, to avoid being overloaded, forces have chosen to avoid using such technologies or, if they do, only focus on what they perceive to be high-risk cases, which in itself can be difficult to determine.

Analysis software for pre-captured data

The software tools that are more frequently used by law enforcement are those that can help analyse digital data that may have previously been gathered or seized as part of an ongoing investigation. A typical online sex offending case could involve law enforcement collecting chat log data from a victim's PC and/or extracting chat fragments from a disk dump of a perpetrator's seized computer. In both cases, significant resources would be required to perform the analysis manually.

The software toolkit that is most commonly used in the field is EnCase, developed by Guidance Software (http://www.guidancesoftware.com/computer-forensics-ediscovery-software-digital-evidence.htm). EnCase provides a powerful set of features for extracting data from a variety of sources (disk dumps, hard disks, mobile phones, hidden volumes, etc.), organizing it in a way to aid investigations (classifying by type – for example, images, videos, chat logs, etc.) and providing support to search the data. As well as its support for data extraction, Encase's key strength is in its ability to take a snapshot of a source and preserve it in a manner that is legitimate for court hearings. However, from a chat analysis perspective, its support is limited, requiring investigators to rely heavily on keyword-based search mechanisms to mine for relevant logs.

Internet Evidence Finder (http://www.jadsoftware.com/go/?page_id=141) also provides features for extracting chat logs and emails from a given source (including social networking sites such as Facebook) and organizing them by client. Similar to Encase, it only provides simple keyword search support for actually mining the extracted conversation data. Microsoft, working with various law enforcement partners around the world, has developed the Child Exploitation Tracking System, CETS (http://www.microsoft.com/industry/publicsector/government/programs/CETsabout.mspx). CETS is intended as a global database for collecting evidence of online child exploitation that can be contributed to and searched by its law enforcement partners. Similarly to other systems, however, its search support is limited and the system performs no proactive trend analysis or cross-referencing of stored evidence.

Internet-based offending: a moving target

As noted earlier, the open nature of the Internet drives a social interaction landscape where there are an ever-increasing number of heterogeneous online social interaction mediums. This open and constantly evolving and expanding landscape presents a fast-moving target which technological solutions must keep pace with if they are to service the need for online child protection. The solution cannot be to pin the target down because offenders adapt their tactics in response to specific types of intervention; we will discuss this in some detail below. Successful technological solutions must be nimble and adaptive in such a rapidly changing landscape. Next, we discuss some of the major challenges that technological solutions must overcome if they are to maintain their agility in the face of change.

Evolving offender tactics

Offenders use many different tactics to either obscure their online offending behaviour or gain the trust of their victims. These range from the use of sophisticated anonymization and privacy technologies to 'social engineering' in order to gain the trust of their victims. A common social engineering tactic is for an offender to create a fake child persona that is used to make initial contact with their victim. Once a certain level of trust has been reached, the offender will pass the victim on to an adult persona by introducing this new persona as a friend or relative of the fake child. Furthermore, offenders frequently change and evolve their tactics in response to solutions utilized by those aiming to protect children and apprehend the offenders. As a consequence, a cat-and-mouse scenario is created where offenders always attempt to stay one step ahead of police by updating their tactics.

In terms of file-sharing activities, offenders commonly label the content (i.e. filenames and other metadata attached to the files) they are distributing with terminology and vocabulary defined within their community, which, to outsiders, is often not related to the actual content. The purpose of this is to attempt to obscure the content and make it difficult for law enforcement agents to identify illegal material, whilst still making it simple for other offenders (who also know the vocabulary) to find the content they desire. Of course, law enforcement agents are able to decipher this vocabulary by manually processing suspicious files, which involves viewing the content and identifying the connection between the content and the vocabulary used to describe it. Identifying such suspicious files can, therefore, be a very time-consuming process. Law enforcement agents also utilize hash-values, a technique used to uniquely identify files. A list of known hash-values can be used quickly to identify illegal material being shared, and from this law enforcement agents can quickly build up the vocabulary used to describe the content.

However, the vocabulary used by offenders evolves frequently, making it difficult for law enforcement to keep up with the changes. Furthermore, the process described above only works for files which are either already known to law enforcement (i.e. via their hash-values) or can be identified via their filenames/metadata due to it containing known vocabulary. Completely new files, that are described using new vocabulary, cannot be easily identified. In fact, as noted above, manual identification of such files is virtually impossible due to the large number of new files appearing in peer-to-peer networks on a daily basis. On the other hand, identification of such files is critical as those sharing new material are more likely to have access to victims.

Public to private shifts

To identify new files, law enforcement agencies frequently carry out covert operations that involve monitoring peer-to-peer and other file-sharing networks. On public file-sharing networks, such as Gnutella, this type of investigation can be quickly and easily set up. On such networks, messages that contain both search terms and search hits (i.e. the files being shared) are passed between nodes participating in the network. As a consequence, it is very easy for software to examine these messages to determine what people are sharing (and also searching for). However, more technically sophisticated offenders have recognized the risks posed by use of such networks and so have begun moving to more private networks. These private networks can have two forms of protection. First, they often have some form of registration process that has to be followed before a user can even connect to the file-sharing network. This registration process typically involves proving to the network administrators that the new member will contribute to the network's community (e.g. by providing new material). Once granted access, the network also typically employs some form of end-to-end encryption that prevents the sort of eavesdropping that can applied to public networks. In such situations, technical solutions cannot be employed in isolation but also require the use of more traditional policing methods to infiltrate these private networks.

Offenders engaging in grooming behaviour using online social mediums also move from public mediums to more private facilities. For example, offenders typically engage their target initially via some public forum (e.g. public chat room). Very quickly, they attempt to move their conversation to a more private forum (e.g. instant messaging). This is aimed at subverting any efforts by moderators of public forums or law enforcement agents in identifying their activity. Furthermore, in private chat sessions, there is less likelihood of a permanent record of the conversations being kept, thus making the activity harder to trace.

In both cases we see a pattern of engagement on public forums with subsequent shifts to private ones to thwart any efforts to monitor and detect suspect activities. This public-to-private shift poses a significant challenge as technical solutions catch up with offender tactics on public forums, the more likely it is that these illegal activities will be driven further underground. Collecting forensic data from private forums, either in real time or post hoc, is critical yet extremely challenging, given the encryption and privacy technologies and procedural safeguards (to gain the trust of offender rings) that need to be overcome.

Fluid identities

The very nature of the Internet makes it possible to create and maintain multiple online personas (Quayle and Taylor, 2001). Many people tend to have multiple identities online, either for purely legitimate purposes, e.g. different shopping sites or social networking forums, or for recreational purposes, e.g. in online games or virtual worlds, or to explore gender and identity (Danet 1998). This fluid nature of identity is also often exploited by offenders, who can control multiple online personas. These personas represent different profiles (e.g. age, gender, hobbies, etc.). The offender can then select a persona that a particular victim may be more likely to converse with, and initiate contact using that persona. Furthermore, the offender could pass the victim on to another persona as the relationship develops (e.g. a child persona could be used initially to befriend a victim but then a different persona might be introduced who is significantly older, such as, 'my older boyfriend', 'my uncle'). Identifying whether the same offender is hiding behind multiple personas is a non-trivial challenge, even more so when such personas are spread across a large number of heterogeneous social interaction mediums.

Another challenge posed by this fluid nature of identity is that offenders can share personas with other offenders. As such, a victim could be groomed by multiple offenders at different points in time using the same persona. This, in fact, is the converse of the multiple personas challenge we highlighted above – technological solutions need to be able to make distinction as the physical personalities behind an online persona change.

Data-overloading

Perhaps the biggest challenge of all is the extremely large amounts of data available on various forums on the Internet and the need to process it to apprehend child sex offenders proactively. Even where technological solutions are available, they can flag very high numbers of potential cases, hence leading to issues of scalability of such policing tools. For example, CPS, used by law enforcement agencies to target offenders' activities on peer-to-peer networks, can produce a large number of results in a very short space of time due to the fact that a large number of files whose hash-values are known to CPS are regularly exchanged on such networks. Law enforcement agencies have a duty of care to investigate all potential cases. Consequently, if such tools are run on a 24/7 basis, the large number of results produced makes investigation untenable.

Similarly, when considering online grooming cases, potentially hundreds of pages of chat transcripts could be collected that have to be processed by law enforcement agents to extract any potential intelligence or evidence. Tools such as EnCase, Internet Evidence Finder and Commission on Engineering and Technical Systems (CETS) are often used to manage this data and support its analysis. From a data analysis perspective, the investigative resources do not scale as intelligence has to be mined via keyword-based search mechanisms, thus requiring manual effort to discover relevant details.

In many ways, the problem is analogous to looking for very specific 'information needles' in a large number of heterogeneous 'data haystacks' and correlating this information for pertinent investigative decisions.

Ethical and legal issues

Another set of challenges that technological solutions must negotiate are those posed by the investigative practices themselves and legislation and ethical issues that cover such investigations. In many ways, such issues are all the more challenging as they must negotiate processes, regulations and ethical expectations that exist to protect the wider public and ensure that law enforcement resources are used efficiently and in the public interest. As technological solutions become available that can be used to monitor online offender activities, issues regarding privacy start to emerge with potentially innocent people being subject to police monitoring. As a result of this, we start to shift to an unknown ethical landscape where there are strong arguments on either side of the privacy vs child protection debate. What kind of suspect behaviour should merit investigating an online user? If tools are deployed to automatically analyse data in a social or file-sharing network, should users be made aware of such monitoring taking place? If yes, would this simply shift offender activity underground – as already seen on P2P networks with offenders moving to more private networks? Would young people themselves welcome such proactive policing as they engage in 'normal' youth sexual behaviour online?

Furthermore, such tools need to operate within relevant legal and regulatory frameworks. The data they collect and process must have been legitimately and legally obtained and stored securely. This is addressed partly through workflows in investigative practices that ensure that legal practices are respected, and partly through secure storage solutions. However, such constraints also restrict how data can be shared between law enforcement agencies, thus creating barriers within investigations. For the developers of technical aids, identifying and understanding the relevant legal legislation and regulatory issues surrounding such investigations is a major challenge, as a particular feature may need to comply with numerous regulations, which may often conflict. The challenge is further compounded by the fact that what is ethical is not always legal and vice versa.

Such issues cannot be overcome by software engineers alone. Close collaboration is required between software engineers, law enforcement and ethics and legal experts to ensure that technological solutions can meet the challenges of evolving offender tactics, shifts to privacy technologies, and the dynamic and fluid nature of online identities and large-scale data analysis while operating within the ethical and legal norms expected within modern society.

Overcoming the challenges: from reactive to proactive policing

As we have seen in the previous sections, there are a number of challenges that must be overcome by technological solutions both from the point of view of offender behaviour and investigative practices. One of the key issues facing law enforcement agencies is the significant volume of data that is stored on offenders' computers and collected during an ongoing investigation. Each seized computer may contain terabytes of image- and text-based data that needs to be sifted through manually. In this reactive mode, hard constraints and time pressures entail investigating officers prioritizing what data to examine and in what order. However, as described in the previous sections, current software solutions do not support this prioritization process very well or in some cases at all. Automatic filtering software can be used on home computers or in online chat rooms to assist service providers in monitoring tasks; however, the automated software is based on techniques that are neither scalable nor robust, i.e. machine-assisted human monitoring of logs and keyword-based approaches. What is needed, therefore, is some way of combining the automatic processing of filtering software with the high accuracy of manual checking.

In the following, we consider technological solutions to these problems that are currently emerging from academic research and discuss how these solutions might support shifts to more proactive apprehension of online child sex offenders. There are two main areas of technological advances that should be considered. First, in relation to file sharing, there are new developments in image processing. Second, related to the analysis of online chat data, recent advances in natural language processing (NLP) are beginning to enable significant advances.

As discussed, due to the widespread use of digital image and video content, law enforcement investigators are faced with a difficult and rapidly growing challenge when analysing suspicious image and video content. Technology for the efficient analysis of large-scale visual databases is required. Commercial solutions, such as Netclean Analyze (http://www.netclean.com) or Videntifier Forensic (http://www.eff2.net), support the categorization and annotation of images, or permit matching against existing databases based on file hash-values, or, more robustly, on visual similarity. In parallel, significant progress has been made in research, for example in projects funded by the EU Safer Internet Programme. The FIVES project (http://fives.kau.se) is developing technologies and tools to help law enforcement agents handle the large amounts of image and video material from seized media. The work in FIVES encompasses both computer forensics components as well as media analysis components. Project i-dash (http://www.i-dash.eu) is targeted at supporting police investigators in the analysis of large-scale (potentially child sexual abuse material) video collections. The project aims at filtering non-relevant material, recognizing known child sexual abuse material (using video finger-printing), and an interactive linking of different videos. Systems for automatic detection of previously unknown illicit content have been developed, based on a statistical analysis of a scene's skin regions (Jones and Rehg, 2002), distinctive local interest points (Deselaers et al., 2008) or motion patterns (Jansohn et al., 2009). Other approaches allow efficient content-based browsing of visual data-bases (Borth et al., 2008) or even the detection of specific objects inside them (Sivic and Zisserman, 2006). In addition, the scalability to very large data-bases has been addressed (Wanke et al., 2010; Hörster et al., 2007). A key focus of our Isis project (http://www.comp.lancs.ac.uk/isis) has been to develop P2P-monitoring technologies to help law enforcement identify new child abuse vocabulary on P2P networks. The Isis monitors operate in a similar way to systems such as CPS, where no discrimination is given to the type of child abuse media being shared. Through analysis of the search queries and results, it is possible to identify unknown search terms and propose candidate links to known search terms using language analysis techniques (Hughes et al., 2008).

Having considered technological advances in relation to file sharing, we now turn to the analysis of online chat data. Current law enforcement methods employ indexing tools such as desktop-based search engines to support the searching of previously seized textual data e.g. through Encase and Intella (http://www.

vound-software.com). However, these still operate at the word level. Techniques exist that make use of statistical methods from computational linguistics and corpus-based natural language processing to explore differences in language vocabulary and style related to the age of the speaker or writer and extract other features automatically with high accuracy. Keyword profiling (Scott, 2000), exploiting comparative word frequencies, has been used in the past to investigate the differences between spoken and written language (Rayson et al., 1997), British and American English (Hofland and Johansson, 1982), and language change over time (Baker, 2009). Rayson (2008) extended the keywords methodology to extract key grammatical categories and key semantic concepts using tagged data in order to make it scalable. The existing methodologies draw on large bodies of naturally occurring language data known as corpora (singular corpus). These techniques already have high accuracy and are robust across a number of domains (topics) and registers (spoken and written language) but have not been applied until recently to uncover offender behaviour, for instance masquerading behaviour or use/sharing of multiple personas. The second relevant set of techniques is that of authorship attribution (Holmes, 1994). The current methods (Juola et al., 2006) allow a narrowing in focus from the text to the individual writer in order to generate a stylistic profile for authors. Specific research challenges in this area are the constraints of small amounts of language evidence, in the region of tens and hundreds rather than thousands of words, as observed in chat room data. Some successes have been reported in gender classification of blog posts (Mukherjee and Liu, 2010).

Within the Isis project we have built on these advances to develop a highly sophisticated language forensics toolkit to help law enforcement officers analyse the vast amounts of conversation data they collect as part of an ongoing investigation. The toolkit provides a range of powerful functionalities that can quickly summarize such data, extract intelligence and enable law enforcement personnel to focus on the high priority aspects of a case. A key facet of the Isis project is close integration of ethics experts with the technical team so that the various features of the toolkit are developed with key ethical considerations at the forefront of the developers' decision-making processes.

Key features of the toolkit include:

- *Data extraction and management* – data can be imported from a variety of sources (IM, forums, email, etc.). Conversations can also be captured in real time (e.g. during an undercover operation). Advanced techniques allow for the extraction of 'chat fragments' from disk and memory dumps, and their reconstruction into a conversation flow.
- *Chat log analysis* – sophisticated analysis allows investigators to quickly see who the participants are within a conversation, when the participants were online/offline, topics, names/places, etc. that are mentioned.
- *User profile building* – enables building profiles of potential suspects or victims. Sophisticated analysis of text determines age and gender characteristics with high accuracy, and extracts language stylistic data such as the key words or phrases a potential suspect or victim regularly uses.

- *Profile comparison* – profiles can be compared against one another to identify potential similarities, for example to help identify if multiple online personas are actually the same person.
- *Timeline analysis* – analyses data over a timescale, highlighting when specific users, names, places, terminology, etc. occur. Side-by-side case analysis is also supported to help identify trends and common characteristics.
- *Terminology extraction* – automatically identifies new and evolving terminology for a given domain, so investigators are always aware of current language use.

Whilst the Isis Language Forensics Toolkit operates on English language texts, in the DAPHNE project at the University of Antwerp in Belgium, a methodology for automatic extraction and analysis of stylistic characteristics (associated to personality, age group and deceptive language usage) is being developed for Dutch. Other NLP techniques such as named entity recognition (Mikheev et al., 1999) can be used to extract dates, times, people and places, offering potential improvements to current law enforcement techniques for data analysis.

A roadmap

In order to bridge the gap between filtering and forensic software and to support the move from reactive to proactive policing, the technological solutions must first allow for prioritization of seized or collected data from individual computers. Subsequently, this would allow scaling up of the techniques to monitor much larger data sets online (e.g. entire forums or social network pages) and in a real-time fashion. Law enforcement officers would benefit from large-scale proactive policing for three main reasons. First, it would permit more complex models of offender behaviour to be built based on much richer data sets. Second, a much deeper understanding of previous case data archives could be gained – currently, these are not used once a case has closed. Finally, it would permit law enforcement officers to identify online forums that should be monitored manually in the future.

Engineering breakthroughs are needed to provide a step change in both the level and the effectiveness of technological interventions that support police, children's services, criminal justice practitioners, schools, parents and young persons in countering the threats posed by predatory advances of online child sex offenders. This necessarily requires a multidimensional and multidisciplinary approach addressing the needs of these various stakeholder groups from a range of technological, legal and ethical perspectives. Such a step change can only be brought about by focusing on three major research challenges:

1   *Understanding online child sexual abuse and the role of the Internet* – what technological breakthroughs can enable large-scale data analysis to study a range of fundamental questions: what are the patterns of offender and victim behaviour that lead to most risk of offence or harm to children? How do online

child sex offenders operate and organize themselves and how do these patterns of operation and organization evolve?

2   *ProActive technological solutions* – what software innovations can lead to solutions that can act as a shield against or provide early warning of online abuse or a repeat offence? What novel technologies can enable proactive policing that is both scalable and targets the roots of Internet-based child sex offences?

3   *Legal and ethical implications of technological interventions* – are current legal frameworks dealing with online child sex offences effective and in step with technological advancement? How can we ensure that solutions for early warning and proactive policing are compliant with complex legal frameworks and can cope with changes to these? How can we incorporate ethical considerations (e.g. privacy, data protection, etc.) into the core design of technological innovations?

Only by overcoming the above three key challenges can we ensure that technological solutions can cope with the moving target of Internet-based child sex offenders.

References

Baker, P. (2009). The BE06 Corpus of British English and recent language change. *International Journal of Corpus Linguistics, 14*, 312–37.

Borth, D., Schulze, C., Ulges, A. and Breuel, T. (2008). Navidgator – similarity based browsing for image & video databases. *Proceedings of the KI*, Kaiserslautern.

Cooper, A. (1998). Sexuality and the Internet: Surfing into the new millennium. *Cyberpsychology and Behavior, 1*(2), 181–7.

Crystal, D. (2006). *Language and the Internet*. New York: Cambridge University Press.

Danet, B. (1998). Text as mask: Gender, play, and performance on the internet. In S.G. Jones (ed.), *Cybersociety 2.0: Revisiting Computer-mediated Communication and Community*. Thousand Oaks, CA: Sage Publications, pp. 129–58.

Deselaers, T. (2008). Image retrieval, object recognition, and discriminative models. In proceedings of *Ausgezeichnete Informatikdissertationen*, 51–60.

Finkelhor, D., Mitchell, K. and Wolak, J. (2000). *Online Victimization: A Report on the Nation's Youth*. Alexandria, VA: National Center for Missing and Exploited Children.

Henry, O., Mandeville-Norden, R., Hayes, E., and Egan, V. (2010). Do Internet-based sexual offenders reduce to normal, inadequate and deviant groups? *Journal of Sexual Aggression, 16*(1), 33–46.

Hofland, K. and Johansson, S. (1982). *Word frequencies in British and American English*. Bergen: NCCH.

Holmes, D.I. (1994). Authorship attribution. *Computers and the Humanities, 28*(2), 87–106.

Hörster, E., Lienhart, R. and Slaney, M. (2007). Image retrieval on large-scale image databases. Proceedings of the CIVR. Amsterdam.

Hughes, D., Walkerdine, J. and Lee, K. (2006b). Monitoring challenges and approaches for P2P file-sharing systems. *Proceedings of the 1st International Conference on Internet Surveillance and Protection (ICISP'06)*. Cap Esterel, France.

Hughes, D., Walkerdine, J., Coulson, G. and Gibson, S. (2006a). Is deviant behaviour the norm on P2P file-sharing networks? *IEEE Distributed Systems Online, 7*(2).

Hughes, D., Rayson, P., Walkerdine, J., Lee, K., Greenwood, P., Rashid, A., May-Chahal, C. and Brennan, M. (2008). Supporting law enforcement in digital communities through natural language analysis. *Proceedings of the 2nd International Workshop on Computational Forensics (IWCF 2008)*. Washington DC, Lecture Notes in Computer Science 5158, 122–34. Available online at http://dx.doi.org/10.1007/978-3-540-85303-9_12.

Jansohn, C., Ulges, A. and Breuel, T. (2009). Detecting pornographic video content by combining image features with motion information. *Proceedings of ACM Multimedia*, Beijing.

Jones, M.J. and Rehg, J.M. (2002). Statistical color models with application to skin detection. *International Journal of Computer Vision, 46*(1), 81–96.

Juola, P., Sofko, J. and Brennan, P. (2006). A prototype for authorship attribution studies. *Literary and Linguistic Computing, 21*, 169–78.

Middleton, D. (2009). Internet sex offenders. In A.R. Beech, L.A. Craig and K.D. Browne (eds), *Assessment and Treatment of Sex Offenders: A Handbook*. Chichester: Wiley-Blackwell.

Mikheev, A., Moens, M.and Grover, C. (1999). Named entity recognition without gazetteers. *Proceedings of the 9th Conference of European Chapter of the Association for Computational Linguistics*. Morristown, NJ: Association for Computational Linguistics, 1–8.

Mukherjee, A. and Liu, B. (2010). Improving gender classification of blog authors. *Proceedings of the 2010 Conference on Empirical Methods in Natural Language Processing*, 207–17.

Quayle, E. and Taylor, M. (2001). Child seduction and self-representation on the Internet. *CyberPsychology & Behavior, 4*(5), 597–608.

Quayle, E., Holland, G., Linenan, C. and Taylor, M. (2000). The Internet and offending behaviour: A case study. *Journal of Sexual Aggression, 6*, 78–96.

Rayson, P. (2008). From key words to key semantic domains. *International Journal of Corpus Linguistics, 13*(4), 519–49.

Rayson, P., Leech, G. and Hodges, M. (1997). Social differentiation in the use of English vocabulary: Some analyses of the conversational component of the British National Corpus. *International Journal of Corpus Linguistics, 2*(1), 133–52.

Scott, M. (2000). Focusing on the text and its key words. In L. Burnard and T. McEnery (eds), *Rethinking Language Pedagogy from a Corpus Perspective*. Frankfurt: Peter Lang, pp. 104–21.

Sivic, J. and Zisserman A. (2006). Video Google: Efficient visual search of videos. In J. Ponce, M. Hebert, C. Schmid and A. Zisserman (eds), *Toward Category-level Object Recognition*. Heidelberg: Springer, 127–44.

Thelwall, M. (2008). Fk yea I swear: Cursing and gender in MySpace. *Corpora, 1*(3), 83–107.

Wanke, J., Ulges, A., Lampert, C. and Breuel, T. (2010). Topic models for semantics-preserving video compression. Proceedings of the MIR, Philadelphia.

14 A public health approach to addressing Internet child sexual exploitation

Megan Clarke, Kurt M. Ribisl,
Desmond Runyan and Carol Runyan,
University of North Carolina at Chapel Hill

Introduction

Public health, like medicine, is concerned with decreasing morbidity (illness) and mortality (death) and with improving the quality of life. However, in contrast to medicine, which responds with diagnosis and treatment for sick, injured or abused individuals after a disease or injury has occurred, a public health approach seeks to *prevent* disease and injury, by making changes that will affect entire populations. Early public health approaches to problems were based on responses to infectious diseases, such as cholera and bubonic plague, and focused on the interplay between the infectious agent, its host (the person harbouring the disease) and the environment. As public health has been applied to address interpersonal violence, it has provided an alternative to a strictly criminal justice approach that, like medicine, tends to give more emphasis to addressing the problem in individuals after events have occurred. Public health is increasingly being recognized as providing a powerful systematic approach focused on the prevention of violence through social and environmental changes at the population level.

In this chapter, we will introduce fundamental public health principles and their emphasis on population-level approaches, primary prevention and environmental change, describing how these principles could be implemented in order to prevent the production, use and distribution of online child sexual images. Although not the explicit focus of this chapter, the public health approach described here also has clear implications for preventing the online solicitation and enticement of children for both online and offline exploitation. We will present various examples demonstrating how the public health approach has been applied to other health issues, such as crime reduction, motor vehicle safety, unintentional child injury in the home and teenage tobacco use. Finally, we will present a planning model often used in public health to aid practitioners in translating these concepts into practice.

Overview: the public health burden of the issue

Scope of the problem

Due to its illegal and hidden nature, exploitation of children through sexual images is a difficult issue to measure with precision. However, the evidence that does exist suggests that it is a widespread and growing global problem. At any one time, it is estimated that there are over one million images of children available on the Internet, with 200 new images posted daily. It has been reported that one child pornography website alone received a million hits in one month, and there are an estimated 50,000–100,000 paedophiles in organized pornography rings around the world accessing indecent images of children. In one year, the period from 2000 to 2001, US law enforcement made an estimated 2,577 arrests for Internet sex crimes against minors (Wolak et al., 2003).

Negative health effects

Children who are sexually abused are subject to feelings of shame, guilt and fear, depression, post-traumatic stress disorder and aggression (Finkelhor et al., 2000; Jonsson and Svedin, Chapter 2, this volume; Kendall-Tackett et al., 1993). In addition to the effects of the initial exploitation, children portrayed in sexual images may be subjected to ongoing exploitation, as the record of their initial abuse is circulated over the Internet and accessed by viewers (Beech et al., 2008; Quayle et al., 2008; Wolak et al., 2008). Systematic studies of the consequences of exploitation in the form of the taking and circulation of pornographic photographs are lacking. Former victims of child pornography have reported ongoing trauma from the knowledge that images of their abuse are continually circulating and that people may be using those images to stimulate themselves sexually. They have also reported fears that they could be recognized or that the materials may encourage the abuse of other children and/or be used to lure other children into sexual activity (Jonsson and Svedin, in press; Prichard et al., 2011).

The impact of indecent images of children is not limited to the child suffering the abuse. ECPAT's 'Report on Child Pornography and the Sexual Exploitation of Children Online' states: 'We argue that the crime of possession, making or distri-bution of child pornography, whether virtual or not, is a crime not only against a particular child, but against all children' (Quayle et al., 2008). The circulation of child sexual images harms children as a whole, as it contributes to a view of children as sexual objects and potentially as the objects of real abuse (Quayle et al., 2008). Existing images can fuel the production of new images, as offenders' increasing consumption often leads to an increase in demand for new (and sometimes more extreme) materials (Quayle and Sinclair, 2011). In some cases, offenders use existing materials to groom future victims (Quayle et al., 2008). The growing availability and sophistication of technologies will continue to intensify these problems. In light of these threats, an international public health response is warranted in order to protect the health and well-being of children globally.

What is a public health approach and how does it apply to Internet child exploitation?

Population vs individual approaches

In a classic article, Geoffrey Rose (1985) outlines the differences between a population and an individual approach. Many public health interventions include both population and individual-level strategies, but public health practice prioritizes change that can occur at the population level, which has greater potential to have widespread effects.

Individual approaches

When determining how to approach a health problem in a community, a common-sense first step may seem to be the identification of individuals or groups who are at the most elevated risk for the problem. Programming and resources can then be targeted toward these groups. For example, in attempts to decrease obesity rates, practitioners may identify overweight populations in a community in order to develop interventions that will teach these individuals the importance of physical activity and a healthy diet. Rose (1985) refers to this style of intervention as an individual approach. Most counselling and education programmes fall into this category. However, Rose argues that this is premised on the wrong focus – understanding and preventing the most high-risk individuals from acquiring the health problem. Rather, he argues that public health should focus on changing the whole population and reducing the rate of the health problem at the community level. This approach relies on universal strategies that address entire populations. Everyone receives the same intervention and, as a result, the prevalence of a problem in a population shifts, rather than shifting only in those individuals targeted through a high-risk individual approach.

Figure 14.1 is a visual depiction of the difference between an individual and a population approach applied to the prevention of exploitation via online child sexual images. These figures show the hypothetical distributions of children's risk for being victimized through the production and distribution of indecent images. In these figures, the average level of risk is shown at the centre of the curve, and most children will have a level of risk at or around this point. To the left and right of this point, in the 'tails' of the distribution, are the children with lower than or higher than average risk. In an individual strategy, practitioners attempt to identify those children at the far right side of this curve, at higher than average risk. Practitioners would then focus their resources and attention to prevent the production of sexual images among these individuals specifically, where it is most likely to occur. By doing so, they attempt to truncate this curve and to reduce the occurrences of exploitation among those with highest risk (Rose, 1985).

Risk factors that may heighten children's susceptibility to being exploited through indecent images include more frequent and interactive Internet use, depressive symptomatology, lack of attachment, sexual orientation concerns,

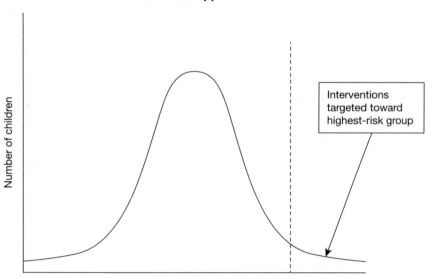

Individual approach

Number of children

Interventions targeted toward highest-risk group

Level of risk for exploitation through online child sexual images

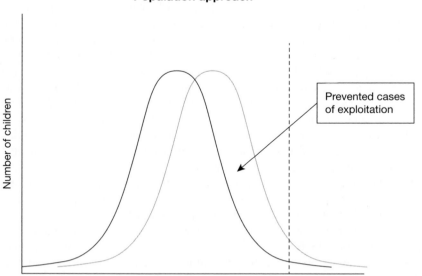

Population approach

Number of children

Prevented cases of exploitation

Level of risk for exploitation through online child sexual images

Figure 14.1 Population vs individual approaches to prevent the production and distribution of online child sexual images

neglect and experiences of offline physical or sexual abuse (Jonsson and Svedin, Chapter 2, this volume; Mitchell et al., 2007; Wolak et al., 2008; Ybarra, 2004). One individual high-risk strategy is to conduct educational programmes for high-risk children and their parents, including raising awareness about online child sexual images, guidelines for safe Internet use, and the importance of parental Internet use supervision. Some educational programmes have been shown to increase knowledge of safe Internet behaviours among youth, and some useful parental education materials have been developed (Quayle et al., 2008). However, there has been little evaluation of educational tools, and there is a tremendous need for more research that can be incorporated into the development of evidence-based educational programmes (Quayle et al., 2008; Wolak et al., 2009). In addition, many children do not meet the individuals who exploit them online, but rather are exploited by people they already know, such as parents, relatives or family friends (Quayle et al., 2008).

Individual strategies can also be directed at persons who are at high risk for becoming offenders. Most offenders are male, and they are more likely than the general population to have never been married, be unemployed, have substance abuse issues, have experienced physical and sexual abuse, and have diagnosable paedophilia (sexual attraction to prepubescent children) or hebephilia (sexual attraction to pubescent children) (Babchishin et al., 2011; Beier and Neutze, Chapter 12, this volume; Wolak et al., 2009). However, it is important to note that many offenders do not share this risk profile, and many people with these characteristics are not child pornography offenders. Another risk factor is having exploited children in the past (Beier and Neutze, Chapter 12, this volume).

Individual strategies targeting offenders can include treatment, counselling and education aimed at changing attitudes or increasing offenders' skills to cope without acting on their desires. There are innovative self-help programmes, such as the Stop It Now! Helpline, Croga and Project Dunkelfeld, which provide support, treatment, and referrals for people who have self-identified themselves as at risk for child sexual abuse or accessing indecent images of children (Beier and Neutze, Chapter 12, this volume; Beier et al., 2009; Croga, n.d.; Stop It Now!, 2010). These projects have shown that it is possible to identify people at high risk before they act on their desires. Efficacy of treatment is currently being evaluated (Beier and Neutze, Chapter 12, this volume).

When targeting high-risk individuals, interventions can be designed to have a greater depth and specificity, which could increase potential for a positive effect among those most likely to become victims or perpetrators of child sexual images. However, individual strategies are often short-lived with respect to impact and may be completely ineffective. Though these interventions may prevent some cases, they require accurate identification of high-risk characteristics and finding and recruitment of appropriate individuals for participation. In addition, most interventions at this level require immense ongoing efforts by individuals in order to maintain healthy results (Frieden, 2010; Rose, 1985). For efforts targeting children, some argue that it is neither ethical nor effective to place the burden of risk reduction on the victims of sexual images.

Even if these interventions do have a positive impact on a small number of highly motivated individuals, the population impact of such resource-intensive, specific interventions is very small (Frieden, 2010; Rose, 1985). As shown in Fig. 14.1, all children in a population are at some level of risk for exploitation. By using exclusively high-risk strategies, only a subset will be affected, neglecting prevention for the majority of children.

Also, as future generations give rise to new high-risk individuals, interventions will have to be sustained and repeated (Rose, 1985). This cycle will continue as long as the underlying causes for the production and distribution of indecent images of children remain in place. According to Rose (1985), 'The health education phase aimed at changing individuals is, we hope, a temporary necessity, pending changes in the norms of what is socially acceptable.' Changes in broader social conditions that can affect the 'root causes' require population solutions. Unfortunately, many environmental changes are not quickly implemented. In the meantime, it is important to educate and counsel individuals in order to empower them to make the healthiest choices available (Frieden, 2010).

Population approaches

Population strategies provide an alternative and more promising approach (Rose, 1985). Rather than determining the causes of high-risk status in individuals, these strategies seek to determine and control the causes of a health problem in a population as a whole. When implementing a population strategy, each individual may experience only a small change in his or her individual risk level, but, collectively, the reduction in susceptibility of an entire population may, in fact, avoid more cases than an intervention targeting a smaller high-risk group. According to Rose's prevention paradox, 'a large number of people at a small risk may give rise to more cases of disease than the small number who are at a high risk' (Rose, 1985).

For example, a 1995 study compared the projected effectiveness of a population-wide lifestyle intervention, such as sodium reduction, to medical treatment in its ability to decrease incidence of coronary heart disease (CHD) and stroke. The study found that almost 60 per cent of CHD events and 45–50 per cent of strokes occurred among people with a high *normal* diastolic blood pressure (DBP), who were ineligible to receive blood pressure medication. Therefore, although the high-risk strategy of medical treatment was expected to decrease an individual's DBP by 5–6 mm Hg, it was not having any effect on over half of the people who were experiencing CHD events or strokes! The population-wide intervention was projected to have a much smaller effect on each individual participant's DBP, a reduction of about 2 mm Hg. The study found that when implemented across the entire population, this 2 mm Hg reduction would lead to a 6 per cent decrease in the number of CHD events and a 15 per cent decrease in the number of strokes. In fact, when this study factored in medication non-compliance, the population-wide intervention was expected to prevent *more* CHD events than medication prescribed to high-risk individuals (Cook et al., 1995). In other words, this small 2 mm Hg change across a large population was expected to have a greater impact than the targeted medical intervention administered to high-risk individuals.

Population strategies address mass influences that lead to negative health behaviours and outcomes, such as policies and environmental structures. The Health Impact Pyramid (Frieden, 2010), a model comparing various levels of intervention according to their potential population impacts, posits that changing the context to make individuals' default decision a healthy option is more effective than an individually focused intervention. Contextual changes affect all members of the communities where the changes are implemented. People in the target communities do not have to expend any personal effort to experience the health benefits of such interventions, because the context in which they live is altered. In fact, Frieden (2010) describes interventions at this level of social and environmental change as requiring great effort by individuals in order for them *not* to experience the benefits of the changes.

Improvements in motor vehicle safety are a great example of the effectiveness of population strategies to change the context. For example, in 1967, it was mandated that all new passenger cars sold in the United States must be equipped with energy-absorbing steering columns. From that point on, the default for new car owners was to drive safer cars, through no effort of their own. In fact, many car owners were not even aware of this new feature in the cars they were driving. This intervention had no impact on the way that individuals drove, but by changing the context, it is estimated that it decreased the risk of driver fatality in a frontal crash by 12 per cent (Hemenway, 2009).

Injury related to the use of infant walkers provides another example. In the early 1990s, walker-related incidents led to 20,000 emergency room visits per year, mostly due to head trauma caused by infants falling down stairs. Various public awareness campaigns, physician advice to parents and warning labels were implemented. In spite of these efforts, the rates of walker-related injury remained steady. In the mid-1990s, the US Consumer Product Safety Commission worked with manufacturers to widen the base of walkers so that they could not fit through a doorway and to add a feature that stopped walkers when they approached the edge of a stair step. After the development of these new standards, walker-related injuries dropped 76 per cent, from 23,000 in 1994 to 5,100 in 2001 (Hemenway, 2009). Prior to these interventions, all efforts to reduce infant walker-related injuries required consistent action and vigilance by individual parents. However, it can take only a moment for a child to get into a dangerous situation. Because of this, parental supervision alone cannot completely eradicate the risk of child injury or exploitation. This intervention was successful because it made children's environments safer, and it did not depend on the effort of individuals for children to be positively impacted by the increased protection.

As shown in Fig. 14.1, a population strategy attempts to shift the entire distribution by reducing risk of exploitation through sexual images for all children in the population rather than attempting to affect only those at the highest risk. Population strategies attempt to create a safer Internet, by making it more difficult for offenders to contact children online, reducing the number of indecent images of children available online, and making it more difficult or risky to access such images.

One population strategy is the use of online safety tools on websites that have the potential to be dangerous for children, such as chat rooms and social networking sites. These safeguards may include abuse buttons (for easy reporting of any suspicious interaction or web content), chat moderation and more stringent default privacy settings (Quayle et al., 2008).

Another important population strategy is the identification and removal of indecent images of children from the Internet. Changes in technology have greatly affected the availability of exploitive images. In the US and many other countries, law enforcement has made great strides in reducing the availability of printed magazines with child pornography. However, the advent of the camcorder allowed users to produce images without needing to get them developed, avoiding the risk of detection. This technological change was subsequently followed by the growth of the Internet, which also lowered the barriers to producing, sharing and distributing indecent images of children (O'Donnell and Millner, 2007). Future changes in technology will certainly affect the quantity and availability of images, and strategies to reduce availability, even if they seem pretty modest, may add up to significant population impacts. For instance, a study by Demitriou and Silke (2003) examined people visiting a website for free games and software. Once there, they were presented with links to legitimate content, but also links to illegally obtained software and hard-core pornography. The majority of visitors opted for the illegal and pornographic content even though it was not their reason for visiting the site originally.

This screening and removal is currently done by many ISPs (Internet service providers) and could be done by websites (such as peer-to-peer (P2P) file-sharing websites) that are used to facilitate file-sharing and social networks of child sexual image collectors (Carr, chapter 6; Prichard et al., 2011; Quayle et al., 2008; Wortley, chapter 11). Many of these sites display prominent links to child sexual images, some of which are even included in the sites' top search terms. Research has indicated that onset for offenders can be triggered by curiosity and without any pre-existing attraction to children. For example, men who are purely gynaephilic (men who are preferentially sexually attracted to adult women), still showed sexual arousal to images of prepubescent and pubescent children in phallometric studies (Lykins et al., 2010). Therefore, the presence of easily accessed child sexual images is a major risk factor (Prichard et al., 2011), and they should be removed.

Finally, policy change leading to more consistent and effectively enforced laws is a population approach for the prevention of the production, use and distribution of indecent images of children. The harmonization of laws across countries is essential in order to effectively combat this kind of exploitation, as offences often cross country lines, causing confusion in arrest and prosecution (International Centre for Missing and Exploited Children, 2008). In addition, laws must not only criminalize possessing child sexual images, but they should also explicitly include accessing and viewing images (Quayle et al., 2008). Law enforcement efforts should include a focus on arresting and prosecuting producers of these materials, in order to address the supply in addition to the demand (Carr, chapter 6). However, any policy change should be approached carefully, as a proliferation of law criminalizing the sexualization of children can have unintended negative consequences, such as increasing the allure of offending, and expanding exposure to images through legal discourse and court proceedings (Adler, 2001).

Public health practice, although sometimes employing high-risk strategies, still places a priority on population strategies. Frieden (2010) echoes Rose in his statement that 'the need to urge behavioral change is symptomatic of failure to establish contexts in which healthy choices are default actions'. Population strategies seek to remove the underlying causes of the proliferation of child sexual images, such as an unsafe Internet environment and low levels of deterrence for potential offenders. These kinds of long-lasting change, even if they are small, can have significant impacts in preventing exploitation when implemented across large populations.

Rather than just teaching children how to avoid the dangers posed by sexual predators and making prevention the responsibility of the child victims, society must work towards creating a safer, healthy world for children. As Internet access reaches more children in poverty and in developing countries, the importance of this approach is even more profound, as efforts to make the Internet safe for all children reduce the opportunity for differentially high exposure among children who may not have access to more active and targeted approaches.

Haddon Model

William Haddon, Jr. developed a model that has been used widely in conceptualizing injury and violence interventions from a public health perspective (Haddon, 1980). It was later expanded as a decision tool by Runyan (1998). Haddon's model demonstrates that hosts, agents and environments, as outlined in the public health model (Susser, 1973), interact to create health problems. Each of these elements must be taken into account when identifying successful intervention approaches. According to the public health model, the host is the person affected by the health problem (e.g. people injured in a car crash). Haddon conceptualized the agent as 'energy' (e.g. mechanical energy transferred to the host during a car crash). This occurs through a vehicle (inanimate entity like a car) or vector (animate entity – like a human perpetrator of violence). Finally, the environment refers to the physical and social environments which facilitate or impede the injury or violence and which provide multiple opportunities for population-level solutions. Weather, road conditions and the presence of stoplights are all aspects of the physical environment that can affect the likelihood of collisions, while the social environment includes policies such as speed limits and social norms such as those surrounding drinking and driving. Through the rows of the matrix, Haddon differentiated the timing of the intervention effects before, during or after an injurious event. To prevent negative health impacts of an adverse event, programme planners use this matrix to identify multiple intervention points to achieve maximum effect. While intervention at any of these points will reduce unhealthy outcomes of the event, strategies that involve multiple cells of the matrix are more likely to have a large sustainable impact.

In the Haddon Matrix, interventions designated in the 'pre-event' phase are directed at preventing the event from occurring – for example, improving road conditions as a means to prevent motor vehicle collisions or eliminating the production of indecent images of children. At the 'event' phase, interventions are designed to minimize the negative health effects that occur *while* the event is happening. Seatbelts are a clear example of an event phase intervention applied to motor vehicle collisions. If a motor vehicle collision occurs, seatbelts will minimize injury but have little or no influence on whether the collision happens. Similarly, Internet strategies designed to limit the spread of and access to child sexual images minimizes their potential harm. Both pre-event and event phase interventions provide primary prevention for damage, though event phase strategies often interrupt the event early in its progress. In contrast, 'post-event' strategies facilitate the most effective treatment or response possible *after* the event occurs in order to minimize negative outcomes (Haddon, 1980). In the case of motor vehicle collisions, creating better emergency medical response systems or constructing roads with wide shoulders facilitates access of emergency vehicles to collision sites. Similarly, identification and treatment for victims, treatment and/or punishment for offenders, and the removal of images from the Internet are all examples of post-event strategies for exploitation through child sexual images.

Situational prevention in criminal justice is an example of an environmental approach and has been successful in preventing crime by removing opportunity (Wortley, chapter 11). For example, the Washington DC Metro system was designed specifically to reduce crime by creating a safer environment with open, well-lit spaces for natural surveillance, few places where criminals could hide, extensive video surveillance, and limited seating to discourage loitering. Subway crime rates are generally about 75 per cent lower in Washington DC than they are in other large cities, such as Atlanta, Chicago and Boston (Hemenway, 2009). The Internet, the environment in which online child sexual images exist, could be similarly reconstructed to deter crime. Currently, offenders are able to operate covertly, with relatively low risk of prosecution, and with plenty of opportunities to contact children and to share images. Changes should be made to the Internet that make the creation and sharing of child sexual images more risky and less opportune.

By employing Haddon's model to the production and distribution of indecent images of children, one can develop multiple intervention strategies to reduce the occurrence and/or effects of distribution.

Haddon Model and online child sexual images

Table 14.1 shows the Haddon Model applied to the creation and distribution of online child sexual images. In this figure, 'pre-event' strategies are identified to prevent the distribution of such images, primarily through preventing their creation. 'Event' strategies are identified to reduce the negative impacts when images

Table 14.1 The Haddon Model applied to the prevention of production and distribution of online child sexual images

	Host *Children*	Vector *Offenders*	Physical environment *Internet*	Social environment *Social norms, policies*
Pre-event Preventing the distribution of images	• Awareness education • Guidelines for safe Internet use • Parental education about the importance of Internet use supervision	• Counselling for adults at risk for offending • Self-help programs for adults at risk for offending	• Internet controls in homes and public places • Online abuse buttons • Chat moderation • More stringent default privacy settings on social networking sites	• Media campaign encouraging safe internet use and parental supervision • Pressure on entertainment and advertising agencies to discourage sexualization of children • ISP codes of practice to impede contact between children and offenders • More effective laws and penalties for producing images
Event Reducing the negative impacts when images are distributed	• Helplines for reporting of abuse and referrals for treatment	• Preventing sellers of images from entering online payments systems and establishing merchant accounts • Credit card companies blocking transactions from identified sources • Increasing difficulty of accessing known or suspected image file-sharing sites	• Pop-up warnings and ads linked to known child pornography search terms • Increase difficulty of accessing sites known or suspected of being sources of images	• Changing, blocking, or removing sites that facilitate supportive social networks of image users • ISP codes of practice to impede distributing and accessing images • More effective laws and penalties for accessing, viewing and distributing images
Post-event Reducing negative health outcomes of images after they have been distributed	• Assistance and recovery programs for children portrayed in images	• Prosecution of offenders • Offender counselling	• Identification and removal of images • Hotlines for reporting of websites containing images	• Enforcement of all laws • Adequate child protection and law enforcement policies to allow for effective investigation, assessment, intervention, support, and follow-up services for children

are distributed, by applying harm reduction strategies in order to control widespread distribution. 'Post-event' strategies are identified to reduce the magnitude of the potential negative health outcomes after indecent images of children have been distributed, primarily through providing counselling to children and offenders and by removing images from the Internet so that re-victimization does not occur and recovery can begin.

Host: children portrayed in online child sexual images

In this model, the children portrayed in online child sexual images are defined as the hosts, or the people victimized by the exploitation. Through 'pre-event' strategies directed at changing host behaviour, children and parents can be educated about indecent images of children, safe Internet use, and the importance of parental Internet supervision. These approaches will only address cases in which children meet their exploiters online. However, these strategies can still provide some protection from cases of online solicitation.

Although public health prioritizes primary prevention, it is sometimes necessary also to implement harm reduction and treatment strategies in order to minimize the negative effects of events that do occur. 'Event' strategies such as helplines can minimize the harm caused by the production and distribution of exploitative images by facilitating fast and simple reporting of abuse (Stop It Now!, 2010). This reporting mechanism may be a strategy to interrupt any ongoing abuse of children, and through early identification of offenders, they may serve to prevent or disrupt the distribution of images prior to them being shared widely. 'Post-event' strategies such as assistance and recovery programmes can provide important support, counselling and treatment for children who have been portrayed in child sexual images.

Vectors: offenders

'Pre-event' strategies directed towards adult offenders or potential offenders include treatment, counselling, education and self-help programmes aimed at changing attitudes or increasing their skills to cope without acting on their desires. These interventions, targeted toward changing offenders' behaviours, can help prevent the creation of indecent images of children.

'Event' strategies minimizing the widespread distribution of child sexual images can also be directed towards adult offenders by making it difficult for them to share the materials that they have produced. This could be done by blocking sites or increasing the effort required for them to access known or suspected locations where they could share their files (Taylor and Quayle, 2008). For example, the Financial Coalition Against Child Pornography is a coalition of leaders in the online banking and payment industries and Internet service companies. This coalition works to prevent sellers of child pornography from entering payment systems and establishing merchant accounts (Financial Coalition Against Child Pornography, 2007). Similarly, some credit card companies have begun to block transactions from sources that have been identified as child pornography sellers (Wortley, chapter 11). This approach has great potential – in 2005, websites selling cigarettes, which often facilitated illegal cigarette sales to minors, were banned from accepting credit cards, such as Visa and MasterCard, and other online payments (e.g. Paypal), as well as prohibited from using commercial shippers, such as UPS or FedEx. After these policies went into effect, the number of websites selling cigarettes that went out of business increased significantly, and monthly traffic at popular sites went from approximately 36,000 unique visitors per site before the payment and shipping bans to approximately 8,000 visitors after the bans were put in place. In fact, summing across the fifty most popular sites, over 1,250,000 visits per month were cut, even though this policy left some loopholes whereby personal checks were still accepted for payment and the US Postal Service still allowed deliveries (Ribisl et al., 2011). The key lesson is that efforts to increase the difficulty in accessing, selling or purchasing child sexual images, even if they are imperfect, can have notable population impact.

'Post-event' strategies directed at offenders include arrest and prosecution, as well as treatment for those willing to seek care so as to prevent them from contacting the child victim (or victims) again or distributing child sexual images widely. However, the efficacy of existing offender treatments is highly debatable, requiring additional research and evaluation in order to increase the utility of this approach (Middleton et al., 2009).

Physical environment: Internet

Research addressing environmental factors of the distribution and production of child sexual images has shown that it is important to recognize the role of the virtual environment where the solicitation of child victims and the distribution of images take place (Wortley, chapter 11). Therefore, although this environment is better described as virtual than as 'physical', it is an essential intervention point and has been identified as the physical environment in this model. Elements of the Internet environment that facilitate or impede the effects of the vector on the host can be altered to be more supportive of the protection of children.

In addressing the physical environment in the 'pre-event' phase, interventions will seek to create an Internet environment that inhibits the creation of indecent images of children, primarily through preventing contact between offenders and children. Again, although these particular environmental changes will not apply to all instances of exploitation (such as images produced by children's parents or other offline acquaintances), they do address the prevention of online solicitation and grooming of victims. This can be done through a variety of strategies. Effective Internet controls, such as filtering software, could be used on home and public computers to prevent children from accessing potentially dangerous sites and to prevent offenders' contact with them. Although widely advocated, evidence on the effectiveness of filtering software has been mixed, suggesting that while it may have a modest effect, it is far from foolproof (Fleming et al., 2006; Mitchell et al., 2003; Perrin et al., 2008; Quayle et al., 2008). Internet controls could be implemented on a wider scale, as per a more population approach, by implementing online safety tools on websites that are potentially dangerous for children (i.e. abuse buttons, chat moderation and more stringent default settings) (Quayle et al., 2008).

An 'event phase' intervention addressing the physical environment could be the use of popup warnings or ads linked to known child pornography search terms while the terms are being entered into a search engine, with the goal of deterring some would-be offenders from accessing child sexual images (Prichard et al., 2011; Taylor and Quayle, 2008; Williams, 2005). However, Williams (2005) emphasizes that the potential effectiveness of such messages will largely depend on their content. Messages framed as legal or official warnings may actually have the unintended consequence of increasing access to messages by magnifying the deviant status of the behaviour. Messages that are more likely to be effective will explain the criminal nature of accessing indecent images of children and will emphasize the added harm that is done to children by those who view the images (Taylor and Quayle, 2008; Williams, 2005). Pop-up messages and ads such as these could also be used to inform users of treatment and self-help programmes. Another 'event phase' intervention could be to increase the difficulty in accessing images, by blocking or slowing access to known child pornography sites or routing users through information pages before they are able to access suspected sites (Taylor and Quayle, 2008).

'Post-event' strategies could also be directed towards environmental changes to the Internet, through the identification and removal of child sexual images. One strategy for removing materials is for ISPs to conduct ongoing screenings to identify and remove sites containing indecent images of children. The Second World Congress has recommended the establishment of hotlines that can be used to report such websites. Hotlines have been developed, funded and implemented by organizations such as the Association of Internet Hotline Providers (INHOPE) and the Safer Internet and Safer Internet Plus programmes (Quayle et al., 2008). In order to improve the effectiveness of this strategy, it has been suggested that guidelines should be developed for law enforcement to better receive and investigate reports from hotlines or that hotlines should report directly to self-regulating ISPs (Perrin et al., 2008; Quayle et al., 2008).

Social environment: policies and social norms supporting or discouraging the creation and distribution of online child sexual images

The social environment can also facilitate or impede the effects of the offenders on children. Elements of the social environment that are particularly relevant to the discussion of child sexual images are policies and social norms that either support or discourage their distribution.

Pre-event strategies can be aimed at creating a social environment that discourages the creation of indecent images of children. Social marketing campaigns and educational programmes could be implemented to influence social norms encouraging safe Internet use and parental supervision. Media advocacy campaigns could be used to put pressure on entertainment and advertising agencies to dis-courage social norms that are permissive of the sexualization of children. Policy change is also important in affecting the social environment. Codes of practice could be developed so that ISPs would enact policies to prevent contact between children and offenders (such as requiring online safety tools) (Quayle et al., 2008). In addition, more effective laws and penalties for producing child sexual images create an environment that is more difficult and risky for potential offenders.

Another important element of the social environment surrounding the pro-duction and distribution of indecent images of children is the development of social networks of offenders online, facilitating file sharing but also forming a subculture or community (Carr, chapter 6; Prichard et al., 2011). Some of these websites condone the use of child sexual images passively, such as P2P sites that allow child pornography links to appear in their lists of top search terms, and others condone them more actively, by normalizing child sexual offending and portraying it as natural and loving (Prichard et al., 2011). Changing or removing these sites to eliminate this source of social support for producing, viewing and/or sharing indecent images of children are examples of 'event' strategies to affect the social environment.

Other 'event' strategies affecting the social environment are similar to the 'pre-event' strategies. Codes of practice for ISPs to impede the distribution of child sexual images could include policies concerning the regular screening and removal of images or the use of website safeguards (Quayle et al., 2008; Wortley, chapter 11). Additionally, more adequate laws and penalties for accessing, viewing and distributing indecent images of children can deter offenders from using images and therefore reduce demand and distribution.

In order for laws and penalties to be effective as interventions, they must be adequately and consistently enforced. The enforcement of laws is a 'post-event' strategy, ensuring the prosecution of offenders after materials have been dis-tributed. In addition, the social environment affects the quality and consistency of services delivered to children who have been abused through the creation and distribution of sexual images. Another 'post-event' strategy is advocacy for ade-quate child protection and law enforcement policies that allow for effective investigation, assessment, intervention, support and follow-up services.

As shown in Table 14.1, the Haddon Model identifies multiple points of intervention and many possible intervention strategies that can reduce negative health effects due to online child sexual images. Although public health strategies emphasize primary prevention and environmental approaches, each of these intervention points could be effective in reducing the negative health impacts of the production and distribution of indecent images of children. Programme planners can use the Haddon Model to identify a wide variety of interventions and then prioritize their efforts, using criteria such as effectiveness, cost and feasibility (Runyan, 1998).

Logic models

The principles emphasized in public health approaches have the potential of being demonstrably effective in reducing negative health outcomes across populations. However, careful intervention planning is crucial in translating these concepts into effective practice. A logic model, often used in planning public health interventions, is a systematic method of visualizing the relationships between resources invested in the programme, programme activities and desired outcomes. These models explicitly outline the causal pathways through which programme activities, if implemented as intended, are expected to affect change (W.K. Kellogg Foundation, 2004). Logic models can be created in various formats, but they generally include inputs, activities, outputs, outcomes and impacts. Arrows connecting each of these components show the causal connections between them. Logic models are read by starting with the inputs and reading left to right in order to see the planned progression of activities and results over time (W.K. Kellogg Foundation, 2004). However, they are often constructed by starting with the desired results and working backwards in order to discern what resources and programmes will be necessary in order to produce those results.

Online child sexual images prevention logic model

Selected interventions identified in the previous models have been organized into a logic model in Fig. 14.2. Logic models are generally programme specific, so this example does not include all of the interventions that have been identified for the prevention of the production and distribution of child sexual images. In fact, even the few interventions included here may be too broad in focus for one programme to implement all of them. When programmes are unable to target multiple levels of intervention, it is important for them to partner with other organizations that are implementing programming that complements their own. This model outlines the resources needed in order to implement the selected interventions and the causal pathways by which each of these activities will lead to the ultimate goals of the proposed interventions – decreased sexual exploitation of children online and offline.

Logic models begin with inputs, the resources that are to be invested into a programme. The inputs included in this logic model are fairly typical, including funding, staff, curricula and partnerships. It is important to recognize that prevention programmes addressing online child sexual images do have some unique input needs. For example, it may be necessary to hire staff members with particular skill sets, such as information technology skills or policy advocacy experience. Access to specific technologies may also be a unique need for programme implementation, such as hotlines, filtering software, website safeguards and ISP-screening technologies. Another important input for these programmes is the partnerships. Partnerships are essential to making changes that will impact policy and law enforcement internationally, and they can be challenging to build. This input is important for programme planners to take into account.

The next element of the logic model is the activities, the tasks that a programme intends to complete. These activities will lead to the intended results of the

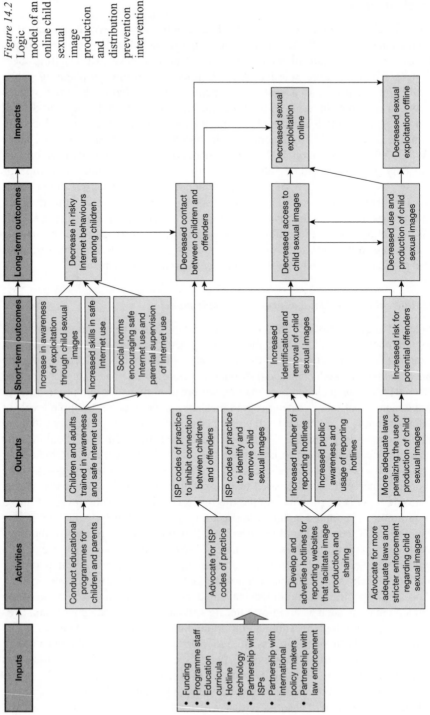

Figure 14.2 Logic model of an online child sexual image production and distribution prevention intervention

programme – outputs, outcomes and impacts. Outputs are the immediate products of the activities. Outcomes are the changes that the programme intends to cause, and they are often divided into short-term and long-term outcomes. Short-term outcomes usually refer to changes in knowledge, skills, opinions and motivation. Long-term outcomes generally include actual changes to behaviour, physical environments or policies. Finally, impacts are the fundamental changes that a programme intends to cause. Impacts can include changes in health status, environmental conditions and quality of life.

The first activity included in this logic model is to conduct educational programmes for children and parents. As shown in the logic model, conducting educational programmes would yield children and adults trained in awareness and safe Internet use, which would lead to an increase in awareness of exploitation through child sexual images, increased skills in safe Internet use, and if implemented widely enough, social norms that are more encouraging of safe Internet use and parental supervision of Internet use. The assumption of this intervention strategy is that increased knowledge and skills, combined with more supportive social norms, will change the Internet behaviour of children. A decrease in risky Internet behaviours among children should lead to decreased contact between children and offenders.

The second activity, advocating for ISPs to develop codes of practice that inhibit indecent images of children, is intended to lead to the development and adoption of ISP codes of practice. This logic model outlines two specific industry-based policies. The first output is a code of practice that would inhibit contact between children and offenders. This may include policies requiring certain website safeguards. If implemented effectively, this logic model assumes that an ISP code of practice would decrease contact between children and perpetrators. The second output is a code of practice to identify and remove child sexual images. Again, the assumption of this model is that a formalized industry-based policy outlining required action would in fact lead to increased identification and removal of images.

Another activity leading to the same short-term outcome is the development and advertisement of reporting hotlines. This activity has two outputs, an increased number of reporting hotlines and increased public awareness and usage of reporting hotlines. The model assumes that the hotlines would be effective, and therefore having more hotlines and greater usage would lead to increased identification and removal of child sexual images. The model proposes that this short-term outcome, the removal of these websites, will lead to a decrease in access to images as a long-term outcome.

The final activity included in the logic model is to advocate for more adequate laws and enforcement regarding indecent images of children. The intended output of this advocacy is the passage and enforcement of consistent laws with stricter penalties for the use or production of child sexual images. These laws and increased enforcement will increase risk for potential offenders. By increasing risk, the model assumes that offenders will be effectively deterred from contacting children, using images and producing images as long-term outcomes.

The final assumption of the model is that each of these long-term outcomes – decreasing contact between children and offenders, decreasing access to child sexual images, and decreasing the use and production of such images – will lead to the ultimate impacts of the programme: decreasing sexual exploitation of children both online and offline.

Utility of logic models

By making the assumptions throughout the intended process explicit, programme planners using a logic model have more insight into how they expect their planned activities to lead to their ultimate goals. They are able to articulate their assumptions about why their programme will work, and they can identify possible gaps in logic that need to be made clear. By mapping out potential interventions in this way, programme planners are able to identify the most critical points of intervention.

For example, by constructing a clear depiction of the causal pathways leading to a decrease in sexual exploitation, a programme planner intending to conduct only an educational programme would be able to see clearly that this approach would be limited to affecting children's risky behaviour and their potential connection with offenders. Considering that only 12.7 per cent of identified children portrayed in sexual images were exploited by someone they met online (Quayle et al., 2008), this approach, while important, is insufficient to affect the majority of exploitation cases and create the kind of population change required. That intervention alone would neglect other key environmental factors leading to exploitation, such as the supply and demand factors of indecent images of children. A programme planner could use this logic model to recognize that they may want to incorporate more programme activities addressing environmental factors, or they may want to seek partnerships with complementary organizations that are able to address these factors.

These models remind us that although knowledge, skills and counselling are important, they are not sufficient to keep current and future generations of children safe by preventing the growing threat of exploitation. Public health principles can guide programme planners to think beyond the solutions immediately available and to expand their thinking to include all of the various intervention points that can prevent cases of exploitation, including the environment, social norms, organizational guidelines and policies. Programme planners can use these principles carefully and strategically to consider these options and to prioritize their efforts in order to have the most significant and lasting impact.

Conclusion

We can create interventions that will transform this generation of parents and children into savvy individuals who are better equipped to navigate an environment fraught with hazards. However, even the most educated of individuals are susceptible to missteps. When dealing with a hazard such as sexual exploitation, the smallest of missteps can have devastating consequences for a child. With each generation of children and each wave of new technologies, we will have to repeat our efforts.

Public health focuses on prevention, while recognizing the value of treatment and prosecution. Instead of focusing these prevention efforts towards high-risk individuals, public health approaches seek to transform the population through transforming environments, often requiring either engineering or social policy reform. Rather than teaching individuals to navigate hazards, public health approaches seek to remove those hazards altogether. Our goal is not to produce children who are skilled at avoiding danger, but to create an environment in which they do not have to. In doing so, these approaches have the potential to prevent harm not only for this generation of children, but also for the generations to follow.

References

Adler, A. (2001). The perverse law of child pornography. *The Columbia Law Review, 209*, 1–101.

Babchishin, K.M., Karl Hanson, R. and Hermann, C.A. (2011). The characteristics of online sex offenders: A meta-analysis. *Sexual Abuse: A Journal of Research and Treatment, 23*(1), 92–123.

Beech, A.R., Elliott, I.A., Birgden, A. and Findlater, D. (2008). The Internet and child sexual offending: A criminological review. *Aggression and Violent Behavior, 13*(3), 216–28.

Beier, K. M., Neutze, J., Mundt, I. A., Ahlers, C. J., Goecker, D., Konrad, A. and Schaefer, G. A. (2009). Encouraging self-identified pedophiles and hebephiles to seek professional help: First results of the Prevention Project Dunkelfeld (PPD). *Child Abuse and Neglect, 33*(8), 545–9.

Cook, N.R., Cohen, J., Hebert, P.R., Taylor, J.O. and Hennekens, C.H. (1995). Implications of small reductions in diastolic blood pressure for primary prevention. *Archives of Internal Medicine, 155*(7), 701–709.

Croga (n.d.). Croga.org. Available from http://www.croga.org.

Demitriou, C. and Silke, A. (2003). A criminological Internet 'sting'. Experimental evidence of illegal and deviant visits to a website trap. *British Journal of Criminology, 43*(1), 213–22.

Financial Coalition Against Child Pornography. (2007). *Internet Merchant Acquisition and Monitoring Best Practices for the Prevention and Detection of Commercial Child Pornography.* Financial Coalition Against Child Pornography, available online at http://www.fdic.gov/news/news/financial/2007/fil07072a.pdf.

Finkelhor, D., Mitchell, K.J. and Wolak, J. (2000). *Online Victimization: A Report on the Nation's Youth.* Alexandria, VA: National Center for Missing and Exploited Children.

Fleming, M.J., Greentree, S., Cocotti-Muller, D., Elias, K.A. and Morrison, S. (2006). Safety in cyberspace: Adolescents' safety and exposure online. *Youth and Society, 38*(2), 135–54.

Frieden, T.R. (2010). A framework for public health action: The health impact pyramid. *American Journal of Public Health, 100*(4), 590–95.

Haddon Jr, W. (1980). Advances in the epidemiology of injuries as a basis for public policy. *Public Health Reports, 95*(5), 411–21.

Hemenway, D. (2009). *While We Were Sleeping: Success Stories in Injury and Violence Prevention*. Berkeley: University of California Press.

International Centre for Missing and Exploited Children. (2008). *Child pornography: Model Legislation and Global Review*. Alexandria, VA: ICMEC.

Kendall-Tackett, K.A., Williams, L.M. and Finkelhor, D. (1993). Impact of sexual abuse on children: A review and synthesis of recent empirical studies. *Psychological Bulletin, 113*(1), 164–80.

Lykins, A.D., Cantor, J.M., Kuban, M.E., Blak, T., Dickey, R., Klassen, P.E. and Blanchard, R. (2010) Sexual arousal to female children in gynephilic men. *Sexual Abuse: A Journal of Research and Treatment, 22*(3), 279–89.

Middleton, D., Mandeville-Norden, R. and Hayes, E. (2009). Does treatment work with Internet sex offenders? Emerging findings from the Internet Sex Offender Treatment Programme (i-SOTP). *Journal of Sexual Aggression, 15*(1), 5–19.

Mitchell, K.J., Finkelhor, D. and Wolak, J. (2003). The exposure of youth to unwanted sexual material on the Internet: A national survey of risk, impact, and prevention. *Youth and Society, 34*(3), 330–58.

—— (2007). Youth internet users at risk for the most serious online sexual solicitations. *American Journal of Preventive Medicine, 32*(6), 532–7.

O'Donnell, I. and Millner, C. (2007). *Child Pornography: Crime, Computers and Society*. London: Routledge.

Perrin, P.C., Madanat, H.N., Barnes, M.D., Carolan, A., Clark, R.B., Ivins, N., Williams, P.N. (2008). Health education's role in framing pornography as a public health issue: Local and national strategies with international implications. *Promotion and Education, 15*(1), 11–18.

Prichard, J., Watters, P.A. and Spiranovic, C. (2011). Internet subcultures and pathways to the use of child pornography. *Computer Law and Security Review, 27*(6), 585–600.

Quayle, E., Loof, L. and Tink, P. (2008). *Child Pornography and Sexual Exploitation of Children Online*. Bangkok: ECPAT International.

Ribisl, K.M., Williams, R., Gizlice, Z. and Herring, A.H. (2011). Effectiveness of state and federal government agreements with major credit card and shipping companies to block illegal Internet cigarette sales. *PLoS One, 6(2)*, e16745.

Rose, G. (1985). Sick individuals and sick populations. *International Journal of Epidemiology, 14*, 32–28.

Runyan, C.W. (1998). Using the Haddon Matrix: Introducing the third dimension. *Injury Prevention, 4,* 302–307.

Stop It Now! (2010). *Stop It Now!* Available online from http://www.stopitnow.org.

Susser, M. (1973). *Causal Thinking in the Health Sciences*. New York: Oxford University Press.

Taylor, M. and Quayle, E. (2008). Criminogenic qualities of the Internet in the collection and distribution of abuse images of children. *Irish Journal of Psychology, 29,* 119–30.

Williams, K. (2005). Facilitating safer choices: Use of warnings to dissuade viewing of pornography on the Internet. *Child Abuse Review, 14*, 415–29.

W.K. Kellogg Foundation (2004). *Logic Model Development Guide*. Battle Creek, MI: W.K. Kellogg Foundation.

Wolak, J., Finkelhor, D. and Mitchell, K. (2003). *Child-pornography Possessors Arrested in Internet-related Crimes: Findings from the National Juvenile Online Victimization Study*. Washington DC: National Center for Missing and Exploited Children.

—— (2009). *Trends in Arrests of 'Online Predators'*. Durham, NH: Crimes Against Children Research Center.

Wolak, J., Finkelhor, D., Mitchell, K.J. and Ybarra, M.L. (2008). Online 'predators' and their victims. *American Psychologist, 63*(2), 111–28.

Ybarra, M.L. (2004). Linkages between depressive symptomatology and Internet harassment among young regular Internet users. *CyberPsychology and Behavior, 7*(2), 247–57.

Index

Note: Page numbers in *italics* are for tables.